09104865

IN ALL THINGS FIRST

IN ALL
THINGS
FIRST

NO. 1 SQUADRON
AT WAR 1939-45

PETER CAYGILL

AVIATION

First published in Great Britain in 2009 by
PEN & SWORD AVIATION
An imprint of
Pen & Sword Books Ltd
47 Church Street
Barnsley
South Yorkshire
S70 2AS

ISBN 978 1 84884 050 8

Printed and bound in England
By CPI

Pen & Sword Books Ltd incorporates the Imprints of Pen & Sword Aviation,
Pen & Sword Family History, Pen & Sword Maritime, Pen & Sword Military,
Wharncliffe Local History, Pen & Sword Select, Pen & Sword Military Classics,
Leo Cooper, Remember When, Seaforth Publishing and Frontline Publishing

For a complete list of Pen & Sword titles please contact
PEN & SWORD BOOKS LIMITED
47 Church Street, Barnsley, South Yorkshire, S70 2AS, England
E-mail: enquiries@pen-and-sword.co.uk

Website: www.pen-and-sword.co.uk

Contents

Introduction

For the vast majority of those interested in aviation history the term 'It's Quicker By Bus' will be meaningless, indeed any connection with flying at all seems unlikely on first glance. I first came across this phrase just over forty years ago thanks to the father of a school friend and was left in no doubt as to its link with the RAF's premier fighter squadron. The man's name was Walter Ramsey and during the Second World War he was a pilot with No. 1 Squadron whose official motto was (and is) *In Omnibus Princeps*, or In All Things First. At an undefined point in the squadron's history someone came up with a slang version of the Latin (presumably in the bar) and it was immediately accepted. Walter Ramsey did not talk in any great detail of his wartime experiences before his sad death in 1977, but his pride in having served in No. 1 Squadron was apparent for all to see. By the time that he joined No. 1 Squadron in 1942 it had already been in existence for thirty years but its origins went back even further to the first military experiments in Britain with balloons. Since then it has had a near-continuous history and as the unit approaches its official centenary in 2012, it continues to meet the challenges of the 21st Century.

This book is a detailed history of No.1 Squadron's involvement in the Second World War from its deployment to France during the Phoney War, to bomber escort and armed reconnaissance missions over northern Europe in 1945. In the intervening years it fought with distinction during the Battle of France and the Battle of Britain and was at the forefront of Fighter Command's offensive policy in 1941 in which it sought to wrest the initiative from *Luftwaffe* units based in northern France. Later it took on a night role and had considerable success during Intruder operations, racking up an impressive score of enemy aircraft shot down. Having flown the Hawker Hurricane, No. 1 Squadron went on to fly its successor, the Typhoon, which was used to counter the so-called hit-and-run raids in which Focke-Wulf Fw 190 fighter-bombers raided towns along the south coast. With the gradual demise of the *Luftwaffe* No. 1 Squadron took on a ground-attack role and took part in operations against V-1 construction sites situated along the Channel coast. It later converted to the Supermarine Spitfire and shot down many V-1 flying bombs in the summer of 1944. No. 1 Squadron continued to fly Spitfires until the end of the war using advanced bases in Holland and Belgium so that it could escort bombers attacking targets in north-west Germany.

Pilots from all over the free world served with No. 1 Squadron during the Second World War and the actions that they took part in are pieced together from Combat Reports and first-hand accounts. These paint a vivid picture of the air battles that took place in the skies over northern Europe. There are also extensive appendices that record aircraft losses, details of selected operations and the operational careers of two No. 1 Squadron pilots.

CHAPTER ONE

Early Days

No. 1 Squadron officially came into existence on 13 May 1912, although its history can be traced to the origins of military flight in the UK in 1878. It was in this year that the first experiments were undertaken by the Royal Engineers at Woolwich into the use of hydrogen balloons to provide Army commanders with information on the disposition of enemy troops. The benefits were immediately obvious and in 1884 three balloons were deployed to Africa to assist with Sir Charles Warren's expedition to Bechuanaland. Funding via a parsimonious Treasury remained a problem however and it was not until 1890 that military ballooning was established on a sound footing at South Farnborough. Four balloons were used during the Second Boer War of 1899–1902, and in addition to their normal reconnaissance duties, the directing of gunfire was attempted for the first time. It was also at this time that the first experiments were made in air-to-ground communications with the use of Marconi wireless sets.

With the coming of a new century, a new type of aerial craft emerged when the first British dirigible airship, the *Nulli Secundus*, was flown for the first time in September 1907. This was followed by two other airships, the *Beta* and *Gamma*, but with further experimentation in balloons and man-carrying kites taking place as well, the expansion of the flight had rather overtaken the organisation that had previously been set up to support it. So it was that the Air Battalion of the Royal Engineers was formed in 1911 with No. 1 Company responsible for airships, balloons and man-carrying kites, while No. 2 Company operated the first aeroplanes. The rapid advances in aviation in other countries, notably France and Germany, led to the setting up in December 1911 of a sub-committee of the Committee of Imperial Defence to review military aviation in the UK, the findings of which were that a service should be formed for military flying. This recommendation led to the setting up of the Royal Flying Corps (RFC) on 13 May 1912 in which No. 1 Company became No. 1 Squadron.

The fact that No. 1 Squadron was to specialise in lighter-than-air operations was to be unfortunate in the short term as the rapid improvement in capability of the aeroplane led to questions being asked as to how useful airships would be in time of war, and with increased tension in Europe, this was becoming a distinct possibility. The Royal Navy had no doubts about the usefulness of the airship as it was ideally suited to maritime patrol and at the end of 1913 all of No. 1 Squadron's airships were handed over to the Senior Service. This left the squadron without any meaningful equipment and it was not until 1 May 1914 that a decision was made to re-equip No. 1 Squadron with aeroplanes. These were extremely slow in arriving so that when war was declared on 4 August 1914 the fledgling RFC had to fly to France without No. 1 Squadron.

It was not until 1 March 1915 that No. 1 Squadron was given the order to go to war by which time its commanding officer was Major Geoffrey Salmond. Having arrived in France on 7 March, No. 1 Squadron was pitched straight into the Battle of Neuve Chapelle and carried out its first reconnaissance sorties two days later. On the 12th the first offensive mission was undertaken when four BE.8s attempted to bomb a railway bridge at Douai. Only three aircraft returned as Lt Oswald Mansell-Moullin became the unit's first loss when he had to land in enemy territory due to engine failure and was taken prisoner. On 15 March the squadron's mixed bag of BE.8s, Avro 504s and Moranes flew to Bailleul, which was to be its base for the next three years.

During the rest of 1915 the squadron flew the usual mix of observation, artillery spotting and bombing sorties behind the front line, but these operations increasingly came under threat not only from anti-aircraft fire but also from German aircraft. It was clearly advantageous for an army to deny access to its rear areas and this led to the development of fighter aircraft (known as scouts during the First World War) whose principal aim was to shoot down enemy reconnaissance machines. The first aerial combat involving a No. 1 Squadron crew took place on 5 July when Capt D.E. Stodart and 2nd Lt M.S. Stewart, who were flying an Avro 504, shot down a German machine. On the very next day Lt Oliver Filley and Lt Lambert Playfair were carrying out a reconnaissance for the 11th Infantry Brigade in an Avro 504 but having already driven off a German aircraft, two more appeared and Playfair was mortally wounded by a bullet from one of these machines.

To keep losses to a minimum it became necessary to operate aircraft in tactical formations instead of singly and in March 1916 No. 1 Squadron received a few examples of the single-seat Nieuport 16 scout, which was powered by a 110 hp Le Rhone rotary engine. These were fitted with a single 0.303-in Lewis machine-gun on a Foster mounting, a curved fixing which allowed the pilot to pull the gun back and down so that he could change drums easily and also fire vertically upwards. These aircraft flew with the two-seaters to ward off attacks by German scouts and were also used in the run up to the Battle of the Somme, which commenced on 1 July. They proved to be extremely effective against German observation balloons that were ranged along the British front and for this task they were armed with Le Prieur rockets fixed to the interplane struts. By August however the Nieuports had been handed over to No. 60 Squadron as the RFC began to establish specialised scout squadrons. For the rest of the year No. 1 Squadron continued with its regular tasks for the Army but it would not be long before it too was to change its role.

In January 1917 the two-seaters were gradually replaced by the Nieuport 17, a development of the Type 16 flown previously, and at the beginning of February No.

1 Squadron became operational as a scout squadron. With a gradual improvement in the weather, aerial activity began to increase and from 25 March No. 1 Squadron was heavily involved in balloon-strafing ahead of the Battle of Arras, which lasted from 9 April to 16 May 1917. At the end of April the squadron was joined by 2nd Lt Philip Fullard who was to become the unit's top-scoring pilot in a short but meteoric career. Fullard was a fresh-faced nineteen-year-old and an excellent athlete having played football for Norwich City. Although he had more flying time than most new pilots as he had been retained for a time as an instructor, he still found the Nieuports tricky to fly compared with the docile Sopwith Pup that he was used to. Fullard was professional in his approach to flying and would spend hours dis-assembling his Lewis gun and rebuilding it so that he never had a stoppage in the air. When he came to lead a flight he was mindful of the other pilots and over a three-month period none were shot down.

Combat victories accumulated at a steady rate and in October No. 1 Squadron was able to claim its 200th German aircraft. Other successful pilots at this time were Lt Tom Hazell who claimed twenty victories with No. 1 Squadron (plus another twenty-three with No. 24 Squadron), 2nd Lt William Campbell with twenty-three and Lt Louis Jenkin with twenty-two. By mid November, Philip Fullard (by now promoted to Captain) had shot down forty German aircraft, his last victims being two Albatros D.Vs shot down near Zandvoorde on the 15th when flying Nieuport 17 B6789. Two days later he was playing in a football match when he suffered a bad leg break, which prevented him from flying operationally for the rest of the war. Fullard was the highest scoring 'ace' on Nieuport scouts and considering his achievements in just six months, had he been able to continue flying it is possible that he may have become one of the top scorers of the war.

By the end of 1917 the Nieuport 17 was becoming increasingly outdated and in early 1918 No. 1 Squadron converted onto the SE.5a. This was powered by the 200 hp Wolseley Viper liquid-cooled engine and had a top speed of 126 mph. The first German aircraft to be shot down by a No. 1 Squadron SE.5a was an Albatros D.V, which was forced down on 16 February by 2nd Lt P.J. Clayson. Whereas Fullard had been pre-eminent in 1917, Percy Clayson was to take his place in 1918 and by mid July he had accounted for twenty-nine German aircraft. The most difficult time for No. 1 Squadron was after the German offensive of March 1918 in which it was used primarily for bombing and ground strafing. With the advance of German forces Bailleul had to be evacuated and the squadron's SE.5as flew to St Marie Cappel on 29 March and Clairmarais on 13 April. During this period the RAF came into existence on 1 April although as its fighting elements were flying from dawn until dusk in a desperate attempt to stem the German advance, they can be forgiven for hardly noticing.

By the end of April the Germans had been halted (the use of tactical air power being a deciding factor) and some stability returned to the front line. With the USA having joined the war there was now the prospect of a significant breakthrough later in the year and several Americans were to join the ranks of No. 1 Squadron including Lt Duerson Knight who shot down ten German aircraft between May and August 1918. The decisive battles were fought in August with the opening of the Allied offensive around Amiens on the 8th. Initially No. 1 Squadron was tasked with bombing operations behind the front line and later as bomber escorts. On many occasions these were contested and on 30 August Lt Harold Kullberg (an American serving with the RAF) shot down two Fokker D.VIIs. With the German armies retreating in disarray No. 1 Squadron had to move three times to maintain contact and its final victories of the war occurred on 29 October when Lt W.A. Smart and Capt Reginald Hoidge each shot down a Fokker D.VII.

By the end of the war on 11 November 1918 No. 1 Squadron had accounted for over 300 German aircraft shot down but this had come at considerable cost as sixty pilots and observers had been killed and another thirty-three wounded. In addition thirty-six had been taken as prisoners. The squadron remained on the Continent until the end of February 1919 when the remaining members returned to London Colney before moving to Uxbridge the following October. With massive demobilisation of personnel and the cutting of the RAF to a fraction of its wartime size, the future for No. 1 Squadron was uncertain, but eventually its continued existence was confirmed, albeit 4,000 miles away in Risalpur in north-west India.

As the original unit disbanded on 21 January 1920, the new No. 1 Squadron was reformed the following day. The first squadron commander in the post war period was S/L Jack Graham and his flight commanders were F/L Geoffrey Robarts and F/L Frank 'Mongoose' Soden. The squadron's equipment consisted of Sopwith Snipes, which were powered by a 230 hp Bentley BR.2 rotary engine and had a top speed of just over 120 mph. As India at the time was relatively stable there was little need for operational flying, which was just as well as the sourcing of adequate spares was a major problem. As so little flying was available, news that the squadron would be moving to the Middle East was greeted with considerable delight. In early 1921 it was decided that the most cost effective way of policing the mandated territories was by utilising the RAF so that the majority of the ground-based forces that had been carrying out the job could be deployed elsewhere. The main offensive element was to comprise several squadrons of two-seat Bristol F.2B Fighters and DH.9s, however a fighter squadron was also needed and the move from India to Mesopotamia (shortly to be renamed Iraq) began at the end of April 1921.

No. 1 Squadron was based at Hinaidi near Baghdad but most of the tribal unrest in Iraq was in the Kurdish area to the north. The Sopwith Snipes were generally not called upon as in most cases the other units were able to operate unopposed. Other factors were the short range of the Snipe and lack of suitable forward airfields. For a short time the squadron also flew a small number of Nieuport Nighthawks, which were the first RAF fighters to feature a radial engine. Development had been taken over by the Gloucestershire Aircraft Company following the collapse of Nieuport and the original ABC Dragonfly engine was replaced by the Armstrong Siddeley Jaguar II or Bristol Jupitor III. The Nighthawk was not a success in the Middle East due to problems with its engines and all had disappeared by the end of 1923.

It was not until April 1925 that No. 1 Squadron saw any action when a detachment of Snipes flew north to take part in attempts to quell unrest that was being instigated by Sheikh Mahmud, the Governor of the Sulaimaniya province. As battle raged between the rebels and the Army, the well-timed arrival of a flight of Snipes led by F/L Francis Luxmoore proved to be the deciding factor and many Kurds were killed during the strafing attack that followed. This put an end to the fighting but it flared up again the following year and in May 1926 part of the squadron headed north once again for operations against the rebels who had recuperated over the winter period. The detachment was maintained for four months, however it was becoming clear that the Snipe was not suited to the type of flying it was being asked to do and No. 1 Squadron was disbanded on 1 November 1926. Although most personnel stayed in the Middle East and were posted to other squadrons, a small nucleus returned to the UK to be part of the reformed No. 1 Squadron, which opened for business on 1 February 1927.

On its return No. 1 Squadron was based at Tangmere, an idyllic airfield situated three miles east of Chichester in Sussex and close to the South Downs. Its position meant that it was ideally located for the defence of the main south coast ports of Southampton and Portsmouth. Although Tangmere had been used during the First World War it had closed in 1920 and had only recently re-opened. It was also home to No. 43 Squadron with whom No. 1 Squadron would develop a healthy rivalry over the next twelve years and between them they would transform Tangmere into the best fighter station in the whole of the UK. No. 1 Squadron was re-equipped with Armstrong Whitworth Siskin IIIAs which, although it was powered by a supercharged Armstrong Siddeley Jaguar IV engine of 420 hp, had a top speed only slightly higher that the levels achieved during the First World War at 153 mph. No. 43 Squadron was similarly equipped and soon applied black and white chequerboard markings on its aircraft. Not to be outdone No. 1 Squadron opted for two red bands that ran the full length of the upper wing and also along the fuselage sides. The rest of the airframe was in natural metal finish that was polished until it shone.

Tangmere was unique in the RAF's Home Establishment in operating to a tropical routine during the summer months with flying commencing at 0730 hrs and ceasing at 1300 hrs. This left the whole of the afternoon for leisure pursuits, which added to the attraction of a posting to Nos 1 and 43 Squadrons. This seemingly relaxed way of life did not detract from the effectiveness of the squadrons, which managed to fly more hours than any other unit and regularly beat them at the annual gunnery practice camps. In early 1929 Nos 1 and 43 Squadrons formed No. 3 (Fighter) Wing of the Air Defence of Great Britain (ADGB) along with No. 25 Squadron from Kenley. All three squadrons took part in the Hendon Air Pageant of that year, performing a routine in which twenty-seven Siskins flew opposition passes over the aerodrome to the delight of the crowd.

In complete disregard of seniority, No. 43 Squadron was re-equipped with

Furies in May 1931, No. 1 Squadron having to wait a further nine months before it also received the new thoroughbred from the Hawker stable. The Fury was the first RAF fighter capable of flying at a speed in excess of 200 mph in level flight and its fine handling qualities and exquisite looks marked it out as a classic. It was powered by a 525 hp Rolls-Royce Kestrel IIS water-cooled V-12 inline engine, the close cowling and pointed spinner proving to be aesthetically pleasing and a marked contrast to the uncowled Jaguar of the Siskin. Its arrival marked an escalation in the competition between Nos 1 and 43 Squadrons with each trying to outdo the other at the annual Hendon Air Pageant. At the 1932 event No. 43 Squadron performed 'tied-together' aerobatics while No. 1 Squadron flew a formation team of three aircraft, with another two performing synchronised aerobatics.

Although No. 1 Squadron had occasionally been upstaged by No. 43 Squadron it got its own back in 1934 when it was invited to perform in Canada, thereby becoming the first RAF squadron to take part in displays in North America. Five Furies were transported by ship across the Atlantic and rebuilt at Hamilton, Ontario. The occasion was the centennial of the city of Toronto and No. 1 Squadron's Furies performed on 2–4 July and also took part in displays throughout Ontario and Quebec over a three-week period before returning to the UK. The highlight of 1935 was the Silver Jubilee Review of the RAF by George V at Mildenhall on 6 July. This was followed by a flypast at Duxford in which No. 1 Squadron flew past the saluting base at the head of No. 3 (Fighter) Wing.

At Tangmere life carried on as before but the worsening political situation in Europe hinted that the period in which the RAF had been known as 'the best flying club in the world' was about to come to an end. Soon it became clear that Germany was re-arming and that Italy had ambitions to extend its influence in the Mediterranean and in Africa. The start of the Spanish Civil War in July 1936 soon escalated as Germany sent forces to fight with the fascists under General Francisco Franco, while the Soviet Union sided with the Republicans. Britain was left with no alternative but to re-arm as well and the first of several expansion schemes for the RAF had already been put in place. This was to affect No. 1 Squadron in March 1937 when 'B' Flight was removed to form the nucleus of No. 72 Squadron, which was about to reform. The age of the biplane was not quite over as No. 1 Squadron participated in the International Aviation Meeting at Zurich in July and competed against top display pilots from Europe with a four-aircraft team.

By early 1938 the prospect of another European war had become a distinct possibility but events then deteriorated further, culminating in the Munich Crisis in September of that year in which the German annexation of Czech Sudetenland was agreed by Britain's Prime Minister, Neville Chamberlain, and Edouard Daladier of France. The humiliation of Britain and France did at least allow more time for its armed forces to re-equip with more modern machinery and towards the end of 1938 No. 1 Squadron's obsolete Furies began to be replaced by the eight-gun Hawker Hurricane. The new monoplane fighter was powered by a Rolls-Royce

Merlin II of 1,030 hp, which propelled the Hurricane to a top speed of 339 mph. By April 1939 No. 1 Squadron was fully operational and at the end of May its Hurricanes were detached to Sutton Bridge for gunnery practice. This was to be the last opportunity for the squadron to hone its air-to-air firing skills before war was declared. Within a matter of months the targets would not be drogues but real aircraft crewed by a deadly foe.

CHAPTER TWO

The First Team

When war was declared on 3 September 1939 no other unit in Fighter Command could claim to have more experience within its ranks than No. 1 Squadron. It had remained in existence during the inter-war years despite the Ten Year Rule, which saw Government funding for the armed forces reduced based on the assumption that there would not be another war for ten years. Having survived, the RAF's premier fighter squadron had the benefit not only of a near-continuous history, it had also profited from the fact that it was made up of many pilots and ground crew who had been together for a long time and had built up a tremendous esprit de corps in that time.

It was commanded by S/L Patrick J.H. Halahan, a blunt Irishman whose nickname was 'The Bull'. He was thirty-one years old and was the son of a soldier in the Dublin Fusiliers. Following an education at Weymouth College he passed out from the RAF College at Cranwell and served in Palestine and Iraq before taking command of No. 1 Squadron in April 1939. He had a pugnacious appearance courtesy of his stocky figure and prominent jaw, but at the same time there was an Irish twinkle in his eye. Although he was a recent arrival, his pilots immediately saw his abilities, both as a pilot and as a leader, qualities that would soon be put to the test.

His senior pilots included F/O Prosser Hanks and F/L P.R. 'Johnny' Walker. Hanks, who was often referred to as 'Ducks', came from York where he was born on 29 July 1917 and joined the RAF in 1935 before learning to fly with 6 FTS at Netheravon. He joined No. 1 Squadron in September 1936 and became a prominent member of the unit's aerobatic team, taking part in the International Aviation Meeting at Zurich in July 1937 having celebrated his twentieth birthday the week before. His mastery of the air was not just confined to piloting an aeroplane as on one notable occasion he and F/O Caesar Hull of No. 43 Squadron managed to change seats whilst flying a Hawker Hart over Tangmere. He would eventually take over as 'B' Flight commander. Walker was another member of the Fury aerobatic team and was three years older than Hanks. He originally came from Hacheston near Framlingham in Suffolk and had attended Woodbridge School before being commissioned in the RAF on 21 October 1935. Walker's position in the aerobatic team was No. 3 to the left of the leader (F/L Teddy Donaldson) with Hanks in the No. 4 or 'box' position. The No. 2 was F/O H.E.C.

'Top' Boxer. The team astounded the onlookers at Zurich by completing their full display on the second day in atrocious conditions which included a 200 ft cloud base.

George Plinston was another recent arrival on No. 1 Squadron having been posted in as an acting Flight Lieutenant from No. 56 Squadron. His journey to be a fighter pilot was an unusual one as following an education at All Fellows School at Honiton in Devon he had attended the Royal Military College at Camberley and had subsequently been commissioned in the Army with the rank of 2nd Lieutenant. However, after two years' service with the 2nd Battalion of the Yorkshire and Lancashire Regiment he resigned his commission and learned to fly at a civilian flying school at Bristol. He gained his RAF 'wings' in 1936 and during his time with No. 56 Squadron flew the Gauntlet II and Gladiator I from the Gloster stable, before converting onto the Hawker Hurricane.

As well as pilots from the British Isles, several others had been tempted to join up by the worsening political situation in Europe, including Flying Officers Leslie Clisby and Mark 'Hilly' Brown. Clisby was born in McLaren Vale in South Australia on 26 June 1914 to a music-loving, Methodist family and initially it seemed as though his future lay in engineering as he eventually took a night school course at the South Australia School of Mines. In 1935 however he enlisted as a mechanic in the RAAF and was soon accepted for flying training at Point Cook, Victoria. During this period he had to bale out of a Gypsy Moth trainer when he lost control during formation flying practice. He survived the experience unscathed with only a dent to his pride. On arrival in the UK he underwent further training at 1 FTS at Leuchars before being posted to No. 1 Squadron in 1938. A good athlete, he was 5 ft 9 in tall with light brown hair. His attitude was typical of many Australians in that he was tough and uncompromising, with a determination to do his best as a fighter pilot.

Hilly Brown was twenty-seven years of age and had been brought up in Glenboro in Manitoba, Canada. On completing his education he worked as an employee of the Bank of Montreal and during this time he became a member of the Brandon Flying Club. He arrived in the UK in May 1936 and after training was posted to No. 1 Squadron in February 1937. The top button of his tunic was unusual in that it dated back to the First World War and had been presented to him shortly before he left Canada by a young boy whose father had been a pilot in the RFC. The button became a kind of lucky charm for him. Also from the colonies was F/O Bill 'Stratters' Stratton who was twenty-three years old and came from Hastings in New Zealand.

P/O Paul Richey who was also twenty-three came from a privileged background. His father was Lt Col George Richey DSO who had a long Army career, which saw him wounded in action three times, twice during the Boer War and at Ypres during the First World War. During the latter stages of that conflict he commanded the 1st Battalion of the Royal Fusiliers and the 25th Regiment of The King's Regiment in Palestine and Egypt. The military history of the Richey family

11

went back even further than that however as Paul's grandfather had been a Captain in the Royal Artillery and later was City Marshal of London. In the inter-war years Richey senior was responsible for organising the *gendarmerie* for King Zog in Albania and during this period Paul was educated at the Institut Fisher in Switzerland and later at Downside School near Bath in England. At the latter establishment Richey was a contemporary of Michael Robinson who would later command the Biggin Hill Wing in 1941 although their friendship only blossomed after they had left school.

Paul Richey was an accomplished athlete and excelled at virtually any sport. At school he was captain of boxing for three years as well as being captain of the First XV at rugby. He was a superb gymnast and also excelled at hockey and running. In 1935 Richey took the entrance examination for Cranwell on two separate occasions but despite passing both he missed out due to the small number of places that were available. For a time he gave up on the RAF and instead became a favourite at the debutante balls where he was a hit with the girls (if not with their parents) thanks to his good looks and fair hair, together with his occasionally outrageous behaviour. A job in the City of London followed but he was dismissed from his firm of stock brokers after forgetting to bank a cheque for £50,000 following an excellent lunch (in today's money this would be around £1.5m).

By this time his friend Michael Robinson had joined the RAF on a short service commission and was with No. 111 Squadron. Richey decided to join up by the same means and was accepted in 1937, commencing his flying training at a civilian organisation before being posted to 2 FTS at Digby in Lincolnshire. Despite being classed as 'exceptional' in the air, certain misdemeanours on the ground (including being late back from leave and an altercation with a policeman who refused him entry to a dance in Oxford) resulted in him acquiring a reputation for being something of a rebel. Unfortunately the latter incident occurred when he had been confined to camp and he was put under close arrest for disorderly conduct. The matter was eventually sorted by his Air Officer Commanding (AVM L.A. Pattinson) and Richey was transferred to 7 FTS at Peterborough where he completed his training. He was posted to No. 1 Squadron in 1938.

F/O Billy Drake was born on 20 December 1917 and was the son of an English father and Australian mother. His father was a doctor who practised in Australia and Fiji in the early 1920s and the infant Drake, who was an only child, accompanied the family before they returned to the UK where he commenced his schooling. As he was rather a loner Drake was picked on at several schools, but perversely this usually led to his own expulsion after the unfortunate boy was battered into submission. Like Paul Richey, his education was completed in Switzerland and on return (much to the horror of his parents) he expressed a desire to learn to fly. This stemmed from a brief flight in a light aircraft with Alan Cobham's Flying Circus as a youngster and in 1935 he presented himself for a short service commission in the RAF. Although initially rejected as his eyesight was not of the required standard, he was encouraged to try again and on his second attempt he was successful. His first operational posting was to No. 1 Squadron at Tangmere where he flew the biplane Fury before converting onto the Hawker Hurricane. Strikingly handsome, Drake was never short of female company and in the air wore a silk scarf that had been presented to him by a lady friend that bore the colours of Hyperion, the winner of the Epsom Derby in 1933. As Billy Drake could trace his line directly back to Sir Francis Drake, there was a fitting symmetry that one of the latter's descendants should be on hand to help repel another invader.

A relative newcomer at the start of the war, but one who would quickly make a name for himself, P/O Peter Mould came from Hallaton near Uppingham in Rutland. His first taste of life in the RAF was as an aircraft apprentice at Halton in December 1933, which was the inspiration for his nickname of 'Boy' as he had been a boy entrant. He was later awarded a cadetship at Cranwell where he excelled, becoming a triple 'Blue' at athletics, cricket and rugby. Having completed his training in 1939 he joined No. 74 Squadron for a short time before transferring to No. 1 Squadron a few days before war was declared.

Mould's arrival at Tangmere came within days of that of twenty-year-old P/O Peter Matthews from Hoylake in Cheshire. But for the coming of war it is likely that he would have followed in his father's footsteps and trained as a vet; instead he chose the RAF and joined on a short service commission in August 1937. After completing his flying training he was posted to No. 1 Air Armament School at Eastchurch in Kent in June 1938 and spent just over a year there before joining No. 1 Squadron. Other commissioned officers on strength on 3 September 1939 included F/O Cyril 'Pussy' Palmer, F/O C.G.H. 'Leak' Crusoe and P/O David Blomeley. Palmer was born in Cleveland, Ohio, in March 1918 to British parents and had been with No. 1 Squadron since 1938. Crusoe had arrived a little earlier (about the same time as Hilly Brown) and had spent some time as the squadron Adjutant, gradually submerging under a sea of paperwork as the situation deteriorated from week to week and preparations were made for the squadron to deploy to France. David Blomeley was from Stafford and after attending King Edward's School he worked for a firm of agricultural valuers and surveyors. Having secured a short service commission in March 1938 he was trained at 7 EFTS, Desford, and 11 FTS, Shawbury, before being posted to No. 1 Squadron. He arrived just before the departure of the unit's old Hawker Furies. No. 1 Squadron's complement of officer pilots was completed by F/O S.W. Baldie and P/O Colin Birch.

The unit also had a number of highly experienced NCO pilots most of whom had taken the same route as 'Boy' Mould by becoming boy entrants as aircraft apprentices at RAF Halton before learning to fly. These included Sgt Arthur 'Darky' Clowes who was originally from New Sawley in Derbyshire and joined the RAF in January 1929. The aircraft apprentice scheme had been introduced in 1920 at the instigation of Lord Trenchard, the father of the RAF and Chief of the Air Staff. The course lasted for three years and the intention was to provide a pool of skilled aircraft mechanics to service and maintain the RAF's aeroplanes, which were becoming increasingly complex. Academic and practical training was provided, together with basic military training, for the 155 entrants to each course, which was made up of boys between the ages of fifteen and seventeen and a half. Sgt Frank Soper was another ex-Halton 'Brat'. He came from Devonport in Devon and had enlisted as an apprentice at the age of sixteen in September 1928.

Sgt Fred Berry had also been to Halton having joined as an apprentice in August 1929 as a fifteen-year-old. He was the son of a physical training instructor who had served with a fusilier regiment at Fort William, Calcutta, in India. Having achieved the rank of AC1 (Rigger), he served at 5 FTS at Sealand before being posted to No. 24 Squadron, by which time he had been promoted to LAC. In early 1935 he went back to Halton for further technical training but eighteen months later he successfully applied for flying training, which took place at 9 FTS at Thornaby. His first operational posting as a pilot was to No. 43 Squadron at Tangmere in February 1937 but he was transferred to No. 1 Squadron shortly before war was declared. The list of NCO pilots in September 1939 was completed by Sgt Rennie Albonico.

In his autobiography *Billy Drake – Fighter Leader* (with Christopher Shores, Grub Street, 2002) Billy Drake gave assessments of some of his colleagues. For him the most important member of the squadron was 'A' Flight commander Johnny Walker. The length of time he had been with No. 1 Squadron together with his abilities in the air and on the ground meant that he was respected by everyone. It was a similar story with Prosser Hanks who was well-liked but Drake remembers George Plinston as being rather difficult, in particular when he had had too much to drink. He was then liable to take a dislike to random individuals for no apparent reason and attempt to land a punch on them. He quite often succeeded and the weight of the blow was often such that the unfortunate recipient was unlikely to be in a fit state to retaliate.

No. 1 Squadron's Commonwealth contingent were known as the 'colonials' and were a varied group. Hilly Brown and Bill Stratton fitted in well enough but the Australian Leslie Clisby was another who could be difficult at times with his hard-line attitudes. He was not well disposed to the English, who were usually referred to as 'Poms', although if his views were accepted and due allowance was made, a decent enough relationship could be maintained. Drake roomed with Clisby for a time and the two got on quite well and became friends. Although Drake rated Pussy Palmer as 'a brilliant pilot...potentially better than any of us' he was something of an outsider and tended not to speak unless spoken to. His abiding memory of Palmer was that he was rarely seen without a cigarette; indeed when he was later shot down and had to take to his parachute he even managed to 'light up' during his descent.

Billy Drake also commented on the gulf that separated commissioned and non-commissioned pilots. Although all pilots were equal in the air and depended on each other, it was a different matter on the ground and the two groups tended to go their own way and did not socialise together. Each would have their own Mess and so at this stage of the war at least, it was rare for officers to get to know NCO pilots well. There was however scope for NCOs to be promoted to officer status. P/O Boy Mould had started his RAF career modestly at Halton. Drake remembers him as 'a lovable chap' but one who had a few issues on the NCO/officer divide that he was so familiar with. Often it was the case that officer pilots did not get to know their non-commissioned counterparts until the latter had been commissioned. This happened with Billy Drake and Darky Clowes and it was only later that Drake discovered that Clowes had narcolepsy, a neurological condition affecting part of the brain in which he was liable to doze off at any time of day. This usually occurred for a few minutes only and although slightly embarrassing for the sufferer, was nevertheless amusing to everyone else.

CHAPTER THREE

The Phoney War

The inexorable descent towards another European conflict was finally confirmed when Prime Minister Neville Chamberlain announced, in a sombre tone, that Britain and Germany were once again at war with each other. No. 1 Squadron's pilots heard the announcement in the Mess at Tangmere. There was no celebration, they had known that war was inevitable for some time but there was also a realisation that many in the room would not survive. There was however a deep resolve that No. 1 Squadron would give a good account of itself in the battles that were to come. So far the *Luftwaffe* had had a fairly easy ride but it would be a different matter when it came up against the best fighter squadron in what everyone knew to be the finest air force in the world.

The assumption that German bombers would be seen in the skies over Britain with immediate effect led to a number of false alarms. A section of three Hurricanes of No. 1 Squadron led by Johnny Walker, with Paul Richey and Frank Soper as his Nos 2 and 3, were scrambled at 0315 hrs on 4 September to intercept a reported raid. Although there was considerable ground mist in places, it was a pleasant moonlit night so that the coastline between Brighton and Portsmouth could easily be seen despite the recently imposed blackout. Having climbed to 20,000 ft the three pilots flew up and down the patrol line but as soon as it became apparent that the radar screens had picked up 'friendly' aircraft they were allowed to return.

No. 1 Squadron had known for several days that in the event of war it would be moving to France. The controversial policy of sending fighter squadrons across the Channel had been hotly contested by Air Chief Marshal Sir Hugh Dowding, the C-in-C of RAF Fighter Command, who argued that their loss would lead to a serious weakening of Britain's air defences, which were still considered to be under-strength despite the expansion plans of recent years. In the event Dowding lost the argument and Nos 1 and 73 Squadrons were to form 67 Wing of the Advanced Air Striking Force, with Nos 85 and 87 Squadrons becoming the Air Component of the British Expeditionary Force.

For No. 1 Squadron the move to France began on 4 September when the ground party left by rail under the command of S/L David Pemberton who was to be Operations Officer at HQ 67 Wing. The squadron's Hurricanes did not leave until the 8th when they took off from Tangmere just before midday led by Johnny

Walker. By coincidence Paul Richey had been visited by his father that morning but the call to readiness brought a swift end to their time together. As the pilots had been ordered to remove the squadron badges from their overalls, Richey gave his to his father who watched from the airfield boundary as the pilots ran to their aircraft and taxied to the end of the take-off area. No doubt the former soldier was contemplating the fact that the war to end all wars that he had fought in had not prevented his own son from a similar experience and an uncertain future.

After one last low level beat up of Tangmere, one that incurred the wrath of the station commander, the Hurricanes joined up into squadron formation and under a clear blue sky, set course for France. Just over an hour later they landed at Octeville to the north-west of Le Havre, the airfield being at the top of cliffs that were 400 ft high. Prior to doing so, and in customary fashion, the squadron flew low over Le Havre to let everyone know of their arrival. They found that accommodation had been provided in a nunnery on the edge of the airfield and the evening was spent moving from one drinking establishment to another. The following day any hangovers were soon overcome during a sweltering morning when Bull Halahan ordered the digging of trenches for use in the event of an air raid. At 1135 hrs the Hurricanes took off for another demonstration over Le Havre including squadron, flight and section formations, air drill and the obligatory low level beat up which impressed everyone who saw it. Having toiled once more in extreme heat to complete their trench-digging duties the pilots were not best pleased to be told that they were to fly to an airfield near Cherbourg with immediate effect. After yet another low level demonstration they landed at 1910 hrs. Patrols were carried out the following day by sections of three aircraft but a return to Octeville was ordered on 11 September.

By now the squadron was certainly making a name for itself amongst the people of Le Havre together with those who were just passing through, although according to Paul Richey most of the drinks that had been meant as a token of appreciation for No. 1 Squadron's pilots were consumed by No. 73 Squadron instead! Over the next few days most of the flying that was carried out was non-operational, including testing the Hurricane's eight-gun armament by firing into the sea and practice attacks. On 19 September Bull Halahan led the squadron on a reconnaissance of the local area, which took in Rouen, Beauvais, Amiens and Dieppe. However, a week later it was announced that the squadron would be on the move again, this time to Norrent-Fontes to the north-west of Béthune. The MT convoy and advance party left on 26 September with the main party departing two days later. The Hurricanes left on the 29th, the pilots discovering that their new base was little more than a large grass field with all accommodation under canvas. This was far removed from the pleasant little airfield at Octeville but a week later another move was underway, to Vassincourt about fifty miles to the south-east of Reims.

The airfield at Vassincourt was situated on a hill and to the north-east was the small village of Neuville where the squadron was billeted. Although much of the accommodation was deemed satisfactory, the property chosen by the advance party as the Officers' Mess left a lot to be desired as it was a farmhouse that reeked of damp, a situation that was likely to get a lot worse over the winter. The air was also rank with the smell of horses or pigs, depending on which way the wind was blowing. Eventually a solution was found and the Mess was transferred to the top floor of the *Mairie* (town hall), much to the annoyance of S/L David Pemberton who had been using it as an operations room. The local Mayor was not particularly welcoming to the RAF at first as he was of the opinion that the presence of the squadron would lead to German air attacks, but as the Phoney War continued he quickly changed his mind, especially when money began to flow into the pockets of the villagers. The area was very poor and although all houses had electric lighting, few had running water or mains drainage.

The nearest town of note was Bar-le-Duc, formerly part of the medieval duchy of Upper Lorraine, which was located about ten miles to the east. It was here that No. 1 Squadron's pilots found the delights of the Hotel de Metz, which was run by the Ensminger family. Jean Ensminger, together with his wife who was known to all as *Madame* Jean, took a particular liking to everyone from No. 1 Squadron and worked hard to ensure that they received the best service and the finest food that was available. When the war finally came the hotel provided a sanctuary where pilots could unwind for a short time before they were needed to be on readiness to ward off German reconnaissance missions.

By now No. 1 Squadron had been joined by Tony Henniker, a Rolls-Royce service engineer who had arrived in France in mid September to ensure that the Hurricanes' Merlin engines were well cared for. He was usually referred to as 'Knackers', a nickname that owed more to phonetics than anything that could be considered remotely rude. Over the coming months his duties would extend far beyond those for which he had been trained and when everyone else on the squadron was fully committed he would become an extremely useful 'additional' member. He was eventually commissioned and for a time became the squadron's Intelligence officer.

No. 1 Squadron's first real offensive sorties took place on 15 October when fifteen Hurricanes departed at 0800 hrs for the airfield at Etain-Rouvres. Three hours later they took off again in five sections of three aircraft and patrolled from Saarlautern to a point forty miles inside the German frontier. Led by Bull Halahan, the Hurricanes flew below a layer of stratus cloud at 7,000 ft and were subjected to anti-aircraft fire near Saarbrucken. Four enemy fighters were seen but these dived away into low cloud to the east before they could be attacked. After the patrol the squadron returned direct to Vassincourt and all aircraft were down again by 1230 hrs. Over the next few days local patrols were maintained by sections of three aircraft, weather permitting.

The move to the east had brought No. 1 Squadron close to the frontier with Germany and the huge defensive fortifications of the Maginot Line lay about seventy miles to the north-east of their new base. For now the Germans were content to probe the French defences and high-flying reconnaissance aircraft were often seen heading west to obtain photographs of what they would be up against come the invasion. No. 1 Squadron's first combat success of the war occurred on 30 October when Boy Mould managed to shoot down a Do 17 that flew directly over the airfield at an altitude of around 20,000 ft. Several pilots took off in pursuit, including Paul Richey and Frank Soper, but only Mould was able to maintain contact with the Dornier. It was a beautiful late summer day, the only cloud being high level cirrus. Mould found the German aircraft at 18,000 ft and moved in from astern to fire one long burst, which set the Do 17 on fire. It then fell into a vertical spiral and no parachutes were to emerge before it dived into the ground ten miles west of Toul. This was the first German aircraft brought down by the RAF over France and two trophies from it, an extremely misshapen gun and a bullet-riddled oxygen bottle, were added to No. 1 Squadron's collection. The Dornier was from 2(F)/123 and had been flown by an experienced crew comprising Hptm Baldwin von Normann und Audenhove, Oblt Hermann Heisterbergh and Fw Friedrich Pfeiffer.

One aspect of this combat that is worthy of note is the fact that the guns of No. 1 Squadron's Hurricanes had been harmonised to converge at 250 yards instead of the so-called 'Dowding Spread' at 400 yards, which had been adopted so that junior squadron pilots, who would invariably not be the best marksmen, could actually do some damage to the enemy. This system detracted from No. 1 Squadron's performance however as all its pilots were extremely experienced and could do much more damage at the closer harmonisation. The change had been made at the last armament camp at Sutton Bridge in April 1939 but the Air Ministry had not been told to avoid any problems with officialdom. Without doubt the reduction in harmonisation range was to have a huge impact on the success of No. 1 Squadron during its time in France.

It was during October that a show was put on at the village hall, which was now being used as the airmen's Mess. This was to ensure that morale remained high among the men and as there was very little to do at Neuville, apart from consuming the local beer, it was also hoped that the entertainment would prevent boredom and over-reliance on drink. One of the stars of the show was Pussy Palmer who had a little acting experience and together with Tony Henniker appeared in a number of sketches that lampooned Hitler and also made fun of senior RAF officers. Anything in which officers embarrassed themselves was bound to be a huge success and although a second show was put on, a Christmas panto that was adapted by Palmer did not go ahead. (By this time concert parties were arriving from the UK and although most got no further than Reims, the squadron was entertained by several well known names including Billy Cotton's Band and Ralph Reader's Gang Show.)

A period of adverse weather around this time badly affected the flying programme although on 6 November the squadron again flew to Etain-Rouvres, this time with the intention of carrying out a frontier patrol with No. 73 Squadron, which had moved there the previous month. Soon after arriving a German aircraft flew over the airfield at high level and five of No. 73 Squadron's Hurricanes took off to intercept it. They were unable to catch up with the high-flying aircraft however and their late return meant that the intended patrol over the front line had to be postponed. No. 1 Squadron flew back to Vassincourt later in the day in sections of three (and by various routes) but no enemy aircraft were seen. Over the next few days standing patrols were flown whenever possible, together with practice attacks on the Fairey Battles of No. 15 Squadron and recognition training flights in the somewhat vain hope that the French might be able to identify the Hurricane as a friendly aircraft (Paul Richey had already been attacked by a French Air Force Morane-Saulnier MS.406 but had emerged unscathed).

In early November a familiar figure arrived to join No. 1 Squadron in the shape of F/O John Ignatius Kilmartin who was well known to everyone having served for two years with No. 43 Squadron at Tangmere. Like his new commanding officer, Kilmartin came from Ireland and had been born in Dundalk on 8 July 1913. He was one of eight children and was the son of a forester, but sadly his father died when he was only nine years old and he became part of the 'Big Brother' programme, which saw many children of school age taken out of care institutions and sent to Australia. Before the Second World War most boys who were part of this child migration scheme were given farm training and Kilmartin was no exception as he spent five years working on a cattle station in New South Wales. He subsequently lived with an aunt in Shanghai in China, working for two years as a clerk in the Shanghai Gas Works. It was during this period that he saw an opportunity to become an RAF pilot and set out in 1936 on the Trans-Siberia railway together with a group of Japanese sumo wrestlers heading for the Berlin Olympics. His first operational posting was to No. 43 Squadron. He was strikingly good looking with wavy black hair and his powerful frame and countenance reflected his difficult childhood.

The weather finally began to clear on 22 November and a glorious sunset heralded a fine day on the 23rd. The change in the weather did not go unnoticed by the Germans who sent over an increased number of reconnaissance flights, the first of which was seen flying west at around 20,000 ft over Vassincourt at 1030 hrs. F/O Pussy Palmer took off to intercept it and two other aircraft flown by 'Killy' Kilmartin and Frank Soper who had just commenced a defensive patrol were also vectored towards it. Kilmartin saw the aircraft (later identified as a Do 17) as he was passing 10,000 ft and finally overtook it at an altitude of 24,000 ft by which time it was over Chalons-sur-Marne. He climbed 500 ft above the Dornier as the other two Hurricanes were by now attacking and as they broke away he fired two long bursts using a little deflection. Before his second attack he noticed that black smoke was pouring from the port engine. Soper also made two attacks and after the second he saw two of the crew take to their parachutes.

Palmer's hurried departure led to problems in the air as the oxygen bottle in his Hurricane had not been replaced after a previous sortie and what was left was soon used up. He decided to carry on and eventually overhauled the Dornier, firing a number of short bursts from 2–300 yards range from astern. By now both engines were trailing an ominous plume of smoke and after the two crew members baled out he decided to draw level with the aircraft. He could see the pilot clearly and his head appeared to be lolling from side to side as the Dornier maintained an erratic course. As the fuselage was riddled with bullet holes Palmer was certain that the pilot had been killed but he then got the shock of his life as it suddenly decelerated and swung in behind him to begin firing. Several bullets passed through the hood and petrol began leaking onto the cockpit floor from the reserve tank, which had been punctured. He quickly dived away so as to be out of range but on descending though 5,000 ft acrid smoke began to pour into the cockpit and he undid his straps before preparing to bale out. As he did so the propeller stopped dead and the smoke cleared so he did his straps up again before force landing, wheels up, in a ploughed field near Moiremont.

At 1145 hrs a section of three Hurricanes led by George Plinston took off to patrol at 20,000 ft between Verdun and Metz. After about fifty minutes a burst of anti-aircraft fire prompted him to look to his left where he saw a Heinkel He 111 of 2(F)/122 proceeding west at an altitude of around 24,000 ft. As he gave chase the German aircraft turned back towards Germany but Plinston managed to get on its tail and open fire, although his attack was spoilt by a single Hurricane from No. 73 Squadron (TP-F) flown by F/O Newell 'Fanny' Orton. Despite this his fire hit the port engine of the Heinkel but he was unable to make a follow up attack as four of his guns ceased to work due to the extreme cold.

The attack was then taken up by Darky Clowes who made two passes before six French Air Force fighters, identified as 'Moranes', commenced an attack (these were in fact Curtiss Hawk 75As of GC II/5). The method adopted by the French pilots was to attack from all directions, which was in marked contrast to the formal Fighter Command attacks of the RAF. Seeing another opportunity Clowes moved into line astern to fire three long bursts after which the Heinkel dipped its port wing and dived to ground level, one member of the crew leaving by parachute at 6,000 ft. As he was on the verge of breaking away his aircraft shuddered violently as one of the French aircraft collided with its tail unit. Although control was extremely awkward, his Hurricane continued to fly and he was able to watch as the German aircraft crashed in a forest to the north-east of Saarbrucken. In fact half of the rudder and one elevator had been ripped from Clowes' Hurricane and he was fortunate to be able to make a successful crash-landing back at Vassincourt in which he stepped out unhurt. It was Paul Richey's turn to man the operations room that day and he was one of the first on the scene. Although Clowes was uninjured, the experience had unnerved him. Richey later recalled that he attempted to laugh it off but for a time shook uncontrollably and had difficulty relating exactly what had happened.

There was further contact between the opposing forces later in the day when Bull Halahan and Hilly Brown were patrolling between Verdun and Metz in the early afternoon. A cluster of ten anti-aircraft bursts at about 20,000 ft south of Metz alerted them and on flying in that direction they saw a Do 17 flying in a westerly direction. As they approached the Dornier it turned to the south and attempted to climb but the Hurricanes were able to move in with ease to deliver attacks in turn. After two passes the Do 17 went into a tight spiral but pulled out at 12,000 ft and turned back towards Germany. After a further attack it again fell into a spiral dive and also began to burn behind the cockpit area. On this occasion it did not recover and continued spiralling before diving into the ground (this was a Do 17P of 3(F)/122 and the crew of Fw F. Hallauer, Fw S. Dressler and Gefr W. Schultz were killed). On returning to base Halahan discovered a slight rip in the fabric of one wing of his Hurricane, which he assumed had been caused by debris as no return fire had been experienced. In his combat report he emphasised the usefulness of AA fire which, although generally ineffective, was of tremendous use as a pointer for patrolling fighters.

The full story of the shooting down of Pussy Palmer only emerged later in the day. It transpired that the German pilot (Uffz Arno Frankenberger of 4(F)/122) had seen Palmer moving in alongside and had pretended to be dead before throttling both engines and then leaping out of his seat to fire the forward-facing gun with deadly effect. He then regained his seat and expertly force-landed his aircraft, before being captured by the French. Of the two crewmen who baled out, Uffz K. Ehlers fell to his death and Uffz A. Roeder was hospitalised with a leg wound. No. 1 Squadron's pilots (with the possible exception of Palmer) were so impressed with the German's exploits that they were determined to invite him to dinner. This was easier said than done however as he had been taken to a jail at St Menehould and the French were not particularly keen to let him go, even for a short time. After much negotiation a deal was struck and Billy Drake, who spoke German, was dispatched to bring him to the Mess. Tony Henniker later recalled that Frankenberger looked 'scared stiff' when he arrived but after a few uncomfortable moments he began to open up as more alcohol was consumed and a good time was had by all. At the appointed time he was taken away again to resume his incarceration having been the recipient of three cheers as his car sped off. In the event he did not spend too long as a captive as he was released after the German invasion and was back with his unit by the end of June 1940.

The combat involving Pussy Palmer was to have a big impact on the degree of protection offered to pilots as at this stage of the war there was no back-armour fitted to fighter aircraft. As thirty-four bullets had struck his Hurricane he was very fortunate to have survived. Bull Halahan was determined that something should be done and took armour plating out of a wrecked Battle and had it installed in one of the squadron's Hurricanes. The need for back-armour had been raised before but the Air Ministry had always argued that its inclusion would degrade performance and affect handling characteristics. The modified aircraft was flown to RAE Farnborough by Hilly Brown who put it through his usual repertoire of aerobatics, which finally convinced the would-be experts that there was no performance penalty. After this convincing demonstration, armour plating was fitted to all RAF fighters and saved countless lives.

The relentless approach of winter with occasional snowfall and freezing temperatures meant that No. 1 Squadron did not encounter the *Luftwaffe* again until the following spring. The winter of 1939/40 was one of the worst on record and the relatively primitive conditions at Vassincourt, which included canvas hangars, meant that it was a feat in itself just to maintain operations throughout this period. At the end of November three new pilots joined the squadron, Pilot Officers Raymond Lewis, John Mitchell and John Shepherd. The weather relented sufficiently for the newcomers to carry out local flying to become more accustomed to the Hurricane and to their new surroundings. Not long after George Plinston was posted out, his place as 'B' Flight commander being taken by Prosser Hanks.

On 7 December a standing patrol of six aircraft was maintained between Metz and Pont-à-Mousson from 0715 to 1350 hrs. Shortly after taking off on one of these patrols Peter Matthews had to return as the locker flap on his Hurricane had come undone. He was airborne again as soon as it was fixed but failed to make contact with the others and decided to return to Vassincourt. After flying on course for thirty minutes he was unable to locate the airfield and was soon hopelessly lost. Low on fuel, he attempted to put his aircraft down near St-Dizier but failed to see rising ground in poor visibility and his force-landing became more of a crash-landing. Fortunately he was not hurt but his Hurricane (L1971) was badly damaged.

Over the next two weeks little operational flying was carried out and pilots had to content themselves with local flying and air tests. It was not until 21 December that further patrols were flown, again from Metz to Pont-à-Mousson. The following day sections of three Hurricanes patrolled the line from 1420 hrs until dusk, although one led by Leak Crusoe nearly had a disastrous ending. Sent off at 1500 hrs to intercept a raider reported to be approaching Verdun, the section (comprising Crusoe, Bill Stratton and Frank Soper) found no German activity and so returned to base. The canal that ran alongside the airfield was eventually located but visibility by this time was extremely poor and Crusoe was unsure whether to turn left or right. He evidently turned the wrong way as the airfield did not appear out of the murk and, with darkness approaching, the three Hurricanes force-landed near Loxeville to the west of Commercy. Two were damaged on landing but were deemed repairable.

Winter tightened its grip on northern Europe towards the end of December and the ground crews had a difficult time in getting the squadron's Hurricanes started. Even removing the twelve outer spark plugs to pre-heat them did not guarantee that the Merlins would start and the engines were not all that was frozen. As the airmen had to sleep in unheated accommodation many came down with colds and flu during the winter, which only added to the problems being experienced. Although the pilots' billets were of better quality, many of these did not have a fire and it was not unusual for water to freeze in the rooms overnight.

It was around this time that No. 1 Squadron acquired the services of Lt Jean Demozay who joined the unit as an interpreter. Demozay, the son of a weaver and a native of Nantes, had been refused entry into the French army on three occasions on health grounds but was determined to be of service and he was attached to the unit to help it get on with its French neighbours. He also came into his own as a general 'fixer'. Some accounts have stated that Demozay was already a pilot, having acquired a civilian licence before the war, although there is no confirmation of this. With his local knowledge he was to become an indispensable member of the squadron, especially after the German invasion and the withdrawal through France.

The new month of January brought no respite from the weather and a new problem was a rash of broken tailwheels due to the airfield surface being rutted and frozen. These usually occurred when landing but on occasion happened even when taxiing. There was little of note until the 10th when section patrols were flown between Metz and Nancy and from Verdun to Sorcy-sur-Meuse. In the afternoon Prosser Hanks led nine aircraft in a patrol over Metz although three pilots were forced to drop out with various engine maladies. The Merlin of Frank Soper's Hurricane suffered a drop in oil pressure and rough running. After force-landing he discovered that a con-rod had broken and had penetrated the crankcase. Darky Clowes returned to Vassincourt with oil pressure problems, together with excessive vibration, and Sgt Rennie Albonico left the patrol as his engine was cutting out at regular intervals to make a precautionary landing at Ecury.

On 12 January patrols of three aircraft covered the line between Metz and Nancy and during one of these P/O John Shepherd became lost and eventually landed at a French airfield. In the afternoon Prosser Hanks led five Hurricanes of 'B' Flight in a patrol of the area around Thionville and encountered an aircraft that was believed to be a Heinkel He 112. An interception was attempted but the German aircraft quickly dived for home. This was the first of several sightings of an aircraft that did not see operational service with the *Luftwaffe*. It had been designed to the same specification as the Bf 109 but had lost out to Willi Messerschmitt's contender and the aircraft seen by No. 1 Squadron's pilots would undoubtedly have been a Bf 109.

Bad weather, including significant snow, badly affected flying for the rest of the month. The conditions were causing such concern that on 29 January three Hurricanes were flown to a French airfield at Mourmelon due to a forecast of rain followed by a severe frost. Here they could at least be kept undercover. One patrol was possible on the 29th by a section led by Hilly Brown but the engine of P/O David Blomeley's Hurricane cut and he was obliged to force-land to the south-west of Verdun.

Conditions deteriorated even further in February to the point where Vassincourt became unserviceable for a time. On 21 February Pilot Officers Mould, Shepherd and Mitchell left for Etain-Rouvres to carry out operations from there. On the 22nd the trio patrolled around Triaucourt, however Shepherd and Mitchell lost their leader and had to return. Mould carried on alone and saw a He 111 at 19,000 ft two miles north-west of St Menehould. As he had a height advantage of 5,000 ft he was able to drop onto the Heinkel from up sun and fired a short burst, which prompted the German pilot to dive steeply to ground level. Mould followed firing short bursts whenever he could until his ammunition was exhausted and the bomber was last seen at low level heading into Belgium. On landing at Etain-Rouvres Mould found that four of his guns had stopped firing due to faulty 0.303-in rounds. With a slight improvement in the state of the landing area at Vassincourt, Mould's section returned there on the 25th.

By the end of February No. 1 Squadron's pilots were becoming restless at the lack of activity, a situation that was compounded by the problems that had been experienced with the landing area at Vassincourt. In contrast No. 73 Squadron had fared rather better at Etain-Rouvres and had at least been able to continue flying without restrictions. There was a marked difference in the character of the two squadrons that made up No. 67 Wing. No. 73 Squadron was commanded by the dynamic S/L Brian 'Red' Knox and its two most famous pilots were Flying Officers 'Fanny' Orton and Edgar 'Cobber' Kain. Paul Richey (and others) regarded Kain in particular as a 'split-arse' pilot who would think nothing of leading his section forty miles into Germany on the lookout for *Luftwaffe* aircraft. This kind of behaviour was anathema to Bull Halahan who preferred to play by the book and ordered his pilots not to fly over the frontier unless the tactical situation was in their favour or a combat dictated that they do so. He was of the opinion that the war would come soon enough and was not prepared to risk his pilots on offensive sorties.

The new month of March began with Leak Crusoe being carted off to hospital with measles and not long after P/O John Shepherd was heading in the same direction with jaundice. For those that remained there was the prospect of increased activity as the clouds of recent weeks cleared to be replaced by warm spring sunshine. Patrols were carried out during the morning of 2 March between Metz and Nancy and whilst on one of these a section comprising Hilly Brown, Frank Soper and P/O John Mitchell saw what appeared to be an enemy aircraft well to the east of Pont-à-Mousson. Brown signalled the others into close formation and they flew to investigate, eventually seeing several AA bursts and three aircraft which appeared to be fighters. However, in turning to the south and climbing, so as to come at them from up sun, Brown lost sight of them.

Having reported to base, Brown turned his radio back to 'Receive' just in time to hear Frank Soper shout 'Tally Ho' and on looking round saw a Do 17 flying south at 24,000 ft. The Dornier made a rapid 180-degree turn and dived but could not prevent Soper getting on its tail. As Mitchell was some distance behind, Brown manoeuvred into a position so that he could attack as soon as Soper broke away. The latter fired two bursts but just as he was moving in, the engine on Brown's Hurricane suddenly belched smoke and there was a rapid rise in rpm. It felt as though he had suddenly hit the slipstream of another aircraft and he immediately assumed that he had been hit by return fire or AA fire. With the height that he was carrying he was able to glide to a French aerodrome at Nancy thirty miles to the west where he made a wheels-up landing as he could not get the undercarriage selector into the down position. On inspection there was no combat damage and it transpired that the propeller had failed at the hub (the prop was new and had only flown ten minutes during an air test).

During the course of Frank Soper's attacks flames began to emerge from the port engine of the Do 17 together with an ominous trail of black smoke, however it continued a jinking dive to around 50–100 ft with the rear top gunner firing frequent bursts of tracer. On passing 400 ft there was a hiss as Soper's ammunition ran out and seeing another Hurricane to his right, he broke away to let it move in. He assumed that this was the aircraft of Hilly Brown but he was already on his way back and it was Mitchell who took up the attack. He made four further passes but on the last of these he turned away with his engine smoking having been hit by return fire. The two Hurricanes turned to the west and eventually Soper selected a small grassy patch about 300 yards long by the side of a stream near Sarre-Union where he indicated Mitchell should put his aircraft down. Soper was disturbed to see the undercarriage coming down on the other Hurricane as the field was extremely marginal for a wheels-down landing but as Mitchell had left his radio on 'Transmit' in acknowledging the call, he was unable to tell him to raise it. In turning he lost sight of the other aircraft and despite searching the area for ten minutes and calling continuously he did not see it again. Later in the day news was received that Mitchell had crashed on landing and had been killed. He was credited with a half share of the Do 17 that came down at La Petite-Pierre. This aircraft belonged to 4(F)/11 and two of the three-man crew, including the pilot Oblt Adolf Leupold, were wounded.

The following day patrols between Metz and Nancy were flown throughout the day. At 1120 hrs two Hurricanes flown by Hilly Brown and Frank Soper took off. Half an hour later they were flying at 22,000 ft near Pont-à-Mousson when Soper sighted an enemy aircraft ahead, around 4,000 ft above, which was soon identified as a He 111. Soper flew towards it and when still about 1,000 ft below was fired on from the ventral gun position, which put three bullets into the Hurricane, including one that knocked out one of his own machine-guns. He pulled up and managed to fire a short burst before his aircraft stalled. As he was recovering he saw Hilly Brown move in for a beam attack, which apparently silenced the upper rear gunner. Soper attacked again from underneath before Brown swung in from the rear to fire a long burst from 300 yards down to 50 yards, which hacked various bits off the Heinkel and left it pouring smoke from its engines. As he broke away Brown's Hurricane was covered in petrol and oil, which streamed back from the stricken aircraft. Soper then moved in to deliver an attack from astern, which further disabled the German machine, and by the time that Hilly Brown swung in once again its undercarriage had come down. It then descended to land in a ploughed field near Forbach. The Heinkel had been engaged on a reconnaissance sortie and came from 3(F)/121. Of the four-man crew only the pilot escaped injury, two were killed and the final member suffered a leg wound. A small explosive charge was placed under the nose by the surviving crew so that by the time the French arrived on the scene, the centre section had burned out and all that remained were the outer wings, engines and bullet-riddled rear fuselage.

Patrols were maintained, with a few breaks for bad weather, for the rest of March but there was little further activity for No. 1 Squadron until the very end of the month. It was noted that on a number of occasions the RAF's patrols seemed to coincide with those of the *Armée de l'Air* so that each air force spent a considerable amount of time investigating each other, a situation that was described by No. 1 Squadron's diarist as 'quite a nuisance'. Having endured the atrocious winter weather for so long the RAF's procurement system belatedly clanked into gear and on 4 March several Nissen huts were erected for the maintenance and armament sections, with others for use as Operations and crew rooms. By the 12th all the squadron's Hurricanes had been modified with back-armour, which improved the pilots' confidence considerably.

During the middle of the month two new pilots joined No. 1 Squadron in F/O H.N.E. 'Sammy' Salmon and P/O R.H. 'Dopey' Shaw. Both pilots undertook practice flying and reconnoitred the local area but it was immediately apparent that they lacked training with too few hours on the Hurricane to be familiar with its limitations. They also appeared to have had little or no R/T (radio telephony) practice and were unfamiliar with the aircraft's oxygen system. This meant that time had to be taken from squadron duties to give them the necessary training for active service. In doing so, it also used up valuable aircraft hours to allow them to do non-operational flying.

By now Nos 1 and 73 Squadrons had adopted a new operational programme that allowed pilots a regular break from operations. On the first day No. 73 Squadron was the duty squadron with two flights operational. In case of emergency, No. 1 Squadron had one flight available while the other flight was released for the day. On the next day No. 1 Squadron took over as duty squadron with No. 73 Squadron having one flight available and one released. By alternating the flights that were released, each flight thus had a day where they were excused from duty every fourth day.

Up to now there had been little interaction between Nos 1 and 73 Squadrons but this did change to some extent when Tony Henniker acquired the services of an 8 hp Renault, which made it much easier for him to visit No. 73 Squadron at Etain-Rouvres. On some of his trips he was accompanied by No. 1 Squadron pilots. On one occasion he took Prosser Hanks and Leslie Clisby, however their visit resulted in them causing something of a stir as he recalled in his book *Rolls-Royce on the Front Line* (Rolls-Royce Heritage Trust, 2000)

During the afternoon 'Ducks' came across a British Army motorcycle belonging to an anti-aircraft battery, which had recently arrived. He

27

grabbed it and started to ride it about the village. Then some of the other boys thought they would like to join in so the wretched machine was made to carry Ducks, Leslie, Graham Paul and Fanny Orton (both 73) on the village street. Ducks was the pilot and all went well until they rounded the church and were on their way back – slightly down hill. By this time many of the locals had turned out to watch the fun. On the homeward journey a drain in the road had to be negotiated and the bump threw one of the boys heavily onto Duck's arm causing him to open the throttle. The bike started to gather speed, while four very scared aviators clung on like grim death, and it looked as though the fun and games had got a little too serious. However, another bump in the road brought the incident to a happy and amusing ending, although by now Ducks had completely lost control and was heading for disaster. As luck would have it, the four went straight over the handlebars into a large heap of manure, much to the delight of the onlookers. Hank More had now taken over 73 Squadron and he took rather a poor view of the proceedings, so made Ducks take the motorcycle back and apologise to the Army. After supper we left Rouvres under a bit of a cloud. However, by the next time I visited 73, Hank had decided it had been a good show and told us to come over again soon.

On 29 March the weather was fine but with numerous patches of cloud from 15–28,000 ft. Patrols were maintained along the Metz front from 0700–1530 hrs and at 0910 hrs Pussy Palmer took off at the head of a section of three Hurricanes with Paul Richey as his No. 2 and Peter Matthews in the No. 3 position. By the time that they had climbed to their operational height French AA fire alerted them to the presence of a hostile aircraft, which was seen flying north east at around 20,000 ft. As they attempted to close they lost sight of it in cloud but flew on in the hope that it would eventually re-emerge, in the meantime climbing to 25,000 ft. This particular machine was not seen again but instead they stumbled upon two Bf 109Es, which were heading in a southerly direction about 1,000 ft above. Palmer led his section in a climbing turn but they had been seen and the Messerschmitts manoeuvred to come in from behind. As Peter Matthews shouted a warning, Palmer flung his aircraft into a steep turn to the left but in doing so spun and lost 12,000 ft before regaining control. Although he climbed back to 20,000 ft he did not see either of the German aircraft again.

After the break had been called Paul Richey continued to climb whilst maintaining a good lookout behind. He eventually saw an aircraft appear in an attacking position but was unsure whether it was one of the 109s or Matthews' Hurricane. As it opened fire on him he was left in no doubt and so wrenched his aircraft into a twisting dive to the left followed by a violent pull-out. At this point the 109 flashed by just above before turning to the left and diving. Richey followed it down but was not able to get within range until the German pilot pulled out and began climbing. This gave him the opportunity to open fire at about 300 yards but he found that his gun button was prone to sticking when it was released and so some of his ammunition was wasted. Even so three long bursts were enough to hit the 109 in the starboard wing and it fell away slowly to the right into a steep vertical spiral. As the second 109 was still above him Richey was not able to follow his victim any further and it was last seen descending behind German lines, smoking badly and seemingly out of control (although this aircraft was claimed as destroyed, its pilot, Lt Joseph Volk of 9/JG 53, was able to crash-land, albeit wounded). During this brief exchange Peter Matthews attempted to fire at the other 109 but was not able to get within range.

At 1400 hrs Johnny Walker, Bill Stratton and Darky Clowes took off to patrol in the same area at 25,000 ft. Half an hour later they saw a number of aircraft to the east of Metz, which turned out to be Bf 110s of LG 1. These were Goering's famed *Zerstorers*, or Destroyers, another product of the Messerschmitt factory at Augsburg. It was confidently predicted that the Bf 110 would sweep all before it with its long range and heavy weapons and its reputation had not gone unnoticed by the RAF as Air Marshal Sir Arthur Barrett, the AOC-in-C of BAFF, had promised dinner to the first RAF pilot to shoot one down. Although the Bf 110 had a similar top speed to the Hurricane it was not as manoeuvrable as a single-engine fighter as No. 1 Squadron's pilots were about to find out.

Although they were outnumbered three to one the Hurricane pilots did not hesitate in engaging the German formation and very soon a dogfight developed in which it was a case of every man for himself. The German pilots certainly handled their aircraft with élan doing half rolls, before diving out and coming up in stall turns but it was not long before Johnny Walker had one in his sights. His first burst was wide of the mark but after a second the Bf 110 dived down to 18,000 ft before pulling up into a stall turn, which enabled Walker to catch up and both started to 'mix it' as he later put it in his Combat Report. By this time a small amount of smoke was seen to be coming from the port engine of the German aircraft and its manoeuvres were easily followed. Walker was then joined by Stratton who put in several good bursts (he had rejoined the combat having spun when attempting to turn in behind one of the 110s). By now they were in the cloud layer but the 110 did not use any evasive tactics at all except to dodge in and out of clouds from time to time. Both engines were now streaming smoke and as he had used up all of his ammunition Walker returned to base, leaving the 110 at 3,000 ft in a glide to the east. Stratton also returned at this time and estimated their position as near St Avold.

During the initial stages of the combat Darky Clowes had become aware of two Bf 110s diving from the rear and slightly to the right and having warned his leader had turned into the attack. His turn was rather too tight however as he blacked out for a time, eventually coming to in a dive. He pulled out at 18,000 ft to find that the 110s had followed him down and so came inside their turn and fired three short bursts at the lead aircraft, which pulled up before stalling onto its back and entering a vertical spiral dive. Clowes was then in front of the second 110 but was able to

29

out-manoeuvre it with ease. He then went after another which dived past him but even using full boost he was unable to close the gap between the two aircraft. As he pulled out of his dive he noticed a 110 being attacked by a Hurricane, with another away to the left about to move in behind the RAF machine. Having selected full throttle he was able to close for a beam attack down to 100 yards but overshot and plunged into clouds at 5,000 ft. On climbing above the cloud layer again he was completely alone and so returned to Vassincourt via Metz.

Of the three Bf 110s to be claimed only one was destroyed, that attacked by Walker and Stratton, which was flown by Fw Friedrich Lindemann who baled out into captivity having already ascertained that his gunner (Uffz K. Radeck) had been killed during the attacks. Air Marshal Barrett honoured his pledge to pay for the first conqueror of the Bf 110 to have dinner with him but graciously invited all three members of the section. Two days later his personal aircraft (a twin-engined Percival Petrel) arrived at Vassincourt to transport Walker, Stratton and Clowes to Paris where they dined at Maxim's and, according to the squadron diary, had a 'corking' time. No. 1 Squadron's pilots had been impressed by the speed of the Bf 110 and although manoeuvrable for a twin-engine aircraft, it could not compete with a Hurricane. They were also of the opinion that the rear gunner was incapable of returning fire during steep turns as he was probably 'blacking out' or was too uncomfortable to take proper aim.

On 30 March another new pilot arrived as P/O Peter Boot reported for duty. He had enlisted in the RAF in 1937 and had re-trained as a fighter pilot two years later when he took the course at 6 OTU. He was commissioned on 1 December 1939 and No. 1 Squadron was his first operational posting. He soon fitted in with his experienced colleagues and was to make several claims during the summer.

Further patrolling took place along the Metz front on 1 April from early morning. Just before midday Prosser Hanks was leading a section at 23,000 ft with Boy Mould and Leslie Clisby as his Nos 2 and 3 when the latter saw flak bursts near Thionville. A few minutes later nine Bf 110s were seen about 4,000 ft above and Hanks put his section into line astern with the intention of getting on their tails. As the Hurricanes were climbing below and a little to one side of the 110s they were seen and the German aircraft turned to attack. The leader made straight for Hanks and both pilots fired at each other head-on. The 110's burst consisted of cannon and incendiary bullets and one cannon shell penetrated the port leading edge of Hanks' Hurricane, passing through the main spar and petrol tank on its way with shrapnel piercing the hood. Oil poured out of the mainplane but Hanks decided to fire all of his ammunition before leaving the battle. He fired at about four aircraft altogether and saw one go spinning down completely out of control but as it did another got onto his tail so he was unable to confirm its demise. After evading this aircraft he left the fight and force-landed at Etain-Rouvres.

After the initial exchanges Leslie Clisby broke away to his left and attacked one of the enemy formation, which alternately climbed and dived, executing stall turns and steep wingovers. He was able to fire a total of six bursts with deflection before exhausting his ammunition, by which time smoke and flames was beginning to appear from the port engine and fuselage. The 110 fell into a near vertical dive but having followed it down Clisby lost sight of it to the north of a line between Thionville and Longuyon. He was another to land at Etain-Rouvres, in his case just to get refuelled and re-armed, and he then flew back to Vassincourt

During the dogfight Boy Mould managed to get in several deflection shots at one of the Bf 110s, which began to stream black smoke from the starboard engine and behind the cockpit. It also went into a steep dive and he too was of the opinion that it was out of control. His attention was then taken by another 110 that was firing at him from behind so he turned towards it and continued firing until he had no more ammunition left. At one time in the fight he turned too steeply and his Hurricane flicked into a spin but on recovering after about 1,000 ft he found that the 110 was still on his tail. The Messerschmitts were from I/ZG 26 and although No. 1 Squadron claimed three destroyed, only one suffered combat damage with Obfw E. Blass being wounded. Another was damaged on landing. On this occasion the anti-aircraft flak bursts were no help whatsoever in indicating where the enemy formation was, in fact if the Hurricanes had gone to investigate the fire they would never have seen the Bf 110s.

Although the weather was rather cloudy on 2 April with intermittent rain, patrols were again carried out. During one of these four Hurricanes of 'A' Flight led by Leslie Clisby, together with Laurie Lorimer, Pussy Palmer and Killy Kilmartin, were orbiting Metz at 15,000 ft when flak bursts began to appear to the east. A twin-engined aircraft was seen but as they tried to get closer it turned away and out-climbed them. A group of six to eight aircraft then appeared flying at a great height and to the east. These were chased for some time but again the Hurricanes could not close the gap and fell further behind. By now they had reached 20,000 ft and not long after Killy Kilmartin saw another formation away to the south. He turned towards them but these turned out to be French fighters.

Palmer then attempted to warn Clisby that another two aircraft were moving in from the north and were about 4,000 ft above but someone's R/T was switched to 'send' and the message never got through. He then flew past him to attract his attention but in turning towards the aircraft, by now identified as Bf 109Es, he became detached from the rest by about half a mile. The 109s immediately peeled into an attacking dive, the pair being quite widely separated, but then another was seen only 30–40 yards behind Palmer's Hurricane. This was flown by the German ace Hptm Werner Mölders, the *Gruppenkommandeur* of III/JG 53, and his shells struck Palmer's reserve fuel tank, which went up in a sheet of flame, some of which entered the cockpit. He wasted no time in turning the aircraft on its back before releasing his straps, opening the hood and pushing forward on the stick so that he was thrown clear of his stricken machine. He then delayed opening his parachute for 4–5,000 ft and landed only 500 yards away from German outposts but was eventually rescued by French troops from no-man's land and returned to his squadron. (Palmer had become Mölders' twenty-first victim in a combat career that would see him shoot down 115 aircraft before he was killed flying as a passenger in a He 111 in November 1941.)

In the meantime Leslie Clisby had dived after one of the Bf 109s and opened fire at 250 yards with slight deflection. It straightened out of its left-hand diving turn, which allowed him to fire again and white and then black smoke was seen to come from the engine. It went over onto its back and plunged straight down but disappeared in clouds at around 5,000 ft. Clisby wound his tail trim back and pulled on the control column to climb but did so a little too strenuously and blacked out. When he came to he was south of Saarbrucken and returned to Vassincourt via Nancy. Kilmartin also fired at a 109 which swung up in front of him. He fired a long burst from full deflection to dead astern and the 109 seemed to hover for a moment before flicking onto its back and descending in a spiral dive. In attempting to keep it in sight he got himself into a spin and on recovering saw what he assumed was his 109 crash into some houses in a village and blow up, however it was discovered later that this was in fact Palmer's Hurricane.

Paul Richey should have taken part in this action but had been delayed on take-off as he had trouble getting his engine started. After finally getting airborne he climbed to 25,000 ft to the north of Metz but could not find his colleagues. He did encounter the same fighters (identified as Moranes) that Kilmartin had seen but having already had a run in with the French in the air, he stayed well clear of them. Having estimated his position as near Thionville, he dived through clouds only to discover that he was some way into Germany. Leaving a trail of flak bursts behind him he flew down the Moselle valley at high speed before landing at Metz by which time he was extremely low on fuel. Unfortunately as he was taxiing his tailwheel broke, and although a replacement was quickly delivered, a change in the weather meant that he was to be a guest of the *Armée de L'Air* for a couple of days.

When the weather finally cleared Killy Kilmartin took F/O Sammy Salmon and P/O Peter Boot on a local flight on 5 April to try to teach them some of the arts of combat flying. There was little of note over the next few days and most of the flying that was carried out was of a training nature, plus air tests on three new Hurricanes that had been collected from Reims. Off duty activities included a concert by the Alhambra Concert Party at Bar-le-Duc on the 6th and a cross-country run followed by a cinema show three days later.

On 11 April the squadron was expecting a visit from Lord Trenchard but instead received orders that they were to prepare for a move to Berry-au-Bac, to the north-west of Reims, at any time. This was prompted by the German invasion of Norway and it was thought that a similar move might be made into France, Holland and Belgium in which case the Battle light-bombers based at Berry would be called into action and would need fighter escort. The order to commence the move came at 1500 hrs and No. 1 Squadron's Hurricanes took off from Vassincourt two hours later, becoming fully operational on landing. All equipment and personnel were transferred without incident, except for the unit's thirty-two-seat Leyland bus, which overturned en route when the driver fell asleep at the wheel.

Luckily there was only one other person on board as it had been loaded with kit bags belonging to members of the ground crew. He escaped injury although the driver had to be treated for lacerations to his face. On arrival the officers were accommodated in Ville-aux-Bois and Juvincourt, however the quality of their billets left a lot to be desired.

By noon the following day Maintenance and Flight tents had been erected and the pilots took over a windowless concrete hutment normally used for ammunition stores. With the aid of a stove, a gramophone and a few petrol boxes, it was made reasonably comfortable. Bad weather over the next few days precluded any flying and on 14 April the wind picked up in the late afternoon to such an extent that it blew away the Armoury tent. This was followed by heavy rain, which did nothing to improve the mood of the armourers. Problems had been experienced in that the airmen's billets were some distance from the airfield and with a shortage of transport this was proving to be impracticable. The billets were quickly moved to Pontavert just to the west, much of which had been re-built after the 1914–18 war and offered clean accommodation. It was also noted with some pleasure that the cafes were larger and better. Above all the citizens were apparently keen to have the squadron in their village, something that could not be guaranteed everywhere in France. The Officers' Mess was a bungalow owned by a champagne merchant from Reims who used it as a summer cottage.

The new patrol line was from the airfield to Vouziers but most of the flying that was carried out was affiliation with the Battles of Nos 12 and 142 Squadrons. This was excellent practice for the new and inexperienced, but the more experienced pilots were fed up with the lack of activity. On 17 April Bull Halahan made a reconnaissance flight to the Belgian and Luxembourg borders, noting much road traffic with Allied transport moving towards the frontiers. The next day a replacement Hurricane was delivered, which was fitted with a three-blade constant speed propeller in place of the two blade, fixed-pitch wooden prop of early aircraft. This delivered a much improved performance and pilots were particularly impressed by the sprightly take-off and higher rate of climb.

No sooner had No. 1 Squadron become accustomed to its new surroundings when it was announced that they would be returning to Vassincourt. On 19 April the transport moved off in its own time (not by convoy) and the Hurricanes took off by section and flew by various routes so that the move was carried out as unobtrusively as possible. Some difficulty was experienced in getting the village *Mairie* for use as the Officers' Mess as before, but everything was sorted 'in time for tea'. The officers were the guests of the Hotel de Metz in the evening where *Madame* Jean welcomed her squadron back with a sumptuous dinner.

The frustration of recent days came to an end on 20 April with patrols commencing at first light. Pussy Palmer, Killy Kilmartin and Paul Richey had just returned to Vassincourt when the distinctive sound of a German aircraft made them search the sky. The day was perfect with unlimited visibility and they soon saw it at about 20,000 ft directly over the airfield. By the time that Richey had taken it in,

Kilmartin was already running as fast as he could towards his Hurricane and took off in pursuit. Richey was not far behind although his ground crew had not finished replenishing his aircraft after the previous sortie. Kilmartin flew towards St-Dizier and was fired on by French anti-aircraft guns as he climbed through 10,000 ft but by this time he had lost sight of the German aircraft. Turning right towards Chalons-sur-Marne he saw it again and climbed towards it (in his subsequent combat report he referred to it as a He 111 but it was in fact a Ju 88).

As he closed in he was seen by the crew of the Junkers, which went into a high speed dive. Kilmartin was several miles behind at this stage but then the German pilot inexplicably pulled his aircraft into a climb which allowed him to close the gap considerably. The Ju 88 then continued its dive to ground level, jinking from side to side, but at every change of direction Kilmartin was able to cut the corner and get a little closer. Eventually the pilot realised this and flew straight and level, which resulted in a long stern chase. After several minutes the range had been reduced sufficiently for Kilmartin to open fire but as he did so the Junkers was thrown into a skid, which spoilt his aim. When it straightened up once more he fired again but at the same time the rear gunner was firing at him and one bullet entered the cylinder head on the port bank of his Merlin engine. On breaking away he was aware that the starboard engine of the Junkers was out of action, but of more immediate concern was the fact that his own aircraft was on fire. As he was too low to bale out he had no alternative but to carry out a force-landing at Les Clerimois, about ten miles east of Sens. The damaged Ju 88 came from 4(F)/121. It flew south instead of east and was subsequently attacked by Asp Amouroux in a Bloch 151 of GC III/9 before crashing at Ozolles near Macon. The four-man crew led by Oblt K. Pritzel were captured.

Paul Richey was airborne a couple of minutes after Kilmartin but lost sight of the Junkers as he climbed to 20,000 ft. He was low on oxygen as there had been insufficient time to refill the bottle so he used it sparingly. Even so he began to experience the onset of hypoxia but fortunately was still lucid enough to realise that something was wrong and that he had better get down fast. In the event he descended a little too quickly and having forgotten to throttle back in his slightly befuddled state, it was no real surprise when his propeller disintegrated with a loud bang, although he initially thought that his tailplane had failed. As he still had plenty of height he was able to glide back to Vassincourt to make a well-judged dead-stick landing, which was applauded by Johnny Walker, Prosser Hanks and Boy Mould who had watched him circling silently overhead.

A patrol of five Hurricanes of 'A' Flight led by Prosser Hanks encountered an He 111 around midday flying at 20,000 ft with two Bf 109Es and an 'He 112' near Bouzonville. As they were 5,000 ft above at the time and had the sun behind them they were in the perfect position to attack and having put his section into line astern formation Hanks half-rolled to come in behind the Heinkel. After two bursts it performed a flick-roll onto its back before diving vertically with flames coming from its starboard side. Sgt Rennie Albonico who was flying as the No. 5 in the formation went for the second Bf 109 and in the ensuing dogfight managed to fire three deflection bursts before it broke away to head for the frontier. As it did so it left a trail of thick black smoke. Holding a position 100 yards behind the 109 he fired the remainder of his ammunition and it was last seen in a steep dive apparently on fire.

Boy Mould was not quite near enough to his leader to join in during the first attack so waited at around 22,000 ft for an opportunity. He did not have long to wait as the 'He 112' climbed up in front of his aircraft and he was able to get in a good deflection shot. The German aircraft immediately turned to the east and continued its climb with Mould firing a long burst at ever increasing range as his adversary pulled away. Like the aircraft attacked by Albonico black smoke was seen to pour from the engine. The final member of the section to fire his guns was Sgt Fred Berry who attacked the remaining Bf 109, which also dived towards Germany. It turned on its back and continued diving and disappeared from view at about 5,000 ft between Bouzonville and Saarlautern.

Following this action the He 111 was claimed as destroyed with two of the single-engined fighters being given as unconfirmed destroyed and the other as a probable. From German records however it would appear that no aircraft were lost. In combat, RAF fighter pilots were often fooled into thinking that their fire had caused significant damage to the aircraft they were attacking when the smoke that they could see being emitted was merely that produced by the engine as the pilot went to full power. This was certainly the case with the Bf 109Es that were attacked on this occasion, the 'He 112', of course, just being another Bf 109.

At around the same time that the above combat was taking place, Johnny Walker was leading five Hurricanes on patrol near Metz as Red section with Billy Drake as his No. 2 followed by Darky Clowes (No. 3), Hilly Brown (No. 4) and Bill Stratton (No. 5). Flak bursts appeared in the sky about 5,000 ft above announcing the arrival of an unidentified aircraft flying west but on chasing after it, this was discovered to be a Spitfire (this was probably a photo-reconnaissance machine of No. 212 Squadron based at Seclin near Lille).

Walker then closed up the formation (with the exception of Red 3 who had become detached) and returned to the patrol line. At 1220 hrs, when east of Thionville, Billy Drake informed his leader of condensation trails to the east but Walker continued to take his section towards the north in the hope that they could be drawn over to their side of the frontier. Eventually they came over and were discovered to be nine Bf 109Es in a long, drawn out formation. The 109s were so far apart that Walker was able to attack one in the leading section without fear of being bounced by those behind. They appeared to have been taken completely by surprise and after two bursts the 109 turned over onto its back and went down in flames. In the excitement of watching it go down Walker got into a very steep dive and found it impossible to rejoin the battle. On this occasion at least there was no doubt as to the fate of the 109. It was an aircraft of 7/JG 53, which crashed ten miles south-east of Thionville, killing its pilot Lt F. Sievers.

As Walker went for the left-hand machine in the leading section, the three 109s at the rear turned tail and headed for Germany. Hilly Brown positioned his Hurricane behind the last one but held his fire until he could identify the aircraft for certain as being hostile. By the time he was sure that it was a 109 the German pilot knew that he was being followed and put his aircraft into a steep dive. It then pulled up suddenly, which nearly caught Brown by surprise, but he was able to match the German's manoeuvre and fired a burst as it climbed. It then began to descend faster than before and Brown fired several more bursts before breaking off the attack. The 109 was last seen going straight down near Sierck-les-Bains.

Having given the initial warning Billy Drake had rather an eventful time. He attacked the leader of the first section and after 'milling around' for some time found that he was outnumbered three against one. One of the 109s attempted a full-beam shot, which luckily missed, but having gained an excess of speed it passed directly in front and underneath his Hurricane and pulled up to the right, presenting a reasonable deflection shot, which he took. The 109 then dived vertically and appeared to be out of control. Drake was unable to follow it down however as the section leader dived onto his tail, but it was not long before the situations were reversed. The 109 half-rolled and then dived, turning at the same time, thus giving Drake the opportunity to fire three deflection shots. It then levelled out just above the ground and flew at high speed for the border, jinking constantly from side to side. One evasive tactic was particularly impressive as the German pilot deliberately flew towards high-tension cables and flew underneath them. Fortunately Drake saw them in time and also went under them. By now the border had been crossed and he was flying deeper into Germany but there was one final opportunity to fire when the 109 commenced a turn as the two aircraft sped along a river valley. A trail of black smoke was seen before the German aircraft crash-landed on a hillside. During all of this time the remaining 109 had been trying to get onto Drake's tail but had not been able to close to firing range (the 109 that Drake attacked was from II/JG 53, the pilot escaping unhurt).

In the early afternoon news was received that Killy Kilmartin had been rescued by the French who had entertained him royally, plying him with liquor until he was quite merry. He was returned to the squadron during the evening and was gratified to discover that the Junkers he had attacked had not made it home after all.

The day's events were soon being digested back home as a report under the dramatic headline 'RAF Chasers Roar Into Enemies – 5 Nazis Down' was printed in the *Daily Mail*. It was written by Noel Monks, an experienced Australian journalist who had also covered the bombing of Guernica and was now working as a special war correspondent in France

> After a few days of quiet, aerial activity began again over the Allied front today. Our fighters went out searching for trouble and became engaged in a series of fights, with the odds heavily against them, but all of which were brilliantly successful. The Germans lost four machines which we know to

have crashed, in addition to one that is known to have been put out of action, but was able to creep home before coming down in enemy territory.

I saw the German aircraft over us today, at a considerable height in the clear sky, with only a few fleecy clouds to afford them the shelter that they so eagerly seek. The super-cool atmosphere made their exhausts into a tell-tale streak and several actions followed. In the first, when it was only four against four, a Heinkel 111 was being escorted by three Messerschmitt 109s and was tackled by four British machines near Charnay. In an action that was fiercely fought the Germans lost the Heinkel, whose crew was taken prisoner, and one of the Messerschmitts. The other enemy 'planes disappeared and made for their own lines.

In the second battle the odds were nine to four against the RAF, but the British fighters accept any odds and went straight in. The nine Germans were Messerschmitt 109s – Goering's mass-produced aircraft – and in the first onslaught a Messerschmitt was sent plunging earthwards, to crash inside the Allied lines. Another was so badly punished in the long fight that followed that it, too, was shot down and fell in enemy territory. The pilot of the German 'plane that fell inside our lines made a desperate attempt to escape by parachute, but the parachute failed him, and the pilot was killed.

In the third fight, the British fighter shot down a Heinkel 111 (sic) on reconnaissance over Allied territory. When the British fighter sighted the enemy, he immediately went in pursuit and the fight, which lasted for some time, resulted in the German being so shot up, that he crashed within Allied territory, blazing furiously. Within a few moments the machine was a mass of burnt and twisted metal.

The weather on 21 April was again sunny and bright with excellent visibility but as it was a rest day with 'A' Flight held at thirty minutes available, the only flying carried out consisted of training flights for new pilots. On the 21st Prosser Hanks was leading a morning patrol comprising Laurie Lorimer, Leslie Clisby, Boy Mould and Dopey Shaw when fifteen Bf 109Es were seen above them flying at an altitude that the Hurricane pilots could only dream of attaining. Two eventually came down and were fired on by Clisby and Mould but they immediately broke away and headed for Germany. With the others still above and ready to pounce, the Hurricanes made no attempt to follow and the respective formations were content to keep a wary eye on each other. Eventually each side made the decision to go home with No. 1 Squadron happy that it had achieved a moral victory.

There was little flying for the rest of the month as another period of bad weather with heavy rain caused further problems and for a time the landing area at Vassincourt became extremely muddy. The topsoil consisted of a layer of clay, which meant that it was poorly drained and tailwheels in particular became choked with mud. On 22 April there was a discussion amongst the pilots on tactics. For some time No. 1 Squadron had been flying patrols using five aircraft, with two acting as 'weavers', or 'arse-end charlies' as they were often called. These flew above and behind the basic three-aircraft section to warn of attack. This was an idea that had been pioneered by the French and once adopted the squadron was never taken by surprise. On 28 April six pilots went to Paris for the night, which at least gave them a break from the 'tedious monotony' of Neuville, as the squadron diarist put it. The month ended with electrical storms that meandered over the French countryside and the occasional deluge did nothing to improve the state of the airfield.

Having come face to face with the Messerschmitt Bf 109E in combat, several No. 1 Squadron pilots managed to get a closer look at their most dangerous adversary on 3 May when Bull Halahan led a section of six aircraft to Amiens to inspect a 109 that had been captured by the French. This was an E-3 (Werke Nr 1304 formerly 'White 1' of 1/JG 76), which had force-landed the previous year at Woerth in the Bas-Rhin Department about twenty-five miles north of Strasbourg. In the intervening time it had been tested extensively by the French at Orleans/Bricy and now it was No. 1 Squadron's turn to have a go. After examining the 109 closely on the ground, it was flown by Hilly Brown in a mock combat with Prosser Hanks in a Hurricane. In doing so he became the first RAF pilot to fly the *Luftwaffe*'s principal single-seat fighter. Unfortunately the oxygen system could not be made to work on the 109 and the trial had to be restricted to a height of 15,000 ft. This tended to flatter the Hurricane, which was much happier at medium altitudes.

The Hurricane was fitted with the latest constant-speed propeller but even so Brown left Hanks behind on take-off and during the initial climb. At 15,000 ft the two aircraft approached each other head on to commence a dogfight. Hanks performed a stall turn followed by a vertical turn, which brought him down on the 109 from behind. He then had little difficulty staying there until Brown tried a tactic often used by *Luftwaffe* pilots, a half roll followed by a vertical dive. He began to pull away but had great difficulty pulling out of the dive due to the amount of force that had to be applied to the stick. In contrast Hanks was able to pull out much more easily but in doing so found that he had a tendency to black out. This was attributed to the upright seating position in the Hurricane, which was in contrast to the 109 where the pilot's seat was semi-reclined so that the occupant was rather more 'g' tolerant.

After this dogfight Brown moved in behind Hanks who carried out a series of climbing and diving turns at high speed. During the course of these Hanks was able to reverse the positions within four turns and at no time did Brown manage to get his sights on the Hurricane. This superior manoeuvrability gave the RAF pilots much encouragement but they tended to gloss over the fact that the 109 was around 30–40 mph faster than the Hurricane. It was also significantly better during climbs and dives. After the post flight debrief Halahan was of the opinion that the balance would always be in the RAF's favour once the 109s had committed themselves to combat, provided that the Hurricanes were not surprised and that the odds were no more than two to one. Up to now the Bf 109 had only been seen infrequently but it would not be long before his judgement would be put to the test. Another fact to emerge in the comparison was that the duck egg blue undersides of the 109 made it very difficult for it to be seen from below, unlike the RAF's Hurricanes, which were painted with one wing black and the other white. Halahan strongly recommended that they should be painted with similar camouflage on their under-surfaces and this was adopted in time for the Battle of Britain.

The following morning Johnny Walker led his flight to Amiens but the weather proved to be impossible beyond Reims and they were only able to complete their journey in the afternoon. They arrived just as Hilly Brown was taking off in the 109 to fly to Boscombe Down with an escort of three Blenheims and one Hudson. Once in the UK the German aircraft continued to be evaluated and was given the RAF serial AE479 (this aircraft ended its days in the USA after it was shipped there in April 1942).

In the last few days several new pilots had arrived on No. 1 Squadron including Pilot Officers Charles 'Red' Stavert, George 'Randy' Goodman, Roland 'Rip' Dibnah and Don Thom. Stavert was only eighteen years old and had joined up on a short service commission at the age of seventeen. He had been in the middle of his training at Grantham when war was declared and this was his first operational posting. Goodman was the son of a railway engineer and was a year older, having also secured a short service commission in June 1939. For the time being the new faces were kept out of the firing line so that they could get to know their surroundings and gain experience. It would not be long before every squadron pilot, however raw, would be thrust into the battle.

Just when there were signs that the impending conflict was about to begin, several lorries arrived at the airfield on 7 May and proceeded to offload a large wooden Mess in sections on the ground. Considering that the squadron had been at Vassincourt for the last seven months this did not say much for the efficiency of the RAF's provisioning. It was also noted that the local 'peasantry' took great interest in the arrival of the new Mess and the squadron diary speculated that they were eyeing it up as a source of fuel for the following winter. In the way of light relief 'Mel' (an artist working for *The Tatler* magazine) spent some time with the squadron sketching those who were deemed to have any claim to fame. The caricatures that he produced were eventually published and featured such luminaries as Billy Drake, Boy Mould and Prosser Hanks, together with F/O D.M. Brown (Medical Officer) and F/L J. Vaughan-Roberts (Adjutant). The latter had various nicknames including (predictably) 'Robbie', together with slightly less obvious ones such as 'Sabu' after the film Elephant Boy and 'Fish-hooks', which was a term he often preferred to use instead of uttering a swear word.

On 8 May alarms resulted in the entire squadron being brought to readiness at 0400 hrs but deteriorating weather meant that the immediate panic subsided and the rest of the day was quiet. There was very little activity the following day and many sensed that this was the calm before the storm. For those lucky enough to have the day off there was a chance to appreciate a glorious sunny day and spend time in the ancient city of Metz. Paul Richey travelled with Killy Kilmartin in Sammy Salmon's vintage Lagonda, a car that he had somehow managed to get back from Malaya during a spell on a rubber plantation. On the way they picked up a French girl that Richey had got to know and having disposed of Kilmartin and Salmon the two spent the afternoon walking in the park. The day became even more magical in the evening with the setting sun casting golden embers over the Cathedral St Etienne but in the distance a feint rumbling noise could be heard, like far off thunder, and there were few who did not appreciate its significance. The rumours had thus been true after all and the firing of the main armament of the Maginot and Siegfried Lines left no one in any doubt that the invasion had begun.

CHAPTER FOUR

Blitzkrieg

The German invasion of Holland, Belgium and Luxembourg commenced in the early morning of 10 May and combined the massive use of air power together with the might of the *Wehrmacht* as its mechanised forces smashed their way forwards. Paratroops were also dropped ahead of the advance to seize key locations such as the bridges over the River Maas. From first light air strikes were flown against airfields and communications targets in France and for No. 1 Squadron it was a day of ceaseless activity. 'B' Flight, with Prosser Hanks in the lead, was the first away at 0500 hrs and soon encountered a formation of Dornier Do 17s, which were in the process of attacking Thionville. Hanks accounted for one and Boy Mould shot down another but in doing so he overshot his victim and was hit by return fire. This caused minor damage and punctured a tyre, but of more concern was the fact that one bullet passed through the cockpit and ripped the right leg of his overalls.

Johnny Walker took 'A' Flight into the air not long after with orders to patrol Metz at 20,000 ft. A thick haze persisted up to 5,000 ft and although it was clear above, the ground was nearly obscured, with the low sun only making matters worse. Despite a plethora of targets elsewhere, the five Hurricanes of 'A' Flight had to wait nearly forty minutes before being warned of an enemy aircraft that had been sighted near Etain-Rouvres. Walker put his section into line astern formation and Hilly Brown and Paul Richey swung into their allotted positions, with Killy Kilmartin and Frank Soper bringing up the rear. It was not long before a lone Do 17 was seen, an aircraft of KG 3 on a reconnaissance mission.

Walker went into the attack as the Dornier dived for home but the latter's rear gunner fired the telling blow by putting several bullets into his Merlin engine, leaving him no choice but to leave the fight to crash-land to the east of Verdun. Brown and Richey fired in turn but were hampered by ice that had formed on the inside of their windscreens as they plunged into the warm, moist air at low level. Having had to resort to scratching it off with their gloves, it eventually cleared, which was just as well as by now the Do 17 was flying at extremely low level and there were numerous obstructions. The chasing pack now comprised Brown, Richey and Soper and eventually their attacks began to tell as the Dornier suddenly lost speed before crash-landing at Mont-St-Martin. Of the four-man crew, one was killed and three were captured unhurt.

The primary role of No. 1 Squadron in time of war had always been to provide protection to the Battles of the AASF and around noon 'B' Flight was detailed as cover to an attack that was intended to slow down the German advance. With Prosser Hanks leading, the Hurricanes patrolled over Luxembourg for twenty minutes but no other aircraft were seen and having fulfilled their commitment they turned for home. On the way back around fifteen Do17s were seen with fighter escort but as they were in a poor tactical position, Hanks told his pilots not to engage. Three Hurricanes of another squadron then appeared on the scene and having failed to appreciate the danger, immediately went into the attack. One of these was shot down in quick time as the other two, suddenly aware of the position they had put themselves in, beat a hasty retreat.

During the morning orders had been received that the squadron was to move once again to Berry-au-Bac and 'B' Flight were the first to leave Vassincourt in the early afternoon. On the way they encountered Heinkel He 111s of KG 53 and two were shot down by Billy Drake and Boy Mould. A third was shared by Prosser Hanks with Richard Lewis, although this was claimed as a Do 17. The danger of attacking bomber aircraft in close formation with their ability to cover each other was highlighted once again when Laurie Lorimer was shot down by return fire. He took to his parachute over Chalons-sur-Marne and was unhurt. The rest of the squadron's Hurricanes flew to Berry not long after, led by Bull Halahan. No sooner had they arrived than a He 111 made a bombing run on the airfield and dropped anti-personnel bombs, which fell with an ear-splitting shriek. Pilots flung themselves to the ground but were able to get up and dust themselves down as silence returned. Less fortunate were a farmer and two workers who had been ploughing a nearby field. Their mutilated bodies were found at the bottom of bomb craters and the horses that they had been using had to be shot.

On 11 May the pilots were roused from their sleep at 0245 hrs as they had to be ready to take off half an hour before daybreak. After the previous day's attack it had been decided that the concrete building used as the pilots' hut was too much of an obvious target and a tent was erected 250 yards away in the cover of some trees. As the *Luftwaffe* was carrying out further raids on airfields, all pilots were at cockpit readiness from 0800 hrs so that they could take off at a moment's notice. It was not long before the distant drone of approaching aircraft was heard and one by one the Merlin engines burst into life. As 'B' Flight accelerated over the airfield and into the air, Paul Richey was alerted by his rigger who waggled one aileron of his Hurricane to rock the control column from side to side in his cockpit. At the same time he pointed urgently in the direction of the German aircraft, imploring his pilot to get into the air. Richey wasted no time and once he was airborne found himself flying next to Billy Drake.

It seems likely that Berry-au-Bac was the intended target of the bombers (He 111s) as they immediately turned away and started to climb when No. 1 Squadron took off. In doing so they made it impossible for the Hurricanes to intercept them as their height advantage was too great but this did not prevent Richey and Drake from trying. When he eventually gave up the chase Richey looked round and saw another aircraft silhouetted against the creamy layer of haze that clung to the ground for a few thousand feet. It was a Do 17, but its pilot saw Richey at virtually the same time and he put his machine into a steep dive away to the east. A long stern chase developed with Richey firing several long bursts, which appeared to strike the engines as wisps of smoke were seen and oil splattered onto the Hurricane's windscreen. As he had flown a long way to the east Richey eventually decided to leave the Dornier and turned for home but was unsure of his position.

After some time, he flew over a French airfield as evidenced by Potez 63s dispersed around the perimeter, and landed amid numerous bomb craters. Unfortunately in swerving to avoid one of these, his Hurricane tipped onto its port wing, which damaged the wing tip. As it was deemed unflyable, he had to leave it behind and returned courtesy of the *Armée de l'Air*. The airfield he landed at was Mézières and it seems likely that the Do 17 he attacked was a machine from 3(F)/31 on a reconnaissance flight. It returned with damage, one crew member having been wounded in the left arm.

There was no further action until mid-afternoon when 'B' Flight heading out on patrol came upon a formation of Bf 110s being attacked by Hurricanes from another squadron. Prosser Hanks led the attack and damaged the starboard engine of one of the 110s. Boy Mould went for another, putting its starboard engine out of action, and as he broke away the attack was taken up by Leslie Clisby who shot up the port engine. In the meantime Charles Stavert, the final member of the section, was firing at a third 110 and saw large pieces fall from the tailplane and fuselage. Hanks and Mould returned to attack the second 110, which was diving towards the ground, and not long after it crash-landed at Vendresse to the south of Laon. The crew, which comprised Lt Walter Maurer and Uffz Stefan Makera of I/ZG 26, were captured unhurt. (This was the first occasion that Walter Maurer encountered No. 1 Squadron, he would do so again in September 1942 with similar results, see page 161.) Clisby and Stavert then attacked the third 110, which was last seen diving from 10,000 ft with one engine out of action and the other emitting white smoke. This aircraft was reported to have crashed south-east of Rethel. Clisby also fired at the first 110 and stated that when he last saw it the starboard wing and engine were on fire.

'A' Flight, comprising Walker, Brown, Richey, Kilmartin and Soper, took off in the early evening and at around 1915 hrs came across a large force of forty enemy bombers escorted by a dozen or so Bf 110s. The Hurricanes turned to the west to engage the escorts and went for the left flank of the enemy formation as it was straggling slightly. Johnny Walker fired from astern at one of the 110s but another swung round on to his tail. He was able to reverse the positions quite easily and fired again, hitting the 110 decisively as it went into a climbing turn. It immediately burst into flames and crashed into a wood, the pilot baling out. Walker then fired at another 110, which went over onto its back and dived from 4,000 ft but was not seen to crash.

The 110s then adopted one of their favourite tactics when faced with single-engine fighter opposition, the defensive circle, but it was soon broken up and a general dogfight ensued. Hilly Brown followed one of the 110s into a climbing turn and fired as it straightened out. He then attacked another but soon had one on his tail. After increasing speed in a dive, he pulled out before turning tightly towards it and was able to get behind his opponent. He fired the remainder of his ammunition and the 110 went down in a shallow dive but he lost sight of it as it flew behind some trees. Killy Kilmartin attacked a 110 from the starboard bow with a short burst after which it 'broke into pieces in the air'. After this he dived on another, which rolled on its back and dived straight down into a wood. He then saw a lone Hurricane surrounded by four 110s and went to its assistance but after a short burst at one of these aircraft his ammunition ran out and he was forced to break away and return to Berry.

The Hurricane that Kilmartin had attempted to help was that flown by Paul Richey. After accounting for two 110s, Richey found himself outnumbered and as he was flying an old Hurricane fitted with a two-blade, wooden propeller, he had little, if any, performance advantage over the Bf 110s and had to rely on its excellent rate of turn to stay out of trouble. Every time he managed to get into position to have a shot at one of the 110s that were milling around him, another got behind him and he had to break away again as tracer flashed past his aircraft. Only by turning as tightly as possible with his Hurricane shuddering on the point of a high-speed stall was he able to spoil the aim of his adversaries who were intent on exacting retribution for their comrades who had been shot down.

Most air combats last a few minutes at best but Richey was still in a desperate struggle after a quarter of an hour, by which time the exertion of constant manoeuvring was beginning to have an effect. Eventually he approached a 110 head-on and both fired at each other, Richey slamming his control column violently forwards at the last moment to avoid a collision. As he did so a cannon shell smashed into his engine and his vision was obscured by black smoke. He also felt a blast of hot air and saw a flicker of flame appear beneath his feet. Sliding the hood open, he released his straps and threw himself out of the right-hand side of the cockpit, pulling on the trailing edge of the wing to assist his exit. His parachute opened with a reassuring jolt which temporarily winded him but the Bf 110s that were still circling left him and he floated down to land in a wood near Mont St Jean, to the north of Brunehamel. Soon after coming down he was accosted by two armed French soldiers who were initially suspicious but embraced him warmly as soon as they realised he was British.

Although No. 1 Squadron claimed to have shot down nine Bf 110s with another unconfirmed during this action, this bears no relation to actual German losses. In fact only two had been destroyed including that flown by Lt Friedrich Auinger who baled out with a leg wound after Obgefr Bernhard Hofeler, his radio operator, had been killed. The only other 110 lost was that of Uffz Willi Weis who baled out safely and was taken prisoner (his radio operator, Uffz Erich Ebrecht, was also killed). All the Bf 110s were from 1/ZG 26.

By now the Germans were advancing rapidly through Holland and Belgium and it was vital that the two remaining bridges over Albert Canal near Maastricht should be destroyed (these should already have been blown up by ground forces). This was to be achieved by five Battles of No. 12 Squadron, which were to be protected from fighter attack by No. 1 Squadron's Hurricanes plus two other fighter squadrons. The Battle was hopelessly inadequate in terms of performance and capability. It was highly vulnerable to fighter attack and ground fire so that this operation was likely to be a one-way mission. In the event all five aircraft were shot down and the first posthumous VCs of the war were awarded to F/O Donald Garland and his observer Sgt Thomas Gray.

No. 1 Squadron took off at 0820 hrs led by Bull Halahan with Brown, Clisby, Kilmartin and Soper forming Red section, and Blue section comprising Lorimer, Lewis and Boot. They arrived over Maastricht fifty-five minutes later at 10,000 ft but immediately ran into large numbers of Bf 109Es of 2/JG 27, although several were again identified as He 112s. Hilly Brown was hit twice by a 109 and escaped by diving into cloud, taking no further part in the battle. Leslie Clisby attacked a 109 and saw it hit the ground, having already witnessed another that crashed after being fired on by Frank Soper. Laurie Lorimer and Soper then combined to attack another 109, which was last seen diving towards the ground leaving a trail of smoke behind it. Peter Boot went for two 109s, firing a long burst at one before being attacked by the other, which damaged his starboard wing. In the meantime Killy Kilmartin was dicing with two 109s that had tried to dive on the rest of the squadron below but as soon as these shot into adjacent clouds, they were replaced by two more. After a few steep turns and a few desultory bursts of fire both sides decided to call it a day and dived for home. Only one Bf 109E suffered significant battle damage, that flown by Lt Friedrich Keller, which force-landed near Liege.

The final claims for No. 1 Squadron were made by Leslie Clisby who on emerging from cloud at 3,000 ft over Maastricht saw seven 'Arado biplanes'. These were probably Henschel Hs 126s of 4(H)/13 being used for observation duties. Clisby later claimed to have shot down two, the others escaping in cloud. Of the eight Hurricanes that had set out, only six returned to Berry. Bull Halahan had force-landed to the west of Maastricht when his Hurricane was hit in the engine during combat with a 109 (possibly that flown by Oblt Gert Framm, the *Staffelkapitän* of 2/JG 27). He returned later having witnessed a battle between French and German tanks. He also claimed that the Belgian troops he had seen were running away from the front faster than the refugees. Richard Lewis had his aircraft set on fire and he baled out minus an eyebrow. He came down virtually on the front line and was locked in a cellar for a time, but apparently not all Belgians were running away and a brief counter-attack led to his release and he was soon on his way back in a French car. Of the Hurricanes that did make it back those flown by Brown, Boot and Soper were damaged but were repairable.

In the early morning of 13 May 'B' Flight, led by Prosser Hanks, took off to carry out a patrol and soon encountered a formation of Heinkel He 111s escorted by Bf 110s about ten miles south-east of Vouziers. By this time the Hurricanes were already one man down as Billy Drake had been forced to make an early return due to a faulty oxygen supply. Leslie Clisby went for one of the 110s and saw it crash in flames. He then fired at a Heinkel, which was left with both engines smoking, but this attack could not be pressed home as he was set upon by a French Potez 63 that appeared on the scene. On his way home however he was able to give another He 111 of *Stab* KG 55 his undivided attention and forced it to crash-land with its wheels up near Coulommes. To complete the job he then landed alongside the German aircraft and apparently secured five prisoners who he handed over to the French at Bourcq. However, his efforts were to be in vain as within twenty-four hours they had been freed by the advancing German forces. To make matters worse Clisby's Hurricane was damaged on landing and as it could not be immediately repaired, it had to be abandoned. (The account of Clisby capturing the entire crew single-handedly has been called into question as one member of the crew was so badly wounded that he subsequently died and another died as a result of wounds inflicted by *gendarmes* as he resisted arrest. The three remaining crew were captured as they attempted to reach German-held territory.)

Boy Mould also fired at one of the 110s before attacking a He 111 that had become separated from the rest. This was forced down near Landres and the crew had to take cover in a wood after Mould made simulated attacks on them. He was relieved to see their position soon surrounded by French soldiers who were able to capture the German crew. Another Heinkel was claimed by Prosser Hanks, George Goodman and Laurie Lorimer. The latter's Hurricane (L1681) was hit but he made a successful force-landing at St-Loup-Terrier, although his machine was wrecked in the process.

When the remaining Hurricanes landed at Berry-au-Bac there was no sign of Billy Drake. By nightfall there was still no word about him but the following day a report was received that a British airman had been admitted to the hospital at Rethel and Paul Richey was sent to check on his identity. The pilot was indeed Drake and the full story soon emerged. After leaving his section he saw three Do 17s and as he was in a perfect position to attack he immediately dived on the nearest, but without checking behind to see if there were any escort fighters present. Having disposed of the first Dornier he was moving into position to attack the leader when bullets and shells ripped into his Hurricane from behind and he was aware of a sharp pain in his leg and also in his back. His aircraft burst into flames so he released his Sutton harness and disconnected his oxygen and R/T leads but then realised that he had not yet opened the hood. This momentary hesitation probably saved his life as he suddenly realised that with the aircraft the right way up the flames would be likely to enter the cockpit and set fire to his overalls, which had been soaked in petrol. Instead he inverted the Hurricane before releasing the hood and was able to fall free at a height of about 8,000 ft. As he drifted down he was aware of the Bf 110 that had shot him down and thought that it might have fired at him, although as there was still a battle raging overhead the bullets may have been errant shots from further up.

As he approached a French field his troubles were far from over as he could see a group of farmers who were armed with a variety of lethal-looking implements, including scythes and pitchforks. As he was wearing old pre-war white overalls and had blonde hair, he had reason to worry. Luckily he came down far enough away from them so that he could show them his RAF wings when they arrived. Once his identity had been established they were extremely courteous and helpful and arranged for a car to take him to a nearby medical clearing station. Here he was informed that a doctor was not available and they had run out of anaesthetic. The best they could do to ease the pain was to offer morphine and it was not long before Drake was moved to the hospital at Rethel. When Paul Richey arrived he had just been operated on to remove shrapnel from his leg and back and was lying face down. For the time being Billy Drake's war was over and Richey left him, little realising that five days later he would be in a similar situation. (There is some documentary evidence to suggest that Billy Drake was actually shot down on 11 May, however other accounts, notably that of Paul Richey, identify the 13th.)

The level of German air activity meant that all pilots were being stretched to the limit as calls for them to respond were incessant from dawn to dusk. Fatigue inevitably began to set in and the strain of constant operations led to many instances of irrational behaviour. In his autobiography Tony Henniker gives an insight into the pilot's mood at that time, an account that also shows the level of stress felt by other squadron members.

Our little Mess was very comfortable but we really did not have time to appreciate it. The boys were doing so much flying that they were always dog-tired when they got back in the evenings and all they wanted was food and sleep. Unfortunately they did not get enough of the latter and it was obvious that they could not keep up the flying and fighting all day long with little rest. As time went on, we all – even the non-flying personnel – became a little jumpy. One evening this was brought home to us rather forcibly. We had left the ante-room and were about half way through our supper when we suddenly heard a voice shout 'Take cover!' followed by another 'Take cover!' With one accord, we all jumped up and rushed out of the dining room only to find that someone had left the wireless on. We went back and finished our meal rather sheepishly. The programme was from England where they were apparently still light-heartedly putting on plays about air raids and war – perhaps to remind the populace that there was one going on.

One evening just before dark a Frenchman came rushing into the Mess and said that a parachutist had landed in a field close to the village. Led by The Bull about seven of us, who happened to be there at the time, grabbed our pistols, jumped into the Humber brake and, directed by our informer, made across the fields to a small lake surrounded by bushes where the enemy was supposed to be hiding. We surrounded the spot and closed in, but having beaten up all the bushes, we found nothing. Maybe it was a good thing we didn't have to start shooting as we were more likely to hit each other on either side of the pond. This was the first of a spate of parachutist rumours going round about at this time and apart from those dropping all over the place the thing we really had to take note of was the threat to capture the aerodrome. More sleep had to be sacrificed to mount a night guard, although it mostly involved the ground personnel.

Robbie (a retired RAF pilot), our new Adjutant, did great work in organising our own 'RAF Regiment'. The aerodrome scare had by then turned to the next threat and that was of assassination of personnel of the squadron. Rather than have the pilots scattered around the village in their various billets, The Bull ordered all officers to sleep in the Mess – a reversal of his original plan. This meant that we were going to be slightly crowded but everyone found some floor space somewhere. Laurie Lorimer put his camp bed in the room I shared with Donald Hills [equipment officer], leaving literally no floor space at all. Poor Laurie was very tired and nervy and slept with his gun in one hand. I had to stay up late doing combat reports and went into my room several times and each time I entered Laurie sat up and pointed his gun at me and said he would shoot the next person who came into the room. I felt he wasn't fooling. When I finally went to bed, I opened the door first and went in well afterwards! That night we all slept with our pistols under our pillows. Laurie slept badly and must have had numerous nightmares as he made strange noises throughout the night. He should have been rested for a few days but couldn't be spared and, in any case, he was determined to keep going with the others.

On 14 May 'B' Flight were the first to be engaged when a formation of Bf 110s of 2/ZG 26 flew over Berry-au-Bac. In a hectic action Prosser Hanks claimed to have shot down two, with Richard Lewis, Peter Boot and Boy Mould claiming one apiece, but this came at considerable cost. Hanks' Hurricane was hit in the reserve fuel tank and immediately burst into flames. He was able to bale out successfully but his goggles had not been in place at the time of the attack and he had been bathed in glycol. According to the squadron diary by the time he returned his eyes resembled poached eggs. Of more concern was the fact that Leslie Clisby and Laurie Lorimer were missing. News was eventually received that both had been shot down to the south-west of Rethel. It was confirmed that Clisby had been killed and he was buried in the local communal cemetery, however his remains were to be exhumed in 1950 and re-interred in Choloy War Cemetery near Nancy. Laurie Lorimer's grave has never been formally identified and to this day he is still officially referred to as 'missing in action'.

In the afternoon 'A' Flight carried out a patrol in the Sedan area as Battles and Blenheims attempted to attack bridges over the Meuse. Once again there were large numbers of Bf 109Es in the vicinity, in this case from I and III/JG 53, but there were also Junkers Ju 87 *Stuka* dive-bombers of StG 77. The Hurricanes managed to slip in unnoticed and were able to dive on the Ju 87s before the 109s could intervene. The *Stuka* had a fearsome reputation as a symbol of *Blitzkrieg*, but it was almost as vulnerable to attack by single-engine fighters as the Battles of the RAF. It was even slower than the Battle and its only means of defence, apart from two fixed machine-guns and another on a flexible mounting firing to the rear, was its excellent manoeuvrability. No. 1 Squadron made the most of its opportunity and in a short time five had been shot down, two by Killy Kilmartin, with one each to Hilly Brown, Darky Clowes and Bill Stratton. On this occasion the claims were more than justified as StG 77 lost a total of six aircraft including that flown by its commander, Oberstlt Gunther Schwartzkopff, who had been closely associated with the development of the Ju 87 in the close-support role.

The Bf 109Es did eventually come down but suffered significant losses themselves. Brown and Clowes added to their scores and were joined by Pussy Palmer and Frank Soper. Once again these claims are matched by actual losses on the German side, the most high-profile victim being Oblt Wilfried Balfanz of the *Geschwader Stab* who was wounded in combat and crash-landed near Sedan, his aircraft being written off. Others to be shot down were Obfw Walter Grimmling who was killed when his aircraft crashed between Sedan and Bouillon, and Fw J. Kroschel whose 109 came down south-east of Rethel. He was unhurt but was captured by the French. Two other 109s flown by Uffz Grothen and Uffz H. Tzschoppe suffered combat damage and later force-landed out of fuel, the latter's aircraft being damaged beyond repair.

With serviceable aircraft becoming scarce, an attempt was made to retrieve the Hurricane that Paul Richey had damaged on landing at Mézières three days before. Sammy Salmon was dispatched with a lorry and a small group of airmen but arrived at the French airfield just as the Germans were in the process of obliterating it. For an hour they stayed well clear and when they were congratulating themselves on having seen the last of them, eight Dorniers flew low over the airfield to shoot up the few French machines that had not already been put out of action. Salmon and his men were impressed by the Teutonic thoroughness, which included putting a burst of machine-gun fire into Richey's beloved Hurricane (L1679 'G').

The day ended with the arrival of a replacement pilot, P/O N.P.W. 'Pat' Hancock who probably wondered what he had walked into. Hancock was twenty years old and had spent his early years in Streatham, South London. He had been educated at Croydon High School before attending Wimbledon Technical School. But for the war his future would probably have been as a technician as he worked briefly as a laboratory assistant for British Rototherm, which produced industrial instrumentation. Having joined the RAF on a short service commission, he was posted to No. 266 Squadron in November 1939. Shortly afterwards this unit converted to Spitfires so at least he had some operational experience on fighters, even if it was on the wrong type of aircraft.

An hour before noon on 15 May Holland surrendered following the bombing of Rotterdam the day before. In this attack 980 people were killed and a square mile of the city centre was devastated. Elsewhere *Panzer* divisions were pouring through a gap in the French defences and racing anything up to sixty miles beyond the front line, sweeping aside everything in their path. In the meantime the *Luftwaffe* maintained its attacks on airfields and communications targets, such as railheads, to disrupt the movement of troops intended to reinforce key areas. However, knowing which 'key area' needed additional resources was virtually impossible as command centres had also been targeted and to a large extent the bombing had isolated the various elements of the Allied armies. The battle was also of such a fluid nature that any information that was available was likely to be out of date before it could be acted upon.

Berry-au-Bac was one of the airfields ear-marked for treatment on 15 May and was heavily bombed. Frank Soper who had just landed flung himself face down but the blast of nearby explosions lifted him clean off the ground before thumping him back down again. 'A' Flight was in the air and the Hurricanes were soon embroiled with Bf 110s of III/ZG 26, which were escorting Do 17s of I and II/KG 53. One of those airborne was Paul Richey who had been considerably shaken by his bale-out on the 11th and had only just returned to operational flying after a short break to let his nerves recover. Johnny Walker led his men in a climbing turn to the left towards a formation of 110s but on hearing a warning from Richey that there were more above he turned away and began climbing flat out. On seeing the Hurricanes this second group went into a defensive circle but with numerical advantage the 110s soon became more aggressive.

Johnny Walker fired at one of the 110s, which he later claimed as having shot down, but his engine was hit by return fire and he had to put his Hurricane down in a hurry. He stepped out unhurt but his aircraft was damaged and had to be abandoned. Other claims were submitted by Brown, Kilmartin, Stratton, Mould, Clowes and Soper with Paul Richey claiming two more to make a total of nine. In fact only two Bf 110s had been shot down with another two crash-landing with combat damage. The crew of one of the 110s baled out successfully near Arlon but Fw Josef Kistler and Gefr Kurt Wengler were killed in attempting a one-engine landing near Kirchberg in the Hunsruck. The other two came down near Liege and Maizborn. In each case the crew were unhurt and the aircraft was subsequently repaired. By coincidence ZG 26 also claimed to have shot down nine of their opponents, which they identified as French Moranes.

In addition to Johnny Walker, Paul Richey also failed to return. After the defensive circle broke up he saw a Hurricane below him being attacked by a 110 and dived onto its tail. The German aircraft pulled up into a steep climb and Richey fired a long burst into its fuselage, which began to trail smoke and flames, but another had moved in behind him unseen and the first indication that it was there was then his Hurricane began to shudder under the impact of its shells. A large hole appeared in his port wing and his engine began to pour glycol. To get away he threw his aircraft into a violent half-roll to the left and dived vertically down to ground level from about 18,000 ft. After levelling out he climbed again to 1,500 ft and as the smoke did not appear to be getting any worse he attempted to find his way home. However, even at low speed and low revs it was only a matter of time before his engine overheated. As the smoke suddenly thickened and began to obscure his vision it was obviously time to leave and he baled out for a second time, landing in a field with a bump that nearly knocked him out. His luck was in as he spotted an RAF vehicle travelling along a road and on flagging it down, got a ride to HQ 75 Wing. From there he travelled to Reims where he met some of No. 73 Squadron's pilots, including Cobber Kain, before returning to Berry-au-Bac.

The day's other excitement involved Sammy Salmon who was detailed to take three replacement pilots, including Pat Hancock, to 501 Squadron by road (Hancock's 'detachment' was to last all of two days and he was back on 18 May). On the way they witnessed a scrap between some of No. 501 Squadron's Hurricanes and some Do 17s of II/KG 3 during which a crew member of one of the Dorniers landed by parachute in a field next to the road on which they were travelling. The German was fortunate in that Salmon got to him ahead of an angry French mob and he was bundled into the car and taken to No. 501 Squadron's Mess. On the way they had to fend off some French soldiers who attempted to stop them to claim the prisoner as theirs. On his way back Salmon saw another low level dogfight, this time involving Hurricanes of No. 73 Squadron and Bf 110s of 6/ZG 76. During this F/O Fanny Orton was shot down in flames and had to bale out at 600 ft with a shoulder wound and burns. Salmon then looked on as another Hurricane (possibly that flown by Sgt L.Y.T. Friend) fought a desperate battle with four 110s, which took turns in shooting various bits off the RAF machine as it stayed in a tight vertical bank. It finally got away and tore off in the direction of Reims at zero feet. Two of the Bf 110s were shot down during this combat and another was damaged.

The pace of the German thrust into France was now threatening the airfields of the AASF. Rethel had fallen (Billy Drake had managed to get away from its hospital just before) and it was imperative for the squadron to move further to the west. During the hours of darkness orders were received to re-locate to Vraux, near Conde-sur-Marne with the Hurricanes flying over at first light. This was midway between Reims and Paris and would have placed No. 1 Squadron directly in the firing line if the Germans had made a thrust directly towards the capital. Instead they were more intent on heading for the Channel and so 16 May was a relatively quiet day in terms of contact with the enemy, if not in the number of rumours flying about as to the extent of the advance. The final members of the ground party left Berry-au-Bac just in time as the bridge over the Marne-Aisne canal was blown up as soon as the last lorry had got across.

No. 1 Squadron shared the airfield at Vraux with the Blenheim light-bombers of No. 114 Squadron and were looked after in this unit's Mess. Having eaten their meals in the evening, there was none of the games or music normally associated with off duty hours. Instead the rigours of the last six days had taken their toll and all of the squadron pilots, including Bull Halahan, fell asleep at the table and eventually had to be aroused from their slumbers by F/O Vaughan-Roberts. During the night of 16/17 May a column of French tanks sped past the airfield heading towards Paris, its commander stopping briefly to inform them that the Germans had taken Reims and were not pausing in their headlong dash to the west. As he was not able to contact 67 Wing or HQ, AASF, for confirmation, Bull Halahan gave orders on his own initiative for an advance party to head for Anglure, thirty miles to the south-west, while Johnny Walker took over at Vraux with orders to fly there after daybreak. As half of the squadron headed west, a phone line was eventually established to 67 Wing, which informed Walker that the French had been misinformed and that the squadron was to stay where it was. This put Walker in a difficult position as he only had sufficient fuel and ammunition for one day's operations, hardly any ground crew and no spares.

Patrols were recommenced at dawn and it appeared that there were indeed no German troops or armoured units in the immediate vicinity. At 0900 hrs Johnny Walker took off at the head of Red section with Brown (No. 2), Palmer (No. 3), Kilmartin (No. 4) and Soper (No. 5). The intention was to attack Ju 87 dive-bombers that had been attacking Allied troops retreating from the Sedan area. On reaching Vouziers at 8,000 ft a strong force of Bf 110s of LG 1 was encountered but with clearer conditions away to the east and strong fighter opposition above, there was little chance of being able to fulfil the mission. Instead Walker took his section up in a steep climb as the 110s turned to the south-west in an attempt to position themselves up-sun. By the time that he had reached 18,000 ft he felt he was in a position to attack and dived on the nearest 110, but as the battle developed more joined in until it was estimated that up to twenty-five Bf 110s were in the fight against five Hurricanes.

During the dogfight Walker, Brown and Kilmartin claimed one apiece with Soper claiming two. Post-war research has shown that three Bf 110s were destroyed including the *Staffelkapitän* of 14(Z)/LG 1, Oblt Werner Methfessel, an eight-kill ace who was lost along with his radio operator Uffz Heinz Resener. The 110 crewed by Uffz Friedrich Schmitt and Uffz Heinz Schmidt was also shot down and both were killed. A third flown by Lt Kurt Schalkhausser and Uffz Joachim Jackel was badly damaged during the combat and both baled out wounded.

No. 1 Squadron's Hurricanes were also badly mauled with Pussy Palmer being shot down in flames by the Bf 110 flown by Fw Gerhard Jentzsch, however he baled out uninjured. Johnny Walker's aircraft took a cannon shell through the wing and aileron, which required him to land at a French airfield on the way back so that a temporary repair could be effected with a hammer and chisel. Although he made it back safely, Frank Soper's machine resembled a sieve in places and was damaged so severely that its repair was beyond the capability of the squadron's ground crews. In the afternoon a section from 'B' Flight was scrambled to intercept a formation of five Do 17s that had been seen loitering around Vraux but these made off as soon as the Hurricanes were seen.

By the early morning of 18 May the move to Anglure was back on again and this time there was no doubt that the Germans were not far away. Refugees had been streaming past for some time and there had been constant rumours of German paratroops being dropped into forward areas. The squadron had also been warned of possible action by fifth columnists but as yet these had not materialised. Suspicions were raised shortly before leaving Vraux when a nondescript party of men were seen shambling along the skyline some distance away. Frank Soper went to investigate and discovered them to be *Armée de l'Air* personnel who had been forced to evacuate their former base and had chosen to walk, as military road transport was being continually bombed and strafed. There were even reports that the endless lines of refugees that were heading west towards Paris were coming under air attack as the Germans sought to create as much disruption as possible behind the front line.

All serviceable Hurricanes were flown to Anglure but this did not include Frank Soper's L1905 'H', which had been damaged the previous day. This had to be rolled into a bomb crater and set on fire to prevent it falling into German hands. As they flew to their new base, P/O Charles Stavert, with all the innocence of a new boy, chased after a Do 17 that he had seen shortly after taking off. This was an aircraft of 3(F)/31 on a reconnaissance sortie and he wasted no time in shooting it down, Fw Kernbuckler and crew surviving. Having disposed of the Dornier he looked round for the rest of the squadron but there was no sign of them. He then flew off in the wrong direction and soon became hopelessly lost. Eventually he saw an airfield but as he approached he saw a He 111 about to land and shot this down as well. After some time he managed to locate Vraux but by this time his fuel was running low and he had to force-land nearby. On finally making it to the airfield he was just in time to join up with the last members of the ground party who were in the final stages of packing up before moving to Anglure.

No. 1 Squadron's new home was a large grassed area near the village of Pleurs. After a few local flights in the morning to get to know the area, an escort mission was laid on in the afternoon in which Blenheims of No. 18 Squadron attacked enemy columns near Le Cateau. At 1430 hrs Hilly Brown took off in the lead of a formation of eight aircraft but on approaching St Quentin at 2,000 ft they were bracketed by very heavy anti-aircraft fire. Thinking that it was a case of mistaken identity, Brown turned slowly through 180 degrees, waggling his wings, but the firing continued, indicating in no uncertain terms that this area had been taken by the Germans. By now the Hurricanes were widely separated and as he turned to the south a Henschel Hs 126 observation aircraft passed under him. Brown attacked twice but on each occasion the pilot used his manoeuvrability to the full and turned rapidly through 180 degrees. After the second attack it was not seen again. When near St Quentin Sgt Rennie Albonico was seen to dive down and not long after his Hurricane was hit by flak and he crash-landed on the wrong side of the lines. He survived unscathed but was taken prisoner.

On 19 May the call to scramble did not come until just after 1000 hrs, which sent twelve pilots racing to their machines. Red Flight was led by Johnny Walker and in number sequence the rest comprised Hilly Brown, Paul Richey, Bill Stratton, Killy Kilmartin and Frank Soper. Blue Flight had Prosser Hanks at its head, with George Goodman, Boy Mould, Pussy Palmer, Raymond Lewis and Charles Stavert. Their orders were to provide a cover patrol for Battles, which were attempting to stem the German advance towards the road linking Montcornet and Neufchatel-sur-Aisne. The patrol line was from St Quentin to Rethel and on the way several enemy formations were seen but had to be ignored. In the event the Battles could not be located but shortly before they were due to retire they saw twelve aircraft in four sections of three, flying west. At first it was thought that they were Blenheims that had also been attacking the German *Panzers* but soon they were identified as Heinkel He 111s, without fighter escort (these were aircraft from III/KG 27).

As the aircraft of Blue Flight maintained their height to provide cover, Red Flight moved into echelon to starboard and went into the attack. This was not pressed home as it might have been due to a shouted warning to 'Look over behind' and most pilots broke away thinking that German fighters were present. Hilly Brown did not hear the message and fired at one of the Heinkels, which was left with both engines smoking and its undercarriage down. It appears that the warning was given by Frank Soper who mistook another Hurricane for a German fighter. Thereafter all aircraft made individual attacks on the bomber formation.

Johnny Walker made several attacks and later fired at a He 111 with its wheels down, which may have been that already damaged by Hilly Brown. It was seen to glide down towards the ground but with his ammunition exhausted, Walker left the fight and returned via a French aerodrome. Brown in the meantime had managed to prise another Heinkel away from the main formation and saw it make a forced landing in a ploughed field about twelve miles west of Chateau-Thierry. As he circled above he saw three of the crew being taken prisoner by French soldiers. Bill Stratton was flying directly behind Johnny Walker and delivered several individual attacks. During one of these the Heinkel he was firing at broke away but it later recovered and rejoined the formation.

Killy Kilmartin had been firing at one of the Heinkels when the initial warning was given and this aircraft was last seen dropping away with white smoke coming from both of its engines. He then fired at a He 111 that had become separated and was seen heading back towards Germany at 1,500 ft. As he opened fire the Heinkel jettisoned its bomb load and descended into a valley with its undercarriage down. Not wishing to be drawn too far away from friendly territory, Kilmartin turned back and flew home. Frank Soper, the final member of Red Flight, attacked the No. 2 of the rearmost section of three and left it with smoke pouring from both its engines. He then fired at the leading Heinkel and damaged its port engine but was forced to break away when his Hurricane was hit by return fire, which punctured the port fuel tank and damaged the engine. With his aircraft on fire, he dived vertically which appeared to put the flames out, although he had no way of knowing this as the cockpit had been sprayed with glycol and he was unable to see. By an amazing piece of flying he carried out a successful force-landing near Chateau-Thierry with his wheels up but he was flung forwards as his machine decelerated rapidly and was knocked unconscious when he hit the base of the reflector gunsight. As the other members of Red Flight withdrew, there was no sign of Paul Richey.

The lack of German fighters prompted Blue Flight to join the fight and Prosser Hanks went after a straggler to find that only two of his guns were working. George Goodman had already returned as his oxygen system was not working so the next to attack was Boy Mould, however his Hurricane suffered engine trouble shortly after he opened fire at one of the Heinkels. Pussy Palmer went for another straggler after a Hurricane had broken away and saw it go down in flames. He then went for a second Heinkel but during this attack he ran out of ammunition and returned to base. Raymond Lewis latched onto a He 111, which had already been attacked by two other Hurricanes, and left it with its starboard engine on fire, while Charles Stavert fired at another lone Heinkel causing one of its engines to pour black smoke.

Paul Richey had already accounted for two of the Heinkels when he went after a third. During the combat however he became complacent and as he broke away from the doomed bomber he presented an inviting target for the German gunners. The flash of their tracer was accompanied by the unmistakable rattle of shells hitting his aircraft, but this was followed by a deafening bang on the right-hand side of the cockpit and a spurt of blood from his right arm. There was no panic, at least not yet, more a rational appraisal of his situation and the realisation that his right arm was now virtually useless. This calmness quickly disappeared however when he found that he could not move his left arm either and so was powerless to arrest the Hurricane's terminal descent.

With his inability to control his aircraft Richey began to scream but stopped when he felt his left arm move. In a flash he grasped the jettison lever for the hood but it was jammed. At the same time his right arm flopped onto the control column and he pulled back on the stick, which brought the Hurricane out of its headlong dive. By now he was aware of severe pain in his neck but tried to blank this out by concentrating on the French countryside, which was now only about 2,000 ft below. As the hood was jammed he had no option but to bring his aircraft down for a force-landing and chose a harrowed field close to a village. As the Hurricane bounced over the field blood from his right arm splattered onto the instrument panel but fortunately the Hurricane did not go over onto its back.

Once it had come to a halt Richey made renewed efforts to open the hood but even when he put both feet against the panel and pushed with all his strength it still would not move. He could smell petrol, and with ominous wisps of smoke coming up from the floor of the cockpit, fire was a distinct possibility. This shocked him into one last big effort, which finally succeeded in moving the hood to the half-way position. This was enough for him to get out of the cockpit and he ran away as quickly as he could, fearing that his aircraft might explode at any time.

Richey's Hurricane did not blow up but it soon became clear just how lucky he had been. He had been shot in the neck by an armour-piercing bullet, which had nicked his jaw before coming to rest against his spine at the base of the neck. This had caused the temporary paralysis he had experienced during the dive but if the bullet had lodged in a different way, his movement would not have come back and he would have dived into the ground. Richey was doubly fortunate as the bullet had also exposed the carotid artery. If it had struck a merest fraction to one side he would have bled to death in a very short time. After a seemingly endless wait, but one that was probably no more than a few minutes, Richey was helped by some French soldiers who took him to a French hospital near Chateau-Thierry. From here he went to the American hospital in Paris where he was operated on by the famous neurosurgeon Professor Thierry de Martel who expertly removed the bullet. It took a long time for Paul Richey's wounds to heal, both physical and psychological, and he did not return to operations until April 1941 when he joined No. 609 Squadron, which by then was commanded by his friend S/L Michael Robinson.

Although the combat situation was becoming increasingly confused it appears as though No. 1 Squadron had come into contact with the 8th *Staffel* of KG 27. The confirmed claims as submitted were one each to Brown and Palmer, Soper with two and Richey with three. Actual German losses were three He 111s including that flown by Oblt K. Bormann, which came down near Chateau-Thierry. Having set fire to his aircraft, he and two of his crew (the other crew member was badly wounded and died later) managed to evade until 24 May when they were finally captured by the French. Of the other Heinkels, one crash-landed near Chantilly and the other was abandoned over German-held territory.

CHAPTER FIVE

The Withdrawal from France

Throughout the hectic fighting of the last nine days No. 1 Squadron had fared rather better than most other fighter squadrons and still retained the majority of the experienced pilots that had flown to France on that bright summer day in September 1939. The stress of constant operations had taken its toll however and this was compounded by a lack of rest, which saw pilots asleep as soon as they could collapse into a chair after landing (assuming they could find one). Bull Halahan was aware that his men could take no more and had already written to Air Vice-Marshal P.H.L. Playfair, the AOC-in-C of AASF, to the effect that if the current level of operations continued most of them would be killed in action within the week. He reiterated these views after the actions on 19 May and was pleasantly surprised when his request for them to be rested was acceded to. This meant that the senior members of the squadron, including the likes of Johnny Walker, Prosser Hanks, Pussy Palmer, Boy Mould, Killy Kilmartin and Frank Soper, would be heading back across the English Channel within a matter of days so that their valuable combat experience could be passed on to the next generation of fighter pilots.

Bull Halahan was also to hand over command, the new CO being S/L David Pemberton who was already well acquainted with the squadron. Pemberton was originally from Stratford-upon-Avon and had attended Stowe School before becoming a Flight Cadet at Cranwell in January 1931. His first posting had been to fly Handley Page Hinaidi and Heyford bombers with No. 99 Squadron but after a time in Palestine and Transjordan he made the transition to fighters and joined No. 601 Squadron in July 1937. Before serving with No. 67 Wing he was a flying examining officer with 26 (Training) Group. Hilly Brown was retained and was soon to be promoted to Acting Flight Lieutenant to take over from Johnny Walker as 'A' Flight commander with F/L P.E. 'Fritz' Warcup being posted in to take over from Prosser Hanks at the head of 'B' Flight. There was further continuity with the pre-war line up as Darky Clowes stayed with the squadron as the senior NCO pilot. Those pilots who had arrived in the last few weeks such as Charles Stavert, Peter Boot and George Goodman also remained, the mere fact that they had survived catapulting them into responsible positions as section leaders.

By 20 May the German armoured columns were advancing relentlessly towards Amiens and took Cambrai during the morning. Early the following day news was received that Amiens had fallen with *Panzers* securing the bridge over the river Somme at Abbeville. By the evening reconnaissance units of the 2nd *Panzer* Division had reached as far as Noyelles-sur-Mer on the Somme estuary, which flowed into the English Channel. On 23 May General Lord Gort, the commander of the BEF, ordered a withdrawal from Arras and over the next few days the British Army retreated towards Dunkirk from where it was to be evacuated during Operation *Dynamo*.

With German forces concentrating on securing north-east France and pushing towards the Channel coast, No. 1 Squadron was relatively secure at Anglure, for the time being at least. Patrols were carried out to the north but the resources that could be deployed were nothing more than a minor annoyance to the German military machine and could in no way influence the battle. This did not prevent the RAF from trying and on 23 May No. 1 Squadron was ordered to send twelve aircraft to attack dive-bombers operating between Arras and Valenciennes. The route taken shows the extent to which German forces had moved into France. From their base at Anglure they could easily have flown direct to Arras but to avoid flying over German-held territory they had to fly to the south of Paris before heading north-west to land at Rouen-Boos where the Hurricanes were refuelled. In mid-afternoon they set out to the north-east but by this time the weather was beginning to close in and on arriving in the designated area at 2,000 ft they were confronted with what appeared to be a solid bank of cloud virtually down to ground level.

This was the least of their worries however as they were greeted by a formidable anti-aircraft barrage and as the squadron was flying at a relatively low altitude it proved to be extremely effective. This situation was made worse as around two-thirds of the pilots were new and were thus under fire for the first time. Fritz Warcup was quickly onto the R/T to get his pilots to spread out and adopt evasive tactics whereupon everyone began to 'aerobat themselves into a stupor'. The height of the flak bursts was always deadly accurate and the air was criss-crossed with the red lines of shellfire from quick-firing guns. As it was obvious that there were no dive-bombers in the vicinity and that the only task being undertaken was to provide target practice for German gunners, it was agreed that the best course of action was an orderly withdrawal. Fritz Warcup did so under the impression that he had eleven Hurricanes behind him when in fact there were none. The aircraft that he could see were six Bf 109Es of 2/JG 3, which took turns to shoot various bits off his tail. The armour plating behind his seat was also hit by several machine-gun rounds. He made it back to Rouen fifteen minutes after the rest of the squadron where he proceeded to tear a strip off everyone else for leaving him.

As the Hurricanes were being refuelled a He 111 was seen flying over the aerodrome and four aircraft were quickly airborne and climbing fast in pursuit.

Having ceased with his remonstrations, Fritz Warcup was in the lead and went into the attack when he had reduced the range sufficiently. As he broke away Darky Clowes and Don Thom moved in from behind and the Heinkel eventually disappeared into cloud trailing smoke and with its wheels down. This was probably an aircraft of 5/KG 55, which force-landed near Trier having also been attacked by French fighters. Although the pilot escaped unhurt, one crew member was killed and two were wounded. When discussing the combat on their return, Darky Clowes mentioned that during his attack the rear gunner had appeared to let out a stream of mesh netting, which he assumed had been intended to wrap around his propeller. A return was made to Anglure in the evening, all except for four pilots who, due to a combination of lack of petrol and light, were forced to spend the night at Le Bourget.

On 25 May patrols were carried out in the morning in the area around Brienne-le-Chateau but no enemy aircraft were seen. In the afternoon the patrol line was moved further north between Laon and Chauny with the intention of covering ground operations. Once again the danger was not so much from fighter aircraft but fire from the ground. The Hurricane flown by Don Thom was badly hit and it came down behind the front line, Thom being made a prisoner. Several other aircraft were also hit and although they were able to return, this type of damage posed a serious problem as regards the squadron's operational capability. When each patrol was over it was often found that two to three aircraft had received flak damage to a greater or lesser extent and due to a lack of proper servicing and maintenance facilities some of these had to be written off as unserviceable. It was calculated that wastage of aircraft had so far been in the region of thirty-eight, but that only ten had actually crashed. As a result it was rare for the squadron to be able to put up more than ten aircraft at any one time. It was also noted that virtually every aircraft that No. 1 Squadron had had to strike off charge would have been in the air again within a week back in the UK.

The following day David Pemberton led 'A' Flight on a 'safety first' patrol at 0530 hrs but nothing was seen. Later in the morning an order was received for 'A' Flight to provide cover to a bombing attack on an airfield at Ochamps, approximately fifty miles north-west of Luxembourg. The leading section comprised Hilly Brown, Sammy Salmon and Roland Dibnah but the Hurricane flown by the latter was hit by flak ten miles south of the objective, which wounded him in the thigh. At the time they were flying deep into German-held territory but Dibnah was able to fly thirty miles to the south before crash-landing near Nancy. In the afternoon 'B' Flight were to have escorted a French Potez 63 on a photographic-reconnaissance mission in the region of Soissons, but this was abandoned when it was discovered that the cloud ceiling was below the operating height of the French aircraft, which also did not appear at the appointed time.

The Dunkirk operation got under way on 27 May but for No. 1 Squadron it was a relatively quiet day with Hilly Brown leading a patrol that passed off uneventfully, although another two aircraft returned with flak damage. Two further patrols were undertaken without incident. By now the *Luftwaffe* was making regular reconnaissance flights in the vicinity of Anglure. These usually appeared between 1600 and 1800 hrs but as the airfield had not yet been attacked it was assumed that it had escaped detection. The landing ground was merely a collection of fields that had been rolled where necessary, leaving crops of wheat, clover, rye and oats to stand elsewhere as a perfect natural camouflage. Tented accommodation had been put up in nearby woods to prevent it being seen from the air.

Although Anglure had not yet been bombed, this did not prevent Sammy Salmon and Jean Demozay from making a preliminary survey of other areas further to the west on 29 May in case a rapid relocation was needed. Having carried out their task they made an impressive return in a luxury, seven-seat transport aircraft loaned by the *Armée de l'Air*. A sudden deterioration in the weather with low cloud over much of northern France saw little activity for No. 1 Squadron over the last two days of May with only practice flying being possible. The cloud also shrouded Dunkirk and led to a marked increase in the number of troops being evacuated to the UK and a genuine hope that the operation to remove the remnants of the BEF might be a success after all.

As all the Merlin engines were running perfectly, Tony Henniker took the opportunity on 29 May to return to Neuville as the squadron's hurried departure on the 10th had left many bills unpaid. To his surprise Bar-le-Duc was undamaged and was resplendent in the spring sunshine. Even Neuville, which had seemed so depressing in winter, had a completely different feel to it and looked positively radiant under a blue sky with the trees and foliage in full leaf. The local people were genuinely pleased to see Henniker and his presence raised hopes that the squadron might be returning. In giving an answer to the inevitable question he had to be at his diplomatic best so that they were not too disappointed.

He then returned to Bar-le-Duc and the Hotel de Metz where *Madame* Jean gave him her usual effusive welcome. She wanted to know all the squadron news but was able to tell Henniker something that he did not know; that Rip Dibnah was in the local hospital. During the patrol on 26 May he had been wounded in the thigh and had initially been taken to hospital in Verdun. Somehow *Madame* Jean had got to hear of his whereabouts and as nothing had been done to relieve his suffering, had him taken to the hospital in Bar-le-Duc where the shrapnel was removed from his leg. She paid him daily visits and even had her own doctor look after him. Henniker went to see Dibnah, along with *Madame* Jean, but he was in a lot of pain and the visit had to be brief. (Soon afterwards he was removed to Bordeaux before returning to the UK. After making a full recovery he flew with 1 (Canadian) Squadron and S/L Douglas Bader's No. 242 Squadron.)

On 1 June twelve Hurricanes took off from Anglure at 0625 hrs bound for Rouen-Boos and were at readiness by 0745 hrs. Half an hour later 'B' Flight was patrolling the line from St-Valery-en-Caux to the Somme estuary under a solid cloud base at 9,000 ft. The intention was to protect British troop movements from attack by dive-bombers but none were seen. Later in the morning 'A' Flight was airborne on a similar cover patrol. Red section comprised Hilly Brown, Sammy Salmon and John Shepherd with Darky Clowes, Peter Boot and Peter Matthews forming Yellow section. At 1109 hrs nine Bf 109Es were seen above and behind and although Brown tried to take his section up, the Germans held the initiative throughout a brief engagement. Brown was himself attacked by three different 109s while John Shepherd was shot down and baled out near Dieppe. Clowes managed a snap shot at one of the German aircraft but Peter Boot's aircraft was badly hit, although he made it back to Rouen without further incident. Another patrol was carried out in the afternoon before the squadron returned to Anglure at 1700 hrs. On arrival there was news that Shepherd was none the worse for his adventure and in the evening he was collected from Rouen by air.

The preparations for a possible move paid off as on 3 June the squadron's Hurricanes left Anglure at 0415 hrs for Chateaudun, seventy-five miles south-west of Paris, with the road party arriving there in the early evening. The routine was the same as previously and for the next few days the squadron took off for Rouen-Boos at first light to carry out the usual patrols from there. According to No. 1 Squadron records the next major action took place on 4 June, although documents produced by 67 Wing indicate that it took place on the 5th. During a patrol at 0600 hrs large numbers of Do 17s and He 111s were seen, escorted by Bf 110s, the number totalling around 120. Several pilots put in claims, including Peter Boot for a He 111 and a Do 17, Peter Matthews a He 111 and Hilly Brown for a Do 17, but most of No. 1 Squadron's Hurricanes were fired upon, either by the 110s or the concentrated crossfire from the bombers.

Having been hit in the radiator by a Bf 110, P/O H.B.L. Hillcoat had to hurriedly put his Hurricane down as it was beginning to burn. Although he was unhurt, his aircraft was a write-off. Sgt J. Arbuthnot suffered a similar sequence of events, however in his case the radiator was shot away by return fire from the He 111s he had been attacking. P/O Pat Hancock's Hurricane was also badly hit, in the course of which his airspeed indicator was smashed. On landing at Rouen-Boos he had the choice of hitting a hangar or a parked Blenheim and decided that the latter was marginally preferable. Although he stepped out unhurt his aircraft was a wreck. Having successfully baled out on 1 June, P/O John Shepherd's luck finally ran out during this action as he was shot down and killed by a Bf 110. Nearly all of the Hurricanes that made it back landed with minor combat damage at the very least.

Over the next few days further patrols were carried out from Rouen-Boos and Beaumont-le-Roger, which carried the code names *Thelma* and *Robson* respectively. On 9 June eleven aircraft (six from 'B' Flight and five from 'A' Flight) took off at 0415 hrs for Dreux (code name *Maudie*). Here they refuelled before undertaking a patrol between Vernon and Pont-de-l'Arche at 22,000 ft during which P/O H.J. Mann saw a large formation of about twenty-seven enemy aircraft about 10,000 ft below travelling north along the course of the Seine towards

Rouen. As his radio had packed up he attempted to attract the attention of his leader by waggling his wings but he was unable to see them. Mann dived towards them and attacked a straggler but in doing so attracted the attention of around ten Bf 110s, which approached in a wide circle on his port beam with every intention of getting onto his tail. Mann immediately turned towards them and fired a short burst at one of the 110s but as the others were becoming increasingly aggressive he dived away and made for Chartres where he landed to refuel. The others completed their patrol without seeing any enemy aircraft.

Shortly after lunch Peter Matthews was ordered by the AOC to carry out a low level reconnaissance along the Seine from Nantes to Rouen to see which bridge crossings were still available for use. This was carried out at 500 ft and the foremost enemy anti-aircraft position encountered was at the junction of the main road from Rouen to Neufchatel-en-Bray approximately six miles north-east of Rouen. On landing Matthews gave a confidential report to the AOC in person. A further patrol of nine aircraft led by Fritz Warcup was intended to be joined by the Hurricanes of 17 Squadron at 1700 hrs but a huge pall of smoke that rose many thousands of feet into the air over Rouen meant that the rendezvous was missed. No. 1 Squadron patrolled on its own but no hostile aircraft were seen and they returned to *Maudie* at 1805 hrs before flying back to Chateaudun later in the evening.

On 10 June more patrols were flown over Rouen and Le Havre and during one of these Peter Matthews crashed at Orleans. The cause and state of damage to his aircraft were not recorded (or if they were they were subsequently lost) but he was unhurt. Having secured the Channel coast the Germans were now turning their attention further south and it became increasingly likely that No. 1 Squadron would be on the move again. On 12 June orders were received from 67 Wing for the squadron to be ready to pull out of Chateaudun at short notice. At 2100 hrs the go ahead was given for the squadron to move a further fifty miles to the west to an airfield near Le Mans (code name *Sylvia*), the intention being that the aircraft would remain overnight before patrolling in the morning and landing at Le Mans. In fact this was to be the last that the ground personnel saw of the aircraft until they arrived at Angers two days later. The convoy was well under way by midnight despite the roads being congested with a mass of refugees heading out of Paris.

The convoy duly arrived at Le Mans at 0200 hrs on 13 June and was assisted on arrival by the Battle-equipped No. 226 Squadron. It was eventually moved four miles from the airfield to a wooded area that provided excellent cover as there was considerable air activity. The day proved to be a frustrating one as communications were virtually nonexistent and it was almost impossible to obtain information and receive orders. With no sign of the squadron's Hurricanes and rumours that the ground party was at Angers, F/L Vaughan-Roberts decided to move the convoy there and they departed at 1800 hrs. On the way they were strafed by low flying aircraft but there was cover nearby and there were no injuries. The convoy arrived on the outskirts of Angers at about 0100 hrs on 14 June and were met by the small advance party that had gone on ahead. A section of 67 Wing was eventually located and at last some definite instructions were received. They were told to remain at Angers and it was hoped that they would be joined by the Hurricanes later in the day. In the meantime these had been operating from an airfield near Caen (code name *Matthew*) and had been flying patrols in the Le Havre area to provide cover for the evacuation of Allied personnel. There had been further contact with the enemy with Hilly Brown and Darky Clowes each claiming a Bf 109E with Brown also claiming a He 111.

The convoy was then led through the town to a less than satisfactory dispersal point on a road about two miles from the airfield but a local reconnaissance revealed a better alternative in the grounds of a chateau a little further away. The Countess was called from her bed and permission was received to use the grounds, but no sooner had a hasty breakfast been arranged than a further order was received for the squadron to move immediately to Nantes. The main convoy moved off again at 1300 hrs and made slow progress as the road was blocked in several places by large numbers of refugees. They eventually arrived in the evening to find the squadron's Hurricanes already there. As Nos 73 and 242 Squadrons had also arrived, together with aircraft from other squadrons, the airfield was made to look like 'several Empire Air Days all at once'. A continuous patrol was made over the nearby port of St Nazaire but during the day Fritz Warcup and Hilly Brown were both shot down (Brown was to reappear at Northolt on 19 June but Warcup was taken prisoner).

On 15 June the day was spent settling into woods on the edge of the airfield as the Hurricanes carried out further patrols. All available guns were dispersed in surrounding fields as protection from possible attacks by parachutists. By the 16th there was a feeling in the air that the squadron's stay in France was about to come to an end and by mid-morning the order was given to leave for St Nazaire. Accordingly F/L Barber, the squadron's Intelligence Officer, left with around 250 men taking only what they could carry and returned to Plymouth via Brest. After their departure, activity on the airfield increased in intensity as arrangements were made for the remainder of the squadron to move to La Rochelle where the last of the ground personnel would be able to escape to the UK.

During the night of 16/17 June there was a terrific thunderstorm so that most personnel woke up rather damp, but spirits remained high. Except for sixteen ground crew who were to remain at Nantes to look after the squadron's Hurricanes, the final party of twenty officers and forty-two men left for La Rochelle where they joined about 2,000 other troops and boarded a collier (which was still half full with coal) for the journey home. At midnight this rather unusual troop transport moved off from the quayside as German aircraft flew overhead, most saying a silent goodbye to France, which had been their home for the last nine months.

The final patrols were carried out on the 17th over St Nazaire but were unable to prevent a tragedy that was to become Britain's worst maritime disaster. Having already take part in the evacuation of troops from Norway, the 16,243-ton HMT

Lancastria dropped anchor at Charpentier Roads off St Nazaire at 0400 hrs prior to evacuating soldiers of the BEF, RAF personnel and civilians as part of Operation *Aerial*. During its days as a liner the *Lancastria* (formerly known as the *Tyrrhenia*) had a capacity of 2,200 passengers and plied the Atlantic between Liverpool and New York until 1932. Thereafter it was used as a cruise ship operating mainly in the Mediterranean although its final peacetime cruise was to the Bahamas. On becoming a troopship the *Lancastria* was converted for military use, which included anti-aircraft guns being mounted over the former swimming pool and its superstructure painted a coat of battleship grey.

On the morning of 17 June Captain Rudolf Sharpe was preparing to take around 3,000 evacuees back to the UK, however many more were in need of transportation and by mid-afternoon the embarkation was still not complete. This gave the *Luftwaffe* all the time it needed to launch a series of attacks and the first took place at 1400 hrs. A second attack was made ninety minutes later during which bombs missed the *Lancastria* by a mere fifty yards. During this time the Hurricanes of No. 1 Squadron had been patrolling above but the Ju 88s of I/KG 30 were able to use low cloud to launch their attacks before the fighter opposition could intervene.

A third attack carried out at 1545 hrs was the most devastating as the *Lancastria* was hit by four bombs, including one which fell directly down the funnel to explode deep within the ship, blowing out a large hole below the waterline. The oil tanks were ruptured so that burning oil began to spread out on the surface of the water. Within twenty minutes the liner went under, taking many of those who had recently boarded with her. Around 2,500 were rescued but the death toll has never been established with any degree of accuracy as no one knows how many were on board. Estimates vary from 6–8,000 putting the death toll at anything from 3,500 to 5,500, more than the *Titanic* and *Lusitania* disasters put together. In the skies over St Nazaire Sgt Fred Berry was leading a section of three Hurricanes but was hampered in his efforts by cloud cover. He was later credited with having shot down the aircraft that had bombed the *Lancastria* (reported to be a He 111 although it was actually a Ju 88). This was probably the aircraft flown by Oblt Sigmund-Ulrich Freiherr von Gravenreuth, the *Staffelkapitän* of I/KG 30. It returned having been damaged in combat with one crew member dead and two others wounded.

Having completed their duties with a final patrol over Nantes and St Nazaire, No. 1 Squadron's Hurricanes took off at 1145 hrs on 18 June to return to Tangmere leaving the remaining members of the ground crew to get out of France as best they could. Their last task was to douse three unserviceable Hurricanes (L1757, L1974 and P3045) with petrol and set them on fire so that they would be of no use to the Germans. The ground crew should have been taken by road to La Rochelle before completing their journey by sea but as this was to be the last opportunity to escape there could be no guarantee that a ship would be waiting for them or even if it was, that they would get there in time. Instead they eyed a fully-fuelled Bristol Bombay transport aircraft, which was perfectly serviceable, apart from a broken tailwheel. They were not the only ones to covet this machine as it had also caught the attention of Jean Demozay.

Although he had spent the last few months as No. 1 Squadron's interpreter, Demozay knew how to handle an aircraft and had flown the squadron's two-seat Miles Magister from time to time. On one occasion prior to the German invasion it is reputed that he flew Billy Drake from Vassincourt to Amiens so that he could collect a new Hurricane from the Maintenance Unit. Drake must have been reasonably confident in Demozay's flying ability as he was quite happy to let him take control and spent most of the flight asleep. On landing at Amiens he was surprised, and not a little startled, to discover that the fabric wings of the Magister were ripped in several places. The Frenchman's explanation was that he had been forced to take evasive action, which involved flying through a tree, when they had been attacked by some Bf 109Es!

Demozay had received an order to report for service in France but had no intention of staying in an occupied country and was desperate to get to Britain so that he could continue the fight from there. The ground crew assured him that a temporary fix could be made to allow the Bombay to take off and as this was being done he climbed up to the cockpit to familiarise himself with the controls. With the help of a sergeant engine fitter who worked the throttles he managed to take off, even though he had never flown a twin-engine aircraft before, and set out over the Channel. The intended destination was Tangmere to join up with the rest of the squadron but having gained confidence, and on hearing that most of his passengers were from East Anglia, he made for Sutton Bridge near King's Lynn where he brought the lumbering Bombay in for a passable landing. Although he was now far removed from his colleagues, it would not be long before they were reunited.

Despite the fact that the Hurricanes of No. 1 Squadron had returned to their spiritual home it did not feel as a homecoming should. Both the station and the squadron had changed, even if the surrounding countryside was the same and cricket was still being played on the village green. The pilots were under no illusions that they would soon be fighting to preserve everything they held most dear, only now they knew just what they would be up against. But for now at least there was the opportunity to catch up on a few things that had been denied them in France, beginning with a good night's sleep.

CHAPTER SIX

The Battle of Britain

The fall of France was swift and came just six weeks after the invasion. The French government fled Paris for Bordeaux on 10 June, leaving the city open for the Germans to enter, which they did on the 14th. Paul Reynaud, the French Prime Minister, was reluctant to call an end to the war but was forced to resign and was replaced by Marshal Philippe Petain, the hero of Verdun in the First World War. Petain was to sign the armistice on 22 June which, to complete France's humiliation, was conducted in the same railway carriage that had been used in 1918 in the forest of Compiègne for the armistice treaty at the end of the First World War. Four days before France sued for peace Winston Churchill delivered his third major speech after becoming Prime Minister on 10 May 1940. He left his listeners under no illusion as to what lay ahead but concluded by saying that if everyone did their duty, then future generations would say 'This was their finest hour'.

The pilots of No. 1 Squadron at Tangmere knew already what to expect and unlike many other units that had fought in France were to play a full part in the forthcoming Battle of Britain. Their gain/loss ratio in France had been better than any other squadron and although three pilots had been killed, with two taken prisoner, other units had fared much worse. In contrast No. 73 Squadron, their counterparts in 67 Wing, had lost eleven pilots killed with another shot down and captured. During his recovery from surgery after being shot down on 19 May, Paul Richey had been able to savour Paris for one last time before the arrival of the Germans. As he strolled down the Avenue des Champs-Elysees one afternoon towards the Place de la Concorde he happened upon Cobber Kain who was sitting at a pavement bar with Noel Monks, the war correspondent of the *Daily Mail*. Kain informed Richey that most of the original members of his squadron had returned to Britain and that he was due to depart in a couple of days. In his book *Fighter Pilot* (Pan Books, 1969) Richey recalled that Kain looked 'nervous and pre-occupied, and kept breaking matches savagely in one hand while he glowered into the middle-distance'. As a fellow pilot he could recognise the signs that the New Zealander had had enough. Two days later he too would be dead.

On 7 June Kain took off in Hurricane L1826 (TP-B) from Echemines to the north-west of Troyes en route for Le Mans. He passed over the airfield at about 800 ft and then commenced a series of flick rolls to the left but as the Hurricane rolled for the third time it lost airspeed rapidly, before departing into a spin to the right. At such a low height there was no chance of recovery and Kain was killed instantly when his aircraft hit the ground and burst into flames. At the time of his death he was just twenty-two but in his short RAF career he had accounted for seventeen enemy aircraft destroyed. No. 73 Squadron left France on 17 June and was to spend the next two months at Church Fenton in 12 Group. During this period they converted to night fighting and in September moved to Castle Camps in Cambridgeshire to operate over London.

In contrast No. 1 Squadron was to remain in 11 Group and two days after arriving at Tangmere was posted as non-operational to Northolt, near Hillingdon in west London. Northolt had been one of the earliest military aerodromes and its history dated back to early 1915. Its strategic location led to it being transferred to 11 Group Fighter Command in May 1936 and by 1940 it was one of a ring of aerodromes that protected the capital. No. 1 Squadron was still commanded by David Pemberton with the recently returned Hilly Brown resuming his duties as 'A' Flight commander. F/O Harry Hillcoat was promoted to Flight Lieutenant to take over 'B' Flight in place of Fritz Warcup. Other long-standing members to remain with the squadron were Peter Matthews, Colin Birch, Darky Clowes and Fred Berry. As all the equipment had been lost in France, this had to be replaced and at the same time the squadron establishment was reduced from 300 to 225. A particular problem was the fact that all the squadron's records had been lost in France and thus it was necessary to compile duplicates. This task was taken on by P/O L.W. Grumbley who took over from F/L Vaughan-Roberts as Adjutant in early July. Grumbley had served in the Indian Army for forty years and had recently retired as a Major, but was determined to do his bit in the new conflict and had lobbied hard to be accepted for an RAF commission. At the same time P/O J.G. Madden-Simpson joined the squadron as Intelligence Officer.

Following a period of intensive training, which included formation flying, practice attacks and night flying, the squadron was declared operational once again on 3 July. The tactics that were perfected were the regimented Fighter Command attacks, which had been formulated in the years immediately before the war. The basic section comprised three fighters in vic formation and the type of attack chosen depended on the number of enemy aircraft that they were confronted with. For example if a single bomber was seen a No. 1 attack was likely to be called in which the three fighters would drop into line astern formation and attack one after the other. Where three bombers were encountered the fighters would approach in echelon from the rear in what was known as a No. 3 attack with each fighter selecting its own target before breaking away. These tactics had been devised under the assumption that German bombers would be flying from bases in Germany without fighter escort. With the fall of France however they were able to operate from bases in the Pas de Calais and were accompanied by single and twin-engined fighters. For No. 1 Squadron's pilots their experiences in France had at least given them a better appreciation of the inadequacies of Fighter Command's tactics. Even though they still flew the basic vic of three, they did so with one or two weavers to warn of attack by enemy fighters, something that was still to be discovered by the majority of 11 Group's squadrons.

On 15 July Pilot Officers John Davey and J.F.D. 'Tim' Elkington arrived at Northolt to join the squadron. Elkington was a fresh-faced nineteen-year-old who had been educated at Bedford School before entering the RAF College at Cranwell as a Flight Cadet in September 1939. He learnt to fly on Tiger Moths at 9 EFTS, Ansty, before moving on to fly nearly 100 hours on Hawker Harts and Hinds and was awarded a permanent commission the day before he joined No. 1 Squadron. It appears that his posting to the RAF's top fighter squadron may not have been entirely coincidental as ACM Sir Cyril Newall, the Chief of the Air Staff, was an old Bedfordian and had served in the Royal Warwickshire Regiment, as had Elkington's father. The young Tim was not only glad to have joined an elite squadron; he was also pleased to have moved on to a rather more up-to-date Hawker design. At least now he would be able to talk to people without blowing down a tube and could look forward to doing aerobatics in an aircraft that did not have built-in drag. The arrival of Davey and Elkington caused a few jaws to drop as both looked as though they had been at school only yesterday, and this from battle-hardened veterans, some of whom were only a few months older than they were.

On 19 July the first interception took place at 1730 hrs when Red section led by David Pemberton, with Peter Matthews and P/O Dennis Browne as his Nos 2 and 3 sighted a He 111 twenty miles north of Brighton at around 10,000 ft. The Hurricanes were also seen by the crew of the Heinkel, which immediately tried to escape in cloud. Pemberton ordered Browne to keep to his left and the latter followed the German aircraft through the clouds until they came to a gap when it turned steeply and flew directly towards him. It then dived before levelling out at 3,000 ft, slowing to around 250 mph. However, Browne was able to follow and swung in from behind to fire two bursts each of around five seconds from 250 yards, receiving return fire from the upper gun position. He felt his Hurricane being hit but as it still flew normally he continued to follow the Heinkel as it jinked from side to side, its pilot using cloud cover whenever he could.

Browne fired the rest of his ammunition in short bursts until he had none left but by this time there was smoke coming from the port engine. He continued to follow the bomber so that its position could be traced via his Pipsqueak (an early form of IFF system) and he continually called base asking them to vector Red 1 and 2 onto him. Having pursued it for around ten minutes it finally escaped in the clouds but by now Browne had other concerns. The return fire had caused a serious glycol leak and with smoke beginning to billow from the Merlin engine of his Hurricane it was imperative for him to get down quickly. Having switched off his engine he glided down and saw a large estate on his right-hand side. He proceeded to make a wheels-up crash-landing into a large paddock and with flames already beginning to come through the floor of the cockpit, he wasted no time in getting out. Shortly afterwards the petrol tanks blew up and his aircraft was burnt out. Although it has been recorded that the He 111 was later destroyed by No. 43 Squadron, it appears more likely that it was shot down five miles off Shoreham by Hurricanes of No. 145 Squadron flown by P/O Michael Newling, F/O Roy Dutton and F/O A. Ostowicz. (This was an aircraft of 7/KG 55 and was coded G1+AR. The crew of five, which included Oblt Rudi Westhaus as observer, did not survive.)

At this stage of the air campaign against Britain the *Luftwaffe* was concentrating on attacking shipping in the English Channel with a view to closing it entirely and at the same time achieving air superiority over it. As German aircraft could be over the Channel quickly, Fighter Command was left with no alternative but to fly standing patrols over convoys. On 22 July No. 1 Squadron flew to Hawkinge, which was being used as a forward base, but in the event they were not needed and by evening they were back at Northolt. The following day saw the squadron move to Tangmere on a temporary basis with No. 43 Squadron heading in the opposite direction. On 24 July 'A' Flight patrolled the Isle of Wight, however the weather deteriorated throughout the day with coastal fog and rain, and another patrol by Blue section of 'B' Flight was recalled after being airborne only ten minutes.

On 25 July Portland was bombed in the morning and the squadron carried out several patrols as cover to convoys but did not encounter any opposition. At 1508 hrs Blue section of 'B' Flight led by Harry Hillcoat with Sammy Salmon (No. 2) and George Goodman (No. 3) took off with orders to patrol base. After a few minutes they were given a vector of 270 degrees and told to climb. As they reached 12,000 ft Hillcoat asked the controller whether they were to go above cloud but got no reply. Acting on his own initiative he took his section up to 15,000 ft but as they were still in cloud they descended again and began patrolling just below the cloud base. It was not long before a number of aircraft were seen maintaining an east/west line at around 3–4,000 ft some ten to twelve miles south of St Catherine's Point, the southern extremity of the Isle of Wight. Hillcoat flew out over the Channel until he was directly over them but could not identify the aircraft due to the poor visibility. There were between twelve and sixteen in all, in sections of three or four, but soon a small group was seen to break away and begin climbing rapidly in wide spirals. They were finally confirmed as Bf 109Es and when they were about 1,000 ft below on the opposite side of the circle the Hurricanes went into the attack.

The respective formations were soon broken up and individual combats took place. The 109s were soon joined by others which descended from above and Harry Hillcoat became involved with one of the latter. He fired several bursts of varying length with deflection and from astern, but was unable to inflict any substantial damage on his opponent. The German pilot was careful to maintain his speed and Hillcoat had a frustrating time as he could not get close enough. Each time it appeared as though he was gaining on the 109 it zoom-climbed to safety about 1,000 ft above him. Having expended all of his ammunition he finally left it about twenty-five miles out to sea and returned to base.

Sammy Salmon went for the 109s in the first group, which by now had adopted a line astern formation. He fired at the two leading machines by cutting across the circle but as the range was around 400 yards his bullets drifted wide of their intended target. He had better luck when a third 109 pulled sharply across in front of him at around 2–300 yards range, firing a full deflection burst as it continued its steep turn. By quickly reversing bank he managed to get in a further burst from the starboard beam and the nose of the 109 dropped into a vertical dive. Salmon's first impression was that it was out of control but he followed it down and fired again from dead astern, although by now the range had increased considerably. He began his pull-out at 2,000 ft (helped by use of the tailplane actuating gear) but blacked out for an appreciable time, finally coming to in a gentle climb. As the 109 was still diving at high speed when he last saw it he considered it impossible for it to have pulled out before hitting the sea.

In the meantime George Goodman had covered the attacks by Hillcoat and Salmon by maintaining his height but was finally brought into the action when he saw four 109s above emerging from cloud. As they came down in a descending spiral Goodman turned in behind the last one and was gaining on it when, at 3,000 ft, he suddenly saw a 109 close by on his right-hand side making a beam attack. In order to avoid a collision the Messerschmitt broke sharply upwards and turned to starboard, but as it did so it stalled and flicked into a spin. This aircraft continued spinning until it hit the water with a huge splash. The other 109s immediately started to climb for the cloud cover at 10,000 ft and although Goodman tried to follow, they were able to draw away and head back towards France. After landing Goodman discovered that his Hurricane had been hit by two machine-gun bullets on the starboard beam behind the wireless installation. In his combat report he expressed the opinion that the German pilots he had fought were not of the calibre of those he had encountered over France. It appeared that there was very little co-operation between them as they frequently got in each other's way.

Over the next few days further patrols were carried out around the Isle of Wight but although enemy aircraft were encountered by other squadrons elsewhere in the Channel, none were seen by No. 1 Squadron. It was not until 31 July that the squadron fought its next action when Red section led by Peter Matthews took off at 1017 hrs to reconnoitre the usual area. He was assisted in this task by P/O John Davey and Sgt Henry Merchant. On being ordered to investigate a ship about five miles south of Ventnor they descended from 16,000 ft to 5,000 ft so that it could be picked up in the haze that hung over the Channel. They were then informed of possible enemy aircraft two miles south of St Catherine's Point and immediately turned in this direction. An aircraft was seen in the distance but it saw the Hurricanes at the same time and dived to sea level heading in a southerly direction. Matthews gave the order for a No. 1 attack and Davey and Merchant swung into line astern formation as they closed on the aircraft, which by now had been identified as a Do 17.

Matthews attacked four times, alternating with Red 2 and 3, opening fire at the recommended range of 3–400 yards. He soon realised that this was too far away and subsequently pressed home his attacks to 200 yards or less. The Do 17 did not return his fire but appeared to jettison four lengths of wire preceded by puffs of smoke from the port side of the fuselage. On his last attack Matthews got closer than before and as a result had to break away sharply, losing sight of the Dornier in the mist. The action was eventually broken off some seventy miles out over the Channel by which time the port engine was trailing smoke and running at low revs. As all three Hurricanes had used up most of their ammunition (amounting to 5,600 rounds) and could only claim the Do 17 as damaged, it showed the need to get in closer. It was also apparent that the 0.303-in Browning machine-guns as fitted to the Hurricane did not deliver sufficient weight of fire to bring down aircraft fitted with armour plating and self-sealing fuel tanks with any degree of certainty.

The following day John Davey and Henry Merchant were in action again as Red section (on this occasion led by Hilly Brown) took off in the early morning to intercept an enemy raid. When flying ten miles south of Beachy Head at about 800 ft Brown saw a Do 17 and chased after it, however he was only able to fire a three-second burst from around 400 yards before the Dornier disappeared into clouds. As it did not appear to be unduly troubled, no claim was submitted. In the afternoon more patrols took place before the squadron flew back to Northolt with No. 43 Squadron returning to Tangmere, the ground staff being transferred by air.

Having taken up residence at Northolt once again, the squadron was back in a situation where it was required to fly to forward bases to be on hand should it be needed. On 2 August the day was spent at Hawkinge but no patrols were flown and a return was made to Northolt in the evening. On the 3rd the only activity of note involved Harry Hillcoat and Pat Hancock carrying out air-to-ground firing at Dengie Flats on the Essex coast (now a conservation area) and the following day there was another trip to Hawkinge. This proved to be abortive once again and the squadron was back at Northolt by lunchtime. In the afternoon six Blenheims of No. 15 Squadron flew to Northolt for fighter affiliation. These were to represent enemy bombers so that sections of No. 1 Squadron's Hurricanes could carry out practice attacks but an otherwise successful day was marred by a tragic accident. In taking violent evasive action, one of the Blenheims (R3771 flown by P/O M. Hohnen) dived into the ground killing the four-man crew. In the evening the squadron flew to Tangmere but returned at dusk. Over the next few days it flew to Manston, North Weald and Tangmere but was either not called upon, or if it was, there was no contact with the *Luftwaffe*. On 5 August Sgt Martin Shanahan joined the squadron and two days later four aircraft flew to Sutton Bridge for further air-to-ground firing and practice attacks.

The preliminary phase of the Battle of Britain in which attacks had been concentrated on Channel shipping was about to be replaced by much heavier attacks, which had the ultimate objective of destroying RAF Fighter Command. Another factor was that the weather in the first week of August had not been particularly good, but now there was the prospect that the Azores high pressure system would move in to offer predominantly fine conditions for the rest of the month. The first hint of a change of emphasis came on 11 August with a heavy raid on Portland, together with feints by formations of fighters in the Dover area.

No. 1 Squadron was ordered off at 0940 hrs with orders to patrol the coast south of Tangmere. Hilly Brown was 'Acorn leader' but when they were well out over the Channel they were attacked briefly from above by Bf 109Es, which had the effect of breaking up the squadron formation. When he was roughly half way between St Catherine's Point and Cherbourg, Hilly Brown saw a Bf 110 slightly below him at 18,000 ft. He followed it in a slight dive and having set +8 lbs/sq in boost, which gave an IAS (indicated airspeed) of around 300 mph, he was able to gradually overtake it. On opening fire various bits were seen to detach from the Messerschmitt as his bullets struck and the port engine was soon obscured by smoke. Strangely the 110 did not evade and merely maintained its shallow dive, nor was there any return fire. As he fired again Brown's windscreen was covered in oil and he had to break away sharply to avoid collision as the 110 suddenly slowed. P/O Harold Mann who was Brown's No. 2 and had been following his leader, later confirmed that the 110 dropped into a vertical dive with smoke and flames pouring out. He also saw the port engine explode and become a mass of flames.

During this combat Brown had used the new De Wilde ammunition and it was immediately apparent that his aim was good by the small flashes that his bullets gave off as they hit. This new incendiary ammunition had been developed by a Belgian chemist named De Wilde but had been subsequently re-designed in the UK by a Major Dixon. De Wilde was paid the large sum (for the time) of £30,000, even though his original design had a flaw in that when it was used in hot or worn barrels, it was prone to premature explosions. The reason for this generosity was that the Belgian had also been in negotiation to sell his ammunition to the Germans and Italians and it was hoped that they would accept the basic design without realising its weakness. It is not known if this subterfuge was successful.

While Brown had been accounting for this Bf 110, George Goodman (Blue 3) and P/O Charles Chetham (Yellow 3) were chasing after another. Two Hurricanes were ahead of them but these broke away, apparently without firing. The Bf 110 went into a steep dive to sea level and Goodman and Chetham indulged in a race to see who could get into a firing position first. During the dive their airspeed went up to around 420 mph and the descent rate was around 5,000 ft per minute. Chetham eventually won 'by a short head' and fired a preliminary burst at about 300 yards when the two aircraft were still about six to eight miles from the French coast. Although the 110 returned fire, all of Chetham's bullets were hitting around the centre section area, including the rear cockpit, and as the return fire soon ceased, it appeared as though the gunner had been killed or wounded. Not long after, what appeared to be a drogue was thrown out suspended on a long wire and this passed close to the port wing tip of Chetham's Hurricane as he followed the 110, which went into a right-hand climbing turn.

As Chetham broke away, Goodman moved in and closed to about fifty yards. There was still no return fire so he was able to put in a long burst of five seconds and the 110 caught fire at the starboard wing root. Soon afterwards it hit the water and disintegrated. As the twin tail was protruding from the water, Goodman flew low over it to take a photograph with his cine gun as proof that the aircraft had been destroyed. He returned at zero feet so as not to be seen by any other enemy aircraft that might be in the area and was joined by Chetham at mid-Channel. On the way back they saw another twin-engined aircraft hit the water with a Hurricane circling overhead, however as they were low on fuel they were not able to investigate and landed at 1155 hrs. Although No. 1 Squadron had been able to account for two Bf 110s, at some point during the fight the Hurricane flown by P/O John Davey was hit. He was able to make it back to the Isle of Wight but in putting his aircraft down on Sandown golf course, he crashed during his attempted force-landing and was killed, his Hurricane being burnt out.

For No. 1 Squadron at least there followed three relatively quiet days and on 12 and 13 August the squadron flew to North Weald in the morning to patrol convoys in the Thames estuary before flying back to Northolt. On 14 August there were only practice attacks and general flying to keep pilots occupied but this was to be the calm before the storm. In fact the *Luftwaffe* onslaught known as *Adler Tag* (Eagle Day) had begun on the 13th with heavy raids on Eastchurch aerodrome, Portland and Southampton and at the end of the day the Germans had flown a total of 1,485 sorties, the greatest number thus far, losing forty-five aircraft (thirteen RAF fighters were shot down and four pilots were killed). The 14th saw much reduced activity with only ninety-one bomber and 398 fighter sorties but on the following day heavy raids were carried out with aerodromes being the primary targets.

In the afternoon of 15 August Red, Yellow and Green sections of No. 1 Squadron took off from Northolt for North Weald where they were soon ordered to intercept a raid (No. 22) that was heading towards Clacton-on-Sea. This proved to be sixteen Bf 110 fighter-bombers of the elite *Erprobungsgruppe* 210 with an escort of Bf 109Es of the same unit, all bound for the aerodrome at Martlesham Heath. Red section led by Hilly Brown with P/O Dennis Browne and Sgt Martin Shanahan as his Nos 2 and 3 were badly bounced by the 109s and all three were shot down. Brown's Hurricane (P3047) was hit in the gravity tank and set on fire. Although he was able to bale out, he suffered burns to his face but was picked up by the trawler *Kenya* and taken to Harwich. Browne and Shanahan were not so fortunate and both were killed. Martin Shanahan was twenty-five years old and had been with the squadron for just ten days. Dennis Browne was four years younger and had joined No. 1 Squadron when it was still in France.

For those that remained there was the opportunity to hit back. P/O Harold Mann who was flying as Yellow 2 was attacked by two Bf 110s from above and behind. In taking evasive action he lost contact with the rest of the squadron but at the same time was pleased to see the cannon fire drifting well wide. He then chased after six of the fighter-bombers but they were diving for home so fast that they slowly drew away. As he turned round he was fired upon by a Bf 109E but by turning steeply to the left he was able to get behind it as it climbed for height. He opened fire as it presented him with a plan view and it then fell into a vertical dive. On passing 5,000 ft he was attacked by another 109 which holed his petrol tank. Luckily it did not catch fire but after firing at three more 109s he had to switch to his reserve tank as the main tank was empty. He landed at Martlesham without further incident.

P/O Tim Elkington (Green 2) was flying due east from Martlesham at 10,000 ft when a 109 approached him from head on and to the left, 1,000 ft below. It began to climb and turned to the left in an attempt to get on his tail but by turning tightly to the left himself he came up behind it. His first bursts did not appear to hit the 109 but on firing again it straightened out and went into a steep climb. He then fired a further two-second burst from astern and the engine of the 109 suddenly belched fumes before it turned over and 'dropped like a plummet into the sea'.

Peter Matthews also fired his guns at what he identified as a Ju 88 although it is possible that this was in fact a Bf 110 as the action took place at the same time and place as the attack by ErprGr/210. Having seen a melee of aircraft at about 13,000 ft over Martlesham, he attacked three aircraft in quick succession before spotting a 'Ju 88' on its own. This he chased out to sea firing all of his ammunition from astern, which appeared to have hit the German aircraft in the starboard motor as black smoke began to pour out and it suddenly yawed to the right. It then continued in a steep dive but as he had run out of ammunition and was by now well away from the coast he broke off the engagement and returned (during the raid by ErprGr/210 one of its Bf 110s crewed by Lt Erich Beudel and Obgfr Otto Jordan returned to Calais-Marck having suffered combat damage, although unfortunately the damage state was not recorded).

The weather on 16 August was clear and sunny with slight haze over the Channel. After a relatively quiet start the radar screens began to pick up signs of activity around 1100 hrs and shortly after midday No. 1 Squadron received orders to patrol Tangmere. They were then vectored onto enemy Raid 47 and over Selsey Bill were attacked by Bf 109Es. In the dogfight that followed most pilots were engaged, however no claims were made. P/O Tim Elkington went after one of the 109s but another came in from behind. His Hurricane (P3173 JX-O) was hit in the starboard fuel tank by a cannon shell and his legs were hit by shrapnel as it exploded in flames.

By an amazing coincidence, although he had not seen his attacker move in behind him, it appears that his mother had. She was watching the battle from nearby Hayling Island but was unaware that her son was fighting for his life in the skies above. In his rush to get out Elkington forgot to disconnect his radio and oxygen leads and was dumped back into the cockpit on his first two attempts to bale out receiving blows to the head. He was successful at the third attempt but lost consciousness as he drifted down on his parachute. As he was coming down over the coast there was a distinct possibility that the wind would drift him out to sea in which case he would probably have drowned. This was even more likely as he had not been able to inflate his Mae West. His predicament was quickly seen by Fred Berry, his section leader, who flew his Hurricane close to Elkington's parachute several times so that its slipstream blew him back towards the land. He eventually came down near West Wittering and was taken to the Royal West Sussex Hospital in Chichester. His mother went to see him, but on arrival she was given the distressing news that her son was dead. Thankfully this information was completely false as there had been a mix up with the previous occupant of the bed. When she eventually saw her son she failed to recognise him at first as his problems in baling out (as he later put it) had 'somewhat rearranged' his face (he was to spend two weeks in hospital and a further month on sick leave as he recovered from his wounds).

It is highly likely that Elkington was shot down by Oblt Helmut Wick, the *Staffelkapitän* of 3/JG 2 who recorded his eighteenth victory by claiming a Hurricane east of Portsmouth at roughly the same time. Elkington's Hurricane came down at Manor Farm, Chidham, about three miles north of West Wittering but much of it was destroyed by fire (the site was excavated in July 1976 and a number of interesting pieces were found including the charred control column and brass data plate confirming the aircraft serial number).

While No. 1 Squadron was in the air Tangmere was attacked at low level, causing extensive disruption. Hardly a building remained that had not suffered damage to a greater or lesser extent with two hangars being completely destroyed and the other three badly damaged. Several of No. 43 Squadron's Hurricanes were also destroyed on the ground. The Hurricane of P/O Billy Fiske of No. 601 Squadron, which had already been badly shot up, landed in the middle of the raid and was then subject to a strafing attack. Fiske was eventually extricated but he had been terribly burnt and succumbed the following day to become the first US volunteer to die serving with the RAF. Essential services such as power, water and sanitation were all put out of action and ten service personnel and three civilians were killed, with another twenty injured.

Having refuelled and rearmed, No. 1 Squadron was back in the air again at 1630 hrs. They were vectored towards an incoming raid comprising around forty Heinkel 111s in three waves escorted by Bf 109Es and Bf 110s but these were not intercepted until they had crossed the coast and were some way inland. David Pemberton led the squadron alongside the bomber formations and when level with the first wave he signalled his pilots to prepare for a frontal attack in line astern on the second wave. His first burst at the front of a He 111 sent it down in flames. After breaking away he zoom-climbed for a second attack but shortly after this his engine caught fire and he got ready to bale out. As he was doing so the flames subsided so he decided to stay with his aircraft and attempt to get back to base. This he was able to do successfully and on examination it was discovered that two armour-piercing bullets had penetrated the top cowling and had then scored the camshaft to a depth of $\frac{1}{16}$ of an inch. It was thought that the fire had been started by oil fumes, which had then burnt out. The He 111 he shot down was from 6/KG 55 (coded G1+HP) and it crashed near Bramber on the South Downs in Sussex. Of its crew the pilot Oblt Wilhelm Wieland, observer Fw Hans Langstrof and wireless operator Uffz Werner Appel became prisoners; engineer Uffz Anton Hattendorf was killed and gunner Uffz Gerhard Pulver died of his injuries.

Peter Matthews was flying as Red 2 alongside David Pemberton but lost contact with his leader during the second attack so climbed to 20,000 ft behind the enemy formation. He saw a single Hurricane being attacked by five Bf 110s so dived and fired at one of these, following it up in a climb to the top of a cloud layer. By this time the port engine of the 110 was on fire and it rolled over into a vertical dive during which its speed exceeded 400 mph. As it disappeared into a bank of low cloud Matthews pulled out of his dive but blacked out in the process. Although he had not seen it crash, the fact that the 110 had gone down on fire was sufficient for him to be awarded it as a confirmed 'kill'.

Green section led by Fred Berry with Sammy Salmon and Charles Stavert as his Nos 2 and 3 had been last in line during the initial attack. Berry fired at the No. 2 Heinkel in the second vic with a four-second burst and saw it drop out of formation towards cloud cover away to the south. He then climbed again to make another attack from in front and below on the No. 2 aircraft of the third vic and hit this machine in its centre section. It also turned away but in the course of a half-roll Berry lost sight of it. Sammy Salmon was another to lose contact with the rest of his section and climbed to 22,000 ft before diving on the last group of Heinkels. As he did so a Bf 110 appeared in front of him so he fired a short burst at it and saw the port engine stop immediately. He then followed it in a vertical dive but had to break sharply as another three 110s attempted to move in behind him. He was able to lose them in cloud but as he was down to his reserve tank he landed at Redhill to refuel. While he was on the ground the aerodrome was attacked by a single Do 17 and as soon as his Hurricane was ready he returned to Northolt. The Bf 110 that Salmon had fired at was probably A2+GL of 6/ZG 2, which broke up and crashed at Aldro School, Eastbourne. The pilot, Oblt Ernst Hollekamp, was killed when his parachute failed to open and his radio operator, Fw Richard Schurk, came down in the sea off Holywell and was drowned.

Charles Stavert, the final member of Green section, followed Fred Berry into the frontal attack and fired at the second bomber in the formation, hitting it with tracer. He then put his Hurricane into a dive and met another He 111 at which he fired head-on. It immediately went into a vertical dive which Stavert followed and when he broke cloud he saw the smoke beginning to rise from the wreckage of a twin-engined aircraft directly below him.

No. 1 Squadron's Yellow section was led by Darky Clowes and as Red section broke away he raked the flank of the bomber formation. He then half-rolled and when in the inverted position saw one of the He 111s he had fired at leave the protection of the others. As he had been firing he had noticed small lights appear at the front of the Heinkel but was unsure if this was return fire or his De Wilde hitting as this was the first time he had used this type of ammunition. After a second attack he dived below cloud and saw a single bomber (identified as a Ju 88) and having closed to firing range, attacked from the beam. This aircraft also came under attack by four Spitfires and made a rapid force-landing in a large field near Petworth.

The last member of the squadron to put in a claim was George Goodman (Blue 3) who picked out a single He 111 on the fringe of the formation and attacked it from astern. He at once put the port engine out of action and saw the pilot attempting to feather the propeller before continuing on the remaining engine. He was unable to do so however and lost control, the Heinkel nosing over into a dive before crashing to the east of Northchapel in Sussex. On circling the wreckage its bomb load blew up with such violence that Goodman's Hurricane was hit by debris and he noticed his oil pressure drop slightly. This did not get any worse and he was able to fly back to Northolt without difficulty. All the crew of the He 111 (G1+LM) were killed including the *Staffelkapitän* of 4/KG 55, Hptm Wladimir Sabler. The only casualty for No. 1 Squadron was the Hurricane flown by P/O Peter Boot, which was hit in the cooling system. He made a successful crash-landing on the Hog's Back between Farnham and Guildford and was uninjured.

After two days of hectic activity in which the *Luftwaffe* had flown 3,501 sorties there was a lull on 17 August and although the weather remained fine there were no major attacks. Most of the German aircraft that were seen during the day were on photographic reconnaissance missions to assess the effects of the raids of the previous two days and losses amounted to only three, with the RAF losing none. No. 1 Squadron also had a quiet day with practice flying in the morning and night flying practice by 'B' Flight after dark. The German onslaught was resumed on 18 August with massed attacks, the emphasis once again being on 11 Group's aerodromes while others targeted radar stations along the south coast.

No. 1 Squadron began the day by carrying out practice dogfights in the morning but the first sign of aircraft massing over the Channel was seen on the radar screens around midday. Patrols were carried out over base at 8,000 ft and 10,000 ft and during one of these 'B' Flight was sent down towards the south coast to counter yet another raid. At around 1340 hrs a large formation of Do 17s was encountered near Dungeness and Blue section led by Harry Hillcoat with Charles Stavert (No. 2) and George Goodman (No. 3) attacked a singleton that was flying well away from the others. Goodman went in first firing a telling burst into the Dornier's belly, which was soon alight, thus prompting the pilot to open the bomb doors to jettison around eighty 'squarish metal tins' containing its load of incendiaries. As he completed his attack a parachute opened up in front of him as one of the crew baled out, the unfortunate individual falling directly through Goodman's line of fire.

The attack was then taken up by Hillcoat and Stavert. The latter, aiming a little in front of the Do 17, fired several long bursts and saw his De Wilde ammunition hitting the starboard engine and the centre section. By this time the aircraft was well alight and three more of the crew baled out. Harry Hillcoat also attacked with two bursts of around four seconds each and as he broke away to the right and climbed towards the sun he saw a large splash as the German bomber hit the sea. Its evasive action had consisted of turning from left to right but from the moment of Goodman's attack it had been losing height rapidly so it was obvious at an early stage that there would only be one outcome to this particular combat.

While he was watching Blue 1 and 2 carry out their attacks George Goodman's attention was drawn to a Bf 110 about half a mile to his left. It was heading back to France but had obviously already been in combat as its port engine was trailing smoke. Due to its reduced speed Goodman was able to move in behind without difficulty and fired a short burst, which set the port engine on fire. The pilot of the 110 attempted to get away by changing direction as quickly as he could but there was no return fire. The next burst hit the starboard engine, which was also set on fire, but in concentrating on the 110 Goodman had neglected to look behind and his Hurricane was hit by fire from a Bf 109E. He immediately thrust the control column over to the right-hand side of the cockpit to obtain a maximum rate turn and as he did so he saw the 110 he had fired at come down in the sea.

During his turn Goodman made about half a mile on the 109 but just as he was about to climb to bale out he saw the 109 closing in rapidly. His only chance was to head for the English coast and hope that his aircraft could get him there. He used boost override (or 'pulled the plug' as he put it) and made for home with the 109 still gaining, but more slowly. On reaching the cliffs near Rye he turned sharply into a valley near the town and deliberately led the 109 over a coastal gun battery, which unfortunately took no action whatsoever. At this point however the 109 turned away for France and Goodman was able to climb to 7,000 ft and return to base. (The Bf 110 that Goodman shot down had already been attacked by Hurricanes of 56 Squadron, pilots of this unit claiming to have destroyed no fewer than four in the Ashford – Canterbury area. It came from 6/ZG 26 and was flown by Fw Herbert Stange who survived to become a PoW. His radio operator, Uffz Gerhard Wollin, was killed.)

Later in the afternoon the squadron flew to North Weald and when emerging through a layer of cloud at 21,000 ft in the vicinity of Southend they encountered a group of around a dozen Bf 109Es. These immediately turned towards the Hurricanes but successful evasive action was taken and no advantage was gained. In fact one of the 109s was soon in trouble as it overshot the aircraft flown by David Pemberton who dived after it and fired a two-second burst from about 250 yards. He followed the 109 as it dived to ground level and began 'hedge-hopping' through Kent. So low was it flying that he was reluctant to open fire at it for fear of also causing damage to property. Eventually he got his opportunity as the 109 gained a little height and a short burst was enough to send it crashing in flames between Tenterden and Cranbrook.

Over the next four days the fine weather of the previous week gave way to cloud and occasional rain and the number of sorties flown by both sides was greatly reduced. Hermann Goering, the commander of the *Luftwaffe*, had confidently predicted that RAF Fighter Command would be wiped out in four days but clearly it was going to take a little longer. This period was used by both sides as a time for reflection, the Germans also considering their future tactics. It was to lead to the crucial phase of the Battle of Britain with 'ceaseless attacks' aimed at giving the RAF no respite and forcing it to commit all its assets to the fight. If this could be achieved the Germans saw no reason why the British fighter force (what they thought was left of it) could not be fatally weakened to the point where it ceased to be effective. The reality was that the German intelligence assessments of Fighter Command's strength were hopelessly inaccurate in that they tended to overplay the amount of damage that had been caused and the number of fighters that had been shot down.

On 19 August No. 1 Squadron indulged in some local flying practice before nine aircraft patrolled base in the afternoon. In the evening they made sure that they would be ready the next time they were called by carrying out a practice dogfight. After dark there was a taste of things to come for No. 1 Squadron when P/O Colin Birch flew a night patrol in Hurricane P3684. Operations at night did not come naturally to a day fighter pilot, especially when airborne over the blackout and with minimal landings aids. Birch took off at 2304 hrs with orders to patrol base at 15,000 ft but six minutes later he was told to return and descend on a vector of 010 degrees. Unfortunately he heard this as 100 degrees, a course that took him directly towards the London balloon barrage and to compound the initial error he did not receive a subsequent instruction for him to alter course. At 2320 hrs he struck a balloon cable to the west of Finsbury Park when descending through 2,500 ft. The impact caused his Hurricane to yaw sharply to the point where it flew in a complete circle, losing height rapidly. He baled out at 1,500 ft and his aircraft crashed in Chatterton Road, Finsbury Park, bursting into flames as it did so. There was some damage to property but no one on the ground was hurt.

Birch landed on the roof of a house in Finchley and having convinced the occupants that he was not German they organised a rescue as he was still a good 25 ft off the ground. Unfortunately the fireman who attended the scene arrived with a ladder that was only 20 ft long so Birch was required to jump the 5 ft gap into his arms. He eventually plucked up the courage to leap for a second time, the fireman maintaining that he had practised this particular manoeuvre frequently. Whether he had or not, it was accomplished successfully and Birch was finally brought to earth where he enjoyed an enthusiastic welcome and the hospitality of the local police. He was soon returned to Northolt in transport provided by the balloon section.

The chief activity over the next two days was aerobatic practice by all members of the squadron, together with more practice dogfights. Night patrols were again carried out on the night of 22/23 August and another pilot found himself in difficulties. Having pursued night bombers on three separate occasions, Sgt Henry Merchant found that he was short of petrol and could only crash-land by the aid of parachute flares to the west of Maidstone. Although heavy daylight raids recommenced on 24 August with attacks on a number of 11 Group aerodromes and the naval base at Portsmouth, the only operational flying carried out by No. 1 Squadron was a patrol over Northolt in the afternoon, which was uneventful. There were further patrols the next day over Tangmere in the afternoon and Northolt at 1700 hrs, but once again the *Luftwaffe* was elsewhere. On 26 August, after two patrols over base, night flying was undertaken once more and this time it was the turn of P/O Charles Chetham to have a fright. During his patrol he emerged from cloud to be picked up by a searchlight, which was soon joined by several others until he was coned. This disorientated him to the extent that his Hurricane (P3897) went into a spin, his position at the time being over Lacey Green to the north of High Wycombe. As he was unable to regain control he was forced to bale out and landed safely near Amersham.

After another uneventful day on 27 August, No. 1 Squadron saw further action on the 28th. The day was generally fine and fair with some cloud around the Dover Straits, but not enough to affect operations. Eleven Hurricanes led by S/L David Pemberton were airborne at 1231 hrs with orders to patrol Hornchurch but when over Southend at 15,000 ft they met a formation of approximately thirty Do 17s of 1/KG 2 escorted by Bf 109Es 5,000 ft above. These had been attacking the aerodrome at Rochford but although many bombs had fallen on the landing area, no serious damage had been caused and it remained operational. For once No. 1 Squadron was able to deal with the bombers without the 109s paying them any attention and in a short engagement all pilots fired their guns. Two Do 17s were shot down, one crashing at Rochford and another in the sea, near the Tongue Lightship. A third was damaged and was last seen flying on one engine being protected by five of the Dorniers. These aircraft were claimed collectively by the squadron as all pilots had been involved.

Everyone was cheered the following day by the return of Hilly Brown after being shot down on 15 August, however there was little else to get enthusiastic about. Two Hurricanes endeavoured to intercept a single enemy bomber returning to France but lost it in cloud; the rest of the day was spent doing practice flying and taking part in the usual defensive patrols, which were all uneventful.

On 30 August there were further heavy attacks on 11 Group aerodromes with Biggin Hill being particularly badly hit. No. 1 Squadron was not called into action until the late afternoon when eleven Hurricanes took off from Northolt at 1631 hrs. As they were flying to the north of London towards Epping Forest a formation of six aircraft was seen being attacked by a number of Hurricanes. David Pemberton immediately turned the squadron so that it could come in from behind but just before pressing home an attack, the 'bombers' were recognised as being Blenheims and it was realised that a fighter affiliation was taking place. There had already been several 'friendly fire' incidents involving RAF aircraft and the sanity of anyone who authorised such activity in a battle zone has to be questioned.

Not long after a formation of thirty to forty bombers protected by a similar number of fighters were seen and there could be little doubt about the nationality of these. Very soon a large dogfight was taking place that attracted other RAF fighters. Colin Birch (Blue 2) fired two long bursts at a Heinkel 111 from the front port quarter and saw a plume of black smoke emerge from the port engine, together with various bits of debris. It continued on its way towards the Thames estuary trailing smoke and losing height but as he was unable to close to firing range again, Birch eventually had to leave it and return to base.

Pat Hancock, who was flying on the opposite side of Blue section in the No. 3 position, went for a He 111 that was lagging behind the others. He gained height so that he could attack it in a dive, but before he could do so a Spitfire cut in to make an astern attack and he had to wait his turn. When the Spitfire broke away he moved in and fired several long bursts with the intention of disabling the engines. It appeared as though he had been successful as smoke, oil and flames were emitted by both engines but at this point he was attacked by Bf 110s and had to take evasive action. The Heinkel was later claimed as a probable.

Red section was also attacked by Bf 110s and Peter Matthews (Red 1) had to break sharply, however these were then engaged by other Hurricanes giving Matthews the opportunity to turn his attention towards a He 111, which had become separated from the main formation. Moving in from behind he fired all of his ammunition causing serious damage to the starboard engine. During his attack he was fired at the whole time by the rear gunner but as he broke away he noticed a Hurricane of No. 56 Squadron move in to finish the Heinkel off. It is likely that this was the aircraft flown by F/L E.J. 'Jumbo' Gracie who claimed a He 111 at this time.

Upon sighting the enemy, Henry Merchant (Red 2) had followed Peter Matthews in line astern but had also been attacked by a Bf 110, which he eventually managed to remove from his tail. Looking round he saw a He 111 on its own and put his Hurricane into a climb prior to attacking from the beam. During his second pass the port engine stopped but at this moment a Hurricane from another squadron dived on the Heinkel from astern and got in a burst. Merchant then made a head-on attack and as he did so saw one of the crew take to his parachute. On his next attack two more parachutes appeared and the bomber went into a dive before crashing near a cemetery to the east of Southend.

Yellow section was not to be outdone and in the melee Darky Clowes claimed an He 111 and Bf 110 as damaged. P/O Harold Mann (Yellow 3) was soon occupied fending off attacks by Bf 110s but was able to fire at two of them, the first receiving three bursts each of around three seconds, which damaged the port engine. Having broken away from this aircraft he went for another, his fire having a similar effect as this 110 was last seen trailing smoke from its port engine. Having used up all his ammunition Mann then left the battle and returned to Northolt.

Fighter Command had one of its most difficult days on the 31 August with thirty-nine fighters shot down (only two fewer than German losses for the day) and fourteen pilots killed. German attacks were concentrated once again on the south-east with aerodromes as the principal targets. Debden was the recipient of a heavy attack, which caused much damage, but its operations room was spared and it remained operational. The first raids were seen approaching in the early morning and No. 1 Squadron was scrambled at 0740 hrs and vectored towards the Chelmsford area. Here they encountered large numbers of enemy aircraft, consisting of Do 17s and He 111s with an escort of Bf 110s. The latter were able to frustrate the squadron's attempt to go for the bombers and many of the engagements that followed were fighter versus fighter.

P/O Roland Dibnah who was flying as Red 3 was impressed by the sheer numbers of enemy aircraft that were flying in sections of three or five stepped up, with the fighter escort above and behind, straggling all over the sky. In all there were around 100 machines from 15,000 ft up to 20,000 ft. He fired a short burst at a 110 that was trailing the main formation and after breaking away downwards, he climbed steeply once again selecting the leading aircraft in a section of three. This machine was approached from the starboard front quarter from below and he opened up at 800 yards and continued firing until the range had reduced to less than 400 yards. Black smoke began to pour from the starboard engine but due to the proximity of other 110s he disengaged and landed at Hornchurch.

Yellow section was led by Darky Clowes once again but at first he was unable to attack the bombers due to the threat posed by the 110s. Finally he found a way by descending under the bombers and climbing up from underneath the main formation, which consisted of fifteen Dorniers in five vics of three. He fired a two-second burst from the front quarter but as he half-rolled and climbed again he noticed that there were only thirteen aircraft in the formation. One was spinning down and the other was leaving the others in a steep turn to the left. He was then set upon by the escorting fighters and looped up to attack them from underneath. He fired at one Bf 110 from long range but was gratified to see a streak of white smoke appear from the starboard engine. Not long after the engine stopped and Clowes continued to fire as it dived steeply towards the ground. As it levelled off its speed was markedly reduced and it flew along not far above the stall at around 120 mph. He fired one last burst from quarter astern but as he did his ammunition ran out and as he left the 110; its pilot appeared to be trying to find somewhere to land.

The other members of Yellow section were Peter Boot (No. 2) and Harold Mann (No. 3). Having investigated what turned out to be a formation of Hurricanes approaching from behind, Peter Boot made an ineffectual head-on attack on a group of He 111s before becoming involved with the escorting 110s. After firing at one, its starboard engine began to smoke, but on breaking away he got left behind and had a long chase to catch up with the German aircraft, which were then heading back to the coast. Together with a section of other Hurricanes he attacked a defensive circle of 110s and damaged one quite badly, seeing pieces fall off the tailplane. He later saw a 110 hit the ground with its tail shot away but was unsure if it was the one he had fired at.

Having followed Yellow 1 and 2 to identify the aircraft that turned out to be Hurricanes, Harold Mann climbed above the bombers in an attempt to cut them off. However, he built up too much speed in his attacking dive and was unable to hold his gunsight on any of them. He pulled away in front and tried his luck with two head-on attacks but his fire drifted wide on both occasions. He was more fortunate with a third attack, which produced black smoke from the No. 3 aircraft in the leading formation. During these attacks there was return fire from all the bombers and he was also troubled by the 110s diving from above. It is interesting to note that Mann thought the leading aircraft in the bomber formation may have been Messerschmitt 'Jaguars'. This name appears in a number of RAF combat reports of the period and refers to the Bf 162, which was a variant of the Bf 110. It was produced in 1936–7 as a *Schnellbomber* (fast bomber) and although it lost out to the Junkers Ju 88, German propaganda released pictures of a so-called Messerschmitt Jaguar. It never saw service and its use as a propaganda tool was similar to the Heinkel He 112/113.

The leader of Blue section on this occasion was David Pemberton. At the time that the German formation was encountered No. 1 Squadron was south-west of it and about 2–3,000 ft below so Pemberton attempted to manoeuvre the Hurricanes for a head-on attack. As they drew alongside he saw another enemy formation above composed of bombers and fighters and the squadron had to break away to engage the Bf 110s which were dropping onto them. After a general free-for-all with the fighters Pemberton found himself alone so followed the main formation until he was able to select a suitable target. This turned out to be a Ju 88 and he was able to fire all of his ammunition from 300 to 250 yards without being disturbed by the fighters. This aircraft was later claimed as damaged after one engine appeared to stop and the other started belching smoke. After this it began losing height, but not rapidly, and as the combat had take place at 15,000 ft there is a good chance that it made it back over the Channel.

The final member of No. 1 Squadron to put in a claim was Sgt Henry Merchant (Red 2), although this was only done some time later after being shot down. Having fired at one of the Bf 110s he broke away downwards before climbing to position himself for another attack. He saw another Hurricane firing at a 110 from astern and as it moved away he attacked from the port quarter seeing De Wilde strikes on the forward fuselage. As he turned away he found that he was in the perfect position for a diving attack from the front on another of the 110s and having built up speed in the dive he was able to turn and come in once again, this time from the rear. His fire struck the starboard engine, which shed various pieces, together with larger bits of cowling. This was followed by copious amounts of black smoke and the 110 performed a slow roll to the right onto its back before going into a vertical dive with smoke and flames pouring from the starboard engine. However as Merchant had been concentrating on this aircraft, another 110 had moved in behind unseen. The first he knew of the danger lurking behind was when his reserve petrol tank exploded and flames began to enter the cockpit. Although he baled out as quickly as he could, he had to be taken to Halstead Cottage Hospital in Essex suffering from burns.

There was no let up on 1 September with another series of attacks on aerodromes including Biggin Hill where the sector operations room was hit and put out of action. Fighter Command was now being stretched to the limit and the pilots that remained were suffering from the insidious effects of accumulated fatigue as a result of having to fly constant operations. The loss of pilots with combat experience was also becoming an extremely serious issue and on this day one of No. 1 Squadron's longest serving pilots would fall to make this problem even more acute.

The call to scramble came mid-morning and nine Hurricanes led by Harry Hillcoat took off from Northolt with orders to head towards the Maidstone area. The *Luftwaffe* had again used a tactic seen in recent days of sending a substantial formation consisting solely of Bf 109Es towards the south coast in the hope that Air Vice-Marshal Keith Park, the commander of 11 Group, would commit his fighters to battle ahead of a later thrust by a large force of bombers. Fortunately Park did not fall for this particular ploy and No. 1 Squadron was one of fourteen squadrons to be committed to battle on signs that a significant number of bombers were on their way. Naturally they were protected by fighter escort and it was these that No. 1 Squadron were to come into contact with.

When flying at about 17,000 ft to the east of Tonbridge, Hillcoat saw the bursts of anti-aircraft fire ahead, which indicated the presence of a hostile raid. He signalled for the Hurricanes to climb and turned so as to keep up-sun of the position he assessed the German aircraft to be. Soon he saw what he considered to be a formation of twelve Do 17s escorted by a much larger force of single-engined fighters, which had dispersed above and around the bombers to stay out of the flak zone. The formation was proceeding south having already dropped its bombs and Hillcoat was faced with a difficult decision; whether to go for the bombers or to concentrate on the fighters. Eventually he decided that there was insufficient time to attack the bombers before the fighters intervened and decided to go for the latter.

After turning his formation of Hurricanes to the left to engage the Bf 109Es he picked on one of the Messerschmitts, which made a break for home and managed to stay ahead until near the coast. Hillcoat's first burst hit the 109 in the radiator but he had to wait about five minutes before it slowed down sufficiently for him to be able to fire again. After firing a second time smoke streamed from the engine and two more short bursts were enough to prompt the pilot to jettison his hood, the slipstream sucking his arm out as if he was waving at the Hurricane. Hillcoat did not attack again and climbed to give the German pilot the opportunity to bale out. He did so and landed near a road close to the shore not far from Folkstone, his aircraft exploding as it hit the ground about 100 yards away. Hillcoat circled overhead for some time and saw the pilot being apprehended by the military and led away.

Yellow section was soon split up as the 109s waded in and Peter Boot, who was in the No. 2 position, climbed to attack others that were circling above. One of these aircraft detached itself from the circle and dived down but Boot decided to follow it as it crossed over the coast. He managed to get in a long burst at about 250 yards range and the 109 continued its dive until it hit the sea midway across the Channel. On his way back Boot saw what he considered to be a He 113 heading in the opposite direction. He turned quickly and fired at long range but the German aircraft continued on its way. P/O Charles Chetham (Yellow 3) also claimed a Bf 109E after throwing his Hurricane into a maximum rate turn to throw one off his tail. On seeing three 109s below he chased after one and fired three bursts from about 300 yards. White smoke began to pour from it and it went into a vertical dive, Peter Matthews (Yellow 1) later giving evidence that it had disintegrated as it went down.

The last No. 1 Squadron pilot to file a claim for a Bf 109E destroyed was Colin Birch but of the four to be submitted his was the least convincing. As he was preparing to attack the bombers a number of 109s came down on him from the rear port quarter and continued down and away. Birch went after one of the 109s and fired five long bursts from 200 to 400 yards. Smoke came back from the body of the 109, together with bits of the fuselage, but at 3,000 ft he had to break sharply as two more 109s were coming in behind him. During the turn he blacked out for several seconds but when he came to he was completely on his own. He estimated that the 109 he had fired at would have crashed approximately ten miles south-east of Tonbridge in view of its direction at the time and the rate at which it was diving.

As the Hurricanes of No. 1 Squadron returned to Northolt it was immediately apparent that one of their number was not among them. This was P3276 flown by F/Sgt Fred Berry who was shot down and killed by a Bf 109E, his aircraft crashing near Brisley Farm, Ruckinge, to the south of Ashford. The circumstances surrounding Berry's death will probably never be known. However, a Bf 109E came down at virtually the same time and only two miles from where Berry crashed. This was the aircraft flown by Oblt Anton Stangl of II/JG 54, which crashed near Bonnington. It has been suggested that Stangl had the misfortune to suffer a mid-air collision with another 109 but there is a distinct possibility that Berry was involved in some way. Could the two pilots, who were both aces having destroyed five aircraft apiece, have fought a final duel in the skies over Kent? Having served with No. 1 Squadron for a little over a year Fred Berry was laid to rest at Pinner New Cemetery, Harrow, in Middlesex.

On 2 September attacks on aerodromes were continued throughout the day with the first wave being picked up at 0715 hrs. No. 1 Squadron was not called into action until the afternoon however when Harry Hillcoat (Blue 1) led nine Hurricanes off on a defensive patrol over Northolt at 10,000 ft. Not long after, anti-aircraft bursts were seen over London at 18,000 ft so Hillcoat led the squadron in a climbing turn towards the sun, the direction that the enemy aircraft were travelling being determined by fresh flak bursts to the south-east of the first cluster. A long chase over Kent followed and it was not until the coast was reached that the bombers were seen, but by this time they were well out over the sea. Although the main force had gone there were many fighters still in the area and several different formations were seen, each of about twelve aircraft flying in line astern in defensive circles.

Hillcoat took No. 1 Squadron up to 20,000 ft and went for a group of Bf 109Es about 1,000 ft below, these aircraft forming a defensive circle, which was joined by other formations. Once again the pilots considered that the majority of the fighters were Bf 109Es, but that there were a few 'He 113s' among them. Hillcoat attacked one of the 109s and after his first few bursts smoke began to appear and a stream of glycol came back from one of the radiators. He then fired again from the rear with slight deflection at point blank range and could see his bullets hitting. The 109 was left in a shallow dive about ten miles inland near Ashford with Hillcoat confident that it would not get home. As about a dozen 109s were endeavouring to get on his tail he had to dive to ground level before returning to Northolt.

The only other claim to be made during this combat was by Charles Chetham (Yellow 2), although as his leader had already returned with a malfunctioning oxygen system, he had been forced to join up with Green section. As they went into the attack he followed and fired three bursts at a 109, which emitted a feint trail of glycol. As he was about to come under attack himself, he had to break away and after climbing towards the sun he saw a number of other 109s in a defensive circle. Keeping the sun between him and these aircraft he climbed a little further before rolling over into an attacking dive. There were about eight or nine in all but he only had time to fire at three of them. As he continued his dive some of the 109s followed him down but lost him in the haze at lower levels and he was able to escape.

Over the next three days the weather remained fine in the south with some haze over the Channel. Fighter Command's aerodromes continued to receive an incessant pounding, however during the Battle of Britain Northolt was to escape relatively lightly thanks to some ingenious camouflage. As the station was surrounded by built-up areas it was argued that the usual method of applying camouflage paint in the form of jagged lines in an attempt to break up the shape of an aircraft hangar would not work at all and that in this particular location something else was needed. Eventually it was decided to disguise the hangars from above by painting on the outline of what appeared to be two rows of houses with gardens in between. The grassed areas between runways and taxiways were marked up with lines formed with tar that from above looked like hedges. The degree of research that went into Northolt's transformation was such that these lines followed exactly the outline of fields before the aerodrome was built in 1915. Other means of deceiving the enemy included the painting of rough circles of varying diameters on runways and taxiways to look like trees and bushes and a stream was even painted along each runway with a pond where they intersected. By such means Northolt did not suffer to anything like the extent of other aerodromes in 11 Group.

On 3 September the squadron had already carried out a patrol over base before it was scrambled in mid-morning, but by this time North Weald had been severely damaged during an attack by around thirty Do 17s. At the end of the day parity was achieved for only the second time as sixteen RAF fighters were lost for sixteen German aircraft shot down. Sadly the statistics showed that two pilots from No. 1 Squadron lost their lives with nothing to show in reply. During the morning actions P/O Dopey Shaw who had joined the squadron back in March was shot down and killed, his Hurricane (P3782) crashing at Parkhouse Farm, Chart Sutton, to the south of Maidstone. F/L Harry Hillcoat was also reported missing in P3044. He has no known grave and his name is recorded on the Runnymede Memorial.

On 4 September No. 1 Squadron carried out a practice dogfight in the morning followed by a patrol at 18,000 ft over Brooklands near Weybridge. This was in connection with a raid on the Vickers Armstrong factory, the principal production facility for the Wellington bomber, but no enemy aircraft were seen. On the following day nine Hurricanes patrolled Biggin Hill at 20,000 ft before the same number of aircraft took part in a combat patrol exercise from Northolt to Langley. In the afternoon the squadron proceeded to Heathrow where they night stopped before returning the following morning.

Having returned to Northolt there was an early start on 6 September as nine aircraft were ordered off at 0845 hrs to patrol Kenley with Hilly Brown in the lead. The weather remained clear, although it was noticeably cooler, but apart from slight haze in the Channel area and the Thames estuary, visibility was excellent. As the Hurricanes climbed to 20,000 ft there were obvious signs of activity above as the sky was streaked with condensation trails as fighters weaved, before spearing down onto their less fortunate counterparts lower down. No. 1 Squadron should have been joined by the Hurricanes of No. 303 Squadron but there was no sign of the Poles and so they carried on alone. A formation of fighters was seen above and to the right but Hilly Brown's attention was then taken by a much larger formation that was heading west. This consisted of Ju 88s and Bf 110s and was stepped up and back, the lowest aircraft flying at around 20,000 ft.

For once the RAF's normally efficient ground organisation had not done its job properly as the sudden arrival of these aircraft came as a complete surprise to Brown, the controller not having informed him of their height and course. As a result of this a favourable attacking position was not gained on the bombers, which not only made their job much more difficult, but left them open to attack by the escort fighters. At one point during the fight Hilly Brown saw a Ju 88 pass underneath him and managed to fire a five-second burst, only breaking away at the last possible moment when a collision seemed inevitable. He was sure that the rear gunner had been silenced as return fire ceased abruptly and a trail of white smoke

NOT BUILT TILL 1946

appeared from the starboard engine. He was not able to pursue this aircraft as he came under attack by Bf 110s and it was last seen heading south-east towards Tunbridge-Wells.

At first the German aircraft were the least of Charles Stavert's worries as he looked in his mirror and saw a Hurricane whose pilot appeared intent on shooting him down. After some desperate manoeuvring, the other pilot finally recognised the aircraft he was attacking as being friendly and, much to Stavert's relief, broke away. He could now concentrate on the job in hand and it was not long before he saw a Ju 88 low down, heading east. He dived down onto it and put in two long bursts, which put its port engine out of action. Turning to the right, he then attacked from the front quarter, which caused further damage and set the Junkers on fire. It then descended to force-land near Tunbridge-Wells, an event that was witnessed by Sammy Salmon, three of the crew being captured by local police.

George Goodman (Blue 3) was also in action. Having evaded an attack by two Bf 109Es by doing a steep climbing turn, he saw a twin-engined aircraft, later confirmed as a Bf 110, heading south. He carried out an attack from astern and a little to one side with slight deflection, aiming for the cockpit and the engines. After a two-second burst the starboard engine caught fire and the 110 slowed, which gave him the opportunity to move in closer to finish it off. During this attack he was fired upon continuously by the rear gunner, Goodman being under the impression that he had more than one gun at his disposal, although this would appear to be extremely unlikely. As he was very close to the 110 when he broke away to the right and down, the gunner was able to put a number of bullets into the Hurricane's oil tank, the cockpit immediately filling with oil smoke. With his aircraft now in a spin, Goodman recovered to level flight before taking to his parachute. As he drifted down he could see below what he assumed to be the 110 he had fired at, its engine on fire. He watched it all the way until it crashed about three miles south of Penshurst. P/O Roland Dibnah also claimed a Bf 110 as destroyed, which crashed near Crowhurst to the east of Redhill. This was Werke Nr 3373 (S9+BH) from 1/ErprGr 210 and was flown by Uffz Gerhard Ruger who was killed. His radio operator, Uffz Edmund Ernst, survived and was taken prisoner.

In the early afternoon the squadron was scrambled again to patrol Maidstone and while airborne the nine Hurricanes were warned of an incoming raid near Dungeness. Climbing to 27,000 ft they were approaching Dover when Charles Stavert, who was flying as Blue 3, saw a group of Bf 109Es diving out of the sun from about 3,000 ft above (once again some of these were identified as He 113s). Two of the 109s opened fire when they got within range but their tracer passed well wide and Stavert was able to turn and follow one of them as it plunged earthwards. It appeared as though the German pilot was unaware that there was a Hurricane behind as he throttled back and reduced speed, which allowed Stavert to close in. By the time that the two aircraft were descending through 10,000 ft he was close enough to open fire and did so with four bursts, each of around four seconds. A stream of black smoke came from the engine of the 109 and it continued its headlong descent towards the sea. As another 109 had followed Stavert down and was beginning to look as though it might launch an attack, he had to turn sharply to the right to evade and lost sight of the aircraft he had fired at. (This 109 was later claimed as damaged although it is likely that it returned unscathed. When the throttle was opened on the Bf 109E the Daimler-Benz DB 601A tended to produce large amounts of exhaust smoke and this was often taken as a sign of combat damage.)

The fine weather of recent days was repeated on 7 September but the expected blips did not appear on the radar screens at the usual time in the morning and as time passed, a sense of unease began to spread. Even by mid-afternoon there had been little activity but by 1540 hrs the first evidence of an attack far larger than any previously experienced was seen building up over on the other side of the Channel. What Fighter Command could not know at this stage was that the *Luftwaffe* had changed its tactics and had decided to attack London in an attempt to deliver the final knockout blow.

During the Battle of Britain German intelligence had attempted to assess the damage that had been caused to the RAF's fighter defences but it had failed to provide an accurate picture, both of the number of aircraft still available and the state of its command and control system. The truth was that Fighter Command was slowly being bled to death with the loss of experienced pilots, either killed or injured, the most worrying aspect. The constant attacks on sector aerodromes had begun to have an affect and Air Vice-Marshal Keith Park was of the opinion that further heavy attacks on aerodromes and operations rooms would leave Fighter Command in a powerless state in the last decisive battles. By moving on London the Germans hoped to draw in every last RAF fighter (it was assumed that aircraft had been withdrawn to the north well out of range of marauding Bf 109Es and Bf 110s) whereas in effect the change of policy was letting the RAF off the hook by relieving the pressure on its sector stations and ground organisation.

For No. 1 Squadron, like everyone else, the morning was quiet and it was not until 1625 hrs that eleven aircraft took to the air to patrol over Northolt at 15,000 ft. A large formation of bombers, together with fighter escort estimated at around 100 machines, was seen over north-east London and the Hurricanes went in to the attack. F/L John Holderness, a Rhodesian who had only recently joined the squadron, shot down one of the bombers (a Dornier Do 215) while Darky Clowes who was leading Yellow section accounted for a Bf 110. Having attacked several fighters without causing too much distress to the crews of these aircraft, he had better luck with a Bf 110, which dived out of control into the sea in the Thames estuary. Clowes then took part in a series of combats that took him as far as Manston but all of these were ineffectual. By shooting down this Bf 110, Clowes created another job for his ground crew as his Hurricane (P3395 JX-B) carried a wasp emblem on its nose, which acquired an additional stripe every time he scored a victory.

On landing back at Northolt the Hurricanes were rapidly refuelled and rearmed and pilots were told to take off independently and if possible form up into sections in the air. F/L John 'Jack' Finnis joined up with part of the squadron but when he was south of Sevenoaks he dived away to attack a Do 215, which he saw flying about 4,000 ft below at 15,000 ft. He began firing from the front port quarter and kept his thumb on the button for a full seventeen seconds, closing right up on the Dornier. By this time its port engine had stopped and white smoke was pouring out. As he had used all of his ammunition he had to leave it to go on its way and could only claim it as damaged. (Finnis was another Rhodesian who had joined the squadron as replacement for Harry Hillcoat. Before the war he had been an airline pilot in Africa and had also been a flying instructor at the de Havilland school in Salisbury, Rhodesia.)

Also flying with No. 1 Squadron was twenty-one-year-old P/O Michael Homer DFC, a former bomber pilot, who was one of a number of pilots drawn from other units to fight in the skies over southern Britain. He was flying as Green 2 and when over London at 23,000 ft saw a single Do 215 flying east, which had become separated from the main formation of bombers. He dived onto this aircraft to fire a three-second burst from the rear starboard quarter, which produced clouds of smoke from the starboard engine. Subsequently he fired at several other aircraft but had to take violent evasive action when he was attacked by Bf 110s. (Homer did not stay with the squadron much longer and was posted to No. 242 Squadron where he was shot down and killed on 27 September 1940 near Sittingbourne in Kent. He is buried in his home town of Swanage in Dorset.)

By now No. 1 Squadron had been operational in 11 Group for two months and despite the fact that it had suffered relatively few casualties during this period, the accumulated fatigue from which it was suffering was enough for it to be given a 'rest' period in an area that was relatively quiet. This unwelcome information became known on 9 September when a signal was received ordering the squadron to move to Wittering in 12 Group. Both 'A' and 'B' Flights, comprising fifteen aircraft in all flew the eighty miles or so to their new base while thirty NCO and other ranks were moved by road. Although no one at the time could have known it, the Battle of Britain was about to reach its climax over the southern counties but it would do so without No. 1 Squadron. During its time in the front line it had achieved one of the best gain/loss ratios within Fighter Command, and unlike many other squadrons it left the fight with its morale still very much on a high, with pilots who possessed something that was of more value than virtually anything – combat experience.

CHAPTER SEVEN

Junkers and Dorniers

RAF Wittering lies alongside the A1 trunk road about three miles south of Stamford in Lincolnshire. It was first used during the First World War when 'A' Flight of No. 38 Squadron was based there for a time with FE.2bs. The name Wittering came into use in 1924 (the aerodrome had previously been known as Stamford) and the Central Flying School was resident until 1935 when it returned to its former home at Upavon. No. 11 FTS was then formed at Wittering, remaining until 1938 when the station was earmarked for use by fighters. No. 1 Squadron swapped places with the Hurricanes of No. 229 Squadron, the latter unit commanded by S/L A.J. Banham flying into Northolt. As a permanent station Wittering was relatively civilised, although No. 1 Squadron also operated from the satellite airfield at Collyweston (originally called Easton after a local village), which was three miles to the west and had been hastily prepared during the winter of 1939/40.

On 10 September work was commenced to equip the squadron's Hurricanes with VHF radios instead of the high-frequency (HF) apparatus previously carried. Tests of the new radios were made over the next few days together with much local flying so that pilots were soon acquainted with their new area of operations. On 12 September there was much celebration when it was announced that David Pemberton and Peter Boot had each been awarded a DFC for gallantry in flying operations against the enemy. Although a total of twenty-one hours flying was undertaken on this date, none of it was operational, which marked the change with life a little further to the south. On the 15th while Fighter Command squadrons were shooting down the highest number of German aircraft for four weeks (sixty aircraft in all), No. 1 Squadron had to be content with patrols over the Duxford sector. These were entirely uneventful and all aircraft were back on the ground again by 1425 hrs.

Over the next few days in addition to practice flying during the day, there was a requirement to undertake patrols by night, either by single aircraft or by a section of three Hurricanes. On 19 September Yellow section patrolled Coventry at 10,000 ft as the *Luftwaffe* was now putting increased emphasis on the night bombing of built-up areas. Further patrols were carried out during the rest of the month by day and night but in marked contrast to its time at Northolt, no enemy aircraft were seen.

During September a number of pilots left the squadron to join other units that were rather more active in 11 Group. These were replaced by pilots fresh out of Operational Training Units and included a number of Czechs. Among them were Sergeants Jan Stefan, Antonin Zavoral, Jan Plasil and Josef Prihoda. There was however the return of a familiar face as Tim Elkington was finally cleared as being fit to fly after his bale out on 16 August. Most of the shrapnel that had peppered his body had been removed during his stay in hospital, but not all. Many smaller pieces remained and these would gradually appear over the coming years, often during or shortly after a hot bath. Although he was happy to be back, there was sadness and disappointment as Fred Berry, the man who had saved his life, was no longer around and so he was unable to thank him for what he had done.

Further practice flying and interceptions were carried out in early October, the latter proving to be useful on the 8th. Blue section led by Peter Matthews with George Goodman as his No. 2 were patrolling Hucknall when a condensation trail was seen high above at an altitude estimated at 26,000 ft, around six miles away and heading west. Both pilots chased after the unidentified aircraft but even by using boost override they had great difficulty in reducing range. It was only when the aircraft began to descend over the Bristol Channel that Goodman was able to get anywhere near it (Matthews having been left behind by this time) and he recognised it as a Ju 88. It continued its dive to sea level and as Goodman closed in the rear gunner opened fire. Undeterred he opened fire himself at 300 yards with a three-second burst and appeared to have hit the gunner who ceased firing at this point. Goodman could see his De Wilde ammunition hitting the fuselage, wing roots and engine nacelles but the Junkers disappeared into clouds and was not seen again. Having chased after this aircraft for around 120 miles Goodman had to land at Filton to refuel before returning to base.

The following day Tim Elkington and Sgt M.P. Davies were engaged on a practice dogfight in the morning, however they were suddenly confronted with the real thing when control vectored them towards a hostile aircraft that had been reported about five miles north-east of base. This turned out to be a Ju 88, which was seen about 1,000 ft below. As Elkington turned towards the German aircraft the rear gunner opened up at extreme range, his pilot making gentle turns in and out of cloud, which made life extremely difficult, however he was able to fire several bursts from 600 yards down to 300 yards on the occasions when he could actually see the Ju 88 and was joined for a time by his No. 2. Davies had been forced to fly a parallel track to the Ju 88 as both it and his leader had disappeared into cloud, but eventually the former re-emerged and he moved in from the beam to fire a four-second burst down to 150 yards. This caused white smoke to pour from the port engine but the Junkers vanished once again and having orbited for some time without seeing anything, Davies flew back to base.

In the meantime Tim Elkington had managed to stay in contact and as the two aircraft crossed over the coast they ran into clearer weather. By this time the Ju 88 was down to around 500 ft and it tried to evade by performing steep turns. At one point it flew straight at Elkington's Hurricane but he climbed towards the sun before diving onto the Junkers again, both aircraft pulling round into a tight turn. Firing with slight deflection from 200 yards down to point blank range, Elkington fired the rest of his ammunition before breaking away in a climbing turn during which he blacked out. When he regained consciousness there was no sign of the Ju 88 even though the visibility was good with no cloud within ten miles. As the combat had taken him well out to sea (approximately forty miles north-east of Skegness) he landed at Manby to refuel before returning. The rest of the day was decidedly mixed as notification of a DFM for Darky Clowes had to be set against the loss of Sgt Stan Warren who had only been with the squadron for a little over two weeks. He disappeared somewhere over the Wash while on a training flight.

By mid-October two more Czech pilots had joined the squadron, Pilot Officers F. Behal and E. Cizek, but there was also another returnee in Jean-François Demozay, by now a fully qualified Hurricane pilot having taken the course at 5 OTU, Aston Down. Demozay had been determined to become a fighter pilot in the RAF and had even managed to get a posting to the squadron he had been associated with in France. Like many other Free French pilots he adopted a *nom de guerre* to provide a degree of anonymity for his family still living in France and he chose the name Moses Morlaix, the surname of which reflected his upbringing in the Breton region. Demozay still had a lot to learn about operational flying but with his determination it would not be long before he was adding to No. 1 Squadron's already impressive list of combat claims. At the same time several pilots left the squadron including Peter Boot and Colin Birch who were both tour expired. Flight Lieutenants John Holderness and Jack Finnis returned to the action by joining 229 Squadron at Northolt.

With the onset of winter, weather tests were flown with increasing frequency during October with practice flying taking place whenever the conditions were suitable. This consisted mainly of air drill, formation cloud flying, searchlight co-operation, fighter attacks and camera gun work, together with occasional firing practice on the ranges at Holbeach. On 15 October, Darky Clowes had a fright when flying to Northolt in a Miles Magister two-seat trainer in conditions of poor visibility. When he was near Hendon he saw a Ju 88 come out of cloud and head straight towards him. His first inclination was to turn towards the nearest patch of cloud but before he could do this he was amazed to see the Junkers turn tail and flee in the opposite direction. Clowes was second only to Hilly Brown in terms of operational experience, the citation to his DFM noting his 'courage and determination' during many combats against the enemy. Shortly afterwards he was commissioned with the rank of Pilot Officer. Two more Czech pilots joined the squadron on 22 October with the arrival of P/O Antonin Velebnovsky and Sgt Josef Dygryn. The latter was another to use a *nom de guerre* to protect his family during the German occupation of his country and was known as Ligoticky. Both were to make a considerable impression over the coming months.

By now the massed daylight raids of September were a thing of the past. Further south there were still occasional attacks by fast, high-flying Bf 109Es operating in the fighter-bomber role, together with incursions by single aircraft on reconnaissance or Intruder missions. These tended to operate when cloud conditions were such that there was a convenient means of escape if attacked. On 24 October one of these aircraft was encountered by Red section led by Hilly Brown, with Darky Clowes (No. 2) and P/O Tony Kershaw (No. 3). It turned out to be a Do 215 (although identified as a Do17) which was first seen by Clowes near Banbury and he was the first to attack. The pilot of the Dornier attempted to escape by turning towards the east and diving but even though his speed was estimated as 260–280 mph, Clowes was able to move in from the rear and above to fire a burst from 300 yards, closing to 100 yards. As he broke away some return fire drifted past his Hurricane from the rear gunner.

As the pilot of the Dornier turned to avoid the attack by Clowes he inadvertently put his machine within striking distance of Brown and Kershaw. The former fired a long burst with full deflection but although the bomber eventually disappeared into cloud, it could have done so much earlier and the conclusion was drawn that the pilot was relatively inexperienced. Brown then became separated from Red 2 and 3 and asked for a separate 'Pipsqueak' whereupon he was vectored towards St Neots and told to orbit. He waited for several minutes for the aircraft to appear but was then informed by the controller that it had crashed nearby. It appears that the Do 215 was also attacked by a section of three Hurricanes from No. 17 Squadron led by Count Manfred Czernin, however the pilots of Red section were of the opinion that it would almost certainly have crashed before getting home, even if No. 17 Squadron had not come across it. (It had been on a reconnaissance mission over the Midlands and came from 3/Aufkl Obdl. There was only one survivor.)

On 26 October the squadron was paid a visit by Sir Archibald Sinclair, the Secretary of State for Air. He toured the dispersal points and gave everyone the impression that he was extremely pleased with the squadron's overall level of efficiency. He also chatted with the pilots and was particularly interested in meeting Jean Demozay, having already been briefed about his flight back from France in the Bristol Bombay.

The next day there was further contact with the enemy when Blue section was returning from a patrol of the area around Clacton having already been in the air for nearly an hour. On this occasion George Goodman was leading with P/O James Robinson (No. 2) and Tim Elkington (No. 3). As they were approaching the bomber base at Feltwell at around 2,000 ft they were alerted by anti-aircraft bursts and a few seconds later saw bombs exploding on the ground. These set fire to a hangar and also hit an air raid shelter. An aircraft was seen about 3,000 ft above and this was quickly identified as a Do 17. Goodman immediately put his section into line astern formation and closed in on the Dornier, however he had to break away again as the gunners at Feltwell maintained their barrage, which was extremely accurate in terms of direction, although the flak bursts were about 1,000 ft too low. In fact for a time there was a greater chance of one of the Hurricanes being hit and the opportunity for a co-ordinated attack was quickly lost.

Eventually the gunners ceased firing and Goodman moved in to fire a lengthy burst from 300 yards before the Dornier disappeared into cloud. The attack was then taken up by P/O James Robinson who fired a short burst at the German aircraft but it flew into cloud and he lost sight of it. He saw it again briefly but was unable to get his gunsight onto it and then had to return as his fuel state was becoming critical. He landed at Upwood having been airborne for 1 hour 50 minutes. Tim Elkington in the meantime had kept to Goodman's right in case the Dornier turned while it was in cloud. At one point he came very close to it but did not risk firing his guns in case Goodman was in the vicinity. He eventually got the opportunity to fire two bursts at a range of about 350 yards but the Do 17 once again vanished into cloud and this time was not seen again.

Having been encouraged by the success of this mission, the *Luftwaffe* decided to try again two days later but encountered Blue section of 'B' Flight with results that were rather more encouraging. On this occasion Sgt Wilfred Page was in the lead with P/O James Robinson and Sgt Vaclav Jicha alongside. Although it was clear above 4,000 ft, below this level there was a layer of 7/10 cloud about 500 ft thick and it was very misty and quite dark. While patrolling below cloud near Feltwell at around 1800 hrs another Do 17 was sighted but this one was in a poor tactical position as it was about 1,000 ft below and flying relatively slowly. As the Hurricanes dived after the Dornier the attack was very nearly spoilt once again by anti-aircraft fire, which burst rather too close for comfort. The Do 17's rear gunner opened up as Page moved in but he was undeterred and pressed his firing button at 250 yards to fire three bursts, each of around two seconds. He then fired again from closer range and succeeded in silencing the rear gunner but before this the German was able to put several bullets into the Hurricane's coolant system, producing copious amounts of glycol fumes. As he broke away Page took one last look at the Dornier and saw that its port engine was on fire.

Although his Hurricane (P3318) was leaving an ominous trail of smoke behind it, Page got in touch with control and asked for a bearing with the intention of reaching base. However, it soon became clear that he would never make it and he had to make an instantaneous decision, whether to bale out or force-land. In fact the decision was made for him as he was flying over a large town at the time (Peterborough) and he put his aircraft down on the outskirts. The landing was not as smooth as he would have liked, but the damage that was caused was repairable and he emerged uninjured. A local searchlight battery at Yaxley organised a guard for the Hurricane and also provided transport to take Page the ten miles or so back to Wittering.

During the initial attack on the Do 17, Page had been closely followed by James Robinson who fired several bursts before his leader broke away. He then climbed above the Dornier to fire a sustained burst of around six seconds, which caused

95

further damage to the port engine and wing root. As he passed underneath he could clearly see that the nose was illuminated, the small Perspex sections being outlined by fire within the fuselage. He then lost sight of the Do 17 but after climbing up through the overcast he saw two more crossing his path, about 600 yards ahead. Before he could close in both aircraft dived into cloud and although he followed in the estimated direction that they would have taken, when he emerged below cloud there was no sign of them. He circled for a few minutes but as his fuel was getting low, he returned to base. On the basis that the Do 17 had been left on fire it was subsequently claimed as destroyed.

'B' Flight's Blue section was also in action on 30 October, the personnel on this occasion comprising George Goodman, Raymond Lewis and Sgt Vaclav Jicha. The call to scramble came in the early afternoon and the section was vectored towards an unidentified contact near Skegness. The 'bogey' was eventually seen at 6,000 ft and turned out to be a Ju 88 but as Goodman swung in for a head-on attack he suddenly thought that it might be a Blenheim and turned away without firing. Jicha was the first to attack but his second burst had to be cut short as Lewis cut in ahead of him. The latter had also approached the German aircraft head-on but as it passed underneath him, he half-rolled to move in from the rear. He opened fire at around 200 yards with a three-second burst but had to cease when the Junkers flew into cloud. Although Lewis and Jicha returned unsure as to the fate of the Ju 88, they had in fact damaged it severely enough for it to crash-land near Ely in Cambridgeshire (it came from III/LG1 and was Werke Nr 5008, L1+GS). The account for the day was not entirely in No. 1 Squadron's favour as Sgt Josef Dygryn caused serious damage to his Hurricane in a landing accident.

Unfortunately the Operations Record Book (Form 540) entries for November are missing, however the month began in tragic fashion as S/L David Pemberton was killed in a flying accident on the 3rd. There is some uncertainty over the manner of his death, some accounts state that he crashed on landing at Wittering in poor weather, whereas others maintain that he attempted a low level aerobatic manoeuvre and died in a manner similar to Cobber Kain of No. 73 Squadron. Whatever the truth No. 1 Squadron lost a much-loved leader who had been associated with the unit since the start of the war as a result of his role with No. 67 Wing in France, before becoming actively involved as its CO in May 1940. He was buried at the twelfth century church of St Eadburgh's at Broadway in Worcestershire, not far from his birthplace at Stratford-upon-Avon.

The choice of Pemberton's successor was widely applauded as it was none other than Hilly Brown, the popular Canadian thus being promoted from Pilot Officer to Squadron Leader in a single (if extremely long) first tour. His flight commanders were Peter Matthews and Darky Clowes. As the latter had only been commissioned in September his rapid promotion was almost without precedent and he appears to have missed out on the rank of Flying Officer completely, as he went from being a Pilot Officer to Flight Lieutenant virtually overnight.

On 8 November Jean Demozay began his highly successful career as a fighter pilot by claiming a Ju 88 as damaged. He had intended to do some aerobatics but when flying near Sutton Bridge at 12,000 ft he saw an aircraft approaching from the sea about 4,000 ft higher. Its nationality soon became obvious. When Demozay turned towards it, the machine immediately swung round through 180 degrees and headed back over the North Sea and as he closed in he quickly recognised it as a Ju 88. It began to climb towards a layer of cloud at around 22,000 ft and the rear gunner opened fire even when the Hurricane was still about a mile behind and way out of range. Demozay was able to close in to around 200 yards before opening fire and this appeared to disable the starboard engine as it began to trail black smoke. After the attack the propeller also seemed to be turning at reduced revs. The Ju 88 then dived towards some clouds away to the left and although Demozay went after it he lost sight of it and could not find it again. He was not helped by the fact that his windscreen had iced up and after circling for ten minutes, by which time he estimated his position as being around seventy miles from the coast, he considered it prudent to return to base.

Although the official records for November have been lost, some idea of what the squadron got up to can be gleaned from Tim Elkington's logbook. Up to 26 November he managed to get airborne on no fewer than twenty days, most of his flying consisting of defensive patrols. There was also much in the way of general training with Elkington taking part in formation flying practice on eight occasions. Other non-operational sorties included practice attacks, dogfights and practice homings. Much of the non-operational flying was for the benefit of the many Czech pilots who now made up a large proportion of the squadron's strength. Most of Tim Elkington's flying during the month was carried out in V7256 JX-O.

December was notable mainly for a lack of action, even when the weather was favourable (which was not that often) and a move back into 11 Group. This occurred on 16 December when the Hurricanes returned to Northolt, together with thirty-two airmen who were transported by air and one officer who was in charge of 166 airmen to be moved by rail. Although No. 1 Squadron had acquitted itself well during its time in 12 Group, the prospect of coming into contact with the enemy rather more frequently was to be welcomed. However, the *Luftwaffe* was by now concentrating on its night bombing offensive and as a result there was very little activity during the day. On 19 December the squadron patrolled Maidstone at 15,000 ft and although no enemy aircraft were seen, the pilots witnessed what appeared to be an oil tanker blow up in the Thames estuary. The first indication of this was when the clouds parted and what was described later as a 'terrific air bump' was felt as the shockwave from the explosion passed by. Shortly afterwards Hilly Brown saw an object falling to earth on fire but was unsure whether it was a balloon or an aircraft.

There were several pilot movements during December including Charles Chetham who was posted out on leave prior to going overseas and Harold Mann who went to No. 96 Squadron in the night-fighter role. Pat Hancock also left to join No. 85 Squadron but it would not be long before he was back. The month ended in disappointment as although the squadron was held at readiness all day on 31 December, the weather was decidedly unfavourable and no flying took place. By now there was new leadership in RAF Fighter Command who were about to adopt a completely different philosophy and it would not be long before No. 1 Squadron would be at the forefront of a strategy that was much more offensive in its outlook.

CHAPTER EIGHT

Sweeps and Circuses

Towards the end of 1940 the two main architects of victory in the Battle of Britain, Air Chief Marshal Sir Hugh Dowding, Fighter Command's AOC-in-C, and Air Vice-Marshal Keith Park, the commander of 11 Group, were both removed from office. Dowding had been due to retire earlier in the year so his departure was not unexpected. The fact that Park was also replaced was rather more controversial, although the stress that the summer battles had created had affected his health. The manner in which they were supplanted however left a lot to be desired and reflected badly on the RAF, as it transpired that their replacements had actively conspired against them.

The new commander-in-chief of Fighter Command was Air Chief Marshal Sir William Sholto Douglas, a former First World War fighter pilot who had flown SE.5as with No. 84 Squadron. During the inter-war years he enjoyed a steady advancement and in 1938 was made Assistant Chief of the Air Staff. Park was replaced by Air Vice-Marshal Trafford Leigh-Mallory who had led 12 Group since December 1937. The new incumbents shared a belief that the war should be taken to the Germans on the other side of the Channel and their aggressive stance shared much with the policy adopted by Trenchard during the First World War. Whenever the weather was suitable it was now advocated that RAF's fighters should seek out their counterparts in France by operating in Wing strength, a fighter Wing typically being made up of three squadrons. Pure fighter sweeps were to be supplemented by Circus operations in which several Wing formations took part. The core element of a Circus was a small number of bombers (usually Blenheims of 2 Group). By incorporating these it was hoped that German fighters would be forced to participate in a battle of attrition, which the RAF was confident of winning. As the initial fighter sweeps were largely uncontested however, Circuses soon became the predominant operation and over 100 would be flown during 1941.

When the weather was not suitable for large-scale operations it was proposed that nuisance raids be carried out by small numbers of aircraft. These were initially known as 'Mosquito' raids, but the name was soon changed to Rhubarb to avoid confusion with the aircraft of the same name. The main intention once again was to seek out and destroy enemy fighters but when these were not encountered pilots were to look for any target of opportunity. Rhubarb operations would typically be carried out by a pair of aircraft, which would use cloud cover to evade German defences and also as a means of escape.

No. 1 Squadron's first mission of 1941 was a 'Mosquito' raid on 1 January, the participating pilots comprising Darky Clowes, Raymond Lewis, Tony Kershaw and Sgt E. Goy. All made it to France except the latter who was involved in a minor accident at the forward aerodrome at Hawkinge where it had been arranged that they would land to refuel. On the night of 3 January instructions were received for the squadron to move to Kenley and although the ground party got there the following day, the Hurricanes had to stay at Northolt for one more night owing to bad weather. They finally made it at 1100 hrs on the 5th but were then grounded for the next three days as the weather closed in again.

Kenley was just a few miles south of Croydon and had first been used in 1917 as an aircraft acceptance park. It became well known in the late 1920s as a fighter station and provided P/O Douglas Bader with his first operational experience when he was posted to 23 Squadron in July 1930 to fly Gloster Gamecocks and Bristol Bulldogs. Kenley was closed in 1932 for building works to be carried out and it re-opened two years later when Nos 3 and 17 Squadrons arrived from Upavon. During the Battle of Britain it took on the role of a sector station (Gatwick and Redhill were its satellites) and it was attacked on a number of occasions, including one raid at night that caused further damage to infrastructure. No. 1 Squadron's arrival was at the expense of No. 253 Squadron, which flew north to Leconfield in East Yorkshire on rest.

Over the next four months No. 1 Squadron often flew with the Hurricanes of No. 615 Squadron, which was also based at Kenley. Their first opportunity to do so was on 9 January when nine Hurricanes, together with twelve from No. 615 Squadron, took off from Kenley at 1329 hrs. They crossed the coast north of Dungeness and flew towards Cap Gris Nez before turning north towards Calais. The average height of the patrol was 21,000 ft but as they did not cross the French coast at any point there was little likelihood of a reaction from the Germans. The English coast was re-crossed at Deal and the formation then proceeded to Manston and Dungeness once again before returning via Hythe. The weather had been glorious throughout with hardly any cloud, but the lack of response meant that the sweep had felt more like a sector recce as the pilots gazed down on the coastline of France, an area they would come to know well. Patrols were carried out over Canterbury and Dover on 10 January but the fine weather that was prevalent on these two days quickly gave way to a rather more predictable mixture of wind, rain, snow and fog and there was no operational flying for the rest of the month. The only bright spot was the return of Pat Hancock on the 29th. He had managed to convince everyone that he was ill-suited to be a night-fighter pilot and re-joined his old unit via No. 615 Squadron.

On 2 February Circus No. 2 took place (the first had been on 10 January). The target was the docks area at Boulogne and these were attacked by six Blenheims of No. 139 Squadron from Horsham St Faith with No. 1 Squadron in attendance as part of the escort. Pat Hancock, who was flying as Black 1 and was the squadron's designated 'weaver', saw a Bf 109E make a diving attack on the Blenheims as they were completing their bombing run. It broke away in a climbing turn to the left but as Hancock was still about 1,000 ft above he was able to get behind it relatively easily. He fired a short burst from 300 yards, which drifted wide of its intended target, but did rather better after closing in to around 200 yards. A second burst produced glycol fumes but at a crucial moment during his attack he had to stop firing as another Hurricane cut in ahead of him. He last saw the 109 in a steep dive being followed by the other Hurricane.

This aircraft may have been that flown by F/Sgt Karel Kuttelwascher who was No. 2 to Hilly Brown. After his CO had fired at a 109 without effect, the Czech fired a two-second burst from 150 yards and was sufficiently encouraged to claim it as a probable when he returned. Kuttelwascher was another of No. 1 Squadron's Czech pilots and had arrived in October the previous year. He was twenty-four years of age and had joined the Czech Air Force in October 1934. On completion of his training he flew Avia B.534 biplane fighters but after the Germans marched into Czechoslovakia in 1938 he escaped to France via Poland. During the invasion of France he was serving with GCIII/6, his first combat success being a one third share in a He 111 that was shot down on 19 May. With the fall of France he fled to the UK where he converted onto the Hawker Hurricane at 5 OTU, Aston Down. No. 1 Squadron was fortunate to have such an experienced pilot on its strength. Over the next sixteen months he would become one of the RAF's top scoring pilots as well as being part of a legendary duo.

Another Circus operation (No. 3) was flown on 5 February with twelve Blenheims (six each from 114 and 139 Squadrons) attacking the airfield at St Omer. No. 1 Squadron was again given the close escort role (together with No. 615 Squadron) with the Spitfires of Nos 65 and 610 Squadron providing forward cover and another Spitfire Wing offering support as the formation withdrew. For the RAF this operation was something of a disaster as nine fighters were lost with six pilots killed and two taken prisoner. Among those shot down was F/O Raymond Lewis who had to bale out over the Channel after being attacked by a Bf 109E of JG 3. The Canadian was another to have returned to No. 1 Squadron after a break as he had re-joined the unit in October 1940 having been among those posted back to the UK from France the previous May. Unfortunately for Lewis at this stage of the war the chances of being picked up alive from the Channel were slim and it was only later in the year that the Air/Sea Rescue organisation came into its own. His body was never found and his name is another to be commemorated on the Runnymede Memorial. (No. 615 Squadron fared even worse and lost three aircraft, with two pilots killed. This includes two Hurricanes that collided near Dover.)

The next offensive sorties took place on 8 February and involved a Rhubarb operation flown by Hilly Brown and James Robinson. They flew to the airfield at Arques where Brown caught a Bf 109E taking off and damaged it sufficiently so that its pilot was rushed into a hurried crash-landing. This was to be the last venture into France for more than two weeks however as defensive patrols began to predominate once again. After one of these over Maidstone on 13 February Darky

Clowes had the misfortune to 'crash' on landing, but the damage was easily repaired and he was unhurt. Two days later when patrolling between Maidstone and Dungeness (with No. 615 Squadron) a Do 17 was seen briefly but it got away in clouds. During another patrol later in the day the squadron was ordered to intercept unidentified aircraft approaching the south coast from the Channel but these turned back towards France before contact could be made.

It was not until the end of February that No. 1 Squadron was involved in anything other than defensive operations. On 26 February a Circus was laid on at short notice to take advantage of a brief improvement in the weather. This operation comprised twelve Blenheims of 139 Squadron, which made a rendezvous over Biggin Hill at 15,000 ft with the Escort Wing (Nos 1, 303 and 601 Squadrons) and the High Cover Wing (Nos 74, 92 and 609 Squadrons). The target was the harbour at Calais and this was successfully attacked. No. 1 Squadron was the close escort squadron and flew 500 ft above and to the rear of the bombers. Heavy flak was experienced over Calais, which burst mainly in front of and above the Blenheims, and about thirty enemy fighters were seen climbing up from the St Omer area at heights varying from 2,000 ft to 10,000 ft. It appeared as though these had been scrambled too late as they were unable to catch up with the main formation. Six 109s were also seen in mid-Channel returning to France at great speed and very low. The operation was completed by Nos 54 and 64 Squadrons which formed the so-called 'Mopping Up' Wing, which made two offensive sweeps from Cap Gris Nez to Calais as the bombers were withdrawing. Although the bombing attack had gone well, the operation as a whole was rather disappointing as it had failed to generate much of a response from the *Luftwaffe*, which for the RAF, was the principal aim.

On the last day of the month the squadron received a rather belated Christmas present with the delivery of brand new Hurricanes IIs to replace their tired old Mark Is. Although the Hurricane was not capable of significant development, various different engines had been proposed including the Rolls-Royce Griffon and Bristol Hercules, however these were quickly abandoned as major airframe modifications would have been required, which would have interrupted production. In the end the Mark II was to emerge with the two-stage supercharged Merlin XX, which initially offered 1,185 hp and later 1,280 hp. Top speed was increased to 342 mph and the rate of climb was also improved. The first Hurricane IIAs retained eight-gun armament but it would not be long before these were supplemented by the Mark IIB with twelve Browning machine-guns and the Mark IIC with four 20-mm Hispano cannon. No. 1 Squadron's pilots lost no time in getting acquainted with their new aircraft and were generally impressed with its all-round performance.

Due to continued poor weather Fighter Command's offensive against the German fighter force in France made very little headway in March and only two Circus operations were possible on the 5th and the 13th. This meant that No. 1 Squadron was mainly engaged in defensive duties during the month, which included patrols of Maidstone, Dungeness and Tenterden. On 19 March the three Hurricanes of Yellow section took off from Kenley at 1725 hrs to escort a convoy moving westwards through the Channel between Dungeness and Hastings. A section of Spitfires from No. 609 Squadron at Biggin Hill also took part but they were powerless to prevent a slashing attack by Bf 109Es of I/LG 2, which dived straight past the No. 609 Squadron aircraft and went for No. 1 Squadron's Hurricanes, which were flying at 5,000 ft. These 109s were led by Hptm Herbert Ihlefeld who latched onto the aircraft flown by P/O Tony Kershaw and set it on fire. Kershaw baled out but either did so at too low an altitude, or his parachute failed to open. His body was picked up by a whaler and taken to Newhaven. The Hurricane flown by Sgt Jan Stefan was also badly shot up and was further damaged in a crash-landing, which led to it being written off.

Despite very poor visibility further patrols were flown over Eastbourne and Beachy Head on 20 and 21 March but these were uneventful. It was not until 24 March that the enemy was encountered again. At 1300 hrs three Hurricanes of Blue section left Kenley to protect minesweepers off Dungeness. As they were patrolling over the sea two Bf 109Es appeared from the south and launched an attack. As the Hurricanes turned to engage, they sheared off and made for France but they returned briefly to fire at extreme range before retiring for good. Blue section was replaced at 1430 hrs by Yellow section led by Jean Demozay and once again Bf 109Es attempted to intervene. Demozay saw a 109 diving out of the overcast onto Yellow 2 and 3 and turned towards it, prompting it to seek the sanctuary of the clouds once more. Having reformed the section it was not long before the 109s tried again and Demozay was forced to take violent evasive action. Shortly afterwards two 109s made a converging attack on him from behind, but by throttling back he forced them to overshoot. As most of the trouble was coming from above he decided to climb through the clouds and on doing so found that he was only 100 yards behind a section of 109s. Selecting the one that was nearest, he gave it a long burst of around twelve seconds, which was sufficient to bring it down in flames.

By now the grouping of Fighter Command squadrons into Wings had formally taken place with the creation of the post of Wing Commander (Flying), a term that was often shortened to Wing Leader. This role was undertaken by extremely experienced pilots who were in charge of the operational side of a fighter base, the more mundane administrative tasks now being carried out by the station commander. The new Wing Leader at Kenley was W/C John Peel DFC who had graduated from the RAF College at Cranwell in July 1932. During the Battle of Britain he had commanded No. 145 Squadron.

Practice Wing formations were flown on 27 and 28 March with W/C Peel leading and three days later a total of twenty-one Hurricanes IIs (ten each from Nos 1 and 615 Squadrons, plus W/C Peel) took part in a Roadstead operation in the English Channel. A perfect rendezvous was made over Maidstone with six Blenheims, which had Nos 56 and 249 Squadrons as close escort, Nos 1 and 615

Squadrons providing medium cover. The objective consisted of two medium sized ships that were two miles north-east of Cap Gris Nez and there were several near misses on the leading vessel. A group of around nine Bf 109Es dived towards the Blenheims but the attack was rather half-hearted and no fighter versus fighter combats took place. There was no flak either and all aircraft returned safely to land at 1325 hrs, having been in the air for 1 hour 10 minutes.

Operations were hampered by poor weather for much of the following week and on 7 April a signal was received for No. 1 Squadron to move the short distance to Croydon. The new aerodrome lay just a few miles to the north and during the inter-war years had been London's gateway to Europe and beyond before it was requisitioned for military use. The last operation to be carried out from Kenley was a Rhubarb over France on 7 April by five Hurricanes (including W/C John Peel). The French coast was crossed south of Berck but two aircraft became detached from the others shortly after. The three led by Peel broke cloud at 3,000 ft directly over the airfield at Berck-sur-Mer and dived down to strafe three Bf 109Es that were seen on the ground in vic formation. As these were on the edge of the aerodrome and facing into wind it was assumed that they were the readiness flight. About twelve men ran towards these machines but Sgt E. Goy opened fire and at least two fell to the ground. He also saw his De Wilde ammunition hitting two of the 109s.

John Peel also raked the 109s and succeeded in scattering a number of troops who were lounging around on the eastern boundary of the airfield. He then climbed up into cloud once again before descending once more on the lookout for any suitable targets. He did not have long to wait as a large concentration of vehicles soon appeared, which were shot up from a height of 200 ft. The final member of the trio (Sgt Jan Stefan) also fired at the 109s and followed Peel in his attack on the motor transport. The other pair of Hurricanes had little to report on return except that P/O W. Raymond claimed to have fired at two lorries seen on a road to the north of Berck. Although he attacked twice, once from behind and again from head-on, little damage appeared to have been done and it seemed as though the vehicles merely pulled up on the side of the road.

The first operation to be flown out of Croydon was a successful one and resulted in the first RAF victory for F/Sgt Karel Kuttelwascher. Four Hurricanes were airborne at 0830 hrs to patrol Dungeness and when flying at 30,000 ft three Bf 109Es were seen approaching from Cap Gris Nez in a very wide vic formation. Two of these aircraft attacked while the other stayed up-sun and a brief dogfight took place. Sgt Jan Plasil (Blue 2) was fired at first but his attacker soon had Kuttelwascher to contend with. The Czech closed in to a range of only 30 yards and fired two bursts, which produced smoke from the starboard wing root. A piece of debris was also prised from the other side of the fuselage. The 109 continued diving gently in a southerly direction at around 260–280 mph IAS and Kuttelwascher fired again, this time from the rear port quarter. He followed the German aircraft down to around 1,000 ft and saw it crash in a small wood about fifteen miles south of Gris Nez.

Over the next two weeks further defensive patrols were mixed with practice scrambles and air-to-ground firing at the Leysdown ranges on the Isle of Sheppey. On 19 April formation cloud flying was practised and two aircraft took part in a search over the Channel for a Spitfire that had been shot down in the early evening. This was for P/O Wally Churches of No. 74 Squadron who had been in combat with Bf 109Es of JG 53. Unfortunately the search was unproductive and Churches thus joined the growing number of Fighter Command pilots lost as the fighting intensified. There were further personnel changes in April with the departure of Pat Hancock for the second time. In his case there was to be no respite as on 27 April he took off from the deck of HMS *Ark Royal* in the lead of a flight of Hurricanes bound for Malta. Another to leave was Tim Elkington who went to 55 OTU. Among those posted in were S/L Richard Brooker and Sgt C.M. Stocken. The arrival of Brooker heralded the end of Hilly Brown's time with No. 1 Squadron as he was long overdue for a rest. He would remain for a few more weeks to ensure a smooth transition in leadership, but by mid May would be on his way to 58 OTU for a spell as an instructor.

On 21 April six Hurricanes led by James Robinson (Blue 1) took off from Croydon to patrol Maidstone at 20,000 ft. When in the Canterbury area the controller warned them of enemy aircraft approaching from the Channel with an estimated height of 25,000 ft. On looking to their right, these were immediately seen as all four were leaving tell-tale condensation trails against the dark blue of the sky above. They were Bf 109Es heading north-west in a wide line abreast formation and were seen to be climbing fast. Robinson climbed the Hurricane formation on a starboard tack towards the sun but by the time they had reached 29,000 ft the 109s were still about 3,500 ft higher. Each side then circled the other as they came closer together and Robinson fired several short bursts at one of the 109s from full deflection round to the port rear quarter. His fire was accurate as he saw De Wilde strikes and pieces coming away from the port wing, however the 109 escaped in a fast shallow dive towards the sun (Robinson was flying one of the first twelve-gun Hurricane IIBs).

Sgt Josef Prihoda (Red 2) was attacked head-on by another 109. As the two aircraft rushed towards each other they both opened fire but the Czech was determined not to give way and the German pilot had to pull up to avoid a collision. Having done so, he then went into a diving turn to the right and Prihoda immediately wrenched his Hurricane round in a steep turn to port so that he was soon in a firing position. He pressed the firing button at a range of 500 yards and continued to pursue the 109 back over the Channel, eventually closing to 200 yards. Several more short bursts led to white and black smoke appearing and the 109 was last seen diving into cloud at around 7,000 ft, apparently out of control. It was later claimed as a probable. Prihoda was another to be flying a Hurricane IIB and although the installation generally worked well, he had two stoppages (one on each side) due to short recoil. During the fight F/O Antonin Velebnovsky (Red 1) was also attacked by a 109 but managed to stay out of trouble by turning inside his opponent.

The next day Maidstone was patrolled again but the squadron was recalled due to bad visibility and deteriorating weather. Tragically another pilot lost his life later in the day although the circumstances were decidedly bizarre. Sgt C.M. Stocken, who had only joined the squadron a couple of days before, decided to take off in the Magister (T9680) despite having no authority from ops. The weather had also deteriorated further and was now unsuitable for flying of any description. Although he got as far as Deal in Kent, the inevitable happened and he was killed when he flew into a hill near Kingsdown in low cloud.

Further patrols were carried out over the next few days, including a night patrol at West Malling on 25 April. Enemy aircraft were seen on most of the daytime operations but they mostly scurried back to France before contact was made. The exception was on 28 April during a convoy patrol over the Thames estuary by four aircraft. They were later vectored towards Dungeness and Josef Prihoda, who was weaving behind the other three, came off worst in an encounter with a Bf 109E. He eventually put his Hurricane down in a field near New Romney but stepped out unhurt.

The last week in April saw the departure of two long-serving pilots in Darky Clowes and Peter Matthews who were both awarded the DFC at the end of their tours. They were posted as instructors at Operational Training Units, Clowes at 56 OTU, Sutton Bridge, and Matthews at 52 OTU, Debden. They were replaced by Flight Lieutenants K.C. Jackman and W.H. Sizer DFC. From Chelmsford in Essex, Wilfred 'Bill' Sizer was twenty-one years old and was an excellent sportsman, having already represented the RAF at boxing and hockey. He had fought in France with No. 213 Squadron and had survived being shot down on 20 May 1940. Despite suffering facial injuries when he was flung forwards into the gunsight, he was flying again two days later. He then took part in the cover operation over Dunkirk but was shot down again and had to return by ship. During the Battle of Britain he added to his score and by the time he joined No. 1 Squadron he was already an 'ace' with six combat victories. In addition to these changes, Sgt Albin Nasswetter, another Czech pilot, was also posted to the squadron.

Although Hilly Brown was still officially on the squadron's strength, by the end of April S/L Richard Brooker had taken over full control of the squadron. A former school teacher from Willingdon in Sussex, he had joined the RAF in April 1937. During the Battle of Britain he had flown with No. 56 Squadron but he came to No. 1 Squadron from the Central Gunnery School at Sutton Bridge where he had spent four months as an instructor. One of his first duties was to oversee another move as the squadron left Croydon for Redhill on 1 May. Redhill was two miles south-east of Reigate in Surrey and had first been used by the RAF in 1937. It was rather rustic compared to what No. 1 Squadron had been used to since its return from France. Its 'L' shaped landing ground was a grassed area with a perimeter track around the outside giving access via taxiways to dispersal pens and blister hangars.

During the first week in May three more pilots joined the squadron, each of whom had travelled a long way just to be there. P/O B.G. 'Buck' Collyns came from Greymouth in New Zealand and after graduating from agricultural college he worked as a sheep farmer. He qualified as a pilot in May 1940 and was commissioned on arrival in the UK. Prior to joining No. 1 Squadron he flew with Nos 238 and 601 Squadrons. P/O Romas Marcinkus was reputed to have been the only Lithuanian fighter pilot in the RAF and to complete the trio, Sgt Gerry Scott came from Canada.

Much of early May was taken up with intensive training with particular emphasis being placed on night flying, a type of aerial activity that No. 1 Squadron would soon become well acquainted with. For the time being they were to perform a dual role and as the London Blitz was still under way there was no shortage of targets at night, the only problem was finding them. As dedicated radar-equipped night-fighters were still in short supply, Fighter Command had to allocate some of its day fighters to operate in a night role, a policy known as 'fighter nights'. Normally single-engined day fighters were hopelessly inadequate at night as pilots had no aids to help him. They therefore relied solely on their eyes but night vision was often adversely affected by the glare of the exhausts on each side of the nose. Some aircraft were fitted with small horizontal plates to act as shields, but night-fighting in aircraft that were designed to operate by day was far from ideal. There were very rare occasions however when the weather was so good that when it coincided with a moon period, even Hurricanes and Spitfires could pose a serious threat to enemy bombers. The night of 10/11 May 1941 was to be one of those nights.

CHAPTER NINE

A Change of Role

As already related, the *Luftwaffe* changed its tactics on 7 September 1940 with its first major raid on London. Gradually the daylight attacks faded out as aircraft losses were unsustainable but the night offensive continued and London was to suffer raids on fifty-seven consecutive nights. By the beginning of May 1941 around 20,000 inhabitants had been killed (a figure that was equalled by those killed in other British cities) and the level of damage in the capital stood at over one million homes damaged or completely destroyed. Although Germany was in the final stages of preparation for its invasion of the Soviet Union, there was to be one more major assault on London on the night of 10/11 May, an attack that would cause widespread devastation and result in the deaths of a further 1,500 civilians.

It started at 2300 hrs with the wailing of the air raid sirens and shortly afterwards the first bombs began to fall. At the height of the raid bombs were falling anywhere from Islington in the north to Southwark in the south. They also encompassed the area from Wapping in the east to the relatively affluent Notting Hill. Here a stick of bombs flattened fourteen houses on one side of Bomore Road, together with another seven houses on the opposite side. In an instant seven died and thirteen more were injured. The Queen's Hall, thankfully empty following a concert by the London Philharmonic Orchestra conducted by Malcolm Sargent, was hit by a single incendiary that fell on the roof. Despite the best efforts of those on fire watch it could not be extinguished completely (a lack of water at a crucial time did not help) and within a matter of an hour the Hall was completely gutted. Bombs also caused damage at the British Museum and Westminster Abbey. Weather conditions were perfect, with a full moon creating conditions of semi-daylight, so that *Luftwaffe* crews could easily identify their targets. However, just as it was straightforward for the Germans, it was also comparatively easy for the defending fighters who were intent on hunting them down.

For No. 1 Squadron it was to be a busy night and the first section of four Hurricanes, comprising Richard Brooker, Bill Sizer, Jean Demozay and Jan Plasil took off from Redhill at 2300 hrs. Each aircraft was to patrol a designated area with a vertical separation of 500 ft. In this instance Brooker was the lowest at 16,000 ft, while Plasil was the highest of the four machines at 17,500 ft. Half an hour after taking off Richard Brooker was circling the fires that were raging in London when he saw a He 111 running in from the Thames Estuary as it prepared to bomb. He closed in at once and opened fire from 200 yards down to point-blank range in one long burst. As he broke away the port engine was streaming glycol and immediately afterwards caught fire. The Heinkel turned to port and dived vertically down towards the flames below. As Brooker's windscreen had been coated in oil he had great difficulty seeing out but he managed to identify another enemy aircraft against the moon. On turning towards it however he lost sight of it. He then saw another pass directly beneath him but it also disappeared before he could launch an attack. He returned to Redhill at 0045 hrs.

Jean Demozay in the meantime had been patrolling at 17,000 ft when three searchlights lit up a He 111 over the East India Docks. The Heinkel was slightly above him so he climbed up from behind and when still below at a range of only 30 yards, he opened fire with a short burst. This was sufficient to wreck the port engine, which poured smoke, and the bomber rolled over into a steep dive. The Frenchman followed it down and watched as it passed over the Thames to crash on the south side of the river (Demozay was flying Z2909, a twelve-gun Hurricane IIB, unlike the other members of the section who all had eight-gun Hurricane IIAs). Success at night usually depended on being in the right place at the right time. Unfortunately for Bill Sizer and Jan Plasil they saw nothing and returned to base without having fired their guns.

The second section took off at 0015 hrs with F/L K.C. Jackman in the lead. He was to patrol at 16,000 ft with P/O W. Raymond, Sgt Josef Dygryn and Sgt Bedrich Kratkoruky stepped up above him at 500 ft intervals. On this occasion the two pilots at the lowest altitudes (Jackman and Raymond) returned with nothing to report whereas the two Czechs had an eventful night. Dygryn was circling over London in an anti-clockwise direction when he saw a twin-engined bomber (later identified as a He 111) flying south on the same course as himself, but a little below and to his left. He dived onto it from astern for a starboard quarter attack, firing a short burst. The rear gunner in the Heinkel also opened up, but his tracer passed harmlessly over the Hurricane. The two adversaries again traded bursts of fire, that coming from the He 111 suddenly ceasing as though the gunner had been hit. This gave Dygryn the chance to close right in and he fired a long burst before breaking away to position his aircraft for another attack. This was completed from the beam with full deflection and just before he ceased firing the bomber shuddered violently before falling into a steep dive. The Czech fired again as the Heinkel went down but his ammunition ran out and he could do no more. As it turned out he did not need to as the German aircraft continued its descent until it hit the ground and exploded with a bright flash. As he pulled out of his dive Dygryn estimated his position as being near Kenley and he touched down at Redhill at 0055 hrs.

Bedrich Kratkoruky was patrolling near Canvey Island when he saw an enemy aircraft above on his left-hand side (it could not be identified but was thought to be either a He 111 or a Ju 88). After climbing he made a beam attack firing a one-second burst, which led to the bomber going down in a steep dive. Kratkoruky followed firing further short bursts and eventually he noticed smoke coming from the port engine. At around 2,000 ft he pulled out of his dive but the German aircraft continued its descent and was last seen to the south-west of Southend. Although the Czech was confident that he had shot the aircraft down, he was only awarded it as damaged as the action had ended over the sea so there could be no proof that it had been destroyed.

The final section of four Hurricanes was airborne at 0130 hrs but had none of the success of the other two, in fact rather the opposite. It was made up entirely of Czech pilots as it comprised Sergeants Jarda Novak, Josef Prihoda and Otto Pavlu, with P/O Frantisek Behal. Novak chased after a Ju 88 that he saw travelling north. It was only about 200 yards away from him when he first saw it and it was flying at the same height. Having got into an attacking position, he fired a three-second burst at close range but although his fire appeared to be hitting the Junkers, it flew on. He fired a second burst as it went into a dive, but no claim was submitted on his return. Sgt Josef Prihoda saw two He 111s over London but just as he was about to open fire, a series of anti-aircraft shell bursts completely surrounded him and he was fortunate to escape without damage to his aircraft. Sadly, P/O Frantisek Behal did not make it back to Redhill. It was later concluded that he had been hit by return fire from an aircraft he had attacked as he had contacted control to say that he was baling out. His Hurricane crashed at Selsdon Park to the south-east of Croydon and he was killed.

Although No. 1 Squadron had carried out its duty in respect of 'fighter nights', there was still much to do. Another eight Hurricane IIAs took off at various times during the night to patrol over Redhill. The weather remained cloudless with perfect visibility until just before 0400 hrs when smoke and mist began to settle on the western edge of the aerodrome and three aircraft that were airborne at the time had to divert to West Malling. The most successful pilot during the second part of the night was Josef Dygryn who made two further patrols. Having taken off at 0135 hrs to patrol base at 15,000 ft he saw a He 111 slightly above him on its way back to France. He pulled round in a climbing turn to give chase but did not catch up with it until it was just south of Gatwick. Several short bursts appeared to be ineffectual but a beam attack from above produced better results and black smoke soon billowed out of the bomber and passed just above his canopy. Not long after the Heinkel burst into flames and fell into a spin, out of control. It crashed at Upchurch in Kent and was A1+CL of 3/KG 53. Two of the crew survived to become prisoners of war.

After refuelling and rearming, Dygryn took off again at 0315 hrs as the last German bombers were depositing their loads on London before turning for home. When he was flying at 16,000 ft just to the north-east of Biggin Hill he saw a Ju 88 at the same height. He was able to close in quite easily and fired three bursts of two seconds, the last from about 25 yards. It is likely that the Junkers had already been attacked as when it was first seen it was gradually losing height and trailing smoke. Dygryn followed it over the coast before firing a final burst, at which point the Ju 88 burst into flames and dived into the sea about ten miles south of Hastings. Having secured a hat-trick of victories during the night he returned to Redhill and landed at 0400 hrs.

F/L K.C. Jackman and P/O W. Raymond took off again at 0225 hrs. The former patrolled at 15,000 ft but as he had seen nothing after thirty minutes he descended to 13,000 ft and immediately saw a He 111 heading north towards London. He chased after it for about three miles at which point he had reduced the range to around 250 yards. As he opened fire with a short burst the Heinkel went into a steep left-hand turn, leaving behind it a thin trail of smoke. The rear gunner was firing but this did not trouble Jackman and he fired again as the German aircraft made a desperate attempt to escape by diving steeply towards the south. A third burst fired at 9,000 ft caused further damage and the He 111 continued its dive, which by this time had become vertical, and it crashed about fifteen miles south of Redhill. Content with his work, Jackman returned and landed at 0335 hrs.

P/O W. Raymond also met with success. As he was flying to the north of base at 18,000 ft he noticed two combats taking place below him but at this stage in his patrol he had not seen any enemy aircraft. It appears however that one had seen him as red tracer suddenly flashed by just above his Hurricane and on looking to his left he saw a He 111 slightly above. Turning towards it he opened fire from close range from the rear quarter, before crossing over to the other side to fire another burst. The bomber went into a steep dive and appeared to be out of control. Raymond followed it down but pulled out of his dive at 2,000 ft and on circling saw a large fire on the ground about ten miles south of base.

The final claim for the night was made by P/O James Robinson who took off at 0115 hrs to patrol over Redhill. When flying at just over 13,000 ft and flying west he saw an enemy aircraft approaching from the north and slightly above. Although he could not identify the aircraft positively, it was obvious that it was hostile as it dived as soon as Robinson was seen and began weaving from side to side. Despite this evasive action, which became more violent as the Hurricane moved in, Robinson opened fire from about 100 yards, his bullets hitting the fuselage and one of the engines, which began to smoke. As the two aircraft descended Robinson found that it became more difficult for him to keep the aircraft in view and eventually he lost it completely in the dark background. He climbed back to 13,000 ft and saw another enemy aircraft but lost sight of it before he was able to give chase.

The score for the night thus stood at seven destroyed (six He 111s and one Ju 88) with another unidentified aircraft damaged. Although other RAF squadron also did well on this particular night, the performance of No. 1 Squadron was far ahead of anyone else. As the drone of German bombers finally receded over London the appalling aftermath became apparent. Large areas of the city had been wrecked and the House of Commons had also been hit, its position betrayed by the River Thames, which had stood out so well in the moonlight. The Chamber of the House was destroyed and three people were killed. The Palace of Westminster was also severely damaged. Although there were a few more raids on British cities, this was the last major assault on London for the time being. By the time that the bombers returned the RAF's night-fighter defences had been vastly improved and the short-term expedient of using day fighters as a temporary stop-gap was no longer needed.

On 12 May dusk and night patrol were again carried out but these were all uneventful. Maidstone was patrolled the next day but the only events of note were the arrival of new pilots, Pilot Officers Vaclav Kopecky and Antonin Liska from 56 OTU at Sutton Bridge and Sgt L. Travis from 55 OTU at Usworth. There were several scrambles and patrols on 16 May taking in Tenterden, Dungeness and Dover and during the first of these Sgt Josef Dygryn added to his already impressive run by shooting down a Bf 109. A section of four Hurricanes led by Richard Brooker took off at 1320 hrs and climbed to 20,000 ft, however Brooker was forced to hand over the lead to F/L K.C. Jackman on account of weak R/T reception. This was shortly after control had warned of an enemy raid coming in from the Channel. As the weather was near perfect with an almost cloudless sky and excellent visibility there was a good chance that any hostile aircraft would be seen.

Jackman took the Hurricanes up to 26,000 ft but this was still not enough as three Bf 109s were seen circling away to the north-east at an altitude estimated at 32,000 ft. The Messerschmitt 109 had a clear superiority over both the Hurricane and Spitfire at altitude and although Jackman tried to coax his aircraft higher, he was unable to get within striking distance. One of the 109 pilots decided to try his luck however and dived on the Hurricane flown by Sgt Albin Nasswetter. Josef Dygryn immediately broke away and went after the 109, firing a short burst from 250 yards from the port quarter before firing a longer burst from the other side. There were no obvious signs that he had hit the German aircraft, although it continued diving steeply. Realising that the other German aircraft above might be tempted to go after him, Dygryn used the speed he had built up in the dive to zoom-climb back up and fired at another of the 109s but again, apparently, with little effect. He then attempted to climb after them and had better luck than Jackman as his Hurricane made it above 30,000 ft but as he got closer, the 109s disengaged by diving rapidly towards France.

After the four Hurricanes returned to Redhill at 1455 hrs news was received from the 'Y' service (British signals intelligence) that a 109 had gone down in the Channel at approximately the same time and place as Dygryn's combat. As no other combats had taken place at that time he was therefore awarded a 109 as destroyed. During one of the other patrols flown on 16 May another 109 was seen in mid-Channel. Every effort was made to intercept it but at the first sign that the squadron was about to engage, it wisely made off and dived for the French coast at high speed.

On 17 May Hilly Brown finally left No. 1 Squadron for Grangemouth on the Firth of Forth and on the same day notification was received stating that His

Majesty King George VI, on the recommendation of the AOC-in-C, had been 'graciously pleased' to award a DFC to S/L Richard Brooker. Two days later it was the turn of Josef Dygryn to be feted as he was awarded the Czech Military Cross and the Medal for Gallantry by Dr Eduard Benes, the President of Czechoslovakia. The story of Dygryn's exploits on the night of 10/11 May was reported in the *Daily Express* under the headline 'Czech Sergeant Gets Three Raiders' and he was quoted as saying 'I wish they had got me to go up again, I know I'd have got another'. Jean Demozay was also honoured for his night's work as he received the French Medal of Liberation from General de Gaulle, and a Palme was added to the *Croix de Guerre* that he already possessed.

Following a day of unfavourable weather, the next operational sorties were flown on 21 May when No. 1 Squadron provided part of the escort for eighteen Blenheims tasked with bombing the oil refining plant at Gosnay (Circus No. 10). Even by this early stage in the offensive against the *Luftwaffe* in northern France the scale of Circus operations had grown considerably and on this particular day sixteen fighter squadrons were involved in various capacities. The Escort Wing comprised Nos 1, 258 and 302 Squadrons and having taken off from Redhill at 1655 hrs, rendezvous was made over Kenley. No. 1 Squadron had been allocated the role of rear top escort at 15,000 ft and the English coast was crossed just to the south of Dungeness. Weather conditions were generally favourable, the only cloud being very high cirrus, although there was some haze up to 9,000 ft.

The crossing point into France was at Le Touquet and an altitude of 15,000 ft was maintained up to the target area. During the run in around eight enemy fighters were seen climbing up from behind and by the time that Gosnay was reached they were in position to launch an attack. One of the Blenheims (V6390 of No. 110 Squadron) was later seen with its engine on fire and it went down to crash at Allouagne to the north of Arras. The crew of three were killed. No. 1 Squadron's Yellow and White sections had broken away in an attempt to ward off the 109s, but they were beaten to it by No. 302 Squadron, so they rejoined.

When just north of the target P/O W. Raymond and P/O B.G. Collyns (Green section) were ordered to attack a pair of 109s away to the right as they were beginning to act aggressively. They dived after them but another four 109s suddenly appeared in front having emerged from cloud cover. Raymond immediately pulled into a climbing turn and saw two 109s go for Collyns and another for the Blenheims. He went for the latter and got in two short bursts at 100 yards. As he closed he saw smoke coming from the starboard side of the 109 but he then had to break sharply as he was attacked by another. This one was extremely persistent and he only escaped by diving to ground level and crossing the Channel at zero feet. He landed at Gravesend to refuel before returning to base. Collyns managed to shake off the two 109s that had gone for him and returned having joined up with two Hurricanes from another squadron. One of these was attacked when over the English coast but its pilot was aware of the threat and his evasive tactics were successful.

113

During the withdrawal the squadron became split up and numerous individual combats took place. Karel Kuttelwascher (Black 1) was weaving behind the rest of the Hurricanes when he saw six 109s followed by another four, dive down to attack. These were soon joined by twelve more. The Czech saw a Hurricane being followed by four 109s in line astern and he went after the rearmost. He fired two long bursts from close range and smoke immediately began to pour from the wing roots. The 109 went into a spin and appeared to be on fire and out of control. Due to the unusually large numbers of *Luftwaffe* fighters that had been committed to the battle Kuttelwascher had to fight his way out and he was helped in this respect by a single Spitfire. In such a situation when high power settings had to be used for a relatively long time, fuel reserves became an increasingly serious issue and both Hurricane and Spitfire had to land at the forward aerodrome at Manston to refuel before returning to their respective bases.

The squadron's other weaver, Sgt Bedrich Kratkoruky (Black 2), was attacked by two 109s from behind. He managed to lose these two but then saw two more ahead. He turned and closed on the second of these and fired a long burst from the port quarter to astern. His fire had a devastating effect as the tail unit of the Messerschmitt parted company with the rest of the airframe and the pilot baled out. Kratkoruky had several more combats on the way home but these were generally inconclusive and he also landed at Manston to refuel before returning to Redhill.

Several other pilots fired their guns but due to the frantic nature of the combat these were little more than snap shots, which stood hardly any chance of causing significant damage. Antonin Velebnovsky (Yellow 1) was attacked from astern by a 109 but by pulling his Hurricane round in a steep turn he was able to get on its tail. He fired a fairly long burst from close range and saw various small pieces fall from the wings and fuselage, but as he came under attack again soon after, he was unable to say how the 109 fared subsequently.

Josef Dygryn, the other member of Yellow section, went to the rescue of a Hurricane that was being attacked by a 109 and opened fire after pulling out of his dive at very close range. His bullets struck the cockpit area then raked along the fuselage, causing the 109 to wobble in flight before it dived steeply. After gaining height again he engaged another 109 but had to break away almost immediately as he came under attack from behind. He attempted to make the 109 overshoot by throttling back and also applied back stick to lose airspeed, a tactic that proved successful. Realising that his advantage had suddenly vanished, the German pilot was quick to disengage and pushed into a steep dive, which Dygryn had no intention of following. In contrast to what had happened before his return home was relatively uneventful although he saw a 109 dive into the sea about twenty miles out from Gravelines (it is likely that this aircraft was in fact a Hurricane of No. 242 Squadron).

Red section, which comprised Richard Brooker and Albin Nasswetter, was also in the thick of the action. Brooker fired at a 109 from around 300 yards but there were no obvious signs that it had been hit. Nasswetter in the meantime was

114

following his leader and noticed another 109 getting into position to attack Brooker from below. He turned to port and fired two bursts from close range, which hit the enemy aircraft forward of the cockpit as evidenced by De Wilde strikes and a trail of debris. At this point he was attacked from behind and had to evade by pulling into a steep climb, however he then encountered three more 109s which chased him over the French coast. Fortunately he met up with a section of Spitfires and these escorted him over the Channel. As Brooker was returning he saw a Mae West in the water to the north of the Goodwin Sands and 'pipped in' to give the position. This was probably P/O Rodolphe de Grunne, one of No. 609 Squadron's Belgian contingent whose Spitfire was shot down in that position. Sadly his body was never found.

No. 1 Squadron also returned minus one of their number as P/O James Robinson failed to return. Bedrich Kratkoruky later reported that he had seen a Hurricane, which was thought to have been Robinson's, being attacked by two 109s. The Czech attempted to help but before he could do so the Hurricane caught fire and went into a gentle dive towards the sea. As no news was received that Robinson was a prisoner of war it soon became obvious that he had not survived. During the course of Circus No. 10 in addition to the Blenheim that was shot down, eight RAF fighters were lost (including two that collided) and six pilots were killed. Total claims amounted to five Bf 109s however the *Luftwaffe* fighters that took part in this action were from JG 3 and JG 51 who reported no losses.

The next three days were relatively quiet. Defensive patrols were flown over Beachy Head, Maidstone and Hastings but no enemy aircraft were seen. During a similar operation on 25 May however Jean Demozay recorded another victory. He led four Hurricanes off from Redhill at 1535 hrs to patrol Canterbury at 10,000 ft but lost the others in cloud. Not only did he carry on, but he went off on a lone hunt on the lookout for any German aircraft he could catch unawares. This was typical of Demozay who was rather more at home fending for himself than acting as a 'team player' with everyone else. Almost at once he saw a Ju 88 heading south and gave chase until over the French coast only to lose it in cloud. He then noticed eight Bf 109s that were circling above a rescue boat as it made its way towards the English coast. He decided to wait for them to return in the hope of picking off a straggler but then saw three Bf 110s flying in echelon port, just to the north of Dunkirk. He stalked them for some miles before choosing the right moment to attack and fired a four-second burst from 250 yards at the rearmost one. The 110 turned to port before catching fire and diving into the sea.

The last few days of May saw two offensive sweeps over the French coast and a covering patrol for the Tangmere Wing, which had also been trailing its coat in the hope that the resident fighter units would come up for a fight. These operations were largely ignored by the Germans and most of the 109s stayed on the ground. Some did put in an appearance but the few combats that took place did not amount to much. There was no operational flying on 30 and 31 May due to bad weather.

On 1 June a return was made to Kenley but only for a two-week period. This was in connection with the next moon period and involved No. 1 Squadron swapping places with the Hurricanes of No. 258 Squadron. The next day Red section patrolled a convoy of minesweepers south of Hastings but conditions were poor with low cloud and bad visibility. Indeed the weather was rather more suitable for Rhubarb operations. Richard Brooker and Jean Demozay tried their luck but returned from France somewhat downcast as they had been unable to find anything to shoot up. The day was rounded off by Green section patrolling Maidstone and practice firing at the Leysdown ranges. P/O R.N.G. 'Bob' Allen joined the squadron on this day from 52 OTU, Debden, and was put into 'A' Flight in an attempt to balance out a preponderance of Czech pilots. Allen later recalled that there was a danger of the 'Czech Flight' becoming a unit within a unit and that at times of stress in the air the Czechs tended to revert to their mother tongue.

The next few days were uneventful, and the only thing of note was the arrival and departure of several pilots. F/L K.C. Jackman left to be an instructor and F/L Bill Sizer was posted to No. 91 Squadron at Hawkinge. Heading in the opposite direction were P/O Bohumil Horak, another Czech pilot, P/O Nick Moranz from the USA and New Zealander F/L Colin Gray. The latter was an extremely experienced pilot and one of Fighter Command's top scorers. He had already overcome adversity as he had suffered from pleurisy and osteomyelitis, which led to him being rejected twice for military service. On finally being accepted in September 1938 he sailed to the UK to commence flying training and joined No. 54 Squadron in November 1939. The fact that he remained with the squadron was little short of a miracle as shortly after arriving he wrote off the undercarriage of his Spitfire having hit an air raid shelter on landing. This would have been bad enough at any time but it happened in full view of the AOC-in-C Fighter Command, Sir Hugh Dowding, who was on an inspection, and the Hornchurch Station Commander. During the summer of 1940 however he shot down sixteen German aircraft with another shared and was awarded a DFC on 15 August.

Having escorted Blenheims to St Omer at dawn on the 14th, No. 1 Squadron was visited by Dowding's successor ACM Sir William Sholto Douglas who spoke to pilots and apparently expressed his satisfaction at the arrangements made for their recreation. Whether he fully appreciated the fact that pilots usually spent most of their off duty hours by drinking copious amounts of alcohol is not known.

On 16 June F/L Colin Gray was leading the squadron on a defensive patrol along the south coast when he saw a Heinkel He 59 about ten miles south of Folkestone being escorted by a section of four Bf 109s. The He 59 was a twin-engined floatplane of biplane configuration that was generally used by the *Luftwaffe* for air-sea rescue operations, although it had been designed in 1930 for attack and reconnaissance tasks and was fully capable of operating in the anti-shipping role. During the Battle of Britain these aircraft had been used to track the course of British convoys. Gray gave the order to attack in line astern formation, at which point the 109s scattered. He went for the Heinkel and initially fired from head-on before swinging in from behind to use up the remainder of his ammunition, hitting the engines which began to stream black smoke. The attack was then taken up by P/O Bob Allen and it finally hit the sea and blew up. The He 59 was from *Seenotflugkommando* 3 and of the four-man crew, only the pilot, Fw Erich Bohrenfeld, and one other crew member survived, although both were wounded during the attack.

In the meantime the rest of the squadron had their hands full with the 109s, which had been joined by a number of others. Vaclav Kopecky (White 1) dived on one down to 200 ft and fired a burst from astern, which produced a stream of smoke. The 109 also 'wobbled' violently. The Czech made three more attacks using up all of his ammunition in the process. As he broke away it slowed noticeably, burst into flames and dived into the sea. Josef Prihoda (Red 1) went to the rescue of a Hurricane that had two 109s behind it. He fired at extreme range but became aware of another that was coming round in a steep turn with the obvious intention of getting on his tail. Fortunately he was able to pre-empt this manoeuvre and got in the first blow by firing from around 100 yards. The 109 dived steeply and as Prihoda followed it down firing further bursts, it made no attempt to pull out and plunged straight into the dark waters of the Channel.

Prihoda's No. 2, P/O Antonin Liska, also attacked one of the 109s firing a five-second burst from the port quarter at fairly close range. His adversary attempted a tight horizontal turn but Liska had no trouble in following and fired again, at which point the 109 went a shallow dive, trailing black smoke. As he was concerned about another getting onto his tail he had a quick check behind but when he looked forwards again he found that the 109 he had been firing at had disappeared in a layer of haze. He subsequently claimed it as damaged although there is a good chance that the smoke he had seen was merely exhaust smoke as the German pilot applied full throttle.

Jarda Novak (Black 1) went for a pair of 109s and attacked the leader from the port quarter, firing a three-second burst from 250 yards. He then swung in to fire again at close range from behind and saw twin trails of white smoke appear from either side of the 109. It went into a gentle dive towards the French coast but following a further burst, flames began to appear and quickly spread. It was last seen relatively low down but still diving steeply and on fire. The battle was far from one-sided as Sgt Albin Nasswetter was shot down in Z3460. Although he was rescued from the sea, he had been badly wounded during combat with one of the 109s and died the following day.

On the 17th No. 1 Squadron joined with Nos 258 and 302 Squadrons to act as Withdrawal Support to Circus No. 14. This was an attack by twenty-four Blenheim bombers on the Kuhlmann chemical works at Choques near Béthune. By now Circus operations were becoming huge integrated affairs and on this occasion the main 'beehive' comprised a large number of aircraft. Perhaps because such a large force could be seen forming up on the radar screens well before their arrival over France, the German reaction was swift and nine RAF fighters were eventually shot down. These casualties came from the Escort Wing as the high cover squadrons had been briefed to fly too high and were unable to intervene. On this occasion No. 1 Squadron was fortunate not to have been chosen for close escort as this was their normal role.

As the bombers were passing Boulogne on their way home, Josef Dygryn (Red 2) saw a single 109 down below. Perhaps with the memory of his comrade Albin Nasswetter fresh in his mind, he immediately went into the attack and approached the 109 head-on. He opened fire at extreme range but with a closing speed of around 600 mph the distance between the two aircraft decreased rapidly and within seconds the 109 was flashing by above him in a climbing turn. Dygryn pulled his Hurricane round in a steep turn and fired a long burst from the beam moving round to astern, closing in to only 100 yards. The German aircraft appeared to stagger in the air, before bursting into flames and diving into the sea about three miles off Boulogne. It is likely that this was the Bf 109E flown by Fw Bernhard Adam of 2/JG 26, which was lost to a Hurricane in similar circumstances.

The next day No. 1 Squadron again flew as a Wing with Nos 258 and 302 Squadrons as escort to six Blenheims of No. 107 Squadron attacking a hutted camp near the Bois de Licques to the south of Calais. In addition to elements of JG 26, this raid was also contested by JG 2, which had recently arrived in theatre but the bombers and their close escorts retained their cohesion, although one Hurricane from No. 258 Squadron was shot down by flak (three Spitfires were also lost). The day was sad in one respect as Jean Demozay, who had been associated with the squadron from the early days in France, was posted to No. 242 Squadron at North Weald. Within ten days however he was on his way to No. 91 Squadron, the 'Jim Crow' unit at Hawkinge, which was, perhaps, more in keeping with his freelance style. Although he had been very successful during his time with No. 1 Squadron he was about to have a 'purple patch' that would see him end the war as one of the top-scoring French pilots.

The next major action took place on 21 June during Circus No. 17 in which six Blenheim bombers from No. 110 Squadron attacked the airfield at Desvres. The German reaction only came after everyone had turned for home but very soon a furious battle was taking place involving fighters from both JG 2 and JG 26. No. 1 Squadron was flying at 14,000 ft as the top squadron in the Escort Wing with Richard Brooker leading. He saw several 109s coming into attack and very soon one of them had taken up an attacking position behind a Hurricane. Wasting no time he got in behind it and opened fire, closing to less than 100 yards. At this range the twelve guns of his Hurricane IIB were deadly and the 109 began to pour black smoke. Soon the canopy was jettisoned and the pilot baled out, these events being confirmed by Colin Gray who was flying close behind.

As the bombers turned away from the target Jan Plasil, who was flying as Black 1, looked ahead and saw about twelve 109s. By this stage the two other squadrons of the Escort Wing had lost position with the bombers so No. 1 Squadron took the brunt of the attacks. At least there was no shortage of targets and Plasil attacked one of the 109s from behind at around 150 yards. Various bits of debris fluttered back as his bullets struck home and the 109 went down in flames out of control 'like a falling leaf'. His wingman, P/O Romas Marcinkus, attacked a Bf 109 with round wing tips (a Bf 109F) firing two short bursts from astern at 100 yards. He followed it down as it went into a steep dive but had to break away at 6,000 ft as he was about to come under attack. This aircraft was later claimed as destroyed on evidence submitted by Jan Plasil that he had seen this 109 break into pieces.

After leaving the target Josef Prihoda (White 1) saw many dogfights taking place and fired at the first of three 109s but without result. The second, which was also identified as a 109F, was attacked from quarter astern at 100 yards. There was a spurt of black smoke as the 109 turned over and went into a vertical dive. Prihoda deemed it to be out of control at this point but was unable to follow it down due to the proximity of other 109s (it was later claimed as a probable). On his way back he attacked another 109F and succeeded in hacking a few pieces off it before it got away.

When just to the north-west of Desvres Jan Stefan (Yellow 2) saw four 109s turning to attack Yellow and White sections. He managed to get on the tail of one of them and fired three short bursts down to 100 yards. White smoke began to pour from the 109 but he was not able to follow. As the fight continued, height was gradually lost and by the time that the French coast was crossed on the way out some aircraft were down to about 7,000 ft. As he looked down, Buck Collyns, who was also flying a Hurricane IIB, saw a 109F about 500 ft below and dived down to fire a full deflection burst as it came across him. This produced a trail of smoke that was more than just exhaust smoke and after turning he saw the 109 crash in the sea about six miles west of Boulogne (although in this case it is extremely difficult to confirm the participants of individual combats, this may have been the Bf 109F-2 of Uffz Heinz Carmienke of 8/JG 26).

The last to fire his guns was Vaclav Kopecky at a Bf 109F he encountered when just over the French coast. Having fired a three-second burst, the 109 went down in a spin and he watched it descend until it was very low. In fact he watched it a little too long as two 109s were able to move in behind him unseen and open fire. He first became aware of his predicament when bullets tore into his cockpit, hitting his throttle control and smashing it. His engine was also hit and began to smoke but the attack was not maintained so that he was able to make it further across the Channel, which considerably improved his chances of being picked up. He decided not to bale out and instead ditched his Hurricane about eight miles south of Folkstone. By now the Air-Sea Rescue organisation was much better and after spending half an hour in his dinghy he was spotted by a Lysander escorted by four Spitfires. Within fifteen minutes he was picked up by a rescue launch and returned to Dover.

As Kopecky later estimated the time of his combat at 1650 hrs, it appears that the 109 that shot him down was flown by Oblt Gustav 'Micky' Sprick, the Staffelkapitän of JG 26's 8th Staffel. He had already been awarded the Ritterkreuz

(Knight's Cross of the Iron Cross) and Kopecky was his twenty-eighth victory. However, a week later he was to be killed when the starboard wing of his Bf 109F folded up during a split-S manoeuvre. No. 1 Squadron also lost P/O Nick Maranz who was shot down over France. It seems likely that he fell to the guns of Lt Johannes 'Hans' Naumann of 9/JG 26 who claimed a Hurricane during the early stages of the withdrawal.

This day also saw the German invasion of the Soviet Union (Operation *Barbarossa*), which led to a marked escalation in Fighter Command's offensive against the *Luftwaffe*. This was intended to prevent fighter units from being transferred to the east; indeed it was hoped that significant success over northern France would actually lead to the withdrawal of assets to reinforce the west. By now the Hawker Hurricane, even in its improved Mark II form, was becoming obsolescent in the day battles over France. The improved Bf 109F was being seen in greater numbers and it would not be long before the second-generation Focke-Wulf Fw 190 was available. The Hurricane's days were numbered in its primary day fighter role but there were a few last opportunities for it to shine.

Over the next few days more offensive operations were carried out but it was not until 27 June that enemy aircraft were encountered. This was during a late evening Circus (No. 25) to the Fives-Lille factory, which was attacked by twenty-two Blenheims drawn from Nos 18, 21, 139 and 226 Squadrons. The raid was not contested until quite late on when the 'beehive' was approaching the French coast on the way out. No. 1 Squadron was part of the Rear Cover Wing but became split up over the Channel and Karel Kuttelwascher and Josef Dygryn (Yellow 1 and 2) went to investigate aircraft that could be seen towards the east. They crossed the French coast between Cap Gris Nez and Boulogne at 30,000 ft but these turned out to be Spitfires.

They then saw two Bf 109Fs make a move towards the Spitfires and Kuttelwascher attacked one of these, firing two bursts of about three seconds each from dead astern. A stream of debris fell away from the 109, including a larger piece, which appeared to be the cockpit hood. The pilot was seen trying to get out and as Kuttelwascher fired again, he jumped. The Czech did not see a parachute open but on looking down the wakes from a number of small boats could be seen below, all heading towards one particular area where he assumed the 109 had gone in. By this time Dygryn had disappeared but his place had been taken by one of the Spitfires and they returned to Hawkinge to refuel and rearm. During discussions afterwards it transpired that several Spitfire pilots had seen the combat take place and confirmed that the 109 had been destroyed.

Three more sweeps in connection with Circus operations were flown before the end of the month but all passed off without any drama. Sadly the squadron lost another pilot on 29 June when P/O Bohumil Horak was killed when he spun into the ground on approach to Gatwick in Hurricane IIB Z3240.

For No. 1 Squadron the end of June brought good news and bad. The good news was that it was about to return to its spiritual home at Tangmere, however having completed the move on 1 July there was a gradual realisation that for the time being at least, its role had changed, and it was about to enter a quieter period in which it would see little action. As there appeared to be no possibility of a change of equipment in the immediate future, no one could be sure how long this situation would last. There was much practice flying by day and night, together with dawn patrols by sections of two aircraft, searchlight co-operation and occasional 'fighter nights'. During one of these on 8 June, which was undertaken by twelve aircraft, Sgt Gerry Scott fired at an Intruder over Portsmouth but lost sight of it meaning that he could not even claim a damaged.

There was also the first of many trips to Merston, or occasionally, Friston. This usually involved a section of four Hurricanes whose pilots then hung about for the rest of the day in case one of the Air-Sea Rescue Lysanders needed escorting. Usually they did not and they returned thoroughly browned off at the end of the day. Defensive patrols and occasional scrambles also took place but with the Germans now concentrating their efforts in the east, the opportunities for combat on the English side of the Channel were much reduced. There was also increased emphasis on night flying with ZZ landings practised on a regular basis. This was a form of instrument let-down with controllers passing a series of instructions to pilots so that they flew a reasonably accurate approach.

On 14 July the first co-operation sorties were flown with twin-engined Douglas Havocs of 1455 Flight, which was also based at Tangmere. These were American aircraft similar to the Boston light bomber and were used by the RAF in the night-fighter and night-Intruder roles. The intention was for a Havoc to fly at night accompanied by a Hurricane, the ultimate development being the Turbinlite version, which featured a high-powered searchlight in the nose. Having acquired a target on its AI radar the searchlight would be activated to allow the Hurricane to move in for the kill. That at least was the theory, which proved to be rather easier said than done. Although 1455 Flight was formed on 7 July it did not become operational until well into the following year.

On 16 July two aircraft took part in searchlight co-operation work, one of which was Hurricane IIC Z3902 flown by Antonin Velebnovsky. After being airborne for forty-five minutes he requested a vector to base and seven minutes later asked for another. Nothing more was heard from him despite several attempts to contact him by R/T. After two hours he was presumed lost and a search party comprising civilian police, soldiers and the Home Guard was organised to look for him in the Petworth area where he was last plotted on radar. Late in the day his body was found still in his crashed aircraft in a wood near Graffham, about ten miles from Tangmere. He had apparently flown into the top of a hill in poor weather. Velebnovsky was the fourth Czech pilot to be killed over a ten-week period and was replaced as 'A' Flight commander by F/O W. Raymond.

By now the squadron had received a number of Hurricane IIC aircraft which were armed with four 20-mm Hispano cannons. The weight of fire from these guns was over three times that of the Mark IIA with eight Browning machine-guns and at the time it entered squadron service the IIC had greater hitting power than any other single-engined fighter. The Hispano was also superior to any comparable weapon in terms of its armour-piercing capability. Its chief drawback however was a disconcertingly high stoppage rate. This made life difficult for the pilot, as the asymmetric recoil forces generated by a stoppage on one side set up a yawing tendency so that the nose tended to wander at the crucial moment. Cannon tests became a regular feature of the squadron's practice flying and in time the Hispano was to become a much more reliable weapon.

The rest of July was taken up with the regular routine of Lysander escorts and Havoc co-operation although there was something a little out of the ordinary on the 22nd and 23rd as four aircraft were detailed on each day to search the Channel for the German battlecruiser *Scharnhorst*, which was reported to have left its former base of Brest. Nothing was seen, which was not really surprising as it was moving further south to La Pallice harbour at La Rochelle. As the *Scharnhorst* was a prime target for the heavy bombers of Bomber Command it was hoped that it would be rather safer at its new base, however this was a rather forlorn hope as it was attacked on 24 July, the day after it arrived. Although No. 1 Squadron was to be frustrated on this occasion, they would come face to face with it the following year.

August brought more of the same with only occasional opportunities to play a part in a war that as far as No. 1 Squadron was concerned, was mainly taking place elsewhere. By now some of the unit's Hurricanes were being sent to Manston to be held at readiness for possible action over the Channel. More often than not they returned to Tangmere having done nothing all day. Much to everyone's amazement they were ordered off on 9 August to shoot up some E-Boats that had been reported just off the French coast. One was attacked, although it did not appear to be badly damaged. Having flown to Manston once again the following day seven aircraft acted as close escort to Blenheims on an anti-shipping strike off Dunkirk. Unfortunately no ships were seen and the sense of anti-climax was almost palpable.

The lack of activity was beginning to get on the nerves of the some of the squadron's more aggressive pilots. These included Colin Gray who was quick to let everyone know that he had not fired his guns in anger since his arrival at Tangmere at the beginning of July. He decided to make amends by flying over to Merston on 22 August to join No. 41 Squadron in an offensive sweep over France. For this operation he flew one of this unit's Spitfire VBs and was able to satisfy his desire for action by shooting down a Bf 109F near Le Havre to record his seventeenth victory.

On 26 August five aircraft flew to Manston and whilst there were ordered to undertake an anti-shipping sweep of the Channel off Calais. Here they found some barges and minesweepers and carried out a low level attack, which caused some casualties on these vessels. All the Hurricanes returned safely. Later in the day they were off again on a similar mission but this time they were accompanied by aircraft from Nos 242 and 485 Squadrons. A force of seven minesweepers was seen about five miles north-east of Gravelines in a diamond formation and No. 242 Squadron

The S/L P.J.H. 'Bull' Halahan (left) with F/L P.R. 'Johnny' Walker. (IWM C1230)

F/L Prosser Hanks shakes hands with a French Officer. Other 1 Squadron pilots (L to R) are Sgt Fred Berry, F/O Billy Drake, Sgt Rennie Albonico and P/O Peter 'Boy' Mould. (IWM C1297)

P/O 'Boy' Mould was the first 1 Squadron pilot to shoot down a German aircraft in the Second World War when he destroyed a Dornier 17 on 30 October 1939. (IWM C1228)

No.1 Squadron group includes (L to R) Drake, Clisby, Lorimer, Hanks, Mould, Halahan, Demozay, Walker, Brown (doctor), Richey, Kilmartin, Stratton and Palmer. (IWM C1293)

Flying Officers 'Laurie' Lorimer (left) and Leslie Clisby were both shot down and killed on 14 May 1940 during action with Bf 110s of ZG 26. (IWM C1229)

F/O C.D. 'Pussy' Palmer was the first 1 Squadron pilot to be shot down in the Second World War when his Hurricane was damaged by return fire from a Dornier 17. (IWM C1226)

F/L M.H. 'Hilly' Brown who served in 1 Squadron for just over four years, latterly as its commanding officer. (via author)

S/L 'Bull' Halahan examines a German machine-gun taken as a trophy. F/O Paul Richey, Sgt 'Darky' Clowes and F/L 'Johnny' Walker look on. (IWM C1111)

F/L Prosser Hanks took over from F/L George Plinston as 'B' Flight commander in late 1939. He ended the war as a Group Captain. (IWM C1225)

Sgt Fred Berry. (via author)

F/O John Kilmartin (left) and F/O Bill 'Stratters' Stratton. (IWM C1227)

F/O Billy Drake was shot down and wounded shortly after the German invasion of France but was to become one of the RAF's top scoring pilots. IWM C1296)

F/L 'Hilly' Brown (left) with P/O Charles Chetham. (IWM CH1566)

P/O Peter Boot. (IWM CH1567)

Lt Jean Demozay was No.1's interpreter in France and later flew with the squadron. (via author)

P/O 'Darky' Clowes with his regular Hurricane P3395 JX-B. (IWM CH17331)

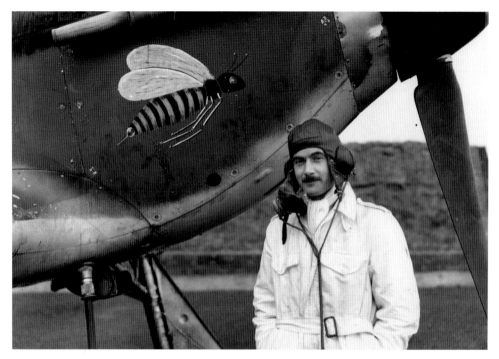

P/O Clowes with the wasp emblem painted on the nose of his aircraft. It is reputed that it acquired another stripe with every combat victory. (IWM CH1570)

P/O Pat Hancock joined 1 Squadron in France in May 1940 and served with the unit until April 1941. (IWM CH1564)

P/O J.F.D. 'Tim' Elkington flew with 1 Squadron during the Battle of Britain and also for a brief period in 1942. (via Tim Elkington)

No.1 Squadron in the air with a squadron of Spitfires in the background. (via Tim Elkington)

Line up of 1 Squadron pilots at Wittering in October 1940 (L to R) 'Hilly' Brown, Zavoral, Hancock, Stefan, Clowes, Demozay, Elkington and Chetham. (IWM CH1565)

Canadian-built Hurricane X AF980 JX-A. (Joan Ramsey)

F/L Karel Kuttelwascher, No.1 Squadron's top scoring pilot during night intruder operations. (via Joan Ramsey)

S/L James MacLachlan in the cockpit of a Hurricane IIC. (IWM CH4014)

No.1 Squadron Hurricane IICs above the clouds. (Aeroplane via Joan Ramsey)

Hurricane IIC Z3778 JX-Y. (Aeroplane via Joan Ramsey)

Hurricane IIC Z3778 breaks away from the camera aircraft. (Aeroplane via Joan Ramsey)

Another view of Hurricane IIC Z3778. This aircraft had previously been flown by 87 Squadron. It was written off in a crash at Acklington on 14 August 1942. (Aeroplane via Joan Ramsey)

Armourers at work on the 20 mm Hispano cannons of a 1 Squadron Hurricane IIC. (Aeroplane via Joan Ramsey)

Although of poor quality this photo shows a 1 Squadron Hurricane IIC equipped for intruder operations with long-range tanks. (Joan Ramsey)

led the attack. One of the minesweepers was set on fire but a Hurricane of No. 242 Squadron was hit by flak and dived straight into the sea (this was Z4001 flown by P/O H. Quilliam who was killed).

On 27 August further intensive Havoc and searchlight co-operation sorties took place but during the latter another pilot was killed when Sgt E. Bloor abandoned his Hurricane IIC (Z3843) two miles north of Horsham. There was another accident two nights later when Sgt G.S. Metcalf was making his first night landing. He approached the aerodrome with too much speed so that he touched down halfway along the runway and went off the end. Fortunately he was able to step out unhurt. The month was rounded off when eleven aircraft escorted two destroyers and seven motor launches which scoured the French coast for enemy shipping, although in the event nothing was seen.

September was another month of intensive training as the squadron worked up to fulfil its new role as a night flying unit. Unless the weather was bad, night flying took place from dusk until dawn including night formation in addition to working with local searchlights and the Havocs of 1455 Flight. On the 19th No. 1 Squadron again entertained distinguished visitors as Lord Halifax, who was HM Ambassador in Washington, spent about an hour touring the dispersals with ACM Sholto Douglas. They appeared to be interested in all that they saw and were particularly curious to learn more of the squadron's experiences with the Turbinlite Havocs.

With little in the way of operational flying September was notable mainly for the arrival and departure of several pilots. On the 4th there was an influx from 52 OTU, Aston Down, including P/O Harry Connolly, F/Sgt S.W. Merryweather, and Sergeants E.S.G. Sweeting, G.H. Corbet, and D.P. Perrin. Of these Des Perrin was to have the longest career with No. 1 Squadron and was to remain on strength for well over two years. He was twenty-two years old and came from Wellington in New Zealand. At the end of the month several Czech pilots left the squadron including Vaclav Kopecky, Josef Prihoda and Josef Dygryn, although the latter would return in the spring of 1942. Another to depart was F/L Colin Gray who finally got his wish for more action. He was initially given the command of No. 403 Squadron but this posting was changed within days to No. 616 Squadron with whom he flew offensive missions over France until March 1942.

No operational flying was carried out in October and the month was marred by two accidents to No. 1 Squadron pilots. On 2 October F/Sgt S.W. Merryweather was flying Z3844 to the Hawker factory at Langley when he crashed on landing. Although his aircraft was a write-off, he was unhurt. Sgt R.H. Oakley, who had joined the squadron on 22 August, had been sent on detachment to No. 1 Delivery Flight and it was whilst serving with this unit that he crashed near Martlesham and was killed. During the month a further batch of pilots arrived to join the squadron including P/O Fred Murray, and Sergeants Jim Campbell, S.P. Dennis, G.C. English and B.C. Williams. However, it is no disrespect to any of these to say that the most important arrival was that of F/L James MacLachlan.

'One-Armed Mac' as he was usually known, was a legend within the RAF as he had returned to active service after losing an arm following combat with a Bf 109E over Malta. He was born on 1 April 1919 at Styal in Cheshire and was educated at Moncton Combe School about two miles south-east of Bath. Here he was an average scholar both academically and at sports, and one of his favourite pastimes was to go for long walks by himself, which goes some way to explaining his predilection for solo night Intruder flights that he was to become famous for. Although he was unsure what to do with his life, this was decided for him following a pleasure flight in 1936 and he instantly knew that his future lay in the air. He joined the RAF on a short service commission the following year and was posted to No. 88 Squadron, which flew Battle light-bombers. Having fortuitously survived the carnage of the German *Blitzkrieg* in May 1940 he transferred to fighters and flew with Nos 73 and 145 Squadrons before serving in Malta with No. 261 Squadron.

By early February 1941 he had already claimed eight enemy aircraft as destroyed but on the 16th he was shot down and severely injured in the left arm when a cannon shell tore into the cockpit of his Hurricane. During his third day in hospital it became obvious (even to MacLachlan) that the arm would have to be amputated, but despite initial misgivings, he was determined that he would fly again, come what may. As he recovered in hospital the bed next to him was occupied for a time by an Italian fighter pilot that MacLachlan had shot down the previous month. He also had a serious arm injury and both no doubt reflected on the crazy nature of war.

Just four weeks after being taken off the critical list in hospital MacLachlan was in the air again at the controls of a Miles Magister, but his request for the opportunity to fly a Hurricane was unfortunately turned down. He had already signalled his capability however by carrying out aerobatics in the two-seater and had also carried out a dummy 'attack' on a gun post. He had even attempted a mock dogfight with a Hurricane. On arriving back in the UK he attended the Queen Mary Hospital at Roehampton for the design and fitting of an artificial limb. Much thought went into the mechanics of the arm as it had to be capable of working all the various controls in the cockpit of a Hurricane, but eventually the design was finalised. In early October 1941, having flown a number of different aircraft types with No. 3 Squadron at Hunsdon, MacLachlan was passed as medically fit to fly and final approval was given by the Air Ministry on 15 October. Three days later he joined No. 1 Squadron to take over command from Richard Brooker who was about to be posted overseas (the official changeover took place on 3 November).

Although MacLachlan was very much a press-on type, he had to bide his time as there appeared to be no immediate prospect of a change in No. 1 Squadron's fortunes. He was soon joined by F/L J.M. Crabb from No. 3 Squadron who arrived on 3 November to take over as the commander of 'B' Flight. Other new arrivals during November included Sergeants S.F. Cooper and J.F. 'Johnnie' Higham.

Having been with the squadron since 3 May, Buck Collyns left on 19 October on promotion to Flight Lieutenant. He joined 60 OTU, which was based at East Fortune in Scotland, and trained night-fighter crews on Boulton Paul Defiants.

Having undergone intensive training, No. 1 Squadron was now a fully operational night-fighter unit and in November much of its patrolling was done at night. There were also occasional night scrambles and Lysander escorts during daylight hours. Unfortunately there were two more fatal accidents during the month. Sgt E. Ruppel, a Canadian who had only been with the squadron just over two weeks, was killed on 18 November when he flew into Bury Hill near Arundel whilst practising ZZ landings. Four days later Sgt L.J. Travis and Sgt Des Perrin were scrambled at dusk and ordered to patrol the Isle of Wight. After being airborne for 1 hour 5 minutes the two Hurricanes collided and Travis was killed when his aircraft (BD940) crashed near Ryde. Des Perrin baled out of Z3899 and escaped with minor cuts and shock.

There was hardly any change in December and with little enemy activity, most of the squadron's work was non-operational. There was however the first sign of a new type of operation as on two occasions during the month a pair of Hurricanes flew to Manston for Intruder operations over German occupied territory. On 5 December they had to return early due to adverse weather conditions, however another attempt on the 16th got far enough into France to attract much searchlight activity and flak. No worthwhile targets were seen and a return was made after 1 hour 10 minutes in the air.

The final action of the year involved Karel Kuttelwascher (by now a Pilot Officer) and Romas Marcinkus. The Czech took off from Manston just before midnight on 28 December to patrol the Channel and came across two vessels, escorted by flak ships, in the approaches to Ostend harbour. He radioed the position of the convoy and two Bristol Beaufort torpedo-bombers were despatched, however they were unable to locate it. Despite a formidable flak barrage, Kuttelwascher descended to carry out a low level attack on the ships and damaged one of them. Marcinkus in the meantime was heading for Le Touquet and flew about ten miles inland before heading south along the coast. He experienced some flak but it was mostly a comfortable distance away from him and he was not unduly troubled. As the moonlight glinted on the water he continued as far as the Somme estuary in search of shipping but was ultimately to be denied and he returned to Manston after being airborne 1 hour 15 minutes. The next day two Hurricanes were ordered to patrol Dover but were recalled after ten minutes due to bad weather.

So it was that the year ended in disappointment and frustration for No. 1 Squadron, a situation it had become rather used to in recent months. As it was now (in theory) essentially a defensive unit, No. 1 Squadron stood little chance of seeing much in the way of action unless there was a change of tactics on the German side. This eventually came about due to the activities of Bomber Command as in the spring of 1942 Germany was stung into retaliation by increasingly heavy raids on the Fatherland. The outcome was a resumption of air attacks against the UK by night during which No. 1 Squadron was to become pre-eminent in a particular role, that of Intruder operations over the continent.

CHAPTER TEN

Night Intruders
(Beginning)

The New Year began as the old one had finished, the predominant factors being bad weather and a lack of German opposition. Bedrich Kratkoruky left No. 1 Squadron on 1 January to become an instructor, which left Karel Kuttelwascher as the sole remaining Czech. A number of pilots were commissioned during the month, Sgts G.H. Corbet and Des Perrin becoming Pilot Officers in the RNZAF, with Sgt E.S.G. Sweeting being granted a commission in the RAF. There were two accidents but thankfully no serious injuries. On 10 January Sgt Gerry Scott had undertaken a searchlight co-operation flight and was returning to Tangmere just after midnight. He experienced engine trouble at the worst possible time, just as he was coming in to land, and as a result he crash-landed heavily. The sudden deceleration flung him forwards into the gunsight, knocking out several teeth and tearing an eardrum. He was admitted to hospital and was out of action for the next four weeks. The other mishap occurred on 24 January and involved Sgt J. Smith who crashed on landing when he lost control in the slipstream of the Havoc he had been flying alongside.

The weather during the first three days of February was so bad that no flying of any description was possible, however there was a slow improvement over the next week, which allowed cannon tests, ZZ approaches and co-operation with searchlights and the Havocs of 1455 Flight. Two new pilots arrived to join the squadron during this period, F/Sgt C.F. Bland and Sgt G.S.M. Pearson.

During the night of 11 February the conditions were suitable for searchlight co-operation work as although there was no moon and there was slight haze near the ground, the skies were clear with visibility of around four miles. Seven pilots of 'A' Flight carried out this task but on his return Sgt E.G. Parsons (Canada) overshot the flarepath and bounced quite heavily. He opened the throttle to go round again but instead of selecting wheels up, he mistakenly raised the flaps instead. This caused his Hurricane (BD945) to stall and as it came down again it clipped a tree before hitting some obstruction wires. With the engine full on, it crashed in a field just beyond the south-east corner of the aerodrome, killing Parsons instantly. On the same day S/L James MacLachlan left for a three-day course on searchlight intercept procedure at the School of Anti-Aircraft Defence at Shrivenham and as a result missed a major flap the following day.

Ever since March 1941, the German battlecruisers *Scharnhorst* and *Gneisenau* had been in dock at Brest and La Pallice where they had been subjected to frequent air attack by RAF heavy bombers. Although no serious damage had been done, Adolf Hitler took the decision that the ships should be moved to German ports and that they should take the shortest route through the English Channel. This audacious voyage commenced in the late evening of 11 February, which meant that the ships would be sailing through the Dover Straits in broad daylight. They were joined by the heavy cruiser *Prinz Eugen* and many smaller warships and E-boats. The *Luftwaffe* fighter force in France was to provide an 'umbrella' over the ships with a minimum of sixteen aircraft at any one time. The breakout had also been timed to take advantage of poor weather as further low pressure systems were expected to track from west to east.

Despite the jamming of British coastal radars, unusual activity was first noted during the morning and further evidence was provided by Spitfires of No. 91 Squadron. This was confirmed by the experienced pairing of G/C Victor Beamish and W/C Finlay Boyd (Station Commander and Wing Commander Flying respectively at Kenley) who were also flying over the Channel. Although the possibility of a breakout had been planned for (Operation *Fuller*) the reaction was painfully slow and inadequate and the initial response was a suicidal attack by six Swordfish torpedo-bombers of No. 825 Squadron, Fleet Air Arm.

It was not until 1337 hrs that No. 1 Squadron became involved when six Hurricanes of 'A' Flight were scrambled to attack some of the escort vessels in the Straits of Dover. Red section comprised F/L W. Raymond and P/O E.S.G. Sweeting, with P/O Karel Kuttelwascher and P/O G.R. Halbeard making up Yellow section. P/O Romas Marcinkus and F/Sgt E.F.G. Blair formed White section. They were escorted by twelve Spitfires of No. 129 Squadron from Westhampnett and rendezvous was made over Hawkinge at 1405 hrs at a height of 300 ft. The formation set a course of 100 degrees over the Channel and after flying for ten minutes Raymond was heard to say 'Target ahead'. Four ships were seen in line astern formation steaming north-east and these sent up a two-colour signal, although defensive fire led to some confusion among the pilots as to the actual colours used. These ships were passed to starboard and two minutes later three more appeared ahead, which immediately opened fire as the RAF formation approached.

The Hurricanes went down to about 50 ft and attacked from the direction of the Belgian coast in line abreast with Red section in the centre, Yellow section to port and White section to starboard. The ships put up a terrific flak barrage but the attack was pressed home, each pilot opening fire with his cannons at a range of about 200 yards to rake the decks and superstructure. Karel Kuttelwascher in particular noticed his shells exploding just beneath the bridge of his target and subsequently claimed a destroyer as damaged. As they withdrew there was no sign of White section and only four Hurricanes made it back to Tangmere. It was soon confirmed that both aircraft had been shot down by flak. Romas Marcinkus survived to become a prisoner of war but F/Sgt Blair was killed. He was a South African and had been with the squadron since 24 June 1941 (one Spitfire of No. 129 Squadron was also shot down and another had to be abandoned due to flak damage on return).

While 'A' Flight were airborne, five Hurricanes of 'B' Flight led by F/L J.M. Crabb took off, also with the intention of attacking the flotilla that was rapidly heading westwards. They set course for Hawkinge but could not locate the target or the rest of the squadron and so landed at Manston at 1455 hrs, Crabb having decided that they would be of more use at this forward aerodrome. However, due to the speed of the Germans and deteriorating weather they were not needed and flew back to Tangmere later in the day.

Like all RAF squadrons No. 1 was keen to foster good relations with the local community but while doing this on 16 February there was another tragic accident. The Mayor of Brighton, Alderman M.W. Huggett, was invited to lunch at Tangmere along with other dignitaries and afterwards was invited to see his town from the air. This opportunity was accepted and he was flown in the unit's Magister (V1013) by James MacLachlan. On their return the Mayor's secretary, Mr George Martin, asked if he could also be taken up and it was arranged for him to be flown by P/O Eustace Sweeting who had taken part in the attack on the German ships just four days before. As the Magister was returning it dropped its port wing as it turned onto final approach and spun in to crash in a field just to the west of the aerodrome. Both men were killed instantly. An inquest was held a few days later in which the Coroner expressed the view that no one was to blame and that it was a pure accident.

On 17 February Karel Kuttelwascher took over as the commander of 'A' Flight in place of F/L W. Raymond who was tour expired. The Czech was promoted to Flight Lieutenant (non-substantive) and thus followed in the footsteps of Darky Clowes by completely bypassing the rank of Flying Officer. A number of new pilots joined the squadron before the end of the month, the most notable arrival being that of Sgt Harrison Taylor 'Moose' Mossip who was to be another long-serving member of No. 1 Squadron. Even though he was only twenty-one years of age, Mossip was an imposing-looking character who came from London in Ontario, Canada, and on first acquaintance he exuded an intensity that impressed everyone. He could not wait to make an impact on the war and it would not be long before he was putting his attack-minded philosophy into action. To help in the final training of pilots new to the squadron a Miles Master was delivered towards the end of the month and it was hoped that this would help them become operational by day and especially by night, at the same time as reducing the squadron's relatively high accident rate.

In early March there was another influx of Czech pilots with the arrival of Sergeants Zdenek Bachurek, Vlastimil Machacek and Jan Vlk from 61 OTU. Others to join came from the dominions (Canada in this case) and were Sergeants G.C. 'Slim' Whitmore and C.J. Herbert. Once again the month was disappointing and when pilots were scrambled on operational patrols they invariably returned with the dreaded 'nothing to report'. The Master was proving useful for instrument flying and by the end of March most pilots had indulged in a number of blind take-offs. On 21 March James MacLachlan took the opportunity to visit his old school at Monkton Combe to talk to the scholars about his achievements to date. The assembled ranks could not have known that he was about to launch on a new phase of his RAF career, one that would see his own status, and that of his squadron, rise to new heights.

On 1 April James MacLachlan took off from Tangmere at 2215 hrs on the first of a series of Intruder operations over occupied Europe. He was followed five minutes later by Karel Kuttelwascher and it was to be the Czech who opened the squadron's account. After crossing the French coast just to the west of Le Havre he orbited the aerodrome at Evreux but as there was no activity there he flew on to Melun where the flarepath was lit. After two minutes a red Very light was fired and he became aware of an aircraft on the runway, about to take off. It climbed to about 1,500 ft but kept its navigation lights on as it turned into the circuit. Kuttelwascher followed and having identified it as a Ju 88 closed in to 100 yards to fire two short bursts from astern. The starboard engine erupted in a bright flash and the Junkers went into a steep dive before exploding on the ground.

By this time he was directly over the aerodrome and saw another Ju 88 lining up. He fired a number of bursts, which caused some damage to it, but he was then lit up by a battery of three searchlights and his Hurricane was bracketed by flak. He escaped by entering a steep right-hand turn down to 500 ft before climbing once again, by which time the searchlights had gone out, as had the approach lights. On his way back he flew over Paris and followed the Seine to Rouen, re-crossing the French coast east of Fecamp and landing back at Tangmere at 0125 hrs. As he trudged into the crew room after a flight lasting just over three hours, he found that MacLachlan had already been back for an hour and in contrast had seen nothing of interest.

The idea of intruding over enemy territory was not new and had been tried by the Germans as early as 1940. At the start of the Second World War German night-fighter defences had been in as parlous a state as those of Britain, but this soon changed. The first confirmed Intruder 'kill' occurred on 24 October 1940 when a Ju 88 of NJG 2 shot down a Whitley of No. 102 Squadron shortly after take-off from Linton-on-Ouse. The idea of Intruder operations was an attractive one as before the development of AI radar it was usually easier to target bombers close to their own bases than try to find them once they had reached their operating altitude.

The Hurricane IIC was ideally suited to the Intruder role as its armament was more than enough to bring down most bomber aircraft and the Hurricane itself was an excellent gun platform. Its wide-track undercarriage also made it much easier to handle during taxiing, take-off and landing than the narrow-track Spitfire. To improve range the Intruder version of the Hurricane carried jettisonable long-range tanks of 44-gallons, which increased total fuel capacity to 185 gallons. By using economical throttle settings for much of the sortie it was possible to stay in the air for anything up to four hours.

The opportunity for effective night Intruder operations came about as a result of German retaliation for the increasingly heavy attacks by Bomber Command, in particular a devastating raid that destroyed much of Lübeck during the night of 28/29 March. This led to the so-called Baedeker offensive between April and June 1942 in which German bombers attacked non-strategic targets purportedly chosen from the Baedeker tourist guide, such as Bath, Exeter, York, Norwich and Canterbury. This led to a rich harvest for No. 1 Squadron's pilots, however the record shows that some were much more in tune with the disciplines of night intruding than others.

Buoyed by the success of the previous night, James MacLachlan left Tangmere at 2340 hrs on 2 April bound for the aerodrome at Rennes. He crossed the Channel at 8,000 ft in clear conditions but encountered cloud as he crossed into France to the east of the Cherbourg peninsula, however this was localised and by the time he arrived at Rennes the conditions were perfect. Unfortunately there was nothing to be seen, apart from the flarepath of a dummy aerodrome, so he flew to Dinard where he orbited at 2,000 ft. This aerodrome was also quiet so he returned to Rennes in the hope that there would be some activity, but was again disappointed. To relieve his frustration he attacked a goods train on the way back near Combourg and left it enveloped in steam with two trucks burning. He then made his way back over the Channel and landed at Tangmere at 0205 hrs.

While MacLachlan had been over France several other pilots had been ordered off on defensive patrols including P/O Harry Connolly who had taken off at 2345 hrs to patrol Selsey. At half past midnight a report was received that his Hurricane (BD947) had crashed in the Channel and that Connolly had baled out. He was to spend three hours in his dinghy before he managed to alert the crew of a trawler with his whistle and he was picked up and taken ashore. After being checked out at the Haslar Royal Navy Hospital in Portsmouth, he was returned to the squadron later in the day none the worse for his soaking.

Karel Kuttelwascher tried his luck with an Intruder sortie on 3 April but he was to be disappointed and returned without having fired his guns. For the next few days defensive patrols were the predominant activity and this led to another accident on the 5th. Sgt Zdenek Bachurek took off at 2215 hrs to patrol base but forty-five minutes later his Hurricane came down near the Arundel to Chichester road at Fontwell and he received severe head injuries. On examination of the wrecked Hurricane it appeared as though Bachurek had forgotten to switch from his mains tank to the reserve tank and so his Merlin had failed due to fuel starvation. (Bachurek was taken to the Royal West Sussex Hospital where he recovered from his injuries. He was to survive the war and subsequently returned to Czechoslovakia.) If this was not bad enough, worse was to follow as there was another fatality on 10 April, again involving a Czech pilot. Sgt Jan Vlk was carrying out ZZ landing approaches shortly after dark but crashed in a field near Barnham, approximately four miles south-east of Tangmere. An ambulance was able to attend the scene within minutes but it soon became clear that Vlk had been killed instantly.

The next Intruder sorties were flown on 16 April and again involved the experienced pairing of Karel Kuttelwascher and James MacLachlan. Once again it was the Czech who would out-score his illustrious leader. Having taken off at 2245 hrs he made for Evreux at 8,000 ft and on arriving flew a complete circuit, but saw nothing. He then decided to try his luck at St Andre and Dreux but again drew a blank. His return journey took him to St Andre once again and this time he saw two enemy aircraft with their navigation lights on. One switched its lights off immediately but the crew of the other were rather more complacent and left them on. Their sloppiness would cost them dear. Kuttelwascher had no difficulty in moving in to fire four short bursts from astern and the aircraft nosed over into a steep dive before hitting the ground with a bright flash. Although it could not be identified with absolute certainty, it was thought to be a Do 217. On his way back via Evreux, Kuttelwascher was confronted by a single searchlight, which fortunately did not pick up his Hurricane and he was able to slip away into the darkness. He re-crossed the French coast near Fecamp and landed at Tangmere at 0135 hrs.

James MacLachlan had taken off twenty minutes ahead of Kuttelwascher and he reconnoitred roughly the same area, also taking in Evreux and Dreux. He also saw nothing at these aerodromes but as he was flying between the two a group of four searchlights flicked on and off for around two minutes, although he was not illuminated. Giving up on this area for the time being he flew to Bretigny which was lit up and visible from thirty miles, but as soon as he had levelled off at 2,000 ft the lights were switched off. He then returned to Dreux and Evreux where he encountered some flak, but otherwise it was still quiet so he flew back to Tangmere, landing at 0125 hrs. These two sorties emphasised that night intruding was something of a lottery when it came to encountering enemy aircraft. To MacLachlan it must have seemed that his Czech comrade was having all the luck but as the Baedeker raids were about to begin, his time would come.

Over the next few days No. 1 Squadron's pilots took part in a number of night scrambles and patrols. On 17 April Des Perrin and Sgt Johnnie Higham were scrambled to patrol base at 3,000 ft but came back after half an hour without having seen anything. The following night three Hurricanes were ordered up at 0210 hrs to orbit a marker beacon that was near a box of searchlights. One pilot received the 'smack' denoting that an enemy aircraft was present but there was no contact. On 21 April F/L J.M. Crabb left the squadron and his place as 'B' Flight commander was taken by P/O (acting F/L) Les Scott who arrived from No. 3 Squadron.

The first bombs of the 'mini Blitz' fell on Exeter in raids over three nights commencing on 23/24 April. A total of eighty people were killed before the bombers turned their attention to other cities, however they were to return in early May. The German offensive prompted a significant increase in the number of night Intruder sorties flown by No. 1 Squadron with many more pilots taking part. Up to now only the most senior pilots had flown over France but this was all set to change. Just before midnight on 24 April Sgt Vlastimil Machacek, who was thirty-three years of age, took off on an offensive sortie with the intention of patrolling the area around Bretigny. He was tracked by radar as far as mid-Channel but the radar return then vanished and he was not heard from again. James MacLachlan and Karel Kuttelwascher also carried out Intruder sorties over France on this particular night, however they were unable to locate any suitable targets. The following night Sgt G.S.M. Pearson spent time near Evreux but found nothing. On his way back he got lost and had to land at Exeter after 2 hours 50 minutes in the air. Offensive sorties were also flown by Des Perrin, Gerry Scott and F/Sgt S.F. Cooper but all returned with nothing to report.

On the night of 26/27 April German bombers raided Bath for the third time in a twenty-four-hour period. The attack was opened at 0125 hrs and as it was conducted in conditions of bright moonlight it caused serious damage. In the space of forty minutes 162 people were killed and as a greater number of incendiaries were used compared with previous attacks, there were extensive fires. The night-fighter forces consisted of Havocs from No. 23 Squadron, Hurricanes of No. 87 Squadron and Beaufighters of Nos 125, 307 and 604 Squadrons. No enemy aircraft were claimed destroyed, although it appears that a Do 217 of IV/KG 2 that was attacked by P/O F.A. Grantham of No. 87 Squadron and claimed as damaged, actually failed to return. In marked contrast No. 1 Squadron was about to achieve rather more in the way of success on the other side of the Channel.

Just after 2200 hrs James MacLachlan took off in his regular Hurricane IIC BE215 JX-I to head for his usual hunting ground, the aerodromes at Evreux and Dreux. As there was 10/10 cloud at 8,000 ft over the Channel he climbed through it and emerged into clear skies above. He descended once again on ETA but found that he had drifted about fifteen miles east of his required track and was over the River Seine just to the west of Paris. In view of his position he decided to pay a call at Bretigny, which was to the south of the capital, but although it was lit up there were no aircraft in the vicinity. After circling for about half an hour he decided to head for Dreux but on the way saw that both St Andre and Evreux were lit and were accepting aircraft. There then followed a game of cat and mouse as each side tried to outwit the other. As MacLachlan began to circle at St Andre the lights were switched off so he flew away to give the impression that he was about to have a go somewhere else. After five minutes he returned by which time the lights were back on again and saw an aircraft taking off to the west. He went after it immediately but lost it as it switched its navigation lights off. He then attempted a head-on attack on a second aircraft with similar results.

As the defences had been alerted to his presence he flew over to Evreux and began circling over the end of the runway at 200 ft. Soon an enemy aircraft took off and climbed to 500 ft. As the night sky was quite bright it stood out quite well against it, its silhouette indicating that it was a Do 217. MacLachlan opened fire at 600 yards but did not have any success until he had reduced range to 100 yards. Sparks came from the starboard engine and the Dornier nosed into a dive that became increasingly steep and it crashed in a field. As he was flying back to St Andre he saw another Do 217 at the same height and on a converging course. He throttled back to allow it to pass in front of him and made two attacks from dead astern, which achieved several hits. After his second burst he could clearly see a trail of smoke in the moonlight but having used up all of his ammunition he had to let it go. He returned via Le Havre, content that he was off the mark and was back at Tangmere at 0105 hrs.

Aware that his CO had had a successful night, Karel Kuttelwascher took off half an hour later hoping that he would be able to catch some of the bombers as they were returning from Bath. After crossing the French coast at Fecamp he noticed white lights at Rouen-Boos, No. 1 Squadron's former base, and began circling. After three minutes he saw a Do 217 against the moon and quickly moved in behind to fire a four-second burst, which destroyed the starboard engine. The Dornier went into a steep left-hand turn and crashed on the aerodrome between some hangars. At this precise moment tracer passed directly over his cockpit and he put his nose down as a Ju 88 passed overhead, the two aircraft missing each other by about thirty feet. He jettisoned his long-range tanks and tucked in behind to fire four short bursts from close range. His shells were seen exploding but the Ju 88 evaded by performing a steep left-hand climbing turn before descending once again. It disappeared from view and very soon Kuttelwascher had different priorities as a searchlight tried to locate him and flak opened up. He decided it was time to leave and returned via the Seine and Etretat, landing at Tangmere at 0325 hrs.

On 27 April a signal was received from AVM Leigh-Mallory congratulating S/L MacLachlan and F/L Kuttelwascher on their highly successful Intruder operations of the previous night. Other squadron pilots tried to emulate their feats over the next two nights with rather less success. On 28 April P/O Fred Murray and Sgt G.S.M. Pearson flew to France but found nothing, as did P/O G.H. Corbet and W/O Gerry Scott on the 29th. The latter pair patrolled the area around Evreux and Chartres but all was quiet. Once again it was left to 'Old Kut' to show the way.

On 30 April he departed Tangmere at 2330 hrs bound for Rennes. He flew a direct track, crossing the Channel at 5,000 ft before descending to 2,000 ft on reaching the French coast. As he was passing Cherbourg he experienced an unusually strong interference hum in his headphones but this soon passed and on his arrival he circled Rennes aerodrome at a distance of about two miles. As no lights were visible he flew away to the coast again and returned, by which time two white lights were showing near a runway. His pulse quickened as he saw an enemy aircraft with a white navigation light in the nose about to take off. As soon as it was airborne this was switched off but visibility was good in bright moonlight and

Kuttelwascher was able to follow it quite easily. He made sure that he kept his Hurricane 'down moon' of the aircraft and identified it as a Do 217. He closed to 150 yards dead astern and fired three short bursts. After the third the nose of the Dornier went down and it dived steeply before exploding on the ground.

He continued to orbit Rennes for the next five minutes but as there appeared to be nothing happening he flew north to Dinard where he orbited at 2,000 ft at a distance of four miles. Another aircraft was seen in the distance by its white tail light but when this was switched off it disappeared. Five minutes later he saw a He 111 about to take off with full navigation lights visible and even though these were doused when still on the runway he was able to follow it as it climbed to 1,000 ft. As he attacked from behind a large piece of metal appeared to break away from the starboard engine. By this time both aircraft were travelling at 180 mph and had crossed over the coast. Two more short bursts were enough to finish the Heinkel off and it dived straight into the sea close to the town of Dinard. The attack was relatively straightforward as Kuttelwascher had not had to contend with return fire, searchlights or flak from the ground. The weather conditions remained perfect with no cloud and only slight haze. As there was clear moonlight over the whole of northern France, visibility was in excess of ten miles. The return journey was made to the west of Jersey and Kuttelwascher landed at Tangmere at 0220 hrs. (James MacLachlan also carried out an Intruder operation on this particular night taking in Evreux, Dreux and Rouen. No aircraft were seen, however he still managed to shoot up two trains and a tug on the way back.)

During all of his Intruder missions Karel Kuttelwascher flew his regular Hurricane IIC BE581 (JX-E). Although it was painted in standard green/grey camouflage on its upper surfaces, as befitting its night role it was matt black underneath (some of No. 1 Squadron's Hurricanes had an all-black scheme). It also carried Kuttelwascher's personal emblem under the exhausts on the starboard side of the nose, that of a yellow scythe with a red banner that had the name 'Night Reaper' written in black. Every effort was made to diminish the effect of the flames coming from the exhausts by using horizontal plates on the upper fuselage to shield the manifolds from the pilot's eyes to preserve their night vision. Little could be done however to lessen the glare itself and once pilots crossed into France they felt extremely vulnerable as exhaust glow was one of the easiest ways of seeing an aircraft at night. The colour that the exhausts produced depended on throttle setting and was at its most blue at high power settings, turning to a redder hue when throttle was reduced.

It had already been decided that Intruder operations should be increased in intensity and diversified with the targeting of the French rail network as well as German bombers. The RAF felt justified in attacking trains as Intelligence had reported that French civilians were barred from travelling at night. On the same night that Kuttelwascher recorded his seventh and eighth victories (30 April/1 May) six pilots took off to attempt to attack moving trains, which on a clear night could easily be seen from the air. The first away was Des Perrin in BN205 (JX-V) at 0040 hrs and he made for the Abbeville area. Having crossed the French coast at Berck he flew five miles inland before returning to the coast at a height of 500 ft. He immediately saw a train travelling south between Etaples and Abbeville and attacked the engine with a two-second burst. It came to a sudden halt, enveloped in steam. He then attacked a second train with similar result. As he had plenty of fuel left he followed the line as far as Amiens but no more trains appeared and having been on patrol over France for forty minutes he made his way back to Tangmere.

Sgt G.S.M. Pearson was the next to take off in BE150 (JX-F) at 0115 hrs and he flew towards the same general area as Des Perrin. Pearson encountered no fewer than five trains around Amiens, two of which were brought to a halt with steam pouring from the engines. On his fifth attack his ammunition gave out and he was left with no alternative but to return to base. Over the Channel there was a thin layer of 10/10 cloud between 1,000 and 2,000 ft and he climbed above this prior to landing at Tangmere at 0330 hrs.

By then four more pilots were in the air, P/O G.H. Corbet, Sgt Jim Campbell, F/Sgt C.F. Bland and F/L Les Scott. Corbet had decided to head further west to Dieppe but on finding no trains had to make do with shooting up a signal box instead. Jim Campbell had better luck and having flown to Abbeville found a goods train with steam up in a factory siding. The engine and trucks were raked in a three-second burst. A short time later another engine was seen being moved into its shed and this was left enveloped in steam after two attacks. Campbell also attacked two engines that were stationary to the north of Abbeville and both emitted steam from their punctured boilers before his ammunition expired.

F/Sgt C.F. Bland went still further to the west to the Bayeux-Caen area and attacked five goods trains before running out of ammunition. Les Scott crossed the French coast west of Dieppe at 2,000 ft and flew south, then west, until meeting a large goods train at Yvetot. He came down to 500 ft and made six attacks on the engine and its trucks. Clouds of steam poured from the engine and at least one truck was set on fire. He returned via Fecamp and landed at Tangmere at 0520 hrs. Attacking ground targets at night could be rather disconcerting at times as the shells tended to ricochet in all directions and occasionally seemed to be heading back in the direction they had come. As they veered off, the trails they left were picked out in a variety of colours from white and red to blue and green, a display that was as beautiful as it was deadly.

During the day James MacLachlan flew over to Oatlands Hill near Amesbury to try out the new North American Mustang that was entering service in the tactical reconnaissance role. His first solo on the type was in no way cautious and turned into a demonstration of aerobatics that put many of the instructors at the locally based 41 OTU to shame. He was impressed by the Mustang's performance at low level and as it also had excellent endurance, the idea of using it for long-range interdiction began to form. On his way back to Tangmere however he had other concerns as the engine of JX-I cut out south-west of Worthy Down and in the ensuing forced landing the Hurricane went over onto its back. MacLachlan was extricated uninjured and later recorded the event in his logbook with a drawing of an aircraft upside down next to the words 'Shakey Do!'

Further train-busting sorties were carried out on 2 May and shortly after midnight F/L Les Scott and W/O Gerry Scott took off for Caen. The weather over the Channel was clear and although some cloud was encountered at 5,000 ft over the French coast, this soon dispersed. Les Scott patrolled the main Cherbourg-Caen railway line for an hour without coming across anything but eventually saw a train just to the west of Caen. Its crew had apparently seen him as well as the train was brought to a halt before it was attacked. He made four beam attacks from 800 ft down to 500 ft and left the engine clothed in steam. His namesake had a disappointing night and despite patrolling for ninety minutes in the same general area, saw nothing. He later reported that his position had apparently been followed by plotting lights on the ground.

During the day some air-to-air firing was carried out with dusk landings by new pilots in the early evening. After dark it was the turn of F/Sgt S.F. Cooper and Sgt G.S.M. Pearson to head for France. Cooper made for Rennes and although the aerodrome at Granville was lit up, there was no activity. He then searched for trains but was thwarted again and eventually returned to land at 0140 hrs. During his debrief he was another to claim that he had seen lights on the ground tracking his position. Pearson also flew towards Rennes aerodrome but had great difficulty locating it as the moon was just rising and it was still quite dark. He did eventually find it and, ironically, was assisted in this task by flak from the Rennes town defences. As there was nothing happening he re-crossed the Channel at 6,000 ft and landed at Tangmere at 0230 hrs. Half an hour later Karel Kuttelwascher and Des Perrin took off to reconnoitre the area between Caen and Rennes. The weather was not particularly conducive to Intruder ops as it was quite hazy with poor visibility horizontally, however the former shot up a train near St Lo and on his way home spotted a small motor boat. He made three attacks on it, which brought it to a halt, and in the moonlight he could see a patch of oil spreading on the water. In contrast Des Perrin had an unproductive night in which no suitable targets were seen.

On 4 May the German bombers returned to Exeter and the raid commenced just after 0130 hrs. By the time that it had finished 156 people were dead and 563 injured, many of them seriously. Serious damage was done to the town centre and many buildings were wrecked along the High Street. The city library was burnt out and all the contents, including many historic documents, were lost. The cathedral was also hit and St James Chapel was destroyed, as were many other old buildings. In the skies above, the Beaufighters of Nos 307 and 604 Squadrons had rather more success than previously and claimed five German bombers shot down. These were backed up by No. 1 Squadron with five aircraft taking off for Intruder operations, although they were soon down to four as Karel Kuttelwascher had to make an early return with engine trouble.

The first Hurricanes were airborne at 0205 hrs as the German bombers were on their return journey. Although it would clearly have been better to have attacked these aircraft before they had dropped their bombs, the chances of success for Intruders operating over France were much higher after the raid had taken place. This was due to the fact that the return of the bombers could be predicted reasonably accurately so that the Hurricanes could be in place and ready to attack. The German crews would also be more tired towards the end of their mission and as they were nearly home it would be natural for some to be affected by complacency. However, one of the main problems associated with night Intruder work was that German bombers often landed at a different airfield to the one that they had taken off from so a certain amount of guesswork was needed to be in the right place at the right time.

The most successful pilot on the night was James MacLachlan who flew to Rennes but on finding this aerodrome unlit he made for Dinard. On arrival he was confronted with a choice of two flarepaths but one was clearly a dummy. At the real aerodrome he saw an aircraft landing but was not in time to be able to attack it. Another was seen close behind with its navigation lights on and this was identified as a Do 217. MacLachlan moved in behind to fire a one-second burst, which produced a sheet of flame, and it appeared that the entire starboard engine fell away. The aircraft went down in a spin and crashed in flames on the ground.

He then spotted another enemy aircraft also with its navigation lights on at 2,000 ft. He turned on to it and fired at 100 yards from the starboard rear quarter. It immediately burst into flames and following a further burst from astern the nose dropped into a shallow dive, which was maintained for about three miles. During this period the port engine was on fire and it eventually hit the ground with a brilliant flash. Although there was no flak, two searchlights tried to illuminate the Hurricane but were unable to do so. On his way back he also attacked the engine of a goods train and it was soon enveloped in steam. As the engine could not be seen for the cloud of steam he fired another burst into the middle of it just for good measure. The other pilots that flew on this night were P/O Fred Murray, P/O Harry Connolly and F/L Les Scott. All spent some time over France searching in the area of Caen-Rennes-Dinard but saw nothing.

Although MacLachlan had identified his second victim as a He 111 it was in fact a Ju 88, as was the first that had appeared to him to be a Do 217. These two aircraft were both from KuFlGr 506. One was piloted by Uffz Josef Palmer who was killed along with two out of three crew members. The other was flown by Fw Robert Bogel and of this crew only the gunner survived after baling out. MacLachlan later recorded his experiences in an Air Ministry Bulletin:

> …when he was just right I pressed the button. I remember seeing the rings round the exhaust glowing beautifully as my four cannons let him have it. A one-second burst was enough – there was a shower of flashes, the engine fell out and the whole place lit up like daylight. I turned and watched the

bomber fall straight down and burn on the ground. There was a pillar of dense black smoke lit with a cheery pink glow on the underside. It looked good. But I'd no time to watch and turned away to see another, a 'He 111', coming straight at me. A one-second burst from my cannon set his port engine on fire. Bunches of sparks, bits of tin and other oddments came flying off and it looked good, too. I gave it another burst for luck at the other engine and then formated on him as he went into a shallow dive. I kept about 100 yards away and watched the Heinkel flying along, flames leaping back from it. As it got lower, the trees and bushes were lit up. It hit the ground and spread forward, like an unopened fan, picked out in bits of flames where the burning wreckage spread.

Having caught up on his sleep during the day MacLachlan was airborne again at 2320 hrs on the 4 May but found Rennes to be covered in fog, conditions that extended as far as Caen and Dinard. With little hope of seeing anything he reluctantly returned to Tangmere and was back by 0135 hrs. Once again it was Karel Kuttelwascher who guessed correctly where the German bombers would be as he flew further east to Evreux and St Andre. He was also to prove that whatever his CO could do, he could go one better.

Kut took off at the same time as MacLachlan and crossed the French coast south of Fecamp at 2,000 ft. Perhaps the first thought that this might be his night crossed his mind at this point as three searchlights that came on from the direction of Fecamp were immediately extinguished after he flashed his navigation lights on and off twice. The omens also looked good as four white lights arranged in a straight line pointed directly towards his intended target. Although there was nothing to be seen at Evreux it was a different story at St Andre, which was lit up with a double flarepath. He saw at least six enemy aircraft (apparently He 111s) in the circuit to land, their positions betrayed by their white tail lights. After circling for two minutes Kuttelwascher moved astern of one of the bombers and fired a two-second burst from astern and slightly below. The starboard engine caught fire and the Heinkel dived into the ground to the north-east of the aerodrome. Amazingly he was able to tuck in behind the next in line, which went straight down to crash in a wood after a one-second burst. A third bomber was attacked using the same tactics and although he lost sight of it, when he was able to turn back he saw three separate fires burning on the ground. It was at this time that the defences finally woke up to the fact that he was around and the lights were put out. He flew on to Dreux and Evreux and at the latter was boxed by four searchlights. He tried the same trick as before but this time it did not work and he only evaded by diving steeply. He landed back at Tangmere at 0205 hrs.

At the same time F/L Les Scott was operating in the same area. Although he saw three aircraft in the process of landing at Evreux he was only able to fire at one of them and there were no obvious signs that he had inflicted any damage. Sgt S.P. Dennis made for Bretigny but on the way encountered activity at an aerodrome that was probably Rouen-Boos. He saw an enemy aircraft at 200 ft just about to touch down but as soon as it had landed the flarepath was switched off. He eventually made it to Bretigny but it was in darkness and after circling for ten minutes he returned to base.

The last member of the squadron to be active over France on the night of 4/5 May was Sgt Jim Campbell who left Tangmere at 0020 hrs on the 5th. He circled the aerodromes at Evreux, St Andre, Dreux and Chartres but as none was active at the time he had to make do with ground targets instead. On a road near Dreux he saw a tanker and went into the attack from 500 ft. There was a bright flash and burning oil was seen spreading over the road. He then returned to St Andre, which was now lit, but as he orbited, his Hurricane was hit by flak and the starboard long-range tank burst. The engine cut momentarily but picked up again as soon as he turned to his reserve tank. Unperturbed he carried on but as there appeared to be nothing in the air he eventually decided to return. On his way back he shot up two trains, the second of which was a heavy goods train pulling trucks containing a material that burned furiously with a bright white light.

The only other incident of note on this night was a rather unfortunate one involving P/O Fred Murray. No. 1 Squadron was still performing co-operation flights with the Havocs of 1455 Flight but the technique was fraught with difficulty and was far from being perfected. The basic idea was that the Havoc and Hurricane would form up over the aerodrome and would then stay in close contact with the aid of formation-keeping lights. Once the Havoc had acquired a target on its AI radar it would close to 1,000 yards at which point it would transmit the code word 'Hot' for the benefit of the Hurricane pilot. On hearing the code word 'Boiling' the Hurricane would then descend 300 ft before accelerating ahead of the Havoc and when it was 300 yards behind the target the airborne searchlight would be switched on for it to be shot down. This was a highly intricate operation, which even if successful in the early stages could often be thwarted by violent evasive action by the target aircraft.

On 5 May Murray was flying with a Havoc piloted by the CO of 1455 Flight, S/L G.O. Budd DFC. A trace appeared on the AI radar of the Havoc and as this was declared hostile the above procedure was followed. Unfortunately the aircraft was a Short Stirling of No. 218 Squadron, which was returning to its base at Marham after a leaflet-dropping sortie in the Laon region of France. For once everything worked as it was supposed to and the Stirling (R9313) crashed in flames in a field at Gatehouse Farm, Lurgashall, fifteen miles west-south-west of Horsham in Sussex. The story does have a happy ending however as Sgt H.J.V. Ashworth and his crew of seven all survived the experience.

Intruder operations were flown over the course of the next four nights but nothing was seen on any of them. By now the moon was on the wane and the weather had also taken a turn for the worse. On 9 May Des Perrin and James MacLachlan made the last sorties of the moon period. The former managed to find the River Seine but visibility was very bad and on arrival at Evreux he could not identify anything except a few lights that were soon switched off. MacLachlan had the same problems and at one point, two searchlights were switched on but the ground mist was so thick that they failed to penetrate. Just as it was becoming more difficult for the Intruders, it was also much more of a challenge for the German bombers to identify their targets and this resulted in a temporary reprieve until the next moon period at the end of May and early June.

CHAPTER ELEVEN

Night Intruders
(Conclusion)

Having enjoyed excellent success and proved the effectiveness of night Intruder operations, No. 1 Squadron had the opportunity to catch its breath over the next three weeks and returned to the usual routine of training flights. During this period there were two awards as James MacLachlan received the DSO, the first such honour for the squadron since the First World War, and Karel Kuttelwascher was the recipient of a DFC. Two familiar faces rejoined the squadron in P/O Otto Pavlu who arrived from No. 65 Squadron and W/O Josef Dygryn from 310 (Czech) Squadron. James MacLachlan also found time to increase his profile even more by taking part in a radio broadcast for the BBC. In it he gave some insight into the art of hunting at night

> I'm afraid the dangers and hazards of flying on night offensive patrols have been rather exaggerated. Certainly the average Intruder pilot is not the cat-eyed, carrot-eating killer that the press sometimes makes him out to be. Most of us night fighters are too fond of our mornings in bed to go flying around in the daytime. Personally, sleeping in the sun appeals to me infinitely more than chasing Me 109s at 30,000 ft. Give me a moonlight night and my old Hurricane and you can have your Spitfires and dawn readiness. We've no formation flying to worry about, and no bombers to escort. In fact, nothing to do but amuse ourselves once we've crossed the French coast. I must admit that those miles of Channel with only one engine brings mixed thoughts and one can't help listening to every beat of the old Merlin engine as the English coast disappears in the darkness. I always get a feeling of relief and excitement as I cross the French coast and turn on the reflector sight, knowing that anything I see then, I can have a crack at. We have to keep our eyes skinned the whole time, and occasionally glance at the compass and clock. As the minutes go by and we approach the Hun aerodrome, we look eagerly for the flarepaths. More often than not we are disappointed. The flarepath is switched off as soon as we arrive and up comes the searchlights and flak. But if you're lucky it's a piece of cake.
>
> Well, when your petrol and ammunition are nearly gone you are faced

with the old Channel again. If you've got something, you leave the enemy territory with a sort of guilty conscience – not for what you've done – that's great fun. But somehow you feel they've got it in for you and that everyone's going to shoot at you. It's a sort of nervous reaction, I suppose. The whole thing seems too easy to be true. Ten to one there's no Hun within shooting distance and the ground defences are quiet. That makes it all the worse and I generally weave about till I'm half way back across the Channel. If you've done nothing, of course, you don't get this feeling as you're still looking for something at which to empty your ammunition. Out over the Channel you can hear your ground station calling the other aircraft of the squadron and you count the minutes and look eagerly for the coast. Often it seems to take so long coming back that you feel sure the compass is wrong and were it not for the North Star I might not be here today. At last, in the distance, you see the flashing beacon and soon you are taxiing in to your dispersal point. I dread the look of disappointment on my mechanic's face if my guns are unfired. But if the rubber covers have been shot off, I've scarcely time to stop my engine before I am surrounded by the boys asking what luck I've had. Then comes the best part of the whole trip – a cup of tea and a really good line-shooting session.

Since 1 April, the squadron has destroyed eleven aircraft for certain and probably three more. The lion's share of this total goes to my Czech Flight Commander Kuttelwascher. He's a first-class pilot and has the most uncanny gift of knowing which aerodromes the Huns are going back to. He'll look at the map and say 'Ill go there tonight', possibly to some unobtrusive aerodrome. Sure enough, even if the others see no activity, he certainly will. One night we agreed to visit a certain aerodrome, but five minutes before we took off, 'Old Kuttel' changed his mind and went to another. I got to my aerodrome to find it covered with fog, while he calmly knocked down three!

With the coming of the next moon period Intruder operations were resumed on 29 May. Just after 0100 hrs six Hurricanes headed for France and although they did not encounter any aircraft they made rather a mess of the French rail network. P/O G.H. Corbet patrolled the railway line between Rouen and Paris and attacked four goods trains, which were all left stationary amid clouds of steam. Sgt B.C. Williams made for Poix and fired at a goods train, which blew up with a brilliant flash and was still giving off steam when he returned later. He also searched the area between Abbeville, Amiens and St Quentin but without success. P/O Fred Murray crossed the French coast just to the east of Le Treport and encountered flak when ten miles inland. Although it was accurate in terms of direction it passed harmlessly beneath him. He then flew north to Le Crotoy and patrolled the line between here and Amiens at 1–2,000 ft, disabling the engines of three goods trains. The other members of the squadron did not fare quite so well and only F/Sgt G.C.

English was able to add to the haul when he shot up two trains between Rouen and Barentin. P/O Des Perrin and Sgt Johnnie Higham had to be content with firing at some stationary trucks and line-side signalling respectively.

On the following night Les Scott and P/O C.L. Bolster were ordered off to intercept a hostile aircraft that had been reported in the Dover/Dungeness area. Whilst patrolling at 5,000 ft Scott saw a Do 217 about 1,000 ft above and immediately jettisoned his long-range tanks to give chase. The Dornier turned for France and dived to 1,000 ft, gradually pulling away even though Scott was flying at around 270–280 mph. After a fruitless five-minute chase he gave up and returned to Tangmere. Further Intruder missions were flown on the same night with mixed results. Whereas P/O G.H. Corbet encountered bad weather in the Béthune area and returned having been airborne for only 1 hour 35 minutes, Sgt Jim Campbell reconnoitred the rail system around Lens and attacked six goods trains. Each engine came to a halt, pouring steam and in one case the trucks were also set on fire. On his way back Campbell was lit up by a searchlight but was able to escape by carrying out evasive action. Sgt G.S.M. Pearson was in the same area and also disabled a train near Lens before moving further to the north-east to do the same at La Bassée.

The night of 30/31 May saw the first 1,000 bomber raid on Cologne and four of No. 1 Squadron's Hurricanes were in the air on the lookout for enemy aircraft over occupied Europe. James MacLachlan took off from Tangmere at 0050 hrs and eventually landed at West Malling three hours later. Although he did not see any aircraft he did manage to attack four trains, one at Peronne and three on the line from Reims to Soissons. The three other pilots were F/L Les Scott, P/O Fred Murray and W/O Gerry Scott who all used Manston as a point of departure. This was to take on extra fuel as their patrols were to be over Holland and Belgium in the hope of catching German night-fighters off guard. Les Scott and Fred Murray both had relatively quiet nights, unlike Gerry Scott.

Having taken off from Manston at 0055 hrs he flew via the Nieuport beacon at 6,000 ft before setting course for St Trond, which was finally reached at 0140 hrs. The aerodrome was brightly lit, including the Visual Lorenz approach-path lighting, and while passing to the south-west of the aerodrome Scott saw the navigation lights of an aircraft about to land. He descended to 500 ft and closed in from behind to fire two one-second bursts that produced several strikes on the fuselage and a big flash from the port engine, which then streamed white smoke. As he was in danger of colliding with the German aircraft he had to break sharply away and as he did so the aerodrome lights went out and a red rocket was fired into the air. Scott then flew to the north climbing to 2,000 ft when he saw another aircraft ahead and about 500 ft above. He was unsure what type it was and followed it as far as Brussels before eventually identifying it as a Blenheim. He returned to St Trond once more but although the lights and Visual Lorenz came on several times, no more aircraft were seen (after returning to Manston he was awarded a Ju 88 damaged, probably an aircraft of II/NJG 2).

The following night Germans bombers were once again over the UK in response to the attack on Cologne and this time it was the turn of Canterbury to be attacked. This was the first of three raids that severely damaged much of the medieval centre of the city, however the twelfth century cathedral was to be spared. Eight aircraft of No. 1 Squadron carried out fighter nights over Canterbury patrolling in layers, stepped up from 8–12,000 ft, however nothing was seen. In addition another seven pilots were operating on Intruder sorties including James MacLachlan who was in the Le Havre area when he had the misfortune to hit a bird. Thinking that the blood on the windscreen might be an oil leak he took no chances and returned rather earlier than he had intended.

Karel Kuttelwascher was on his way to Evreux when he saw a convoy of ships near Fecamp with two larger vessels, possibly destroyers on each side. Although his knack for finding enemy aircraft deserted him on this particular night he attacked two trains between Le Havre and Bolbec and disabled the engines of both. On his way back he saw the same convoy that he had seen on the way in with some E-Boats weaving to the rear. He dropped down to attack one of them from 100 ft and left it streaming smoke, with oil spreading over the water. F/Sgt G.C. English and Sgt Johnnie Higham both made for Poix and Beauvais but saw little. Higham did see a single-engined aircraft lit up briefly by a searchlight over Poix but before he could identify it his own aircraft was lit up by two more and he had to dive away. On his way back he blew up the engine of a goods train at Derchigny.

In the meantime Des Perrin and Sgt S.P. Dennis had flown to Manston to operate further to the east. Perrin flew to Ostend before patrolling the coast between Dunkirk and Knocke. A searchlight lit his aircraft briefly but after a one-second burst aimed in its general direction it went out again. He also saw shipping activity and what appeared to be four destroyers with a similar number of E-Boats between Ostend and Blankenberge. He attacked one of the E-Boats with a two-second burst before returning. Sgt Dennis had decided to go for the aerodrome at Gilze-Rijen in Holland and on arriving saw that the flarepath was lit and also the Visual Lorenz system. When about five miles north-west at 5,000 ft he saw an aircraft on the approach but was unable to get into position in time before it landed and doused its lights. He circled for a further fifteen minutes but everything appeared to have gone cold so he returned via the Maas estuary where he shot up four masted ships, receiving some light, but inaccurate flak in return.

Sgt G.S.M. Pearson had also been ordered to Manston the previous evening to be on readiness for Intruder operations and eventually took off at 0140 hrs to patrol Gilze-Rijen and Eindhoven. He crossed the Dutch coast just south of Flushing at 5,000 ft and was over Gilze at 0235 hrs. Pearson also found it lit up and as he made a half circuit at a distance of five miles he saw the navigation lights of an aircraft, these being repeatedly switched on and off. He approached from the port quarter astern and closed to 150 yards before opening fire with a two-second burst. Further attacks were made from directly astern and multiple strikes were seen on the fuselage, with pieces of debris blown off. The starboard

145

engine also caught fire and the aircraft went into a spiral dive to the right to crash about five miles south of the aerodrome. It exploded on impact and burning fragments were spread over a wide area. Pearson had not been able to identify the aircraft but thought that it was either a Ju 88 or a He 111. On his way back he also attempted to attack a masted ship, only to find that he had used up all of his ammunition. He landed at Manston at 0400 hrs (his victim was a Ju 88C-4 of NJG 2 flown by Obfw Dieter Schade who was killed along with Uffz Jacob Cezanne and Uffz Adolf Jensen).

On the night of 1/2 June seven of No. 1 Squadron's Hurricanes flew over to the continent, five taking off from Manston bound for Holland and two departing Tangmere for northern France. Of those heading for Holland, F/Sgt G.C. English had the most success. He flew via Haamstede to Gilze, which turned out to be quiet, so flew on to Eindhoven. This was lit up but just as things were looking promising the lights went out again. He then attempted to find Venlo but failed to do so and in his frustration fired at a goods train that he encountered in the area. He felt sure that German aircraft would not be far away, it was just a question of guessing correctly. His luck improved when he returned to Eindhoven and although no lights were visible (apart from a red 'Z') he detected movement, which turned out to be a Do 217. It did not have its navigation lights on so contact was lost momentarily, but he soon picked it up again and got on its tail. The German aircraft attempted to dive away to the south but at 500 ft English opened fire from dead astern, hitting the starboard engine. The Dornier dived straight into the ground and burst into flames. He flew one more circuit of the aerodrome but saw nothing so returned via Flushing.

Sgt Jim Campbell also flew to Eindhoven but saw only the aftermath of the combat involving F/Sgt English as the Do 217 was still burning on the edge of a wood. It appears that James MacLachlan also saw the end of the Dornier as he later reported an aircraft going down in flames to the south of Eindhoven as he was patrolling Gilze. He also witnessed something similar to a Turbinlite in operation as an aircraft was lit up, apparently by an airborne searchlight, while another machine entered the beam behind it. The target aircraft was seen to dive to ground level and the engagement then ceased.

P/O Harry Connolly took off from Manston at 0050 hrs with the intention of heading for the aerodrome at St Trond. Shortly before he got there he saw a Ju 88 silhouetted against the moon and he swung in to carry out an attack from astern. As he commenced firing his two port guns jammed and his Hurricane yawed violently to the right due to asymmetric recoil forces. While he was regaining control of his aircraft tracer shot past him as another aircraft (also believed to be a Ju 88) fired from behind. The two machines circled each other in the moonlight, each trying to get behind the other, but after a few minutes contact was lost. On his way home Connolly saw some air firing to the south of Brussels and an aircraft go down in flames. W/O Gerry Scott also flew to St Trond but found no worthwhile targets and returned without firing his guns.

The two pilots who flew over to France returned with nothing to show for their efforts. P/O Fred Murray went to Juvincourt but on the way was lit up by two searchlights, which held him as he dived to 500 ft. He eventually managed to get free but saw nothing of interest during the rest of his patrol and landed at Tangmere at 0400 hrs after 2 hours 30 minutes in the air. P/O G.H. Corbet had chosen to go to Dreux, however the aerodrome was in darkness when he got there and remained so until it was time for him to return.

On the night of 2/3 June German bombers returned to Canterbury and seven Hurricanes of No. 1 Squadron took off at 0240 hrs for 'fighter nights' over the city. It was perfect weather for both attackers and defenders as there was no cloud to shield the moon, thus allowing excellent visibility. As they approached Canterbury it was obvious that the raid was well under way as there were numerous fires already burning. Karel Kuttelwascher decided that it would be easier to locate the bombers on the other side of the Channel and made for the Nieuport beacon. After ten minutes he became aware of a Do 217 going past him on his right-hand side. It was at 4,000 ft and gradually losing height as it prepared to cross the coast. The Czech increased speed to 190 mph IAS and closed in to 150 yards dead astern and slightly below. Two bursts were sufficient to set the starboard engine on fire and the Dornier went into a shallow dive before plunging into the sea about five miles off the Belgian coast. Kuttelwascher continued towards the Nieuport beacon for a time but as it was beginning to get light he returned to Tangmere and landed at 0430 hrs (the Do 217 was probably that flown by Fw Hans Koch of III/KG 2).

One Intruder mission was flown on this night when Sgt G.S.M. Pearson flew to Dreux. This aerodrome could be seen from fifteen miles away but as no aircraft appeared to be in the vicinity it is likely that it was being used as a decoy. He continued to Chartres and circled for fifteen minutes but although the lights came on there seemed to be no activity here either. Coming down to 1,000 ft Pearson followed the Seine valley to Rouen and shot up two goods trains south of the city and another between Rouen and the coast. During the day No. 1 Squadron lost another of its pilots when F/Sgt G.C. English was killed when carrying out a practice attack on another of the unit's Hurricanes. His aircraft (Z3897) stalled off a turn and spun into the ground before he was able to regain control.

No. 1 Squadron was out in force again the following night with James MacLachlan and Karel Kuttelwascher again leading the way. MacLachlan took off from Tangmere at 0100 hrs and crossed the Channel at 6,000 ft before heading for the aerodromes around Evreux. Once there it was a case of paying a call at each one and hoping that his timing was right. Having seen nothing for about half an hour he finally got lucky on his second visit to St Andre, which now had a full Visual Lorenz system operating. Around fifteen aircraft (Do 217s) were orbiting at 1,000 ft preparing to land and were continually switching their navigation lights on and off. One was on final approach as MacLachlan arrived so he followed it, closing to 200 yards and fired as it passed the last bar of the Visual Lorenz at a height of about 100 ft. Its nose immediately went down and it crashed in a shower of sparks just short of the aerodrome.

At that moment six searchlights came on and illuminated the Hurricane but by diving away to one side MacLachlan was able to get away. Despite his presence the approach lights stayed on and he selected the nearest of ten aircraft, which were still circling, and followed it at a height of 500 ft as it approached to land. A two-second burst from astern produced a number of strikes but he was obliged to break away as his Hurricane was again lit up by searchlights and he was fired at by the ground defences. To avoid the flak he climbed to 2,000 ft and encountered another Do 217 with its lights on. He attacked this one from 200 yards hitting the port engine, which caused the Dornier to enter a descending turn to the left, and very soon there was a bright red flash as it hit the ground close to the aerodrome. MacLachlan then went for a fourth aircraft but after about three shells had been fired from each gun his ammunition ran out. Even so there were some hits and it was later claimed as damaged.

Karel Kuttelwascher left Tangmere an hour after MacLachlan having also decided to make for St Andre. When still over the Channel he saw a Do 217 at 3,500 ft heading for France but it had apparently seen him as well as it began to weave and lose height. Although he attempted to follow it down, it dived away to one side and he lost sight of it. He got to St Andre at 0300 hrs and was pleased to see it lit up. After fifteen minutes the sight of navigation lights drew his attention to two aircraft (identified as He 111s), which were orbiting at 1,500 ft. He took up position behind one of them and fired two bursts, each of one second, hitting the starboard engine which caught fire. The enemy aircraft then dived steeply and crashed in flames on the ground.

With so many aircraft in the vicinity it was not long before he saw another. This was a Do 217, the crew of which appeared to be rather more awake than some of their comrades as it turned steeply to starboard and dived away as soon as Kuttelwascher opened fire. He then saw another four Do 217s at 1,000 ft and selected the nearest, firing a burst, which set the right-hand side on fire. It continued to fly straight and level but after a second burst it went down to crash east of the aerodrome. Although other aircraft were seen, Kuttelwascher was unable to get into position to attack any of them and he returned via the Seine and Rouen, landing at Tangmere at 0440 hrs.

Other pilots operating on this night included Les Scott, Des Perrin, Otto Pavlu, Josef Dygryn and Sgt B.C. Williams. Sadly Josef Dygryn failed to return in Z3183 having disappeared en route to Evreux. As he was flying into France Karel Kuttelwascher saw intense flak from Le Havre at about the time that Dygryn should have been returning and it was thought that he might have been shot down at this time. Three months later his body was washed up on the south coast near Worthing.

On 6 June the last Baedeker raid took place on Canterbury and although No. 1 Squadron kept up its Intruder operations, potential targets were much reduced in number. In the early hours of 8 June, six pilots (MacLachlan, Campbell, Dennis, Pearson, Perrin and Les Scott) flew to northern France but all returned with nothing to report. Over the next two weeks Intruders were flown on a slightly more modest scale and it was not until the night of 21/22 June that anything was encountered. The first excitement however involved Sgt J.M. Chalifour who was one of three pilots taking part in operational Turbinlite co-operation. Flying with a Havoc of 1455 Flight piloted by F/L Matthews, a head-on AI contact was made at 10,000 ft south of Worthing. The target aircraft turned to starboard and began weaving so that contact was lost for a time, but it was re-established, only to be lost for good owing to interference off Beachy Head. Rather more success was achieved by the Intruders, which comprised MacLachlan, Murray, Kuttelwascher and Pearson.

James MacLachlan was away at 0045 hrs and not long after take-off witnessed an aircraft coming down in flames near the Isle of Wight. This was probably a He 111 that was claimed as destroyed off Ventnor by a Beaufighter flown by P/O R.J. Foster of No. 604 Squadron. He flew to Rennes and although it had its full Visual Lorenz working, no aircraft were seen and his patrol was uneventful. Fred Murray fared little better. At Dinard he saw a twin-engined aircraft that had just taken off and followed it for around twenty minutes as far as Carentan but it gradually drew away from him so that contact was eventually lost. As he had jettisoned his long-range tanks during the chase he was forced to return a little sooner than he had hoped.

In the meantime Karel Kuttelwascher was heading for his favoured destination of St Andre where he had already had much success. By now he knew this area extremely well and a red flashing beacon and a few white lights were enough to tell him that he had arrived. As he passed the aerodrome on its western side he noticed the lights of a dummy site and continued to Dreux before returning to St Andre. By now more lights were visible and also the Visual Lorenz so he came down to 1,000 ft where he saw a Ju 88 on the other side of the aerodrome with its navigation lights on. He quickly flew across and latched onto its tail, waiting until it was over the last bar of the Visual Lorenz before he opened fire. After a two-second burst the starboard engine and fuselage caught fire and it crashed and spread itself out along the runway. At that moment he saw another Ju 88 at the opposite end of the runway at 1,000 ft so chased after it and fired a two-second burst from 200 yards dead astern. Although the Junkers was hit, both port cannons of Kutterlwascher's Hurricane jammed and it was able to get away by diving to starboard. Having regained control the Czech continued to orbit for the next forty minutes but there was no further activity and he returned to land at Tangmere at 0345 hrs.

Sgt G.S.M. Pearson flew to Evreux, arriving at 0200 hrs. A double flarepath with red perimeter lights came on just as he got there and after circling at 1,000 ft at a distance of three miles he saw an unidentified twin-engined aircraft. A red Very light was fired from the ground and answered by a green from the aircraft, which then proceeded to carry out an approach. Guided by its tail light, Pearson got behind it and closed to what he considered to be the correct firing range. As he was concentrating mainly on a single light he was completely unaware that he was too close and as he opened fire the enemy aircraft was illuminated brightly by the muzzle flashes of his guns. He later estimated that his range during this initial attack was only 30 yards. Although there was no return fire, Pearson saw what appeared to be a red rocket fired from the aircraft. He fired three more bursts, which hit the port engine producing a dull red glow and a trail of smoke but the aircraft climbed suddenly and disappeared from view.

On 24 June four pilots (Dennis, Perrin, Pearson and Gerry Scott) tried their luck over northern France but were thwarted by the weather. As there was 10/10 cloud at 3,000 ft it was very dark below and conditions were made worse by a thick haze, which made it virtually impossible to see anything on the ground, even when flying as low as 500 ft. At one point during his patrol Pearson took a shot at a train but had no idea whether he had hit it.

On 26 June six Hurricanes piloted by MacLachlan, Kuttelwascher, Pearson, Perrin, Campbell and Gerry Scott flew to Manston for operations over Holland. James MacLachlan did not have the best of nights as he was unable to find his target (Gilze-Rijen) due to the fact that his map had blown overboard before crossing the coast. The two most notable sorties were those of Jim Campbell and Des Perrin. The former took off from Manston at 0015 hrs and landed at Ford after a flight lasting 3 hours 50 minutes. During a patrol of Eindhoven, he saw two aircraft crash and burn on the ground; probably RAF bombers returning from a raid on Bremen. Before returning he attacked two trains between Antwerp and Turnhout and blew up both engines. Des Perrin flew to Gilze-Rijen and Einhoven but despite the fact that both were lit up there was no sign of activity. He decided to carry on towards Dusseldorf and thus became the first No. 1 Squadron pilot to fly over Germany during an Intruder operation.

Although the aircraft Campbell saw being shot down were probably RAF bombers (or Blenheims of No. 13 Squadron, two of which were shot down on Intruder operations over Holland) there is a possibility that one could have been the Hurricane of W/O Gerry Scott. He had taken off at 0105 hrs, the same time as Campbell, to reconnoitre Gilze-Rijen, which was less than twenty miles from Campbell's patrol area. Nothing more was heard from him and it was eventually confirmed that he had been killed.

On the following night two more Intruder operations were flown by Sgt Jim Campbell and Sgt Johnnie Higham. Although the two staggered their respective sorties to Evreux, the aerodrome was quiet throughout the night and they had to be content with shooting up trains instead. Campbell damaged the engines of three goods trains around Rouen and Higham disabled another in the same general area. At 0240 hrs six Hurricanes were ordered off on a Roadstead operation as E-Boats had been reported near the French coast, however nothing was seen during a patrol as far as Dieppe. On 28 June two Intruder sorties were carried out by P/O G.H. Corbet and P/O Otto Pavlu but both were unproductive. This day also saw the arrival of thirty-five-year-old André Jubelin, a commander in the French Navy who was posted in from No. 118 Squadron. Following the fall of his country Jubelin was determined to carry on the fight and despite his naval background he wanted to be a fighter pilot. He had a head start as he could already fly and served for a time in the Fleet Air Arm before transferring to the RAF.

A major Intruder effort on 29 June was spoilt by the weather with several pilots finding low cloud over much of northern France, however this did not seem to hamper Karel Kuttelwascher. On finding cloud at 500 ft over St Malo with no signs of activity at Dinard, he decided to explore an alternative target area and flew north for ten minutes before patrolling the base of the Cherbourg peninsula. He had covered this patrol line four times when he saw a Do 217 three miles to the south and 500 ft below. It was flying towards Bayeux and after ten minutes Kuttelwascher was in a firing position. There was a brief burst from the rear gunner but this ceased as soon as the Czech opened up with his cannons. After a second burst from astern the Dornier began to dive and as it did so, it caught fire. It was last seen diving steeply into a bank of low cloud at 500 ft with the wings and fuselage well alight (this was probably a Do 217 of III/KG 2 flown by Uffz Michael Petres who was killed along with three crew members).

Kuttelwascher turned towards the sea and flew towards Barfleur where he saw seven E-Boats putting up intense fire, which was probably aimed at P/O G.H. Corbet who was also in the area. He manoeuvred so that they were between him and the moon before diving to attack. The gunners were ready for him and he met considerable return fire but this did not stop him from attacking an E-Boat, which was left smoking and with a bad list to starboard. Another was given a two-second burst and was hit but this attack could not be continued as he ran out of ammunition. The other pilots active on this night were MacLachlan, Corbet, Higham, Williams and Campbell, the only other success being a goods train that was damaged by Jim Campbell.

On the last day in June three Intruder operations were launched, although P/O Otto Pavlu had to return early with engine trouble. P/O G.H. Corbet patrolled the Rouen-Paris railway line and damaged the engines of three goods trains, which was one better than Johnnie Higham who managed two between Arras and Lens. When the total flying hours were compiled at the end of the month it was found that the figure (on all types of aircraft) came to 1,008 hours, which was a record for No. 1 Squadron.

The final Intruder sorties were flown on 2 July with Karel Kuttelwascher again showing how it should be done. After taking off at 0210 hrs he made for Rennes and Dinard and on finding the flarepath and Visual Lorenz lit at the latter he began orbiting over the sea just off St Malo. The navigation lights of a Do 217 were seen briefly before these were switched off but shortly afterwards two more Do 217s with lights on appeared on his port side. He attacked the nearest, closing to 200 yards from astern and slightly below to fire two short bursts. Fire broke out in the fuselage, particularly on its starboard side, and the bomber dived straight into the ground in flames. By now the other Dornier was slightly above. As he approached, its lights were switched off and he passed about 100 ft beneath it. He was able to keep it in sight however and swung in from behind to open fire from 250 yards. Some hits were observed but contact was then lost and it could only be claimed as damaged.

Kuttelwascher then flew south of the aerodrome and saw another Do 217 at 1,000 ft, also with its navigation lights on. These were soon turned off and at that moment the Hurricane was lit up briefly by a searchlight. Despite having his night vision impaired Kuttelwascher was able to maintain visual contact with the Dornier and closed to very close range before opening fire. The bomber caught fire almost immediately and went into a steep diving turn to the right to explode in a wood north of Dinard aerodrome. The Czech then set course for home meeting some flak from St Malo. He re-crossed the Channel at 5,000 ft and landed at Tangmere at 0445 hrs.

Sgt G.S.M. Pearson was operating in roughly the same area at the same time but had trouble locating Rennes, so flew north between the Channel Islands and made landfall again near Carteret on the western coast of the Cherbourg peninsula. It was here that he saw a Do 217 heading inland and after a five-minute chase closed to firing range. His first burst was wide of the mark, but his second hit the fuselage and at least one crew member baled out at a height of about 800 ft. He was able to fire another short burst before the Dornier disappeared into the night, however shortly after the engagement Pearson saw a bright flash on the ground where it might have crashed. It was later claimed as damaged and although it appeared at one point as though this might have been upgraded, it was finally agreed to leave the claim unchanged.

By the time that Kuttelwascher and Pearson arrived, Sgt Jim Campbell had already been operating in the area around Rennes for about twenty-five minutes. As he crossed the Channel at sea level he had run into three layers of cloud and had been forced up to 9,000 ft to find clear air. At one point however he flew into a thunderstorm and when he finally descended again he broke cloud at 1,500 ft to find it raining. The weather gradually improved so that it was clear by the time he arrived at Rennes on ETA. He orbited for twenty minutes without seeing anything and then patrolled the railway running north to Combourg. He came across three goods trains and damaged the engines of each one before heading for home.

On his way back he saw a Do 217 directly above him at 3,000 ft and travelling in a south-easterly direction. He climbed after it and kept it in sight by the glow of its engine exhausts. He eventually fired a short burst from astern and could see his shells hitting the Dornier on its fuselage, port wing and engine. Campbell fired again but was hampered by stoppages on both port cannons, which was becoming something of a recurring problem. The German aircraft began climbing, eventually reaching the safety of cloud and was not seen again. After orbiting for a few more minutes Campbell set course for home and landed at Tangmere at 0425 hrs.

These sorties were to be the last Intruder operations carried out by No. 1

Squadron as notification was received on 7 July of a move to Acklington in Northumberland. Not only was there to be a complete change of scene, it was also discovered that the unit's faithful Hurricanes were to be replaced by the next fighter design from Hawker, the formidable Typhoon. So it was with mixed feelings that No. 1 Squadron took off from Tangmere at 1700 hrs on 8 July to fly in formation to the north-east. Once again the squadron was being taken out of the firing line in the south but at least there was the prospect of a brand new aircraft to try out. The Typhoon however had a fearsome reputation so for many the tingle of anticipation that was to be expected when confronted with a new type of aircraft, was in this case mixed with a certain amount of apprehension. Whatever happened over the next few months, it was certainly going to be a challenge.

CHAPTER TWELVE

Enter the Typhoon

Acklington was located approximately twenty-five miles north of Newcastle-upon-Tyne and was just inland from the small port of Amble on the Northumberland coast, which had become prominent in the nineteenth century as a gateway for the transportation of coal to the south, and also for export to Europe. The aerodrome at Acklington was opened in 1938 and had been built on the site of a First World War landing ground known as Southfields. At the outbreak of war it was taken over by Fighter Command, initially as a satellite of Usworth, and had been the home of numerous squadrons operating Gladiators, Hurricanes, Spitfires and Beaufighters. No. 1 Squadron was to share Acklington with another Turbinlite Havoc unit, No. 1460 Flight, which became No. 539 Squadron on 2 September 1942.

As was to be expected there were a number of departures as experienced members of the squadron were posted to other units and on rest. One of the first to leave was Karel Kuttelwascher who did not even make it to Acklington, having been transferred as a supernumerary to No. 23 Squadron. Harry Connolly also left to join No. 32 Squadron. Notice was also received that James MacLachlan was to be moving on, in his case as supernumerary Chief Flying Instructor at 59 OTU, Crosby-on-Eden. Heading in the opposite direction was F/L E.J.F. Harrington who took over temporary command of the squadron when MacLachlan left on 22 July. Other pilots to leave around this time were P/O Otto Pavlu, P/O G.H. Corbet and W/O S.F. Cooper.

The movement of pilots between No. 1 Squadron and 59 OTU also saw the arrival of Sgt Walter Ramsey on 21 July on the completion of his training. The fact that Ramsey was available to serve his country during the Second World War probably owed everything to a piece of heroism during the first conflict with Germany. His father, Harry Hugill Ramsey, had served in the Royal Navy and was a member of the crew of HMS *Lion*, the flagship of Vice-Admiral Sir David Beatty's battlecruiser squadron during the Battle of Jutland on 31 May 1916. During exchanges with the German fleet HMS *Lion* was hit by shells from the battlecruiser *Lutzow* and one of its turrets was wrecked. A fire was started and shortly before his death the officer in charge of the turret issued an order to close the doors and flood the magazines, which prevented the ship from being blown apart. Ninety-eight crew members were killed on HMS *Lion*, however three other ships (HMS *Queen Mary*, *Invincible* and *Indefatigable*) blew up with the loss of over 1,000 lives in each case when their magazines exploded. For his actions in saving the ship and the rest of the crew, the officer, Major F.J.W. Harvey, was posthumously awarded the Victoria Cross.

Walter Ramsey was born on 19 September 1921 in Harrogate, his father continuing his association with the sea by serving in the Merchant Navy. He attended Bilton Grange School before a scholarship took him to Harrogate Grammar and on completing his education he worked in a local pathology laboratory. Having joined up, Ramsey was sent to the USA and commenced his flying training in September 1941 on the Stearman PT-13 at No. 2 BFTS (British Flying Training School) at War Eagle Field, Lancaster, in California. His basic and advanced flying was on the Vultee BT-13 and North American AT-6A. Along with other trainee pilots he met many film stars during his stay in California and at a party given by the British Film Colony on Christmas Day 1941 he was able to collect many autographs on his dinner menu including Ronald Colman, Charles Boyer, Joan Fontaine, June Duprez and Ida Lupino.

On completion of his initial training he returned to the UK where he was posted to 5 (P) AFU at Tern Hill. Here he flew the Miles Master I and III before moving on to 59 OTU at Crosby-on-Eden. His first flight in a Hurricane was on 16 May 1942 and the aircraft he was entrusted with on that day was P2877, a former No. 1 Squadron machine, which had carried the code letters JX-P. It had been on strength when the squadron was based at Wittering in 1940 and had been flown by many of the unit's Czech contingent, including Karel Kuttelwascher, Jan Plasil, Jarda Novak and Bedrich Kratkoruky. This was not the only ex No. 1 Squadron Hurricane at Crosby-on-Eden as Ramsey's second trip was in P3170, which had carried the code letters JX-M. This aircraft had been used during the height of the Battle of Britain and had been flown regularly by John Davey and Harold Mann. Others to fly this aircraft were Charles Chetham, Peter Matthews and Tim Elkington. During his stay in the north-west Ramsey was taught air-to-air firing by S/L Alec Ingle who would later command No. 609 Squadron on Typhoons. On arriving at Acklington he still had a lot to learn but he was now in the best place to continue his flying education.

Although everyone had been looking forward to getting to grips with the Typhoon, the new aircraft were rather slow in coming and the first did not arrive until 21 July. However, three more were delivered the next day, with six on the 25th and another five on the 26th. This allowed local practice flying to be carried out but it would be several weeks before the Typhoons were used operationally and in the meantime the squadron's Hurricanes would have to soldier on a little longer. Indeed at the end of the month all the Typhoons were grounded for a short period to await modification.

The Hawker Typhoon had had a troubled gestation and although it possessed tremendous potential, this was still a long way from being realised. Its history dated back to early 1938 and the issue of Specification F.18/37, which called for a fighter capable of 400 mph. It was designed around a Napier Sabre engine of 2,000 hp and it was confidently predicted that the Typhoon would be able to take over from the Hurricane and Spitfire and be more than a match for anything that the Germans could produce. It was developed in tandem with the Hawker Tornado, which was powered by a 1,980 hp Rolls-Royce Vulture, but this aircraft was abandoned after production of its engine was terminated following a series of failures in the Vulture-powered Avro Manchester bomber. The Typhoon was first flown on 24 February 1940 and quickly achieved its design aim of 400 mph, however it was soon beset by a whole host of technical problems.

First and foremost was the massively complex Napier Sabre engine, which was of twenty-four cylinders in an 'H' layout and featured sleeve valves. This type of valve had been used in the car and motorcycle industries for some time and had also been developed for aero engines, particularly by Bristol. The main advantages were that a higher compression ratio could be used when compared with a normal poppet-valve engine and the lack of hotspots that conventional valves tended to create also reduced the chances of pre-ignition. The Typhoon had entered RAF service with No. 56 Squadron in September 1941 but its engine was under-developed and there were constant failures. These were mostly valve-related as the sleeve tended to distort, resulting in a seized engine. By the time that No. 1 Squadron received its first Typhoons to become the fifth RAF squadron to fly the type, time between overhauls for the Napier Sabre was still only twenty-five hours. The continued difficulties threatened to jeopardise the whole Typhoon programme and it was only by utilising the expertise of Bristol's, which had more experience with sleeve valves on its air-cooled radials than any other British manufacturer, that the problem was eventually solved.

The Typhoon was also badly affected by carbon monoxide (CO) contamination, although this tended to vary between individual aircraft. Improved sealing of the cockpit did not completely eradicate the problem and as a result pilots had to be on oxygen whenever the engine was running. There were also a worrying number of in-flight break-ups caused by failure of the rear fuselage at the transport joint. A modification programme was initiated to reinforce this particular area, but structural failures continued to occur and were to do so throughout the Typhoon's career, albeit with reduced frequency. Pilots also had to put up with a high-frequency vibration, which tended to vary with the power setting used and aircraft configuration.

Compared with the Hurricane, the Typhoon was a brute of an aeroplane. Its loaded weight at 13,250 lbs was double that of the Hurricane I and with its chin-mounted radiator and high stance there was an imposing look about it. The massive Napier Sabre engine was fired up by a Coffman cartridge and pilots had to get used to the less than comforting sight of their ground crew standing by with fire extinguishers to put out flames in the air intake after a failed start. Take-off could be a fraught affair if not correctly managed as the huge amount of torque transmitted through the three-blade 14 ft diameter de Havilland propeller was liable to result in a strong swing to the right. Once in the air the Typhoon showed excellent acceleration and picked up speed quickly in the dive. However, early testing had already shown that its relatively thick, highly loaded wing was not conducive to high-altitude manoeuvring and that it was best suited to low and medium altitudes.

No. 1 Squadron's work-up period on Typhoons continued throughout August and during the month all operational flying was carried out by a dwindling batch of Hurricanes as these aircraft departed in small numbers for use elsewhere. The month also saw the arrival of S/L Roy Wilkinson to take over command of the squadron. Wilkinson was an ex Halton 'Brat' who had subsequently re-trained as a pilot, joining No. 3 Squadron as a Sergeant in 1937. He was still with this unit when it was sent to France after the German *Blitzkrieg* on 10 May 1940 and over an eight-day period shot down seven enemy aircraft, with another two shared. For his exploits he was awarded a DFM and Bar. In March 1942 he took command of No. 174 Squadron on Hurricanes but was shot down by flak on 3 May during a Ramrod operation to Abbeville. He was able to evade capture however and returned to the UK via Spain and Gibralter to take up his new appointment as the leader of No. 1 Squadron. Wilkinson's flight commanders were Les Scott and Fred Murray.

During the month of August Sergeants Johnnie Higham and G.S.M. Pearson were commissioned and Cdr André Jubelin left to join the French Naval HQ at the end of his RAF duties. He was replaced (for a short time at least) by a No. 1 Squadron 'old boy' in F/O Tim Elkington who had last flown with the squadron in April 1941. During his second tour he had seen action with No. 134 Squadron, which was transported to Russia by the aircraft carrier HMS *Argus* and operated from Vaenga near Murmansk. In September and October 1941 he had escorted Soviet bombers and had also been involved in airfield defence, sharing in the destruction of a Ju 88 during German attacks on Vaenga. After training Russian pilots to fly the squadron's Hurricanes, No. 134 Squadron returned to the UK in November and reformed at Eglinton in January 1942, however Elkington left in April to join the Merchant Ship Fighter Unit at Speke from where he rejoined No. 1 Squadron at Acklington.

On 9 August P/O J.S. 'Chunky' Chown, the squadron's engineering officer, went to Napier's for a two-week course on the Sabre engine. Chown was one of the real characters on No. 1 Squadron and had a reputation for hard work but at the same time was respected by everyone for his fairness. Having already been with the squadron for nearly a year, he was to remain for another eighteen months. Also on the 9th Sgt Walter Ramsey was detached (as were a number of pilots around this time) for a seven-day course at No. 1529 BAT Flight at Wittering. Here he flew Miles Masters at the satellite airfield at Collyweston and was given instrument flying instruction in let down procedures, homings and beam approaches. Back at Acklington, three Hurricanes departed for No. 257 Squadron at High Ercall on 13 August and four more left for No. 486 Squadron at Wittering on the 15th. Another which took off for disposal had to return due to bad visibility but on its third attempt to land it crashed and burst into flames. The ferry pilot (Sgt W.H. Jones) was thrown partially clear and was pulled to safety by two aircraftmen. He was taken to the station sickquarters suffering from severe burns.

While the Typhoons continued to carry out practice flying including formation, cine gun and air-to-sea firing, the remaining Hurricanes were entrusted with scrambles, co-operation with the Havocs of 1460 Flight and ZZ landings. Although sections of two Hurricanes were scrambled on a regular basis, these operations were usually abortive. A typical example occurred on 29 August when Tim Elkington took off in BN205 with Sgt G.C. 'Slim' Whitmore as his No. 2 in BD983. They were airborne for twenty minutes, however nothing was seen of friend or foe.

By 1 September twenty pilots (out of a total of twenty-six) were operational on the Typhoon and the first Typhoon scramble took place on 4 September. Sgt Ernie Glover (R7863) and Sgt D.C. Thompson (R7865) were airborne at 1325 hrs and landed an hour later. As always seemed to be the case, their patrol was entirely uneventful. The first Typhoon to be lost in an accident was R8690, which was written off in a crash-landing on 5 September. Sgt A.E. Pearce (Australia) was carrying out a sector recce when a connecting rod in his Sabre engine broke, causing much internal damage. He was able to make a belly landing in a field near RAF Longtown in Cumberland but his aircraft skidded through a fence and burst into flames as it came to rest. Pearce escaped with shock and bruises.

The perception that nothing ever happened at Acklington was to be shattered in the morning of 6 September when Blue section, led by Des Perrin in R7922 with P/O Tommy Bridges as his No. 2 in R7923, was scrambled to intercept unidentified aircraft approaching the north-east coast. The two Typhoons were airborne at 1116 hrs and were initially ordered by the sector controller at Ouston to head north for the Farne Islands. This was soon countermanded and Perrin and Bridges were then sent south towards Blyth, at first at 20,000 ft, but after a few minutes they were told to climb to 30,000 ft. Shortly before they reached this altitude the Typhoons switched over to Northsteads GCI control and at about the same time two aircraft were seen heading north-west. At a range of about one mile both of these aircraft began a gentle left-hand turn to the west, with the Typhoons turning to the right to give chase. Despite flying at full boost, which at that altitude equated to an indicated airspeed of 235–240 mph, the overtaking speed was only around 20 mph and range was still about 1,000 yards after three to four minutes. At this point Perrin saw one of the aircraft jettison its bombs in the general direction of Lackenby to the east of Middlesbrough, and both turned steeply away from each other. Perrin ordered Bridges to go for the one on the right while he went for the other. It was clear that the aircraft were hostile although at this stage they could not be positively identified.

They were in fact examples of the twin-engined Messerschmitt Me 210, which had been designed as the successor to the Bf 110. The prototype was flown for the first time on 2 September 1939 but its twin fins and rudders were soon replaced by a single large vertical surface as the original configuration had produced marked longitudinal instability. This was not the end of the Me 210's problems as it was blighted by a propensity to spin at high angles of attack, which led to further modifications including a fuselage extension and leading-edge slats. The Me 210 had been flown on the Eastern Front by II/ZG 1 in late 1941, but following a halt in production to eradicate its poor handling characteristics, the task of turning the Messerschmitt 210 into an effective weapon of war fell to *Versuchsstaffel* 210 based at Soesterberg in Holland. By late August 1942 this unit had become operational as 16/KG 6 and the two aircraft encountered by No. 1 Squadron's Typhoons were from this unit. The aircraft attacked by Des Perrin was Werke Nr 2348 (2H+CA) flown by Fw Heinrich Moesges with Obgfr Eduard Czerny as wireless operator, while that attacked by Bridges was Werke Nr 2321 (2H+HA) flown by Oblt Walter Maurer, the *Staffelkapitän* of 16/KG 6, assisted by Fw Rudolf Jansen.

As he went for the aircraft flown by Moesges, Perrin turned steeply to port and dived, quickly reducing range to about 250 yards. Firing from astern and a little to the left he damaged the port engine before crossing over to deliver another two-second burst from the other side. This hit the starboard engine, which caused the 210 to lose speed so that the Typhoon was then able to overhaul it rapidly. Perrin fired a third burst from dead astern at a distance of only 50 yards, which blew part of the rudder away. The German aircraft immediately turned on its back and dived vertically. Perrin attempted to follow but as he was turning to keep it in view he blacked out at an IAS of over 520 mph and only came to again at an altitude of 3,000 ft off Hartlepool. At first he thought he might have to bale out as he was aware of a terrific hammering noise but it transpired that the safety catches had come out of the starboard cockpit door and it was vibrating violently in the slipstream. As he gradually slowed down the noise became less intense. Perrin searched the sea but could see nothing except for a launch and after a few minutes he returned to base, landing at 1207 hrs.

The latter stages of the combat had been seen from the ground and several people had been alerted by the sound of aero engines and the rattle of cannon fire. Stanley Hill, an eight-year old schoolboy from New Marske, witnessed the last moments of the Me 210 and its crew. The aircraft spun into the ground near a reservoir adjacent to Fell Briggs Farm. Shortly before it did Hill saw a figure leave the aircraft which was that of Heinrich Moesges but before his parachute could open he plunged into the reservoir and was killed. Eduard Czerny fared no better. Although he had baled out earlier his parachute 'candled' and he fell at a high rate of descent. Hill recalls him falling 'ramrod straight, as if standing to attention' and the unfortunate airman plunged to his death little more than 100 yards from where he was standing.

In the meantime the second Me 210 flown by Walter Maurer had come under attack by Bridges. The German attempted to escape by entering a climbing turn to the right and the Typhoon pilot found that he was unable to close to firing range.

Rather than maintain height, Maurer made the mistake of attempting to dive away to the south-east and this allowed Bridges to close in rapidly. His first burst was from astern and slightly to the left, which hit the port engine, fuselage and cockpit cover. A further burst struck the same engine, which eventually caught fire, and a trail of debris was prised from the stricken Messerschmitt. In attempting to stay in contact Bridges also blacked out and regained consciousness at 4,000 ft to the east of Whitby. He then returned to Acklington and landed at the same time as Des Perrin.

The combat had taken place near Robin Hood's Bay and its culmination was seen by another schoolboy, Dennis Crosby who was fifteen at the time. He recalled an eventful few minutes in Bill Norman's book *Broken Eagles* (Pen and Sword, 2001):

> I was waiting by the roadside outside the house for my school-friend, Ernest Brown, to deliver the Sunday newspapers. While I was watching him coming up the hill I could hear distant cannon fire out to sea and to the north of the bay however I thought little of it because aircraft regularly tested their guns over the sea. When Ernest arrived at the gate, the gunfire appeared to be much closer and we both looked out to sea for a while but could see nothing unusual, although visibility was good and we were standing about 300 ft above sea level. Eventually we made out a twin-engine plane coming in from the sea, directly towards us. It was at about 1,000 ft with smoke trailing behind it. We could see no other plane in pursuit and as it drew nearer we could see it was a fighter-bomber. As it approached Fylingthorpe village, two parachutes opened up below it.
>
> The aircraft lost height and crashed below the crest of the hill behind Sunnyside Farm, at the top of Sledgates. There was an explosion, followed by dense smoke and flames but it was impossible to make out the exact spot where it had fallen. Ernest and I raced up the 1 in 4 hill as only fifteen-year olds could and, upon arriving near Parkgate Farm, found the road littered with small pieces of aluminium debris from the plane, which by this time was burning fiercely in the small field behind Sunnyside. The stone wall that bordered the road up to the Park Gates had been flattened by the blast for several yards. Parts of the plane had evidently blown over the road into the garth opposite because there was also a large fire there. We knew that the main fuselage was behind the wall however because there were explosions coming from that direction as ammunition was ignited.
>
> We kept under the cover of the shattered wall and were not foolhardy enough to approach any closer as it was obvious there was little left of the aircraft. As we left the scene, I noticed that one of the small fragments of aluminium on the ground was oblong in shape. Upon picking it up, I was delighted to find that it was an identification plate from a piece of the plane's equipment. Upon examining this much later, I noticed the letters

'ME' and the numbers '210'. This puzzled me because I knew only of the Messerschmitt Me 110 and had never heard of the Me 210. It was sometime later before details of the plane appeared in the spotters' books and I knew for certain what type it was.

Maurer and Jansen both survived their ordeal. The latter came down in a field near Middlewood Farm at Fylingthorpe, while his *Staffelkapitän* landed in the sea just offshore. A race then developed between three boats, one from Robin Hood's Bay and fishing boats from Whitby and Scarborough, to get to him first. The local boat won but on discovering that the airman was German, one of the boat's crew refused to take him on board as he had lost his only son at sea to enemy action. Ultimately Maurer was picked up by the Scarborough boat and was taken there (this was the same Walter Maurer who had been shot down by No. 1 Squadron during the Battle of France on 11 May 1940).

At Acklington confirmation was soon received that both of the German aircraft had been shot down. Perrin had fired 185 rounds in three bursts but there had been a stoppage in the starboard outer cannon due to a link becoming jammed in the ejection chute. Tommy Bridges had fired 280 rounds in four bursts with no stoppages. The fact that both pilots had blacked out and had only recovered consciousness at a relatively low altitude highlighted some of the perils of carrying out high-speed dives in the Typhoon. With its powerful engine and high all-up weight, the Typhoon picked up speed rapidly in the dive and any manoeuvring was liable to produce high 'g' forces. In addition the aircraft soon hit the relatively new phenomenon of compressibility in which shock waves developed over the airframe and ultimately led to loss of control. This was generally not regained until the aircraft had descended into denser air at a lower level and Mach number was reduced.

Also on 6 September the last five Hurricane IICs departed although they did not go very far as they only went to the other side of the aerodrome to join No. 539 Squadron (formerly 1460 Flight). Rather than rely on an affiliated fighter squadron, it had been decided that the Turbinlite squadrons should operate their own single-engined aircraft as there had been numerous occasions when fighters had not been available due to other commitments. As a result of the change in policy several No. 1 Squadron pilots were transferred to No. 539 Squadron, including F/O Tim Elkington, F/Sgt B.C. Williams, Sgt C.J. Herbert and Sgt D.C. Thompson. In the event the advances that had been made with AI radar in Beaufighter and Mosquito night-fighters rendered the Turbinlite squadrons expendable and all had been disbanded by January 1943. Replacement pilots for those who joined No. 539 Squadron were P/O P.N. Dobie and three Australians, Sgt Ned Crowley and twin brothers in Sergeants Charles and Harris Fraser.

The rest of September brought little in the way of action with only an occasional scramble to provide some excitement among the routine of practice flying. Having been the squadron Adjutant since its return from France in 1940,

F/L L.W. Grumbley left on 10 September on transfer to RAF Tangmere. One of his first tasks had been to piece together the squadron's exploits in France due to the loss of original records and when this is added to his period of service, no one had a better knowledge of No. 1 Squadron's wartime achievements than he. His departure so soon after many long-serving pilots had also left meant that yet another link with the past had gone, however at least it offered a good excuse for a farewell party. He was replaced initially by P/O E.L.H. Riche but on his posting to 11 Group HQ; the role of Adjutant was taken on by F/O A.R. Scrope-Davies. On 29 September three more replacement pilots arrived in Sergeants Jack Sutherland, R.W. 'Bob' Hornall and M.R. Wright (Canada). By this time the squadron's complement of aircraft comprised twenty Typhoon Ibs, one Hurricane I, which was used as a general trainer and hack, and one Miles Magister (V1027), however this was to be swapped for a Tiger Moth (DE667) the following month.

October was another disappointing month although one lucky pilot did get the opportunity to shoot down a stray balloon. The month was notable for all the wrong reasons however as on the 21st two Typhoons were lost with both pilots being killed. One was flown by P.E.G. 'Gerry' Sayer, the Chief Test Pilot of the Gloster Aircraft Company, which was responsible for production of the Typhoon. The other pilot involved was P/O P.N. Dobie. The two had taken off at 1415 hrs to carry out air-to-sea firing and it was thought that they had collided in cloud about four miles off Amble. Oil was seen on the water but despite an ASR search, nothing was seen of the pilots or aircraft. During the month Slim Whitmore and Moose Mossip were commissioned in the RCAF as Pilot Officers and new arrivals were F/O C.H. 'Zulu' Watson, Sgt H.K Shawyer and Sgt S.H. Brown.

Two more Typhoons were written off in November although the pilots were unhurt on each occasion. On 9 November P/O Tommy Bridges was about to take off in R7868 when he was hit by R8630. Ground collisions were a particular hazard with the Typhoon as the forwards visibility was very poor, even with the pilot's seat at its highest setting. The other incident occurred on 21 November when F/O Zulu Watson had to force-land R7862 near Charterhall following an engine fire. Watson was able to get out quite easily as the fire was slow to take hold but the aircraft subsequently burnt out. Roy Wilkinson and Chunky Chown inspected the remains for clues as to the cause but with the number of engine-related snags on the Typhoon, there were times when the slang version of the squadron's motto *In Omnibus Princeps* (It's Quicker By Bus) was actually true. Roy Wilkinson had first-hand experience of an engine problem on 30 November when high oil temperature led him to make an emergency landing at RAF Croft, near Darlington.

On 2 December No. 1 Squadron was visited by the new commander of 13 Group, AVM Malcolm Henderson, who spent some time touring the dispersals and chatting with the pilots. Henderson had been awarded the DSO in March 1916 when serving with No. 18 Squadron of the Royal Flying Corps. During a photo-reconnaissance mission his Vickers FB.5 was hit by an anti-aircraft shell, which took off his left leg just below the knee. Despite this he was able to carry out a successful landing, which saved his aircraft and the life of his observer. For much of December the weather was sufficiently bad that no flying took place. There were occasional scrambles as on 22 December when P/O Ernie Glover (R7865) and Sergeant Walter Ramsey (R8752) took off at 1040 hrs only to be recalled ten minutes later as the 'raider' turned out to be friendly. Glover was airborne again at 1340 hrs with P/O Johnny McCullough, the radar contact on this occasion proving to be a Wellington.

The flying programme was also disrupted in January when eight days were lost. Seven operational scrambles took place but five of these involved friendly aircraft and in one of the others the radar plot 'faded' as soon as the Typhoons were airborne, which led to an immediate recall. Two sections were scrambled on 27 January, White section comprising P/O Ernie Glover (R7856) and F/O Zulu Watson (R7877) and Yellow section with Sgt Walter Ramsey (DN241) and Sgt Jack Sutherland (DN490), but neither made any contact, friendly or otherwise. By now the lack of action was beginning to have a detrimental effect on the squadron's morale so the news that it would be moving back to 11 Group in early February was greeted with widespread approval. Compared with its illustrious past, the last few months had been something of a lean spell but at least it had provided the opportunity to come to terms with the Typhoon. Not only were the wilds of Northumberland about to be left behind but the squadron was set to fly to the most famous fighter airfield of them all, Biggin Hill.

CHAPTER THIRTEEN

Low Level Raiders and Ramrods

The move south commenced in the early hours of 9 February but was not the smoothest of No. 1 Squadron's wartime transfers. The main party left Acklington at 0500 hrs and all went well until arriving at Newcastle Central Station whose staff proved that 'finger trouble' afflicted everyone, not just the RAF. The train that was to take the airmen on the long journey to London was not held long enough and set off without twelve senior NCOs who were acting as 'whippers in'. The London and North Eastern Railway then laid claim to the 'The Most Highly Commendable Order of the Irremovable Digit' by scattering many of the wagons containing the squadron's equipment a long way from their intended destination. This meant that lorries had to be sent far and wide, using up precious petrol (always in short supply) to retrieve the gear from around the country.

The Typhoons also had their problems as bad weather caused a number to land at Wittering. Some made it as far as Southend but DN241 flown by Sgt Ned Crowley suffered a hydraulic failure, which resulted in one wheel being locked down while the other remained up. He carried out several circuits but just when it had been decided that he should climb through the overcast to bale out, his fuel expired and he was left with no alternative but to carry out a force-landing. His attempt to smash the undercarriage leg into submission only resulted in a huge bounce and he eventually overshot the runway before overturning in a boggy area on the other side of the boundary fence. He was unhurt apart from a slight facial wound caused by the axe of an over enthusiastic member of the rescue party who was attempting to dig him out. His aircraft however was Cat E and a write-off.

Biggin Hill had shot to prominence during the Battle of Britain as it had been the target of numerous air raids but had managed to stay operational throughout. It became a mecca for the top fighter pilots of the day, its proximity to London's nightlife also being one of the principal attractions. As a sector station its role in the defence of the capital was vital. Its location to the south of London near Bromley meant that its fighter squadrons were ideally placed to intercept raids by aircraft based in northern France before they reached their target. At the time of No. 1 Squadron's arrival Biggin Hill was also home to the Spitfires of Nos 340 and 611 Squadrons.

The main reason that No. 1 Squadron now found itself at Biggin Hill was a change in *Luftwaffe* tactics. Raids by medium bombers were largely a thing of the past, but these had been replaced by fighter-bomber versions of the Focke-Wulf Fw 190A, which were capable of carrying bombs of 500 kg capacity. These hit-and-run raiders flew at high speed and were very difficult to intercept. Apart from the Spitfire IX, the Typhoon was the only other aircraft that could deal with these *Jabos*. The first fighter-bomber sorties were flown in the latter half of 1942 but there was a marked escalation on 20 January 1943 with a large-scale attack on London, which was to be the largest daylight raid since 1940.

Following an early morning reconnaissance in which Lt Hans Kummerling of 8/JG 26 was shot down by a Typhoon of No. 609 Squadron, ninety fighter and fighter-bombers (including the Bf 109Gs of 6/JG 26) attacked London in three waves around lunchtime. Weather conditions were perfect with clear blue sky and excellent visibility. The first wave, comprising the *Jabo Staffeln* of JG 2 and 26 (together with elements of the *Stab* and I/JG 26 as escort), achieved complete surprise and dropped their bombs randomly, one demolishing half of Sandhurst Road School in Catford killing thirty-eight children and six teachers. A further sixty children and staff were injured. A bomb was also dropped at Oakshade Road, about a mile south of Sandhurst Road, which narrowly missed two more schools. There were numerous reports of people being strafed in suburban streets, which led to many casualties. This occurred in Catford and also in Sydenham, Brockley and Penge.

The prelude to this attack was witnessed by Patricia Adamson who was a driver with the ATS. She had just delivered an officer to an anti-aircraft gun battery on a hill near Croydon and was marvelling at the panoramic view over the city when she noticed three aircraft approaching fast and low from the south. Assuming that they belonged to the RAF she was not unduly perturbed but was stunned (and rather disappointed) when they proved to be German and opened fire. Machine-gun bullets and cannon shells impacted all around but the attack was over in an instant and the Fw 190s raced away to the north-east to drop their bombs over the built-up area. The whole raid lasted a matter of minutes and the only German losses from the first wave were the Fw 190A-4 of Lt Hermann Koch who was hit by light flak and had to crash-land in a field, and the similar machine of Obfw Paul Kierstein who was shot down by the Spitfire IX of W/C R.M. 'Dickie' Milne, leader of the Biggin Hill Wing.

The second wave contained some of JG 2's Fw 190 fighters equipped with fragmentation bombs, but by now virtually every available RAF fighter in the immediate area had been scrambled and most of the 190s jettisoned their loads near the south coast and turned for home. Fw Alfred Barthel of 5/JG 26 was shot down by a Spitfire of No. 340 Squadron but the most serious losses were to the Bf 109G-4s of 6/JG 26 who had two pilots killed with two more shot down to become PoWs. The third wave comprised the *Stabsschwarm* and III/JG 26 led by Major Josef 'Pips' Priller who provided cover, Oblt Klaus Mietusch claiming two

Spitfires. A number of III *Gruppe* aircraft returned very low on fuel and Uffz Robert Hager was injured when he crash-landed his Fw 190A-4 at Calais-Marck. As JG 2 had also lost one pilot killed with another injured, the operation had proved to be extremely costly. As a result of the losses inflicted on the German side, attacks on this scale were not to be repeated; however nuisance raids by smaller numbers of aircraft would continue for some time, the targets generally being along the south coast.

The Typhoons of No. 1 Squadron that had put down at Wittering arrived at Biggin Hill on 10 February, whilst those at Southend had to stay a day longer to await a delivery of Coffman cartridges so that the engines could be started. Sector recces were flown by all pilots on the 13th, however Sgt Bob Hornall was able to examine the scenery rather closer than he intended when he experienced engine trouble in R7864 and had to force-land at Danehill in Sussex. Although he had considered baling out at one point, his course of action was limited due to a large number of soldiers who were gathered in open country below. These were part of the 5th Canadian Division, the commanding officer of which was most appreciative that Hornall had steered his stricken aircraft well away from his troops.

The squadron's return to London could not have been better timed as it acquired the services of a new Intelligence officer in P/O Oliver Wakefield who had temporarily given up a stage career to join the RAF. Although he had been born in Zululand, South Africa, Wakefield appeared as the quintessential Englishman with his prominent moustache and on arriving in the UK secured a job with a Shakespearean repertory company. Although he had appeared in films with the likes of Gracie Fields, Glynis Johns and Alistair Sim, he had also made a name for himself as a comedian and appeared regularly at The Savoy and The Berkeley. His theatre connections were to prove extremely useful as he was able to secure tickets for many of the London shows.

The threat posed by *Luftwaffe* fighter-bombers was such that standing patrols had to be flown at all times, weather permitting. This was due to the high speed of the *Jabos*, which also came in at extremely low level, so that if Fighter Command's aircraft remained on the ground there was usually insufficient warning via radar stations for any effective action to be taken. For the rest of the month therefore No. 1 Squadron's Typhoons patrolled off Beachy Head in sections of two aircraft, flying anything up to forty-two hours per day. Although nothing was seen, the squadron diarist was confident when he said '…but it will come!'

Before it did there were several more accidents including two minor prangs on 1 March. The Typhoon of P/O Slim Whitmore burst a tyre on take-off and this led to a heated debate between Engineering and Intelligence as to the Category of damage that had been caused. Engineering only rated it Cat Ac whereas Intelligence considered it to be Cat B. The latter eventually won. The second incident involved Sgt Ned Crowley who omitted to lower his undercarriage on return from a patrol, something that was considered essential for a good landing. Once again Intelligence won out in assessing the level of damage with a Cat B.

A far more serious accident occurred in the evening of 6 March when P/O Slim Whitmore and Sgt Harris Fraser were sent on a patrol. On their return they were flying in thick cloud when it appears that they collided. Slim Whitmore's Typhoon (DN615) was found at Glassenbury Park near Goudhurst in Kent, the wreckage being spread over 150 yards. Harris Fraser's machine (R8942) came down about five miles away at Red House Farm at Benenden and was scattered over an area of 250 yards. Its propeller was located some way from the main wreckage site although this was not a contributory factor in the accident. The funeral of Whitmore and Harris took place on 10 March at St Mary Cray near Orpington. Those present included Roy Wilkinson, Les Scott and Fraser's twin brother Charles. A party of airmen from the RAF Regiment formed a guard of honour and the Sergeants acted as pall bearers. The squadron diary noted that it was a lovely sunny afternoon, the sort of afternoon that both men would have liked to be flying. After the bodies were laid to rest, officers and men paid their last respects and left the cemetery 'to get back to the job of killing Germans'.

The first sign that the squadron's fortunes might be on the way up was on 9 March when Red section, comprising F/L Fred Murray and P/O Moose Mossip, was vectored to Boulogne harbour in pursuit of hostile aircraft. Low cloud prevented a positive sighting and the same went for Green section (P/O S.P. Dennis and W/O W.H. Dunwoodie). During a patrol of the south coast both pilots saw smoke rings where bombs had burst near Brighton. An aircraft was seen behind the section, which was thought to be a 'bandit', but by the time they had manoeuvred into position to give chase it had disappeared into clouds as it made its way south towards the French coast.

Further patrols were carried out over the next three days and on 13 March Blue section led by Les Scott, with Bob Hornall as his No. 2, took off at 1705 hrs. The patrol line was the usual one to the south of Beachy Head and after fifteen minutes 'Cowherd' control vectored the two Typhoons to the west onto an enemy raid. Hornall was having trouble with his radio but managed to hear enough to convince him that at last they had some 'trade'. Soon two aircraft appeared on their starboard beam about three miles away and the Typhoons manoeuvred towards them to come in on their tails. As they did so the aircraft turned towards the Channel and began to climb. By this time they had been identified as Fw 190s and Scott went for the right-hand one, leaving the other to Hornall.

Bob Hornall had no oxygen in his aircraft as it had blown out shortly after they were given the vector and so he did not want to go any higher than 12–13,000 ft. As the 190s were still climbing he was concerned that he might not catch up in time so he opened fire when still about 400 yards away. The 190 immediately began to pour smoke and a piece of debris was seen to fly off. It then went into a shallow dive before flicking into a spin. Hornall followed the 190 down and fired again, however the German aircraft continued to spin until it finally hit the sea.

In the meantime Scott had been able to close in behind the other 190 and fired a short burst from 250 yards. Several explosive puffs were seen as his shells struck and a trail of black smoke appeared. The 190 turned to port in a gentle dive, the smoke by now having changed colour to white. Scott moved in once again to fire a second burst from 150 yards causing further damage. During this attack the cockpit hood was jettisoned. By now the 190 appeared to be gliding down but its pilot was obviously still in full control as he employed clever evasive actions, which spoilt Scott's third attack. After flying a wide circuit around his victim, Scott came in once again firing from 150 yards down to only 50 yards. On this occasion the German pilot was unable to prevent his machine receiving multiple hits after which it turned on its back and dived into the sea about twenty miles south-east of Brighton. The attack, which had commenced at 10,000 ft, was finished off at around 2,000 ft.

News of the double success was greeted with smiles all round and no little relief as the two Fw 190s were the first enemy aircraft shot down in six months. Having got their Biggin Hill account under way however a signal was received notifying the squadron of yet another move, this time to Lympne near Folkstone. The reason for this was that the German hit-and-run raids were now largely concentrated on targets along the south coast and Lympne was ideally located. Although No. 1 Squadron had enjoyed its time at Biggin Hill, it was not displeased to be moving as it was felt that much more could be done operationally at an aerodrome that it did not have to share with other squadrons. The move was supposed to have taken place on 15 March but a thick fog meant a delay and Chunky Chown remained at Biggin to work on the Typhoons. They eventually made it the following day, except for Bob Hornall who had to return with faulty instruments.

Compared with Biggin Hill, Lympne was quite a small aerodrome and so Typhoon operations were not going to be easy. This was emphasised three days later when Zulu Watson overshot on landing and overturned in DN335. The airfield at Lympne had been in use since 1916 and had been heavily bombed during the Battle of Britain. The large General Service hangars that had been erected in 1918 were badly damaged and were replaced by smaller blister hangars in 1941 when Lympne was brought up to the standards necessary for a satellite aerodrome. Having been used to Spitfires for so long, the arrival of the squadron's Typhoons came as a shock to the local population who had to put up with the raucous bellow of the Napier Sabre engines, which had to be run up at regular intervals at night to ensure that they would start when needed.

One big advantage of the new location was that the Mess was located in a mansion known as Port Lympne. This had been designed in 1912 by the fashionable architects Herbert Baker and Ernest Willmott for Sir Philip Sassoon who at the time was the MP for Hythe. It was built in a Dutch colonial style and its external construction featured russet-coloured brickwork with Dutch gables, a roof made from old Kent tiles and window frames that were solid oak. Internally it resembled a Roman villa with marble columns and it had a sweeping stone staircase. The hallway was made from black and white marble in concentric curves and the walls in many of the rooms featured works of fine art. During the Second World War many fine houses were requisitioned for use by the military but this took some beating and having endured an aerodrome that was rather basic, pilots could at least relax in magnificent surroundings when they were off duty.

The routine over the next few weeks was much as it had been at Biggin Hill with standing patrols comprising the majority of the operational flying, the occasional scramble being thrown in for good measure. P/O Ernie Glover and Sgt H.K. Shawyer were ordered off at 1625 hrs on 21 March and got as far as Boulogne but were later informed that they had not got closer than ten miles to the enemy aircraft they had been chasing.

On 29 March F/O C.L. Bolster (R7876 – White 1) and Sgt Jack Sutherland (R8752 – White 2) took off at 1025 hrs for another patrol of Beachy Head. They had been flying for some time when control gave them a series of vectors which took them towards Le Havre. Sutherland was having problems seeing where he was going as his windscreen was covered in oil, a task that was made more difficult as there was considerable cloud at 3–400 ft, which occasionally extending right down to the sea. Eventually the two aircraft were told to return but it appeared that Bolster did not hear the call as he continued to fly towards France. By this time Sutherland's windscreen problem had got worse and he informed Bolster that he was returning but got no reply. The Canadian was last seen heading south at 300 ft about forty miles south of Beachy Head. Sutherland landed safely at Lympne but there was no sign of Bolster and he was not heard from again (it appears he was shot down by an Fw 190 of JG 2).

Although the vast majority of the patrols that were flown were uneventful, some delivered high levels of 'twitch', and not always as a result of enemy action. On 2 April when Roy Wilkinson and P/O Ernie Glover were in the usual patrol area they were told to head to the west as there was a possible 'bogey' in the vicinity. After the third vector they were informed that the 'bogey' was definitely hostile and that it was approaching from France at a height of 1,000 ft. The Typhoons opened up to 350 mph IAS and closed to within five miles but by this time the weather was closing in with a visibility of around 1,000 yards. Wilkinson saw something loom up ahead and only just had time to turn steeply to the right to avoid some cliffs. Almost immediately he passed over what was probably Brighton pier. As the weather was steadily getting worse he contacted 'Cowherd' control for permission to orbit out to sea as the conditions looked a little better in that direction. This was approved but he was soon informed that the aircraft had been shot down by anti-aircraft fire and had crashed near Hove. It was only discovered later that the aircraft had been a Mosquito F.II (DD742) of No. 85 Squadron returning from a Ranger operation. The navigator, F/O S.R. Streeter, was unable to bale out due to injuries received and was killed. The pilot, S/L K.R. Sutton DFC from Oamaru in New Zealand, did bale out but he had been badly injured and was to lose his left leg below the knee and his left hand.

On 6 April the squadron entertained its former CO James MacLachlan who had just returned from the USA. After leaving No. 1 Squadron he had served briefly with 59 OTU, Crosby-on-Eden, and the Air Fighting Development Unit (AFDU) at Duxford but had then travelled to America on the *Queen Elizabeth* liner, which was being used as a troopship. Whilst in the United States he toured various training units and gave lectures to trainee pilots in which he told them what war was really like. Everyone was madly jealous as he was able to shoot an even better line than normal and had photographs to prove it. These included some that were taken during a visit to Hollywood in which he had met the likes of Orson Welles, Joan Fontaine and Betty Grable. Although he had thoroughly enjoyed his time abroad he was desperate to see some action again. Within a matter of days of his visit he had rejoined AFDU where he became increasingly associated with the Allison-engined North American Mustang I, an aircraft that offered high speed at low level and excellent endurance. The germ of an idea, that of using it for long-range interdiction, one that had been present ever since his first flight in a Mustang nearly a year ago, was about to come to fruition.

By now the *Jabostaffel* of JG 26 had been redesignated as 10 (*Jabo*)/JG 54 and in the late afternoon of 9 April this unit launched a raid on Folkstone during which the Fw 190A-5 flown by Uffz Karl Heck was shot down by the No. 609 Squadron Typhoon of Lt Erik Haabjoern. As was standard practice a search of the Channel was set in motion by the Germans but the Spitfire IXs of No. 611 Squadron, together with a section from No. 1 Squadron, were waiting for them and during the ensuing fight another three 190s were shot down. No. 1 Squadron's contribution was Black section, comprising Des Perrin and Bob Hornall, which met up with No. 611 Squadron over Lympne. The mixed formation reached the French coast near Cap Gris Nez and then turned east in the direction of Calais. They were then informed by the controller that bandits were in the vicinity and the Spitfires broke up into sections and climbed above the Typhoons.

Shortly after the warning was given Bob Hornall saw five Fw 190s in his eight o'clock position and dived on the tail of the last in line. Opening fire at 300 yards he closed in and fired two more bursts as the 190 went into a climb. As it did so it shed various bits and its undercarriage came down. It then turned on its side, at which point the pilot baled out. By this time three of the 190s had turned towards him and had begun firing. Fortunately there was cloud nearby in which he was able to lose them. In the meantime Perrin had been concentrating on another group of 190s and so had not been able to help. He also lost them in cloud and quickly headed for home. (Of the three Fw 190s shot down it is likely that Hornall accounted for Werke Nr 7290 'Black 12' flown by Lt Otto-August Backhaus of the *Jabostaffel*. He did not survive.)

This was Hornall's second Fw 190, the squadron diary noting – 'he already has that hungry look'. He would have to wait a long time for his next opportunity however and for the rest of the month the squadron's patrols produced little of note. Most of the activity involved others and on 18 April there was a sign of things to come when eight 'Bomphoons' of No. 181 Squadron flew in to use Lympne as an advanced landing ground prior to a bombing attack on Poix. The future for the Typhoon was as a fighter-bomber and its excellent performance at low level, together with its ability to carry rockets and bombs, was to be its saviour. There had been a concerted effort by some within the upper echelons of the RAF to have the whole project cancelled, however its supporters eventually won the day and the Typhoon would become one of the most feared close-support fighters of the war. The eight Bomphoons of 181 were escorted by twelve Typhoons of No. 486 Squadron and all returned safely.

In the afternoon of 20 April a Ventura of No. 487 Squadron piloted by Sgt G.F. Whitwell carried out a forced landing at Lympne. As it had been about to bomb the harbour at Boulogne an anti-aircraft shell had smashed into the cockpit. Whitwell was severely injured in the blast but remained conscious and was able to jettison the bomb load and head back across the Channel. Having been told to put down at Lympne the bomber made two circuits of the aerodrome as the crew trimmed the aircraft and it finally touched down in what was considered to be a remarkably good landing. This was despite the fact that Whitwell had a compound fracture of the left arm and had lost a lot of blood. He was lifted from the Ventura in a semi-conscious state, but survived. All at Lympne were impressed by his handling of the damaged aircraft and thought that it was a 'damn good show'.

Towards the end of the month two Typhoons were damaged in accidents, one being a write-off. On 27 April Moose Mossip landed in R7865 at 2155 hrs and after touching down normally he then felt a severe bump from the rear of his aircraft. After pulling up he found that the tailwheel had broken off. On the following day Sgt Harry Bletcher had engine trouble during a patrol in R8634 and had no alternative but to force-land on Pevensey marshes, his Typhoon being declared Cat E.

As well as routine patrols, the month of May also brought increased emphasis on offensive sorties to the other side of the Channel. On the 5th six Typhoons led by Roy Wilkinson escorted Spitfires that were carrying out a coastal reconnaissance. During this operation Moose Mossip took the opportunity to look for any targets that he could find and shot up two goods trains near Calais, bursting the boilers of both engines. He then flew to the Dunkirk area and fired at three barges before joining up once again with the rest of the Flight for the journey home.

After this operation the squadron entered a rather quiet spell in which the patrols and scrambles that were carried out were all uneventful. There were also occasional periods of bad weather, one of which led to the cancellation of an escort mission for bombers, the Typhoons having positioned to Tangmere on 11 May. As the conditions were such that a return to Lympne could not be made until the following day, the pilots were forced to night-stop, but at least were able to catch up with a few old acquaintances from the previous year.

On 15 May Ernie Glover and Bob Hornall took off at 2145 hrs for a late evening Roadstead to France. Having made landfall at Cap Gris Nez they flew south to Boulogne where they encountered an R-Boat accompanied by a flak ship. Both pilots attacked the former amid a hail of flak and left it badly damaged. Encouraged by this operation a similar one was flown the following day at the same time by Moose Mossip and Ned Crowley. They also made for Boulogne but this time the Germans were expecting them and put up a curtain of heavy anti-aircraft fire. It was the same at Le Touquet so both decided that it was best to retire gracefully and fight another day. Also on 16 May Les Scott and P/O J.M. Chalifour carried out a Rhubarb operation from Cap Gris Nez to St Omer and Béthune and destroyed one train and damaged another four.

The next offensive sorties took place on 18 May when twelve Typhoons acted as rear escort to bomb-carrying Typhoons attacking Poix. The operation passed uneventfully, the only concern being the late arrival of the Bomphoons at Le Touquet on their return. The next day Ernie Glover and F/Sgt S.H. Brown tried their luck with a Rhubarb operation in the Lille area. The perils of this type of operation were brought home when Glover failed to return. He was last seen by Brown when in a tight turn over Lille and it was presumed that he had been shot down by flak. Brown carried on alone and shot up two trains and a signal box on his way back (it was later confirmed that Glover, who was flying R7863, had survived to become a prisoner of war). On 20 May the squadron started out on a Rodeo operation, the intention being to fly to Abbeville and orbit at 8,000 ft to act as bait for German fighters. The weather conditions were wholly inappropriate for this type of mission however with 10/10 cloud at 500 ft and so an early return was made.

On the other side of the Channel there had been further reorganisation of the *Luftwaffe* fighter-bomber force as the former *Jabostaffeln* had been amalgamated to form *Schnellkampfgeschwader* 10 or SKG 10. On 23 May twenty-six Fw 190s of IV/SKG 10 led by Lt Leopold Wenger carried out a daylight attack on Bournemouth in which 128 people were killed, including fifty-one military personnel, many of whom were serving with the RCAF. At the same time twenty Fw 190s of II/SKG 10 attacked Hastings and it was this raid that was contested by No. 1 Squadron. Red section, led by Walter Ramsey with Zulu Watson as his No. 2, was scrambled at 1258 hrs to intercept enemy aircraft approaching the English coast to the south-west of Rye. The two Typhoons were under Biggin Hill control and were initially ordered to fly on a vector of 230 degrees at a height of 2,000 ft. Ramsey held this course until he was informed by control that German aircraft had been reported in the Hastings area at sea level. He then altered course to 210 degrees and dived to zero feet in order to position the Typhoons over the Channel to cut off the most likely escape route.

The Typhoons crossed the coast just to the east of Rye and as they began to fly over the sea Ramsey and Watson could clearly see clouds of smoke away to their right as bombs exploded in Hastings. They also saw what appeared to them to be red rockets coming from the town that were in fact the trajectories of shells fired by the local anti-aircraft defences. Having flown about three to four miles out over the Channel, Ramsey turned to the right to fly due west and parallel to the coast. He then spotted an aircraft at sea level crossing ahead from right to left. It was flying towards the south and was weaving gently from side to side. As he turned in pursuit and closed from behind, he quickly identified the aircraft as an Fw 190. Due to his high speed he was able to close to firing range with relative ease and opened up with several two-second bursts, which produced a number of strikes.

Although Ramsey did not know it at this stage, he had severely damaged the 190 and the only hope for its pilot was to climb so that he could bale out. As the 190 went up in a steep climb Ramsey fired again but was hampered by a stoppage of the starboard inner cannon, which jammed after firing only sixty rounds. He also had to throttle back and apply coarse rudder to avoid overshooting. During its climb various bits of debris streamed back from the 190 and its hood was jettisoned. With his ammunition exhausted, Ramsey called on Watson to move in, but before he could open fire the 190 turned onto its back at 4,000 ft and the pilot baled out. The Typhoons circled for several minutes to give Mayday calls and the German pilot appeared to be alive as he descended on his parachute. It seems likely that Ramsey's victim was Obfw Herbert Dobroch, but despite his calls for assistance, he was not picked up. (During this raid another Fw 190 flown by Fw Adam Fischer was shot down by the Hastings defences. He also did not survive.)

The rest of the month was mainly uneventful and there was no further contact with the enemy. On 31 May the squadron took off at 1100 hrs to provide cover for Bomphoons but the operation was scrubbed when bad weather was encountered and all aircraft returned to Lympne after twenty minutes. Later in the day eight Typhoons were ordered to attack R-Boats that had been reported between Flushing and Blankenberge. In the event none were seen and the only vessels to be encountered were a number of fishing boats. Some flak was experienced from the Dutch coast but otherwise the operation passed without incident.

Towards the end of May No. 1 Squadron said goodbye to Roy Wilkinson who was promoted to Wing Commander and given the command of RAF Gravesend at the end of his tour. His leaving was marked by the obligatory party in which many ended the night a little the worse for wear. Les Scott took over temporary command until the new CO S/L Tony Zweigbergk arrived on the 30th. He was twenty-seven years of age and had been a civilian pilot before the war having worked for a time providing joy rides in aircraft such as the de Havilland DH.60 Moth before joining Imperial Airways. His last posting prior to joining No. 1 Squadron was with No. 181 Squadron, which had flown Typhoons since September 1942.

June got off to a quiet start with four uneventful scrambles on the 1st. An early morning Rhubarb flown the following day by Moose Mossip and Walter Ramsey was rather more dramatic, especially for the latter. The pair took off at 0940 hrs and made for the area to the north-west of Lille, taking in Bergues, Hazebrouck, Bailleul and Armentières. They were on the lookout for trains and Mossip damaged four in all, but as Ramsey was pulling out of a dive after attacking another near Armentières his aircraft was hit, either by a ground obstruction or by flak, and this caused damage to the leading edge of the starboard wing and its associated fuel tank. The petrol in this tank quickly drained away and Ramsey was left with the prospect of having to fly approximately sixty miles with a damaged fuel system just to make it back to the English coast.

As he flew back in cloud his engine kept cutting out on a regular basis and several times he thought that he would have to bale out. In preparation he jettisoned the cockpit doors but had considerable difficulty in doing so. This was an intricate operation on early Typhoons and involved crossing the arms so that the right hand operated the jettison lever for the port door with the starboard door being released by the left hand. The roof panel was released automatically at the same time. On each occasion that the engine cut out, it picked up again allowing Ramsey to carry on a little further. On his way back he made three Mayday calls but eventually a familiar section of coastline appeared through a gap in the clouds and he thought that he might make it after all. At that moment his engine cut again but this time it did not re-start and he was left with no alternative but to carry out a wheels-up landing, tantalisingly close to Lympne aerodrome. He made an excellent touch down but the field he had selected was a little too short and his aircraft overran through a boundary fence into the adjacent field. This contained a fine crop of peas and with commendable composure considering the circumstances Ramsey got out to eat a few while he waited for assistance. His Typhoon (R8752 JX-L) was examined by Chunky Chown and it was thought that the damage may have been caused by hitting a telegraph pole. Unfortunately Ramsey's favourite Typhoon was not considered to be repairable and it had to be struck off charge.

On 4 June James MacLachlan flew to Lympne in a Mustang I (FD442) that had been modified especially for his use. It was armed with four 20-mm Hispano cannon and was one of the fastest single engined fighters at low level. MacLachlan's lust for action had resulted in a proposal to carry out long-range Intruder missions with this aircraft, the most audacious element being that they were to be carried out by day. MacLachlan had long been on a quest for revenge following the loss of his arm but this had been compounded by the death of his brother, F/L Gordon MacLachlan of No. 616 Squadron, who had been shot down and killed on 16 April. Having obtained the reluctant acceptance of Fighter Command for his scheme, MacLachlan then requested assistance from his former squadron. He took off from Lympne together with three Typhoons of Black section which were to create a diversion, and hopefully no little confusion, as he made for Orleans and Beauvais. The operation was not an unqualified success however as a lack of cloud cover over France meant that it would have been too dangerous to continue and he returned without having fired his guns.

Offensive operations over the next couple of days were mainly abortive with a shipping recce by Tony Zweigbergk and Des Perrin on 5 June being abandoned half way across the Channel due to bad weather. The following day the squadron had been due to escort Bomphoons of 3 Squadron in an attack on Boulogne harbour but this was also cancelled. On 8 June S/L Ray Harries of No. 91 Squadron flew in to Lympne in his Spitfire XII. Following 'certain remarks' in the Mess concerning the relative merits of the Spitfire and Typhoon; a race was arranged between Harries and Tony Zweigbergk from Lympne to Hastings. The Spitfire XII was powered by a Rolls-Royce Griffon III engine with a single-stage supercharger and was optimised for low level operations. It took an immediate lead and the Typhoon was still about 200 yards behind at the finish line, although it was beginning to close the gap. It was felt that if the race had been three miles longer the Typhoon would have won.

Every squadron needed its 'press-on' types, however the attitude of Moose Mossip would have been difficult for anyone to beat. The squadron diary noted that he 'would rather fly than eat, and he would rather eat than anything'. On 11 June he took off in R8631 at 0500 hrs on a Rhubarb operation that covered the area Lumbres – Aire – Lillers. The weather was ideal with a visibility of fifteen miles, although there was some fog in the valleys. His first attack took place at Lumbres where he shot up a train in the station, causing it to blow up. He then flew on to Aire and left a barge burning before attacking another train on a turntable at Lillers. This was left in a cloud of steam but another train in the same area escaped when his cannons jammed. During the day eleven sections patrolled Dungeness, Hastings and Beachy Head without incident.

Having had to abort a Rhubarb operation on 14 June due to unsuitable weather, Les Scott and P/O S.P. Dennis had another go on the 16th. They took off at 0450 hrs and crossed the French coast at Cap Gris Nez before flying to Béthune. Between here and Douai they accounted for nine trains, one of which appeared to be carrying petrol as it was left burning furiously. On their way home they ran into heavy flak and the Typhoon flown by Dennis (DN585) was hit, although not seriously. The flak also had the effect of acting as a pointer for Fw 190s of 4/JG 26 that were in the area and both Typhoons were engaged. Les Scott managed to fire at a 190 that was on Dennis's tail but was attacked himself by two more and was thus unable to help his wingman any further. The latter was last seen heading off at high speed with two 190s directly behind him.

The Typhoon flown by Scott was also hit and he lost the use of his boost override, which put him at quite a disadvantage. During the fight he had selected partial flap to improve his manoeuvrability, but had then forgot to raise them again, which cost him even more speed. He attempted to escape in cloud but this was not extensive enough to be of much use and the Fw 190s had little difficulty in following. During one of their attacks as he came out of cloud his Typhoon was hit again and Scott was wounded in the arm and leg. To add to his predicament his engine began to cut occasionally but he managed to find a slightly bigger cloud than the others and on coming out of the other side was able to dive to sea level before the Germans could respond. The 190 that had fired at Scott was flown by Lt Helmut Hoppe who claimed him as his tenth victory even though he made it back to Lympne without further incident. His Typhoon (R7919) did have to be written off due to the combat damage it had received and was subsequently used for spares. Dennis did not return and was later reported to have been taken as a prisoner (he had been shot down by Lt Dietrich Kehl of the 4th *Staffel* who thus recorded his first combat victory).

Scott was taken to hospital in Orpington where he quickly recovered from his injuries although it would be nearly eight weeks before he was fit to fly again. Over the next few days there was little contact with the enemy although Moose Mossip and Sgt W.A. Booker got a hot reception during a shipping recce off Boulogne on 17 June. Reports had been received that a German ASR operation was under way but apart from five small fishing boats, nothing was seen. Most of the defensive patrols were also unproductive if not without incident. On 25 June F/O Jim Campbell (R7877 – Red 1) and Sgt Syd Cunningham (DN451 – Red 2) were scrambled at 1650 hrs and not long afterwards Campbell hit a balloon cable, which slightly damaged one of the wings of his Typhoon. Of more concern was the fact that Cunningham was flying directly behind and caught the full weight of the cut cable, damaging the wings, propeller and windscreen. He managed to return to Lympne with about 30 ft of cable wrapped around his propeller but landed safely. He was uninjured apart from some minor cuts to his arm.

On 29 June James MacLachlan was ready for another attempt at a long-range sortie over France and this time he was to be accompanied by F/L Geoffrey Page (also of AFDU) in another Mustang. Page was another pilot who had a particular score to settle as he had suffered severe burns when shot down during the Battle of Britain and had undergone numerous operations led by the skilled plastic surgeon Sir Archibald McIndoe. The weather conditions on 29 June were perfect with a solid overcast, good visibility and only light winds. Over the last three weeks the two pilots had been honing their low level navigation skills by constant practice over the UK and by now were as ready as they could possibly be. Once again No. 1 Squadron was to provide a diversion and Red section comprising Tony Zweigbergk (EK176), Zulu Watson (EJ982), W/O W.H. Dunwoodie (R8708) and W/O G. Hardie (DN502) flew with them during the initial stages of the operation, climbing to 1,500 ft over Criel-sur-Mer and firing their guns as the Mustangs 'nipped' into France. After they had departed Tony Zweigbergk shot up a trawler off the French coast on the way home.

The Mustangs of MacLachlan and Page made for the Paris area where they found considerable activity around Rambouillet to the south-west. Here they encountered several aircraft that were identified as Henschel Hs 126s but were in fact Focke-Wulf Fw 56 Stossers of a training group. Four were claimed as being shot down, the actual losses being two, although another had to be written off after a crash-landing by its wounded pilot. The fourth Fw 56 landed safely having sustained some damage. Flying on to Bretigny two Ju 88s were seen about to land. One was shot down and the other was badly damaged and came down on the aerodrome. Having used up all their ammunition MacLachlan and Page began their return journey and eventually landed at Tangmere (in recognition of their feat MacLachlan was awarded a second bar to his DFC and Page was given the DFC). Perhaps insired by their example, Moose Mossip went off on a Rhubarb operation to the St Omer area in the late afternoon and damaged six trains to bring the squadron score up to ninety-two. He also damaged a barge at Lillers, which was left on fire, but had a major fright near Desvres when he nearly flew into several tall chimneys.

By now No. 1 Squadron had settled into life at Lympne, the transition having been eased by the attentions of Mrs Davis who was the camp's Good Samaritan. Also known as Mrs Miniver, or Mrs Mobile, she toured the dispersals three times a day offering tea and snacks and her services came to be indispensible. Mrs Davis was also the proud owner of a Poodle bitch who was heavily pregnant. A sweep was rapidly organised as to the number of pups that would emerge and eventually nine saw the light of day. However, just as the money had been given to the winner, three more arrived and he had to hand it over to Sgt L.E. 'Spike' Watson. One of the pups was given to the squadron where he became known as Honourable-Sergeant Tiffy and featured in several group photographs.

July was to prove to be a rather disappointing month in more ways than one. The trend was set on the 1st when eight Typhoons led by the CO escorted Bomphoons of No. 3 Squadron. Having joined up over Manston they only made it half way across the Channel before bad weather forced an early return. In contrast Moose Mossip was to be thwarted the following day for the opposite reason as clear conditions over France prevented his attempt at another Rhubarb operation. Throughout the month two aircraft were lost in accidents. On 6 July Zulu Watson crashed on take-off in EJ982, however a much more serious event occurred on the 15th.

A two-aircraft section led by P/O J.M. Chalifour (EK228) was scrambled at 2100 hrs but as he was returning to base, the tail of his Typhoon broke away as he was diving through 10,000 ft. Chalifour was killed when his aircraft crashed at Paddlesworth near Hawkinge. This was the first occasion that a tailplane failure had afflicted No. 1 Squadron but it was the fourteenth in all, of which only one pilot had survived. At the end of 1942 a modification programme had been initiated in which fishplates were fitted to the rear transport joint, together with internal stiffening, and the overall strength factor had been increased in the order of 20 per cent. This had the effect of reducing the accident rate but it did not eliminate it completely. It was then thought that harmonic vibrations could lead to failure of the elevator mass balance and that the break-ups might be due to flutter, but despite further modifications in this area, structural failures continued to occur right to the end of the Typhoon's service life. Sadly for No. 1 Squadron in 'Collie' it had lost one of its best-loved pilots and one of its most colourful characters.

There was further bad news on 18 July when it was discovered that James MacLachlan had failed to return from another Intruder mission over France. He had been flying with F/L Geoffrey Page once again but shortly after crossing the

177

French coast near Dieppe MacLachlan's Mustang began to trail smoke and climbed steeply to 1,000 ft. As there were no enemy aircraft present it had either been struck by small arms fire from the ground or had suffered engine failure. MacLachlan slid his hood back as though he intended baling out but then appeared to change his mind and instead attempted a force-landing in a small field. His approach speed was too high however and he overshot the field and careered into a small wood where his aircraft began to disintegrate. Page circled the crash site but could see no sign of life. It transpired that MacLachlan had survived the crash but had sustained severe head injuries, which led to his death on 31 July.

For the rest of the month No. 1 Squadron's duties were mainly defensive with just a few sorties to the other side of the Channel to prevent boredom setting in. On 21 July Moose Mossip and Jim Campbell (the squadron's train and barge specialists respectively) made two attempts at a Rhubarb operation but were frustrated on both occasions by the weather. They had better luck two days later and having crossed the French coast at St Inglevert, they flew on to Hazebrouck, Menin and Ypres before coming out at Dunkirk. Mossip attacked three trains but was hampered by stoppages in three of his four cannons. Campbell had no such worries and he was able to damage three trains and four barges. On their return they were covered by Black section comprising F/O H.J. Wilkinson and F/Sgt James Fairbairn.

The only other activity of note was a Roadstead operation on 26 July in which Tony Zweigbergk led nine aircraft as escort to a squadron of rocket-firing Hurricanes. A number of ships had been reported off Dunkirk and the intention was for the Typhoons to draw fire as the Hurricanes went into the attack, however the 'convoy' turned out to be the local fishing fleet. The next day six Typhoons covered an ASR operation near the Somme estuary. Although enemy aircraft were reported to be in the area, none were seen and the only excitement was when P/O R.A. 'Dusty' Miller bounced a squadron of Spitfires, which 'broke in wild confusion'. Once again No. 1 Squadron was beginning to feel a little hard done by and on most days had to watch large numbers of fighters and bombers as they crossed the Channel to attack targets in northern France. The lack of action was put to Air Vice-Marshal Hugh Saunders (AOC 11 Group) during a visit to the squadron on 28 July and he promised that more offensive work would be forthcoming, which cheered everyone up considerably.

August got off to a quiet start however and on the 2nd just one patrol was carried out from Dungeness to Beachy Head. This only served to provide entertainment for thousands of holidaymakers who despite calls to stay at home had made for the seaside for the bank holiday to take advantage of fine sunny weather. The next day F/L Fred Murray led two sections to Calais in the evening on the lookout for some E-Boats that had been reported in the vicinity but despite unlimited visibility none were seen. Once again the Typhoons had to run the gauntlet of heavy and accurate flak from the gun batteries along the coast.

On 4 August six aircraft took part in a calibration exercise in the morning, which involved flying on a course of 220 degrees at 10,000 ft. This took them towards the Cherbourg peninsula, which they nearly reached before they were allowed to return. In the afternoon an ASR scramble led to frantic activity at Lympne as eight Typhoons all tried to take off at the same time. Only seven actually made it however as one burst a tyre and did not get airborne. This left Spike Watson without a leader and he wisely decided to return. Unfortunately he approached the aerodrome as the squadron diary put it 'with both finger and flaps up' and in the resultant crash-landing the undercarriage was smashed, as was the engine. To make matters worse he was flying R8631, which was Moose Mossip's regular (and favourite) Typhoon which he had used on many of his train-bashing sorties. To say that Watson was unpopular for a time would be an understatement. The patrol flew up the Belgian coast as far as Zeebrugge but apart from two rescue launches, nothing was seen. A busy day was rounded off in the evening with two scrambles over the Channel as enemy aircraft were apparently harassing some Spitfires. On the first operation only the Spitfires were intercepted and although nothing was seen on the second scramble, Control later informed the squadron that they had been very close to an enemy formation that was diving through 8,000 ft as the Typhoons were climbing to the same height.

The next day saw the welcome return of Les Scott who looked fit and bronzed after the recent good weather. Command of 'B' Flight had passed to Des Perrin in his absence and Scott's return was as a supernumerary as it appeared that he was about to be given command of a squadron. Over the next few days a period of bad weather considerably reduced the amount of operational flying that was carried out. On 7 August the CO's Typhoon was flown (with a certain amount of trepidation) by S/L Gordon Sinclair who was known as 'supernumerary Sid' and had been with the squadron since March. Inevitably something went wrong and the power pack for the radio went up in smoke, which led to a hurried landing. Fortunately there was very little damage but Sinclair was rather shaken all the same. The squadron was still operating a solitary Hurricane (AG216), which was used by new pilots and as a general runabout. On 8 August it was being flown by Walter Ramsey. It was nearly a year since he had been in the cockpit of a Hurricane but despite bringing it in for a perfect touch down, the tailwheel fell off, the squadron diarist concluding that the only possible reason for this was 'pure caprice'.

The next day dawned bright and sunny. This came as a considerable surprise to the weather section, which had predicted cloud and rain. The squadron diary had an explanation for this however as any wind from a northerly direction apparently left them with no clues at all. The diary then reverted to the Middle Ages with the following.

There were three occasions when pairs of our warriors mounted their chargers and lowered their visors, but the days of chivalry seem to be past and the panting steeds were brought to rest without entering the jousting arena.

Suffice to say that, once again, nothing happened. In the early evening Tony Zweigbergk and Les Scott flew to Manston to be on readiness for Intruder operations. Unfortunately they were surplus to requirements and returned, somewhat disgruntled, before dark.

The only notable event over the next few days was further abuse to the squadron's aircraft. In the evening of the 12 August F/O Jimmy 'Pickles' Wiley was returning from a scramble when he was another to succumb to 'finger 'trouble' by forgetting to lower his flaps. Unlike Spike Watson a few days before he was at least able to rescue the situation but for a time it looked as though his Typhoon was about to 'savage' the Station HQ. Indeed it was only prevented from doing so by a violent groundloop. Two days later it was the turn of Chunky Chown to go purple with rage amid much gnashing of teeth. Having spent several hours repairing the Hurricane, he then had to watch as it was damaged once again, this time in a heavy landing by P/O H. Gray.

In the early morning of 16 August four sections were scrambled to carry out an ASR operation but during this, EK176, flown by F/O L.J. Wood, developed engine trouble and he had to force-land on the beaches at Lydd. Unfortunately he touched down on extremely rough ground, sustaining severe head injuries from which he did not regain consciousness and he died the following morning. Later in the day Typhoons of Nos 1 and 198 Squadrons escorted a large force of Bostons of 2 Group, which were to carry out a low level attack on an armament and steel works at Denain. The Typhoons flew at 5,000 ft and were able to give cover as far as Albert, approximately fifty miles into France. The bombers were then left to attack the target but before more squadrons were able to escort them on their way home four Bostons (all from No. 88 Squadron) were shot down. This particular trip did No. 1 Squadron's morale a lot of good and it was anticipated that there would be many similar ones in the future.

This proved to be a somewhat forlorn hope, especially after the arrival of No. 609 Squadron at Lympne on 19 August to provide even more competition. This unit also flew Typhoons and was commanded by S/L Pat Thornton-Brown. When they had settled in it was decided that as far as standby sections were concerned, Nos 1 and 609 Squadrons would undertake to do alternate days, so overall there was even less activity than there had been before. On 23 August there was good news as it was announced that Les Scott had been awarded the DFC, however at the same time it was also discovered that he was about to leave to join No. 198 Squadron. To mark his leaving a bumper party was held at Hythe in his honour. After his departure the role of 'B' Flight commander was officially taken over by Des Perrin.

For some time it had been the policy for new pilots to convert to the Typhoon at Tangmere, which provided rather more space than the confines of Lympne. On

23 August Fred Murray flew there followed by P/O H. Gray in the Hurricane as the latter was about to fly a Typhoon for the first time. Gray made two successful circuits and landings before taking off for a third time. The onlookers were then horrified to see him initiate what appeared to be a slow roll, which inevitably ended with the Typhoon entering a spin before crashing three miles north-west of Tangmere, killing Gray instantly.

The squadron's morale at this time was not helped by the fact that it only had ten Typhoons available for operations. It was understood that most other Typhoon squadrons were in a similar position prompting Tony Zweigbergk to utter the ultimate heresy; that perhaps it would have been better to stick to Spitfire production after all. Towards the end of August the squadron, along with all others, was re-established with a CO, twenty-two officer and NCO pilots, an Adjutant, doctor, Intelligence officer and eighteen NCOs and other ranks, who were referred to as 'key personnel'. Everyone else went to an echelon as it had been decided to form maintenance echelons, which would remain in one place rather than follow the squadrons each time they moved, as had been the case previously. There were more unusual happenings as all leave was stopped on 25 August, which led everyone to believe that something big was about to happen. This was the beginning of Operation *Starkey*, a spoof invasion of northern France, which was to reach its anti-climax early in September.

Just as a reminder that they were actually fighter pilots, Tony Zweigbergk and Des Perrin decided to fly a Rhubarb operation on 29 August. They got as far as Boulogne in ideal weather where they saw two Bf 109s. It had been some time since enemy aircraft had been encountered but the German pilots were not particularly aggressive and made sure that they made all their turns at a safe and respectful distance. At the earliest opportunity they beat it back to France leaving the two Typhoon pilots to fly a short and uneventful sweep of the French coast.

The month of August ended with more questions than answers. The roar of large numbers of aircraft heading south for France was accompanied by a significant increase in Allied naval activity in the Channel and yet the squadron was still in the dark as to what it all meant. The squadron diary bemoaned the fact that they had not been told anything and ended with the words 'what will September bring?'

In the event September brought a very congested aerodrome as two Spitfire squadrons (Nos 41 and 91) flew in from Tangmere in the early hours of the 1st in case they were needed to cover minesweepers operating in the Channel. Four new Typhoons arrived for No. 1 Squadron during the day so that each Flight now had seven, but more were needed to allow for unserviceability and for the time being two sections of four aircraft would be the squadron's limit. On 2 September the mass of aircraft now assembled at Lympne spent most of the day covering destroyers and minesweepers in the Channel and in the evening No. 1 Squadron took part in an operation that was described as the largest of the war so far. It involved hundreds of fighters and bombers with Nos 1 and 609 Squadrons providing withdrawal cover for Bostons returning from an attack on a rail target in France. Des Perrin and F/Sgt Con Devey flew close to a Boston that had been shot up but otherwise the operation was uneventful.

Over the next few days the squadron spent most of its time providing cover to minesweepers, which occasionally ventured near enough to the French coast for the Typhoons to be fired on by the guns at Boulogne. During these operations most of the drama centred on Sgt A.R.H. Browne. As he was taking off in DN432 on 5 September he was a little too aggressive in raising the tail of his Typhoon so that its propeller struck the ground. This bent each blade back at right angles by about 8 inches but he then continued with his patrol 'without noticing anything unusual'. Two days later he failed to change fuel tanks soon enough in EK113 and nearly went into the sea before, to everyone's relief, his engine picked up again and he was able to climb away.

Operations on 8 September did not exactly go according to plan and only started as the weather began to deteriorate. The squadron was scheduled to escort twelve Whirlwind fighter-bombers with departure planned for 1715 hrs, however panic reigned after take-off when it was found that the Form D actually said 1815 hrs. Rendezvous was eventually made over Hastings at 12,000 ft with the other escort squadron, but of the Whirlibombers there was no sign. Many formations of Mitchells, Venturas and Marauders were seen flying around rather aimlessly and eventually the Controller admitted that there had been a slight technical hitch. An instruction to orbit was soon amended to 'pancake' and all aircraft returned to their bases. There was no further flying but the night sky was alight with anti-aircraft fire from the other side of the Channel and buildings shook as bombs fell on the enemy coastal defences.

Operation *Starkey* came to its conclusion on 9 September when an invasion fleet set sail from the south coast in the early morning, only to turn around a few hours later under cover of a thick smoke screen and head back from whence it had come. *Starkey* had been intended to disrupt German troop movements to the Russian and Italian fronts by giving the impression that a full-scale invasion was imminent. Unfortunately the Germans were not taken in by the attempted ruse and hardly a shot was fired during the 'assault phase'. During the day No. 1 Squadron flew one escort mission for Whirlibombers attacking a target near Hardelot but once again there was no reaction.

The sense of anti-climax after *Starkey* was not helped by the weather, which included a terrific thunderstorm on 12 September with lightning of amazing brilliance. Conditions had improved somewhat two days later, which allowed Moose Mossip (JP592) and F/Sgt Con Devey (JP483) to fly to Manston for Intruder operations. Compared with the long-range Hurricane IIC that the squadron had flown previously, the Typhoon was not as easy to fly at night and without LR tanks did not have the endurance, the maximum sortie time being around 1 hour 30 minutes. Both pilots took off just before midnight but they were to have contrasting fortunes. Devey saw nothing of interest and then had a scare as he discovered that he had lost all the fluid to his hydraulics. Mossip fared rather better and damaged two trains and three barges in the St Omer – Hazebrouck area. This brought the squadron's total of trains to 100. Having got a taste for Intruder work Mossip was at it again the following night and on this occasion managed to acquire two 500-lb bombs. Flying JP677 he took off from Manston at 2350 hrs along with sixteen RP Hurricanes and seven Bomphoons for an attack on Abbeville aerodrome.

On 16 September it was back to bomber escort work as eight Typhoons led by Tony Zweigbergk formed part of the close escort to Mitchells attacking a power station at Rouen. Six enemy aircraft were seen but such was the level of aerial dominance that had now been created, they made no attempt to attack. It was a similar situation three days later when No. 1 Squadron escorted Bomphoons of No. 3 Squadron in an attack on Woensdrecht in Holland. Once again a small number of German fighters put in a brief appearance but were careful to keep well clear of the RAF aircraft. By now the main threat came from flak defences and on this occasion the anti-aircraft fire was particularly heavy and accurate, although all aircraft returned safely.

Having been impressed by the Typhoon's potential as a fighter-bomber, Moose Mossip persuaded Des Perrin to load 500 lb bombs to his aircraft and they set off on a Rhubarb operation on 20 September escorted by Jimmy Wiley and Con Devey. The principal target was the French rail system but low cloud over the continent turned the mission into an anti-shipping Roadstead from Etretat to Boulogne. Nothing was seen however and the bombs had to be jettisoned in the sea. This particularly upset Mossip who believed in the old adage 'Waste not, want not', and he wanted. On 23 September eight Typhoons of No. 1 Squadron (together with nine from 609) acted as close escort to twenty B-24 Liberators, which were making a feint over the North Sea. The intention was to draw fighters away from a raid taking place elsewhere but only one was seen and it quickly dived for home.

The rest of September was relatively quiet although the squadron was able to assist in two successful rescues from the Channel on the 26th. The first involved Walter Ramsey and Ned Crowley who patrolled for 1 hour 15 minutes as an ASR Walrus picked up S/L Ian Ormston of No. 401 Squadron. The second operation was to save P/O Charles Demoulin of No. 609 Squadron who had ditched following engine trouble. This involved P/O Dusty Miller and W/O W.G. Hardie who were later joined by Des Perrin, Jimmy Wiley, Con Devey and Sgt A.R.H. Browne. P/O Demoulin was rescued just in time as he had lost his dinghy and his Mae West had been punctured. An ASR Spitfire was able to drop another dinghy to him and he was picked up by a rescue launch later.

In early October a number of pilots received their commissions including Con Devey and Walter Ramsey. At the same time Johnnie Higham was promoted to Flying Officer. From an operational point of view very little changed and on 2 October the squadron was involved in another Liberator escort over the North Sea. This involved flying at 23,000 ft, an altitude that most pilots had not seen for a long time, if at all. One can conclude that it was rather cold from the following comment in the squadron diary – 'A brass monkey carried by one of the pilots was heard to say that at that height it had done the most extraordinary things to him'.

Due to a combination of poor weather and squadron release very little happened over the next few days and on 6 October the pilots even had time to visit the Napier factory in Acton, London, to learn a little more about the Sabre engine. It was not until 8 October that another escort operation was laid on and on this occasion No. 1 Squadron was able to put up twelve aircraft instead of the usual eight. They were joined by nine Typhoons of No. 609 Squadron but the Mitchells failed to bomb St Omer/Longuenesse due to cloud over the target. The Typhoons swept St Omer on the way back but did not encounter any enemy fighters. There was no flying for the next five days due to fog and occasional drizzle. On 14 October notification was received that Des Perrin had been awarded a DFC but this news had to be wired to him as he was on leave. He sent a telegram back to say that the drinks were on him, at which point there was a stampede for the bar.

On 15 October Moose Mossip decided it was time for another Rhubarb operation and talked Con Devey into providing cover for him. Mossip's Typhoon again carried two 500 lb bombs and the two aircraft took off from Tangmere. Mossip dropped his bombs with great accuracy in the middle of an electrical transformer near Samer and the pair then sprayed the area with cannon fire. Gun posts and buildings used by gun crews were also attacked by both pilots.

No. 1 Squadron had its busiest day for some time on 21 October with several early morning scrambles. One of these involved Jimmy Wiley and F/Sgt James Fairbairn (Green section) who were airborne at 0758 hrs on reports of German activity over the Channel. After flying at 355 mph IAS on several vectors at sea level, an Fw 190 was seen in their eleven o'clock position, about 300 ft above. It was flying considerably slower than the Typhoons, which had no trouble in closing to firing range. Wiley turned to port and positioned his aircraft behind the 190, opening fire at 300 yards with a two-second burst but as his overtaking speed was relatively high he had to break away to port. As he did so his reflector gunsight slipped down so that on subsequent attacks he had to hold it in position with his left hand.

The attack was then taken up by Fairbairn who fired two bursts from the port quarter as the 190 went into a 360-degree turn to port. Up to this point in the combat the 190 had not been hit but despite his gunsight problems Wiley achieved hits on the port wing root on his next attack prompting the German pilot to dive to sea level and head for the French coast. Wiley followed and used up the remainder of his ammunition but did not see any more strikes. The 190 then began to climb in an attempt to reach cloud cover but this only provided Fairbairn with another attacking opportunity. He opened fire from the starboard quarter with a long burst closing to 50 yards, achieving numerous strikes between the windscreen and engine cowling. This produced a large sheet of flame and various pieces of debris flew off, some hitting the Typhoon in the port tank and port engine panel. The 190 immediately lost height and turned on its back before crashing into the sea. Both pilots returned 'with their tails well up' having recorded the squadron's 234th confirmed 'kill' of the war.

There was further cause for celebration on 23 October when Moose Mossip was also awarded a DFC. This was extremely popular and everyone felt that it was long overdue. Like most other squadrons No. 1 did not need much of an excuse to hold a party and in the evening a suitable event was held in Ashford. The next day a sweep by eight aircraft was flown to Lille – St Omer – Gravelines but apart from extremely accurate flak as the squadron flew over St Omer at 14,000 ft, it was uneventful. This proved to be the last major operation of the month as bad weather prevented all but a few scrambles and defensive patrols.

Having carried out practice flying in the morning of 1 November, the squadron came on state at 1300 hrs and was called upon shortly after. Green section, comprising Bob Hornall and F/O H.J. Wilkinson, was on standby and was ordered off at 1340 hrs to intercept enemy aircraft that had been picked up on radar. These were operating on the other side of the Channel and the Typhoons were given a vector of 110 degrees, which took them towards Cap Gris Nez. As normal they crossed the Channel at zero feet but when six miles short of the French coast they were ordered to climb at 8,000 ft and join up with two Spitfires of 501 Squadron, which had also been scrambled from Hawkinge. The four aircraft flew to Cap Gris Nez at this height where they came across three Bf 109Gs, which approached them from south-east of Calais. These were soon joined by another two from the Gravelines area and a dogfight ensued.

Bob Hornall attacked one of the 109s using full deflection from inside a tight turn and saw his shells hit the port wing. Almost immediately he was fired upon by another of the 109s from his starboard beam and tracer bullets passed close to his tail. Having successfully evaded this attack he joined up with the Spitfires that were mixing it with three 109s over Calais. By now height had been lost to 4,000 ft but the combat soon fizzled out and both sides turned for home. F/O Wilkinson, who had become separated from Hornall, saw a 109 dive towards cloud off Calais but did not have enough time to carry out an attack before it disappeared. After searching briefly for his leader, he returned to Lympne alone.

With darker evenings, Intruder missions could be launched rather earlier and on 6 November Moose Mossip took off from Manston at 2045 hrs to head for northern France. He shot up two motor cars and a train near Le Touquet but received a bullet in his ammunition box, which fortunately did very little damage. The following night he tried again and was joined by Des Perrin. Both aircraft carried 500 lb bombs and the intention was for Mossip to drop his on Abbeville aerodrome while Perrin did the same at Poix. Over France however there was extremely poor visibility and the mission had to be aborted. Perrin jettisoned his bombs in the sea but Mossip, reluctant as ever to waste his precious ordnance, let his go over the French coast.

During 1943 it had become apparent that Germany was developing terror weapons for use against the UK and this had led to the Bomber Command raid on Peenemunde on the night of 17/18 August. Although this attack delayed deployment of the *Wehrmacht*'s V-2 ballistic missile, it did nothing to disrupt the *Luftwaffe*'s V-1 flying bomb programme as it had only been test flown at Peenemunde. By October 1943 photo-reconnaissance of northern France had begun to show unusual construction works, which it was thought were connected with V-1 launching sites.

No. 1 Squadron's first involvement in operations to disrupt use of the V-1 occurred on 9 November when every available Typhoon was required to fly to Tangmere for Ramrod 303. This was for an attack on a site at Martinvast on the Cherbourg peninsula. By now the squadron establishment had been significantly improved and sixteen aircraft (eleven bombers and five fighters) took to the air. On arriving at Tangmere it was clear that this was going to be a maximum effort as the aerodrome was covered with Typhoons in orderly rows. No. 1 Squadron was due to fly with No. 609 Squadron as the fourth wave but there were doubts about the visibility. A thick haze led to the operation being put back until the afternoon but having finally taken off and flown as far as Dungeness, it was eventually scrubbed altogether due to continued concern over the weather and all bombs had to be jettisoned over the sea.

Another attempt was made on 10 November in which seventeen aircraft were made available thanks to the untiring efforts of Chunky Chown and his team in Echelon. The target once again was Martinvast and No. 1 Squadron flew with No. 609 Squadron as the second wave. As the Typhoons approached they were greeted by a curtain of heavy flak, the explosions of which gave one pilot the impression that there was a layer of thick black cloud over the target. It was the first time that many of the pilots had carried bombs but despite this all were dropped in the target area after diving from 11,000 ft to 5,000 ft. Afterwards a strafing attack was made during which light flak caused superficial damage to the Typhoons flown by Moose Mossip and Jim Campbell. The fact that the latter was hit came as no surprise to his long-suffering ground crew as he often returned with a few bullet holes in his aircraft. Later in the day the 'Lympne Wing' did a sweep over Belgium, however the ground could not be seen through 8/10 cloud and thick haze. After being vectored here and there by Control, a return was made with F/O Jimmy King (who had become separated) having joined up with No. 609 Squadron, much to their surprise and indignation.

The next day the squadron had the honour of flying three defensive patrols, the purpose of which were to provide protection to the King and Queen who were travelling by road from Sevenoaks to Brooklands to atttend a service to mark Armistice Day and the twenty-fifth anniversary of the end of the First World War. This was referred to as Operation *George*. Moose Mossip and Walter Ramsey took off at 1355 hrs to fly the first patrol and they were relieved by P/O Con Devey and W/O Fred Wyatt. The final patrol was conducted by F/O Jimmy King and F/Sgt Spike Watson who returned at 1715 hrs.

S/L James MacLachlan
in typically defiant pose
next to his Hurricane IIC
BD983 JX-Q. (IWM CH4015)

Harrison Taylor 'Moose'
Mossip was one of the real
characters in No.1 and
served with the squadron
for almost exactly two
years. (Joan Ramsey)

Sgt Walter Ramsey who
joined 1 Squadron
shortly after it moved to
Acklington in July 1942.
(Joan Ramsey)

Some of 1 Squadron's ground crew (L to R) Sgt Bob Renton, Snowy White and Jim Shelley. (Joan Ramsey)

Sgt G.C. 'Slim' Whitmore. (Joan Ramsey)

Sgt Ernie Glover later flew the F-86 Sabre and became the top scoring Canadian pilot in the Korean War. (Joan Ramsey)

George Edwards, Bill Dyer, Jack Payne and Bert Lacey take a break from servicing a 1 Squadron Typhoon. (Joan Ramsey)

More 1 Squadron ground crew (L to R) 'Tiny' Sharp, Ted Murray, Cpl Turner and Spud Murphy. (Joan Ramsey)

F/L Fred Murray was another long-serving member of 1 Squadron and became its 'A' Flight commander. He is standing in front of R7877 JX-T (formerly JX-K). (Joan Ramsey)

Sgt Walter Ramsey demonstrates the complicated door and hood design of the early Typhoons. (Joan Ramsey)

Des Perrin joined 1 Squadron in September 1941 and by mid-1943 was 'B' Flight commander. He continued to serve with No.1 until April 1944. (Tim Elkington)

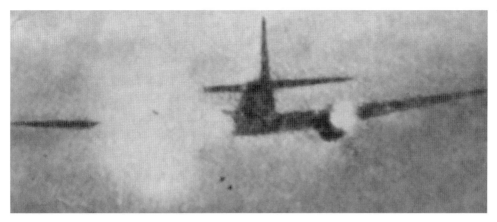

A still from camera gun film showing the last moments of an Me 210 that was shot down by a 1 Squadron Typhoon on 6 September 1942. (via Tim Elkington)

F/L Les Scott.
(Tim Elkington)

R7919 JX-R was 1 Squadron's first Typhoon and survived until 16 June 1943 when it was badly damaged during combat with Fw 190s. (Tim Elkington)

No.1 Squadron July 1943. Back row (L to R) Baker, King, Watson, Jackson, Browne, Hardie, Fairbairn, Gray, Bletcher, Wiley, Devey, Cunningham, Wilkinson, McCullough, Sinclair, Scrope-Davies (Adj) unknown. Front row (L to R) Campbell, Higham, Chown (Eng), Zweigbergk, Perrin, Miller, Heap (MO). (via Chris Thomas)

Typhoon R8752 JX-L after Walter Ramsey's forced landing on 2 June 1943. (via author)

JP592 JX-L was shot down on 25 November 1943 during an attack on a V-1 site at Martinvast killing F/O Jimmy Wiley. (Joan Ramsey)

F/O 'Moose' Mossip on the wing of his regular Typhoon JP677 JX-C. (IWM CH1147)

EK176 JX-K was lost on 16 August 1943 in a crash which killed F/O L.J. Wood. (via Chris Thomas)

Typhoon EJ983 JX-R. (Joan Ramsey)

The nose art on EJ983 shows a Thistle with the motto 'Scotch Mist' underneath. Also apparent are the two victory symbols of F/Sgt Bob Hornall. (Joan Ramsey)

JP841 was written off in a crash-landing at Lympne on 30 January 1944 following engine failure. (Joan Ramsey)

Typhoon JP961 JX-U being salvaged after it was shot down on 22 December 1943. (via Chris Thomas)

JR237 JX-I was also shot down on 22 December 1943, F/O J.W. Sutherland surviving to become a PoW. (via Chris Thomas)

P/O Con Devey and P/O Walter Ramsey (both foreground) at No.7 FIS shortly after leaving 1 Squadron in January 1944. (Joan Ramsey)

MN207 JX-I is seen at Martlesham Heath. It was one of the last Typhoons to be operated by 1 Squadron and features a sliding hood and long-range fuel tanks. (via Chris Thomas)

S/L David Cox who took over command of 1 Squadron on 31 December 1944. (via Chris Thomas)

No.1 Squadron in January 1945 with P/O Ken 'Tony' Weller sitting astride the nose. (via Chris Thomas)

Spitfires of 1 Squadron endure harsh winter weather at Manston in January 1945. (via Chris Thomas)

Spitfire IX MK644 JX-M was wrecked in a landing accident at Northolt on 2 March 1945 in which S/L David Cox was slightly injured. (via Chris Thomas)

Apart from a few Intruder sorties very little operational flying took place over the next two weeks due to persistent rain and by 18 November Lympne was only fit for emergency use. Conditions had improved somewhat by 23 November and on this day eight aircraft, assisted by No. 609 Squadron, bombed another V-1 site at Audingham. Two days later a return visit was made to Audingham in the morning with six aircraft piloted by Tony Zweigbergk, Ned Crowley, Johnnie Higham, Walter Ramsey, Moose Mossip and Jimmy King. After the attack all aircraft returned to Tangmere. Having been refuelled and rearmed they took off again at 1445 hrs for Ramrod 331, another attack on Martinvast, the only difference in personnel being that Jimmy Wiley replaced Johnnie Higham. The attack was carried out by five aircraft (Jimmy King having returned early with engine trouble) and once again bombing results were excellent with gun posts being shot up during the withdrawal. As the Typhoons were racing towards the coast Jimmy Wiley called up to say that his aircraft had been hit. He began to climb so that he had enough height to bale out but at 500 ft he was hit again and his Typhoon burst into flames before turning over and diving into the ground. The rest of the pilots returned in sombre mood knowing that there was no chance that the popular Canadian had survived.

On return the Typhoons landed at Lympne and among those counting the aircraft back was Walter Ramsey's wife Joan. On both missions Ramsey had flown JX-D (JR144) instead of his regular machine JX-L (JP592), which had been used instead by Jimmy Wiley. Joan was unaware of this change as she noted the code letters of the returning aircraft and as JX-L was not among them, she feared the worst. It was only some time later that she discovered that her husband had in fact returned safely.

On 26 November eight Typhoons escorted B-26 Marauders to Audingham and after the attack all aircraft dived to ground level and shot up a number of gun posts as they flew back towards the Channel. It appeared as though one of these blew up as Moose Mossip was flying directly overhead in JR144 as it was covered in mud and received extensive shrapnel damage. Despite this it continued to fly normally and he was able to make a safe return.

Bad weather at the end of November extended into the new month and the only event of note was the arrival of two new pilots. These were Flying Officers Neville Brown and Duncan McIntosh who had both flown Spitfires (Brown with No. 130 Squadron and McIntosh in Malta). As they had also flown Mustangs they were able to become operational on the Typhoon after just a few trips. The first action in December was Ramrod 350 on the 4th when eight aircraft bombed the aerodrome at Moorsele with No. 3 Squadron. Target identification was made difficult by thick haze at ground level but for once the flak defences were relatively tame. The only concern was the engine of P/O H.T. Jackson's Typhoon as it started to cut out badly just after bombing and continued to do so all the way back. He was accompanied by three other Typhoons but fortunately his Mayday calls did not have to be acted on and he made it home.

There was another influx of new pilots over the next couple of days including Flying Officers E.N.W. Marsh, E.G. Hutchin and R.W. Bridgman. By now the RAF's training organisation was beginning to deliver large numbers of pilots, more than was actually needed, and all three had been waiting a long time to be posted to a squadron. Sadly No. 1 Squadron lost another of its Canadian pilots on 7 December during a scramble just before midday. On returning from an unsuccessful attempt to intercept two enemy aircraft, W/O James Fairbairn and F/Sgt Spike Watson were ordered to Hawkinge as the weather at Lympne had closed in. Conditions were not much better at the alternative airfield, however Watson was able to make it. As he was unhappy with his first approach Fairbairn decided to go round again but in doing so he crashed into hills about three miles from Hawkinge and was killed instantly.

As operations were only taking place infrequently Tony Zweigbergk and a small party from the squadron took the opportunity to go to the theatre on 10 December to see the play 'No Orchids for Miss Blandish', which was finishing its run at Streatham. This was a 'shocking tale of vile and ruthless gangsterism', which everyone was particularly taken with. In fact some members of the squadron were so carried away with it that they apparently had to be restrained from taking part, especially in one scene that depicted a bar. Afterwards they met the cast who invited them to a party scheduled for the evening of 13 December. This went very well and also gave everyone the opportunity to forget about the funeral of James Fairbairn, which had taken place that morning at Brookwood military cemetery near Woking in Surrey.

On 14 December No. 609 Squadron left Lympne for Manston and was replaced by the RP Hurricanes of No. 137 Squadron. In the afternoon the order came through to 'bomb up' and eight aircraft were airborne at 1450 hrs for another 'special target' in France. The Typhoons were met by accurate heavy flak on the way in but all sixteen bombs were dropped in the target area from 7,000 ft down to 3,000 ft. Everyone had been instructed to withdraw at low level but due to the hostile reception this was hastily revised and the squadron retired discreetly at 6,000 ft instead. There was a similar operation three days later (Ramrod 371) but eight aircraft soon became seven when Con Devey had to jettison his bombs in the sea and return with engine trouble. The remaining aircraft bombed successfully before shooting up gun posts on the way out. All returned safely, however Walter Ramsey's Typhoon (JP679) was hit by ground fire, which left a large hole in the port aileron. Damage was also caused to the rudder and Perspex behind the cockpit.

Although the Typhoon had been in service for fifteen months its engine problems were far from over and these were to claim another No. 1 Squadron pilot on 21 December. Yellow section comprising Moose Mossip and F/Sgt Syd Cunningham were carrying out an ASR patrol between Dungeness and Boulogne when Cunningham reported that his engine was cutting. He was told to return to base immediately but nothing further was heard from him and it was assumed that he had gone down in the Channel (he had been flying JR144, which had only just been repaired after being peppered by shrapnel on 26 November).

To compound the squadron's recent troubles two more pilots failed to return from operations on 22 December. In the morning eight Typhoons, led by Fred Murray, took off to bomb construction works in the St Pol – Hesdin area. Although the bombing was again carried out successfully the flak defences hit the Typhoons flown by P/O Jack Sutherland and W/O Fred Wyatt, however both survived as prisoners of war. In the afternoon another attack was made on the same target. This was again led by Fred Murray but he had to return early (together with his No. 2, Zulu Watson) due to engine trouble. During the bombing attack Des Perrin had one of his bombs hang up but was unaware of this as he dived down to carry out a strafing attack on some of the gun positions. As he fired his cannons the reluctant bomb finally fell away and the blast from the explosion blew off his trimming tabs and made a large hole in the starboard wing. It was later a matter of some debate as to who had been the more frightened, Perrin or the German gun crew.

After another bombing attack on a V-1 site near St Omer on 23 December the weather deteriorated with several days of fog, which was welcomed by all as it allowed everyone to have a Merry Christmas in every sense, and with a clear conscience. On 28 December Des Perrin and Bob Hornall went to Manston in one of two Airspeed Oxfords that had recently been delivered to collect two of No. 198 Squadron's old Typhoons. This unit was being re-equipped with brand new aircraft that had long-range tanks and the new sliding hoods in place of the old 'Austin 7' doors. The fact that No. 1 Squadron had to put up with another unit's cast-offs did not go down too well. The squadron diary noted that they were not so fussy about the long-range tanks, but they rather liked the new hood design.

The year of 1943 was rounded off with three more bombing operations. The first (Ramrod 398) took place in the morning of 30 December but had to be aborted due to cloud in the target area. There was better luck later in the day when a construction site near Aire was successfully bombed. The next day a similar operation was laid on to a target near Abbeville and although there was considerable light flak in the target area, none of the Typhoons were hit. Of more concern was the withdrawal phase as very accurate heavy flak was experienced, however none of the aircraft were hit and only the pilots' nerves (and laundry) suffered.

The New Year began just as the old one had finished and in the morning of 1 January Tony Zweuigbergk led eight aircraft on Ramrod 407 against a construction works at Hesdin. On this occasion the squadron had a dual role. As well as bombing, it was also tasked with escorting RP Hurricanes of No. 184 Squadron to the same target. As the Hurricanes cruised at a lower speed, the Typhoons had to spend rather longer over 'Indian territory' than was considered healthy and it was unanimously considered that this was a most unsatisfactory type of operation. Although the attack was uneventful there was plenty of drama on return to Lympne. The Typhoon flown by F/O Duncan McIntosh dropped its starboard wing on landing and he opened up the engine to go round again. The wing however hit the ground throwing up clods of earth and in the process made a most unpleasant noise. The aircraft was swung round through 90 degrees and much to everyone's amazement became airborne again. His second landing was much better despite a badly bent wing tip and a jammed aileron. F/O Jimmy King had had a bomb hang up but as his R/T was unserviceable he was completely unaware of the fact. The sight of the ground crews running away from his aircraft as fast as they could go caused a certain amount of amusement on his part, however he soon stopped laughing when he saw a 500 lb bomb not far away, the offending ordnance having finally dropped off at the end of his landing run.

The next day the weather was not conducive to operations at squadron strength so four aircraft led by F/O Jim Campbell took off to attack a target at Ruiseauville but even here the conditions were not favourable and an alternative had to be selected. On 4 January it was back to escorting RP Hurricanes, and as the Typhoons had to attack after the Hurricanes had fired their rockets the bombing was not as accurate as it might have been. Later in the day eight aircraft bombed the V-1 site at Noyelle-en-Chaussee and on this occasion they took two additional Typhoons to act as fighter cover. By now the air was alive with aircraft and although these were invariably Allied, they still had to be watched carefully. The only mishap was when Bill Dunwoodie burst a tyre on take-off and his Typhoon (JP611) stood on its nose. Fortunately he was unhurt and little damage was done.

On 6 January four aircraft led by F/Sgt Harry Bletcher attempted to bomb another V-1 site but were again thwarted by the weather. Instead they bombed an airfield near Aix-le-Chateau. The second raid of the day was in squadron strength, the target being the Red Lion at Hythe. As it was Twelfth Night everyone helped to remove the Christmas decorations, which were tossed onto the fire for added warmth. Not long after there was a knock at the door and this turned out to be the local police who had called to say that the chimney was on fire. As they set to with stirrup pumps, a discreet withdrawal was made to the back room but unfortunately word had already been passed to the Fire Brigade. Reasoning that a fire at a pub was too good an opportunity to miss, they turned up en masse with two fire engines. As the pub had virtually been taken over by the emergency services the pilots decided to retire to the Mess for the rest of the evening during which Bob Hornall's Austin 7 mysteriously found its way inside and under the stairs.

The next day thirteen aircraft (eight bombers, four fighters and one spare) went to Ford in the early afternoon. The target was to have been a site on the Cherbourg peninsula but shortly after take-off the engine of Tony Zweigbergk's Typhoon started to cut out and he returned with his No. 2. Des Perrin then took over but his aircraft also became unserviceable and he had to return with his wingman. This left Dusty Miller in charge, however his machine developed an oil leak and he had to turn back as well. As there were now only two bombers left they wisely thought better of it and decided to call it a day. The next operation was on 11 January when Des Perrin led eight bombers and two fighters to attack a V-1 site near Calais. The

Typhoons were greeted by intense heavy flak as soon as the French coast was crossed and this was joined by light flak in the target area. The bombing was some of the best that the squadron had so far achieved and this particular site was later removed from the target list. The only aircraft to be hit was F/Sgt Paddy Gray's aircraft, which received a piece of shrapnel in the starboard fuel tank.

After two days of heavy rain in which the aerodrome became unserviceable for a time the 14th dawned clear and sunny and twelve aircraft (eight bombers and four fighters) were prepared for an attack on Behen. Due to a timing error by Ops however they were recalled shortly after take-off and the only damage done was to the fish stocks in the Channel. Another operation in the afternoon (Ramrod 455) was rather more successful and a construction works at Bois Coquerel was badly damaged. Gun posts were shot up once again on the way out in which the Typhoon flown by Moose Mossip was holed in the nose tanks and both wings.

During the middle part of the month several pilots who had been with No. 1 Squadron for a considerable time were posted out. These included Fred Murray who had arrived way back on 14 October 1941. He left to take over the instruction courses on the Sabre engine at Napiers and the squadron said goodbye to one of the few remaining links with its time at Tangmere. Other long-standing members to leave were Con Devey and Walter Ramsey who were both to become instructors. During the leaving celebrations Devey's consumption of twenty pints, although not claimed as a record, was nevertheless hailed as a 'good show'. The evening was not without its drama. Tony Zweigbergk's car developed a problem on the way back but a successful 'Air-Land Rescue' got him safely home. Moose Mossip also became separated from the main party, however he eventually returned under his own steam, 'weaving madly'.

Among the replacement pilots were F/O Alex Vale and F/O F.H. Cattermoul who had both fought in Malta. Vale was twenty-one years of age and had been brought up in the tough environment of Peckham in south London. He received a good education at St Alleyn's School, Dulwich, thanks to a scholarship and here he excelled at Greek, Latin and art. The latter skill led to him becoming a trainee in graphic design at a local department store but his world was changed with the start of the Second World War. Although he was a pacifist the destruction wrought on London led to him joining the RAF and he was taught to fly in the USA. By the time that he joined No. 1 Squadron he had considerable combat experience. Others to arrive at this time were F/O Pete Crocker, F/O Ken Langmuir, F/O R.G. 'Red' Ward, W/O J.W. McKenzie and F/Sgt H.H. Price.

A further period of bad weather severely restricted operations over the next ten days and only two more Ramrods were possible. The aerodrome surface was still unfit for operations with bombs on 26 January and the only flying that could be contemplated were a number of weather recces. During one of these sorties F/Sgt Harry Bletcher had a lucky escape as his engine failed on take-off when he was about 12 ft in the air. He immediately raised his undercarriage and put his aircraft down again but unfortunately it hit a concrete pill box, which removed the port wing. With seemingly unabated speed his Typhoon charged into a wood in the north-east corner of the aerodrome. It then dug its nose into a bank of earth, cartwheeled and finished up on its side, with the remaining wing reaching up to the sky. Amazingly Bletcher was completely unhurt and emerged with only a tear in his trousers. His Typhoon (EK139) was most definitely Cat E and several airmen spent much of the day gathering up bits of wreckage, which were spread over a wide area.

Despite reports of 10/10 cloud over northern France on 28 January the squadron was told to bomb up and at 1035 hrs eight Bomphoons escorted by three fighters took off to bomb construction works at Le Grismont. The intended target was indeed covered by cloud but a fortunate break elsewhere allowed the squadron to bomb another site at Bois d'Enfer. All aircraft dropped their bombs successfully except for F/O H.T. Jackson who was unable to get rid of his due to an electrical fault. Efforts to jettison them were to no avail and he was escorted to RAF Ford by F/O Jimmy Campbell. It was emphasised in the squadron diary that this was not because they preferred him to blow a hole in someone else's aerodrome, rather that Ford possessed nice long runways where a smooth landing could be made. Jackson lowered his aircraft very carefully onto the runway and thankfully both bombs stayed where they were.

Ramrod 495 took place in the afternoon of 29 January and No. 1 Squadron again found itself escorting RP Hurricanes. Due to the difficulties already experienced with this type of operation it had been understood that it would not happen again, so it therefore came as something of a disappointment. In an attempt to find a solution it was decided to fly six Typhoon fighters with the Hurricanes, while eight Bomphoons operated independently. The fighters were led by Johnnie Higham (in a new Typhoon with a sliding hood) while the bombers had Des Perrin in the lead. The target was a V-1 site at Behen but when this was reached it was covered by cloud. The Hurricanes returned without attacking but Perrin led his aircraft in search of an alternative target and they found that it was clear around Amiens. The marshalling yards there were attacked and all but two bombs were seen to burst on the tracks and in a factory alongside. Sadly Spike Watson failed to return although there were no fighters in the area and there was no flak. He was last seen just before bombing and nothing more was heard from him.

Although the weather was fine and dry in the UK on 30 January it was rather worse over France and no operational sorties were flown. A large amount of practice flying was carried out, which included one of the new pilots, W/O J.W. McKenzie. Whilst in the circuit the engine of his Typhoon (JP841) developed an internal glycol leak, which led to coolant covering his windscreen, thus making it very difficult for him to see out. To make mattters worse white smoke also began to pour from the starboard exhausts. He managed to lower his undercarriage but on his final approach he undershot the aerodrome slightly and his wheels struck an earth bank on the boundary. This led to the aircraft landing on its belly and after it had come to a halt McKenzie made a swift exit. This was just as well as it burst into flames shortly after and despite the best efforts of the fire crews it was completely burnt out. Considering his short time on Typhoons everyone agreed that he had done as good a job as was possible under the circumstances. At the end of the day it was announced that Johnnie Higham had been promoted to Acting Flight Lieutenant and that he had been put in charge of 'A' Flight. This proved to be a very popular move and was duly celebrated in the Mess in the evening.

On 1 February Moose Mossip (JP677) and F/O Neville Brown (JP679) carried out a shipping recce along the Belgian coast in which the former shot up a trawler off Ostend. A similar mission was undertaken by Jim Campbell (JP751) and Alex Vale (JR126) who headed further south to Dieppe and Boulogne. During this a vessel was attacked and damaged near Pointe d'Ailly. The early part of the month was taken up by a further round of attacks on V-1 sites commencing with Ramrod 504 to La Glacerie near Cherbourg on 3 February. Bombing was carried out from 11,000 ft down to 5,000 ft and although the attack was badly affected by 8/10 cloud cover, several bombs burst in the target area. This target was also attacked on 8 and 11 February, however the latter operation was to be the last from Lympne as No. 1 Squadron moved to Martlesham Heath near Ipswich on 15 February.

Having been at Lympne for eleven months the squadron had built up close ties with the local area and it was something of a wrench to have to leave. Mrs Davis who had provided countless cups of tea for squadron personnel from her NAAFI wagon was presented with a silver engraved cigarette case. The splendours of Port Lympne also had to be left behind but most on the squadron realised that there was bound to be an 'up side' to life at Martlesham. This was evident on arrival as the aerodrome was also the home of the 356th Fighter Group of the US 8th Air Force, which operated P-47 Thunderbolts. The provisioning of the US military was in a different league to that of British forces and having tasted the superb food and helped themselves to free cigarettes, Mrs Davis was soon forgotten.

The first operation to be carried out from Martlesham took place on 24 February and consisted of close escort (together with the Typhoons of No. 137 Squadron) to twenty-four Boston bombers attacking the V-1 site at Hesdin. The next day a force of Mitchells was escorted and this proved to be the last operational sortie for another No. 1 Squadron stalwart, Moose Mossip. He had been with the squadron for just over two years and during this time his offensive spirit and willingness to take on the enemy at every opportunity had been an inspiration to everyone. Like many before him he left to be an instructor.

By now No. 1 Squadron was able to use long-range tanks, which allowed deeper penetrations of occupied Europe. On 29 February eight Typhoons led by Des Perrin took part in Ramrod 603, a low level sweep over Holland, which was aimed at supporting B-17 Fortresses attacking targets in Germany. The squadron flew over the North Sea at 12,000 ft as far as Leeuwarden before diving to ground level in search of targets. About a dozen barges were shot up but on returning to the Zuider Zee an R-Boat was seen about a mile offshore. This was left badly damaged, as was a vessel of about 800 tons that was close by. Height was then regained and despite some flak from the coastal defences all aircraft returned safely after a trip lasting 2 hours 5 minutes which at the time was a squadron record on Typhoons.

On 2 March No. 1 Squadron acted as part of the escort to two raids by B-26 Marauders, the second of which was to the marshalling yards at Tergnier. During this operation W/O Neil Howard experienced engine failure in JP483 and was obliged to force-land not far from the target. On this occasion his squadron colleagues flew home aware that he was safe as he was able to call on R/T to say that he was all right. Howard was one of only two No. 1 Squadron pilots to evade capture and was eventually to return to the UK. Two more escort operations were flown on 3 March, the first involving the escort of twelve Bostons to a 'Noball' target near Hardelot. A similar mission (except that the bombers were Mitchells) was laid on in the afternoon but by this time storm clouds had built up over the Channel, together with bad visibility, and a return was made before the French coast was reached. Bad weather over the Channel area disrupted operations over the next couple of days even though at Martlesham it was clear and sunny.

It was not until 6 March that another offensive operation could be planned and during Ramrod 630 a large force of 108 Marauders attacked the marshalling yards at Poix. Tony Zweigbergk led eight aircraft of No. 1 Squadron as part of the close escort, the rest comprising Typhoons drawn from Nos 3, 198 and 609 Squadrons. Rendezvous was made off the French coast and the target was approached by a rather circuitous route. The bombing was very accurate but during the withdrawal several Fw 190s were seen up-sun. At first they did not seem keen to engage but were prompted to do so by a section of No. 3 Squadron, which appeared oblivious to the threat and elected to fly straight and level, well away from the rest of the close escorts. This 'Prune-like action' led to the section being bounced and the Typhoon flown by P/O C.A. Tidy was shot down by Hptm Klaus Mietusch, the *Kommodore* of III/JG 26 (Tidy survived and was another to evade). Shortly afterwards another 190 dived through the last box of bombers, the whole formation now straggling over ten miles, but fortunately no damage was done. This operation was the longest so far on Typhoons at three hours and six aircraft had to land at Lympne to refuel. Only the CO and his No. 2 were able to return direct to Martlesham.

On 7 March an identical operation (Ramrod 634) was laid on, the only difference being that the close escorts had the protection of two Spitfire IX squadrons as top cover. Unfortunately the target was covered by cloud and although there were much clearer conditions further south, the bombers returned without bombing. The only concern for No. 1 Squadron was the condition of one of the Marauders, which had become detached as it had been reduced to flying on one engine. It was safely escorted back by F/O Jim Campbell and W/O J.W. McKenzie (Red 3 and 4).

This was the last offensive operation of the month and the subsequent lack of activity led many to wonder what the future had in store. Although the weather played its part, even on the good days there was little on offer except convoy patrols and ASR sorties. It was not until 17 March that there was any excitement and even this involved the actions of others. In the afternoon a Lancaster II of No. 514

Squadron made a flapless approach to Martlesham, the pilot having mistaken it for Woodbridge, which boasted a runway 5,000 yards long. Not surprisingly he ran out of runway fairly quickly and ended up ground-looping. This removed the undercarriage and if anyone at Martlesham was not paying much attention, they soon were, the Lancaster finally coming to a standstill having made the most horrendous grinding noise heard for some time. Not long after a USAAF P-47 Thunderbolt made an emergency belly landing with a failed engine but in doing so it hit an obstruction and was flipped onto its back. Happily the pilot emerged unscathed when the aircraft was lifted off the ground.

Having enjoyed the misfortunes of others it was No. 1 Squadron's turn to provide the entertainment on 21 March when Moose Mossip returned to pay a visit. He was now with a fighter affiliation unit tasked with making dummy attacks on bomber aircraft to give practice to the gunners. He arrived in a clapped out Spitfire but decided to make one final flight in his treasured Typhoon. A weakness of the Typhoon on take-off was that it was liable to burst a tyre and this happened to Mossip, the aircraft ending up on its belly. Although he had been extremely popular during his time on the squadron, he felt a sudden mood change as a result of the accident and left rather hurriedly.

The squadron had another black day on 23 March during the course of ASR operations in the Channel. One section comprised F/O Duncan McIntosh and F/O H.T. Jackson but when returning at about 1,000 ft and seven miles off Orfordness, Jackson called to say that his engine was failing. McIntosh turned in time to see the Typhoon of his No. 2 ditch in the sea but it sank immediately. Shortly afterwards Jackson rose to the surface and although he was soon picked up by a Walrus and given artificial respiration, this was unsuccessful and his body was flown to Martlesham. The task of informing next of kin was made even more difficult as less than two months before he had become the proud father of a son.

By the end of the month the rumour mill was in full swing and for once it was fully justified. As far as No. 1 Squadron was concerned the Typhoon era came to a close in early April and this coincided with a move to North Weald. Around the same time Tony Zweigbergk was posted out, as were Johnnie Higham and Bob Hornall. Within a matter of days they would be joined by Des Perrin and Dusty Miller but perhaps the biggest shock of all was the departure of Chunky Chown who had been associated with the squadron for two and a half years. Although this was not the first time that he had 'left', this time it was definite as he was posted to Northolt as the station engineering officer. Among all the other changes it was also discovered that the unit would be swapping its Typhoons for Spitfire IXBs. The Typhoon had had its problems but by 1944 these had largely been overcome and it was about to come into its own as the RAF's principal fighter-bomber in 2nd Tactical Air Force. Although it had become used to operating in the ground attack role No. 1 Squadron was about to revert to more traditional duties with, arguably, the finest fighter of the Second World War.

CHAPTER FOURTEEN

The Spitfire

The move to North Weald was scheduled for 2 April but, like several other wartime moves, it had to be delayed due to bad weather, in this case rain and fog. With very little improvement the following day pilots were becoming resigned to another night at Martlesham when a phone call from North Weald told of a sudden clearance further west. A total of seventeen Typhoons, one Hurricane, one Tiger Moth and an Oxford were airborne at 1530 hrs and were led by F/L H.J. Wilkinson. They arrived safely to be met by the new CO S/L Johnnie Checketts DSO DFC and F/L Ian 'Mick' Maskill who was to be the commander of 'A' Flight. Checketts was from Invercargill in New Zealand and had previously led No. 485 Squadron with whom he had considerable combat success. However, he did have the misfortune to be shot down over France on 6 September 1943, suffering slight injuries and burns in the process. He managed to avoid being arrested and was picked up by the French Resistance. He was then taken to Paris before heading for Brittany where he was transported by boat to a rendezvous with a British launch that brought him back to the UK. He was given the command of No. 1 Squadron after a spell with the Central Gunnery School at Catfoss.

The first of two Spitfire VBs arrived on 4 April for pilots to practise on before the arrival of the Spitfire IXBs, the first three of which arrived on the 9th. These were joined by a brand new Typhoon, which led to a number of puzzled looks considering that the squadron was expecting more Spitfires. They duly arrived on 14 April and as fourteen turned up all at the same time the Servicing Echelon had its hands full carrying out acceptance checks. As well as new aircraft there were new pilots including F/Sgt Ken Weller who arrived on 15 April. By this stage of the war replacement pilots tended to have rather more experience than in previous years and Weller was typical having nearly 500 hours in his logbook. He also had six months' operational experience on Spitfire VCs and IXs with No. 72 Squadron in North Africa, Malta, Sicily and Italy and had survived being shot down by flak on Christmas Day in 1943. Weller was twenty-two years of age and was another to have been trained in the USA. Having been taught to fly at 7 EFTS at Braunstone near Leicester, he completed his basic and advanced training at No. 6 BFTS at Ponca City in Oklahoma. This was also known as the Darr School as it was run under contract to the RAF by Harold S. Darr, the president of Braniff Airlines. Although Weller's Christian names were Kenneth Charles, he was usually referred to as 'Tony' after a character in Charles Dickens' *The Pickwick Papers*, or as 'Red' due to the colour of his hair.

Further periods of bad weather during the early part of April hampered the squadron's work-up period on the new aircraft and also delayed a detachment to Ayr for air firing, which had been scheduled for the 18th. The squadron was finally able to take off two days later although a tragic accident occurred as it was forming up. F/O 'Red' Ward was flying as No. 2 to F/O 'Pussy' Cattermoul but as he moved in to join up he overshot and pulled up in front of Cattermoul's Spitfire. His tail was clipped by his leader's propeller and he flicked over and dived straight into the ground. The Spitfire flown by Cattermoul was only slightly damaged and he landed safely. Although Ward had only been with the squadron a short time he was very popular and his loss was deeply felt. The remaining Spitfires flew to Church Fenton to refuel but here it was discovered that the en route weather forecast had been rather over-optimistic and the rain and low cloud that had affected southern Scotland for several days was still firmly entrenched. This led to a further delay of two days and the squadron did not arrive at Ayr until midday on 22 April.

Ayr was the home of No. 14 Armament Practice Camp and in the run up to the invasion of northern France many squadrons passed through the Scottish aerodrome on two-week detachments to sharpen up their gunnery skills. Although the weather remained rather inclement it was never bad enough to interfere with flying and a very full programme of air-to-air firing and dive bombing was carried out. It was while the squadron was at Ayr that it learned two startling pieces of news. One was that it would not be returning to North Weald but would be proceeding direct to Predannack in Cornwall. The other was that Johnnie Checketts had been promoted to Wing Commander and would be leaving the squadron to become Wing Leader at Horne. So it was that on 29 April No. 1 Squadron began its journey south to an unfamiliar aerodrome and an unknown CO.

Having landed at Rednal on the way the squadron flew into Predannack to be greeted by S/L Pat Lardner-Burke DFC who was to take command. From Orange Free State in South Africa, Lardner-Burke was twenty-seven years of age and had joined the RAF in early 1940. His first operational experience had been with No. 46 Squadron in Malta in 1941 and during this period he shot down five Italian Macchi fighters. He had been fortunate to survive as during his last combat he was badly wounded when a bullet fired from behind penetrated the armour plating behind his seat and entered his chest where it punctured a lung. His next tour was in 1943 as a flight commander with No. 222 Squadron, however he joined No. 1 Squadron after a 'rest' period at HQ Fighter Command.

The aerodrome at Predannack was situated on an exposed location on the Lizard peninsula to the south-west of Truro. It had been formed from rough heathland in 1941 and although it was extremely isolated, it was ideally located for patrols over the approaches to the English Channel. No. 165 Squadron also flew into Predannack around this time from Culmhead and they would join with No. 1 Squadron to form the Predannack Wing, the main purpose being to carry out

'Instep' patrols on the lookout for Ju 88s, which were attacking aircraft of Coastal Command that were searching for enemy submarines. The Wing Leader at Predannack was W/C D.G. 'Splinters' Smallwood DFC. The first day at Predannack was spent getting the 'gen' on the type of operations that were going to be carried out. One thing was immediately obvious and that was the fact that, for the foreseeable future, the pilots would be spending most of their time flying over water. While this was going on, others in the squadron busied themselves trying to trace kit, equipment and men, which were spread over the length and breadth of the British Isles. On 1 May No. 1 Squadron started to take its turn in maintaining a state of two aircraft at standby, four at readiness and six at thirty minutes, with No. 165 Squadron. During the day twelve aircraft were scrambled in pairs and fours but nothing was seen. The following day No. 1 was the duty squadron from dawn to 1300 hrs during which two uneventful patrols were flown. In the afternoon the squadron's Spitfires were fitted with 30-gallon overload tanks as a temporary measure until fittings for the larger 45-gallon tanks could be obtained.

Following a shipping recce in the morning of 3 May, eight Spitfires of No. 1 Squadron (together with eight from No. 165) provided top cover to Typhoons bombing a German destroyer that had been beached. This was actually an Elbing class *Flottentorpedoboot*, or Fleet torpedo boat, but was equivalent in size to a medium-sized British destroyer. Later in the day news was received that F/L H.J. Wilkinson, who had recently left the squadron to take the Fighter Leaders' course at Milfield, was missing after a flight over the North Sea. An ASR search of the area in which he had been flying was unsuccessful and two days later he was listed as missing, believed killed. On 5 May Zulu Watson and Bill Dunwoodie were two more pilots to leave on posting as instructors to 3 TEU (Tactical Exercise Unit) at Annan. Here they joined several ex members of No. 1 Squadron including Des Perrin and Dusty Miller.

Further bad weather over the next few days at least allowed the squadron's Spitfires to be modified to take 150-octane petrol, which allowed the use of an increased boost pressure of +25 lbs/sq in (the previous maximum boost pressure was +18 lbs/sq in). This was limited to a maximum of five minutes' operation but it increased top speed at sea level by around 30 mph (to 364 mph) and also increased the rate of climb by around 950 ft/min, to just over 5,000 ft/min. The downside to all of this was an increased fuel consumption of around 24 per cent so that when operating at full boost and 3,000 rpm, fuel was being used at a rate of 197 gallons per hour. The internal fuel capacity of the Spitfire amounted to only 85 gallons, and even when carrying external tanks pilots would obviously have to be very fuel conscious when flying at full boost, especially as they now had to operate a long way out to sea. The use of higher boost pressures also led to a decrease in engine reliability, which would become more evident later in the year.

On 7 May F/L Alex Vale was appointed as 'B' Flight commander and three days later the first 'Instep' patrol was carried out. This involved Nos 1 and 165

Squadrons (led by W/C Smallwood) and two Seafire squadrons of the Fleet Air Arm patrolling four designated areas around 150 miles west-north-west of the Lizard at zero feet. This was rather an intrepid undertaking, especially as the Spitfires had to take off in the dark so as to be at the patrol area at first light. In the event no enemy aircraft were seen and the patrol was entirely uneventful. A similar operation was carried out on 13 May but the only aircraft seen on this occasion was a Vickers Warwick, which was used for Air-Sea Rescue and general reconnaissance.

After another Instep patrol in the early morning of 14 May in which four aircraft (plus another four from 165) were airborne for 2 hours 45 minutes, Pat Lardner-Burke led eight Spitfires on a Rodeo operation to Kerlin Bastard and Vannes on a search for Ju 88s and Do 217s that had apparently moved into the area. Lardner-Burke decided to have a look at Gael aerodrome to the west of Rennes but although there were no aircraft to be seen, the Spitfires shot up the control tower in the face of intense light flak. On the way out near Morlaix they were fired on by a flak wagon on a goods train and also by gun emplacements nearby. In returning fire, many strikes were seen on the freight wagons. As this was the first successful offensive sortie on Spitfires all pilots returned in high spirits, the squadron diary noting that it had served as a real tonic for them. In addition five uneventful patrols were carried out, together with some practice bombing and air-to-ground firing.

The next day there were only five standing patrols but during one it was made apparent that the enemy were not the only ones who needed to be treated with suspicion. When flying ten miles south-east of Falmouth, Black section, comprising Flying Officers E.G. Hutchin and E.N.W. 'Junior' Marsh were fired upon by four Royal Navy destroyers. This was even though they were flying straight and level at an altitude of 9,000 ft in weather conditions of no cloud and a visibility estimated at twenty to thirty miles. A total of six 3-inch shells burst immediately below them, perfectly accurate for direction, but fortunately just short on range. Both pilots returned safely, albeit considerably shaken.

Another Instep patrol was attempted on 17 May but owing to a chapter of separate incidents it proved to be a bit of a disaster. Eight Spitfires of No. 1 Squadron should have flown with four from No. 165 Squadron but six of No. 1's aircraft failed to make it for one reason or another. The engine of one aircraft failed to start and five others had to turn back shortly after take-off due to engine, R/T and oil trouble. All four from No. 165 Squadron returned early due to R/T problems, leaving just two Spitfires from No. 1 Squadron to complete the patrol. On 19 May Nos 1 and 165 Squadrons provided the escort to RP Beaufighters during a shipping recce to Brest. The strike Beaufighters were also protected by others in the anti-flak role and although a destroyer was set on fire and another hit, one Beaufighter crashed in flames and another was hit in both engines and did not make it back.

On 22 May the squadron suffered one of its worst days for some time with the loss of two pilots during a Rhubarb operation. All restrictions on attacking trains in northern France had just been lifted and Alex Vale decided to lead a section of four Spitfires to seek out rail targets in the area Vannes – Chateaulin – Morlaix. They found two trains, one of which was a troop train, and both were left enveloped in flames, smoke and steam. However, the flak defences hit all four Spitfires and MK890 flown by Sgt E.F. Jacobsen was seen to pull up sharply after the first attack from 50 ft to around 1,000 ft before descending once again. He was not seen again. Alex Vale was also in big trouble as his Spitfire (MK796) was hit by small arms fire during a second attack on the troop train. He attempted to put his aircraft down in a small field, but he undershot and hit a hedge. Still travelling very fast, his Spitfire broke up before finally coming to rest. The other members of the section, F/O Jim Campbell (MK919) and F/Sgt Tony Weller (MK644), circled the crash site but could see no sign of him. Both were able to return to Predannack but their aircraft had been damaged Cat B. Tony Weller's Spitfire had received several hits including one that had entered from below the cockpit before passing between his legs and exiting through the canopy. After landing he had to wait for assistance to get out as his canopy was jammed (news was later received that Vale was a prisoner but that Jacobsen had been killed).

Two days later eight Spitfires of No. 1 Squadron took part in a shipping patrol and were equipped for the first time with overload tanks of 90 gallons capacity. Although these tanks caused a significant deterioration in handling characteristics, their use allowed much greater operational flexibility and they could be jettisoned if required. On this occasion the Spitfires were airborne for 3 hours 10 minutes which, although not as long as some of the night Intruder operations on Hurricanes, was still a squadron record on Spitfires. Everyone's posteriors were 'mighty sore' on return, which led to considerable agitation to have something more comfortable than a dinghy to sit on for over three hours. The CO's suggestion of water cushions led to a few wistful looks. In the afternoon F/O Bob Bridgman was injured in rather bizarre fashion. For some reason he decided to do some 'window cleaning' when flying his Spitfire at about 200 mph but his arm was caught by the slipstream, resulting in a dislocated shoulder. Fortunately his shoulder went back into position almost immediately after he withdrew it, but he still needed treatment from the squadron doctor, F/L W.S. 'Doc' Wallace, on landing. By rights another limb should have been put out of joint considering the amount of leg pulling he received over the incident.

There was little of note during the rest of the month and a late evening Roadstead on 28 May was typical. A report of R-Boats had been received but despite scouring the area from Ushant to the Ile de Batz, nothing was seen. On 30 May eight Spitfires escorted Typhoons of No. 263 Squadron from Harrowbeer on an armed shipping recce. Ten miles south of Ushant a convoy of minesweepers and various auxiliaries were encountered. The Typhoons attempted to bomb the convoy but did not register any hits. The few remaining Typhoon pilots on No. 1 Squadron no doubt felt that they could have done rather better.

After another washout on 31 May, No. 1 Squadron suffered another difficult day on 1 June. Once again the problems occurred during a Rhubarb operation, on this occasion to Chateaulin – Quimper – Kerlin Bastard. The four Spitfires of Red section, led by F/O Pussy Cattermoul were returning after successfully attacking a train when they ran into intense flak on approaching the outskirts of Quimper. This was extremely accurate and Cattermoul's Spitfire was hit in the engine. He called up his deputy to say that he was going to put his aircraft down and he was last seen heading for an open field. Although he survived the crash-landing, Cattermoul was seriously injured and died six weeks later. The other members of the section, F/L R. Brown (ML313), F/O Freddie Town (MK867) and F/O Tommy Wyllie (NH253), all returned safely.

The next day Pat Lardner-Burke led the squadron on its first bombing mission on Spitfires. Each aircraft carried a single 500 lb bomb under the centre section and the intention was to seek out shipping between Brest and Ushant. Unfortunately the area was shrouded in mist and low cloud and with no targets forthcoming, all the bombs ended up in the sea. Another attempt was made in the afternoon by four Spitfires from No. 1 Squadron and three from No. 165 Squadron, all led by W/C Smallwood. This time they found a large merchant vessel of around 10,000 tons entering Brest harbour and a bombing attack was made from 10,000 ft down to 5,000 ft. The attack was well concentrated with an average error of about 100 yards and there were two near misses astern. Another armed reconnaissance was made on 3 June but once again aircraft unserviceability caused problems. Two Spitfires were non-starters due to overheating and two more had to return early with oil trouble. The remaining four aircraft flew to Brest where they bombed a 5,000-ton vessel, one bomb bursting right on the water line and causing the ship to veer sharply to port.

The countdown to D-Day, the Allied invasion of northern France, was in its final stages and No. 1 Squadron was involved in covering the mass of shipping in the Channel. On 5 June an order was received that all ranks, including those living out, were to remain on station from 1800 hrs and bets large and small were made as to the exact date and place that the Allies would land. It came in the early morning of 6 June and during this momentous day No. 1 Squadron flew a total of thirty sorties on two Roadsteads, one Ranger, one convoy patrol and an ASR operation looking for a pilot of No. 165 Squadron who had come down in the sea. During the Ranger operation F/O Tommy Wyllie and F/O Ken Langmuir shot up two goods trains and Langmuir also attacked and hit a German staff car, which swerved off the road and crashed.

Even though the squadron was faced with a sea journey of around 110 miles to get to the French coast, the use of 90-gallon overload tanks allowed deeper penetrations into occupied territory and on 7 June the area around Nantes was reconnoitred. On such an operation the Channel was crossed at zero feet to avoid radar detection, the Spitfires usually flying low enough as to leave a wake behind them caused by the wash coming from their propellers (although there are no recorded instances in No. 1 Squadron, pilots on other units occasionally returned with damaged propeller tips having hit the water). Just before the French coast was reached a rapid climb was made to around 10,000 ft to avoid light flak and small arms fire. Having cleared the coastal defences the Spitfires then dropped down again to ground level to head towards the target.

On this occasion the eight Spitfires were made up of four from No. 1 Squadron, three from No. 165 Squadron, plus W/C Smallwood. On the way to Nantes a goods train was seen and permission was received for this to be attacked. The engine was badly damaged by cannon fire, which punctured its boiler, producing copious amounts of steam. The next target was a tugboat that was seen on the River Loire. This was perfectly placed for an attack by F/O E.N.W. 'Junior' Marsh who fired a long burst, which raked the boat's bridge and hull. These attacks were secondary to the main objective, which was the aerodrome at Nantes, however on arrival there were no aircraft in sight. On the return journey a German-occupied chateau and another train were attacked before the coast was crossed, again at 10,000 ft. The trip back over the Channel was also made at zero feet and the Spitfires landed at Predannack after a flight lasting 2 hours 20 minutes.

In the immediate aftermath of D-Day pilots on all squadrons were asked to fly at maximum intensity, which involved the early risers taking off before dawn, and those flying the last patrol of the day landing after dark. Operations were however frustrated by another period of bad weather and after a Rodeo on 8 June in which two trains and two army lorries were shot up, it was not until the 12th that the squadron was able to fly a successful offensive mission. After an early Rodeo to Vannes and Kerlin Bastard, a late morning Rhubarb by four aircraft to Landivisiau – Chateauneuf – Loudeac led to various military transports being attacked including army lorries, an armoured car and a large pantechnicon type vehicle. In the evening another combined operation with No. 165 Squadron led to a lorry park containing around 100 trucks at Questembert being attacked.

On 14 June the Predannack squadrons operated in Wing strength and led by 'Splinters' Smallwood they carried out a Rodeo to Le Mans. With the increased endurance brought about by the use of external fuel tanks No. 1 Squadron was able to operate over areas that it had not seen since 1940. There was to be another parallel with that particular year as the Spitfires flown by F/O H.L. Stuart (NH246) and Junior Marsh (MK988) landed to refuel at an emergency strip that had been formed to the south-east of Grandcamp. They only stayed for around forty-five minutes but this was the first time that aircraft of No. 1 Squadron had landed in France since its withdrawal, almost exactly four years before.

The next day, six Spitfires of No. 1 Squadron (plus eight from No. 165 Squadron) were loaded with 500 lb bombs and took off at 0920 hrs to fly to Guernsey as there had been a report of a U-Boat in St Peter Port. On arrival this was not evident but a successful attack was carried out on the harbour area with two direct hits on the centre jetty. Despite a curtain of light and heavy flak, which was extremely accurate, all aircraft returned safely. Later another bombing attack was carried out by eight Spitfires on a radar station at Pointe St Mathieu.

Excellent results were achieved and the whole target was obscured by smoke and dust. The day was also notable for a scramble by three aircraft to shepherd a damaged B-17 Fortress into Predannack.

On 18 June the squadron made a return to St Peter Port to attack shipping in the harbour. Having endured poor weather for much of June, conditions were much improved with very little cloud. Unfortunately this tended to favour the defences and the Spitfires were greeted by a barrage of 88-mm flak bursts. As they commenced their attacking dive on a large ship of approximately 7,000 tons, a number of flak ships opened up as well and the pilots began to think more in terms of survival than achieving accuracy. Most bombs fell short of the intended target and no time was wasted in opening up to full throttle and climbing to a safe altitude. Although the attack could not be considered a success, at least everyone emerged from the maelstrom physically unscathed, if not mentally.

Two days later the squadron was on the move again, this time to Harrowbeer, which was around fifty miles to the north-east, near Plymouth. Although the squadron would be working with a new Wing Leader in W/C Harold Bird-Wilson DFC, its area of operations was largely the same. Shortly after arriving he led Spitfires from Nos 1 and 165 Squadrons to bomb a radar station at Lannion. In the evening another mixed force involving sixteen Spitfires (eight each from Nos 1 and 165) carried out an armed shipping recce in the Cherbourg area. On this occasion no ships were seen and all bombs had to be jettisoned over the Channel.

In terms of duration, the move to Harrrowbeer proved to be one of the shortest in RAF history as No. 1 Squadron was notified of a further move to Detling in 11 Group on 22 June. This was in response to the commencement of V-1 attacks and although W/C Bird-Wilson expressed the opinion that the squadron was likely to be back at Harrowbeer in the near future, everyone hoped that their return to 11 Group would be for a very long time. Although the performance of the squadron's Spitfire IXBs had been greatly improved by the use of 150-octane petrol, especially at low level, it remained to be seen how effective the aircraft would be when confronted with Hitler's first terror weapon.

CHAPTER FIFTEEN

The V-1 Campaign

Although No. 1 Squadron had seen plenty of action during its time at Predannack there was no disguising the fact that it was very much on the periphery of the fighter world, which was no place for the RAF's premier single-seat outfit. In returning to 11 Group it felt as though the squadron was back in its rightful place. Detling was situated high on the North Downs near Maidstone and its first military use had been nearly thirty years before. It was selected for home defence operations in 1915 but flying ceased four years later and the airfield was returned to agricultural use. It was not until the expansion of the RAF in the late 1930s that the site was used once again and at the beginning of the Second World War, Detling was home to the Ansons of No. 500 Squadron, Coastal Command. The station was the subject of several devastating attacks during the Battle of Britain, even though it was not a fighter station, indeed it was not taken over by Fighter Command until mid-1942. The location of Detling to the south-east of London meant that it was ideally placed to deal with the V-1 flying bombs that were now coming over in droves from their launch sites in the Pas de Calais, the first having come down at Swanscombe near Gravesend on 13 June 1944.

The V-1 could be traced back as far as 1928 when Paul Schmidt, a fluid dynamicist, began work on a pulse-jet engine that could be used to power a flying bomb. Although his engines were developing 1,100 lbs thrust by 1940 his work was hampered by a lack of funds. The *Reichluftfahrtministerium* (RLM) favoured the Argus Motoren-Gesellschaft of Berlin to develop the pulse-jet as it had already carried out a study of this form of propulsion and Schmidt was ordered to allow his work to be viewed by the company. The official go-ahead was given on 19 June 1942 with Fieseler being responsible for the airframe, Walter KG for the launching ramp and Siemens the guidance system. The V-1 contained 850 kg of high explosive and cruised at a speed of 340–360 mph, at an altitude of 2–3,000 ft. Although the RAF's fastest fighters, the Tempest V, Mustang III and Spitfire XII/XIV, had a small performance advantage at low level, it remained to be seen how effective the Spitfire IX would be in combating the dreaded buzz-bomb.

The British response to the V-1 offensive was known as Operation *Diver* and the first such patrol flown by No. 1 Squadron took place on 24 June. A total of seven patrols were flown from early afternoon but the outcome of these was disappointing and no contacts were made. It was a similar story the next day. The only real chance that a Spitfire IX had of closing to firing range on a V-1 was for it to fly above the flying bomb's cruising altitude and then convert height into speed by diving once it had been seen. However, the V-1 had a wing span of only 17 ft 4 in and a length of 22 ft 7 in and such a small target was difficult to pick up against the ground. This task was made even more difficult if there was any cloud present as occurred on 25 June. The first patrol was airborne at 0510 hrs but operations were hampered by poor weather and it was to prove to be another frustrating day. Although no V-1s were shot down on 26 June there was at least hope of success in the future as the first attacks were made. Some of these were baulked due to 'over-enthusiasm' on the part of several Tempest pilots who cut in ahead of No. 1 Squadron's Spitfires. Although each fighter was under ground control, V-1s tended to attract fighters like wasps to a jar of jam and any pilot who became fixated on his target did so at his peril.

No. 1 Squadron destroyed its first V-1 on 27 June and it was shared between three pilots, F/O Bob Bridgman, F/Sgt Tony Weller and F/Sgt Iain Hastings. They were vectored onto a V-1 coming in from Boulogne and caught sight of it near Dungeness. By the time they were to the south of Tonbridge, Bob Bridgman was in position to attack but he had had to wring every last ounce of performance from his aircraft and his airspeed indicator was showing 360–375 mph. All three pilots fired at the V-1 and it dived steeply to explode near Wadhurst. This initial success was added to by F/O Jack Batchelor who took off at 0930 hrs to patrol the Hastings/Rye area. After being airborne for about forty minutes he was given indication of an approaching V-1 and picked it up about a mile out to sea near Hastings. It was flying on a course of 350/355 degrees at an indicated airspeed of 330 mph and an altitude of 2,000 ft. As it was heading straight for Hastings, Batchelor let it clear the town before opening fire at 500 yards from dead astern, closing to 300 yards. After this attack the jet glow appeared to burn a lot brighter but the V-1 then flew into cloud. Undeterred, Batchelor followed it and fired a second burst in cloud, which appeared to affect the gyro device that controlled the flying bomb's attitude, as it veered off course. Although Batchelor lost sight of the V-1 at this point he was of the opinion that it could not have carried on much further and this was confirmed by the Observer Corps who reported a V-1 crashing at the time and place of his combat. Later in the day No. 1 Squadron (together with No. 165 Squadron, which had also moved to Detling) escorted a force of 104 Halifaxes of 4 Group, which bombed the V-1 site at Mimoyecques.

On 28 July the squadron shot down five V-1s, the pick of the bunch being that despatched by F/O Duncan McIntosh, which was described in the squadron diary as a 'real peach'. Almost immediately after take-off at 1735 hrs a Diver was seen heading north-west at around 1,300 ft. Having barely had time to raise his undercarriage, McIntosh fired a short burst using full deflection and the V-1 exploded in mid air. The time of combat was given as 1736 hrs, or one minute after take-off, which was considered (and with good reason) to be a record. Iain

Hastings added another, which was shot down near Brentwood, and F/L T.D. Williams sent one crashing to the ground near Willards Hill to the north of Hastings. Tom Williams came from Liverpool and was an extremely experienced fighter pilot having achieved his first combat claims with No. 611 Squadron during the Battle of Britain. He had further success with No. 602 Squadron in 1941 and it was whilst serving with this squadron that he was awarded the DFC. Williams' combat on 28 June highlighted another hazard for pilots tasked with anti-Diver operations in that anti-aircraft gun crews quite often continued to fire even when it was obvious that a fighter was moving into attack. On this occasion Williams was nearly hit by fire from the coastal batteries. Although the fighters and anti-aircraft artillery had designated areas in which to operate, the boundaries were not clearly defined and this was by no means an isolated incident.

F/O E.G. Hutchin was patrolling at 1830 hrs when he was informed by Sandwich Control of a Diver six miles south of Canterbury. The performance of V-1s varied markedly and the estimated speed of this one was in the order of 320–340 mph. Hutchin had little difficulty in reducing the range and after firing the V-1 suddenly slowed before turning on its back and crashing alongside a railway line between Halfway Houses and Minster on the Isle of Sheppey. Patrols were carried out throughout the day and the late shift was performed by F/O Junior Marsh. He was in the air at 2300 hrs and was vectored on to a Diver coming in south-east of Dungeness. He eventually saw it near New Romney and closed from 500 yards to 300 yards before opening fire. His shells hit the rear fuselage and port wing, which initally sent the V-1 into a gentle dive. It then recovered to fly straight and level for a short time before performing a steep climbing turn to port before diving down to crash about five miles from Ashford. In marked contrast, operations on the following day were badly affected by low cloud, occasional rain and bad visibility. Of twenty-three patrols by sections of two aircraft, seven pilots fired, but no V-1s were shot down.

On 30 June No. 1 Squadron had its most successful day yet when it destroyed six V-1s with another unconfirmed. F/O Neville Brown was patrolling the south coast near Folkstone when he intercepted a V-1 about five miles to the south-east. This one was heading in the usual north-westerly direction at a speed of 340 mph IAS and an altitude of 4,000 ft. Brown approached from the starboard quarter and fired a four-second burst moving round to astern and closing to 200 yards. This was rather too close should the V-1 have blown up in the air, but instead it heeled over to the right and dived into the sea just south of Folkstone. He then attacked a second but although many strikes were seen on the starboard side it disappeared into cloud and its ultimate fate could not be established.

P/O K.R. Foskett was the most successful pilot of the day with two V-1s confirmed. The first was seen near Faversham at 2030 hrs where it was the subject of an ineffective attack by a USAAF P-47 Thunderbolt. Foskett did a rather better job although as this proved to be one of the slower V-1s, he overshot his target twice. Once he had become accustomed to its cruising speed he achieved multiple strikes and the V-1 rolled over and dived into the ground, exploding among some farm buildings. His second Diver of the evening was shot down at 2220 hrs about one mile north-west of Hastings. At the same time F/O H.L. Stuart was despatching another V-1 between Bexhill and Pevensey Bay. Although the intention was to stop the flying bombs reaching London, those living under the flight path of the V-1s were at severe risk and this one turned over and crashed among some houses. Other pilots to open their Diver account were F/O D.R. Wallace who sent one crashing into the sea off Dover and W/O J.W. McKenzie who completed the work of two other Spitfires by firing at another, which crashed west of Pevensey Bay.

By the end of June just over 2,000 V-1s had been fired at the UK and although the daily numbers varied, once the campaign was under way, the average was 190. There was thus no shortage of potential targets. It was also apparent that the performance boost obtained by using 150-octane petrol to increase the power of the Spitfire IXB's Rolls-Royce Merlin 66 engine had come just at the right time. Given adequate ground control and good weather conditions so that the V-1s could be picked up visually, pilots were having little difficulty in being able to move in to attacking positions. The 20-mm Hispano cannon had been greatly improved since its introduction to service and it was now a much more reliable weapon, which was more than enough to bring down a V-1.

Early July was characterised by a further period of bad weather, which affected the number of intercepts, although it appeared as though the conditions were also affecting the launch rate. The number of V-1s picked up on radar was considerably lower on 3 July than had previously been the case, which was surprising considering that most of the ones that did turn up sailed through the defences unmolested as the cloud base was down to 800 ft with heavy rain. Chasing after V-1s in cloud was not for the faint-hearted and on one occasion F/Sgt Tony Weller had one suddenly appear within feet of his Spitfire before disappearing just as quickly.

The next successes occurred on 4 July. During a patrol near Dungeness, F/O Dennis Davy was vectored towards a V-1, which was approaching Rye above a layer of cloud. This made it much easier to see and Davy was able to get behind it and open fire. His shells struck the pulse-jet, the flame becoming much less bright, and as it lost speed it turned slightly to port and went down to crash on a crossroads about four miles north-east of Hastings. Just after midday F/L Tom Williams and F/O D.R. Wallace shared a V-1, which crashed in the sea just off the coast between Rye and Dungeness, and F/O Duncan McIntosh and F/Sgt Tony Weller accounted for another, which also went into the sea about a mile off Bexhill. It was clearly best to intercept the V-1s as early as possible and many fighter patrols were extended out over the Channel, occasionally as far as the French coast so as to allow more time for the Spitfires to get into position. The squadron diary left no one in any doubt as to what was required when it said – 'the best possible place for these contraptions is in the drink'.

On 5 July two more V-1s were shot down to bring the squadron's score to nineteen, which amounted to 38,000 lbs of high explosive that had not reached its intended target. F/L P.W. Stewart was directed onto an incoming Diver near Beachy Head and although he hit its wings, causing it to trail smoke, it continued on course. Before he could attack again, another Spitfire cut in to fire from astern and the V-1 crashed to the east of Laughton in Sussex. The other successful pilot was F/Sgt Iain Hastings whose attack resulted in a long tail chase, which finished right on the edge of the balloon barrage at Gatwick. As he had been flying in and out of cloud Hastings only saw the barrage at the last moment and pulled up and away in an attempt to avoid it. He was not quite quick enough however and he fouled one of the cables, which spun his Spitfire round, taking off the starboard wing tip and snapping off two of the propeller blades. Fortunately he was close to Gatwick aerodrome at the time and was able to land without further incident. During the day the Detling Wing Leader, W/C Peter Powell DFC*, shot down two V-1s while flying a No. 1 Squadron Spitfire (MK846) but these were not added to the unit's score and were bagged instead by Station HQ.

After a relatively quiet day on 6 July in which twenty patrols were all uneventful, three V-1s were shot down on the 7th. The first fell to the guns of F/Sgt H.J. Vassie, a recent arrival with the squadron. In what was his first combat, Vassie fired at a V-1 near Hailsham and despite 8/10 cloud from 800–1,800 ft he managed to follow it, firing all of his ammunition. As he pulled up and away he lost sight of it but shortly after there was an explosion, the shock wave from which was felt and lifted his Spitfire in the air. F/O H.L. Stuart was advised by control of a V-1 crossing the coast at Eastbourne. He had climbed to 6,000 ft to be able to dive onto any potential targets and was soon in firing range. His shells hit the starboard wing and fuselage and the bomb immediately began a diving turn to the right before crashing into a house adjacent to a hospital to the north of Hailsham. The third and last Diver was shot down by F/O Junior Marsh and also crashed near Hailsham.

By now fifteen pilots could claim to have shot down a V-1 and on 10 July two more broke their ducks. F/O Tommy Wyllie got his first, which crashed in a wood near Crowborough, and another of the squadron's new boys, F/Sgt G. Tate, intercepted another four miles north-east of Sevenoaks and exploded it in the air. The game of musical chairs turned full circle on 11 July when a signal was received that the squadron would be moving back to Lympne. Before it did so four more V-1s were shot down including two by F/Sgt Iain Hastings. F/Sgt G. Tate got his second in two days when he sent one crashing into woods north of Hastings and F/O Freddie Town despatched another to the north of Rye.

Three patrols were carried out in the morning of 12 July but the squadron was released for the rest of the day to facilitate its move to Lympne. The ground crews and road convoy left Detling in the morning and the pilots made their way after lunch following a short session in the bar. On arrival it was apparent that Lympne was rather overcrowded, as an aerodrome that had been intended for just one squadron now had to accommodate three, with Nos 41 and 165 Squadrons also in residence. There was much jockeying for position but No. 1 Squadron managed to capture its old dispersal; it just had to cram in twice as many personnel as before. There was however plenty of room at Port Lympne and its delights were soon discovered by a new generation of No. 1 Squadron pilots.

Lympne was right in the front line as far as the V-1 offensive was concerned and these 'infernal machines' (as the squadron diary referred to them) were regularly seen flying overhead on their way to London. The aerodrome was also close to the anti-aircraft gun batteries situated along the coast and these opened up whenever a V-1 was in the vicinity, which led to many sleepless nights. Personnel were also ordered to wear tin helmets when going about their work as a result of the amount of shrapnel that was falling all around.

The first V-1 to be shot down from Lympne was on 14 July when F/O Junior Marsh attacked a Diver ten miles off Cap Gris Nez. His first attack struck the wings, however a second burst hit the engine, which exploded in a ball of flame. It then turned over before spiralling down to crash in the sea. Another was shot down by F/L P.W. Stewart and this exploded near some farm buildings not far from Tenterden. The next day out of nine patrols the only successful pilot was F/Sgt H.J. Vassie who claimed his second V-1, which was shot down five miles east of Detling. The last flying bomb to be shot down by No. 1 Squadron for several days fell to the guns of F/L Tom Williams on 16 July. His first attack hit the fuselage and wing roots causing the V-1 to enter a shallow diving turn to starboard, however after a second burst it pulled up into a 20-degree climb to port before descending once again to crash in an orchard to the south of Maidstone.

Although the Tempest V squadrons of the Newchurch Wing (Nos 3 and 486) and the Spitfire XIVs of Nos 91 and 322 Squadrons were at the forefront of the battle against the V-1 by day, No. 1 Squadron was also doing a superb job, considering that the Spitfire IXB could not compete with these aircraft in terms of speed at low level. Another factor that had to be taken into consideration was that as soon as the guns were fired, the recoil forces reduced speed by around 20–30 mph. The only other units to fly the Mark IX during anti-Diver operations were Nos 165 and 310 Squadrons. As they had been following each other around for some time now there was considerable competition between Nos 1 and 165 Squadrons and for most of the V-1 campaign their respective scores were extremely close. The pattern of scoring within the squadrons was also very similar and many pilots within No. 165 Squadron had been able to put in a claim for a V-1 destroyed. No. 1 Squadron's current top scorer was F/Sgt Iain Hastings with four plus one shared, the most successful pilots on No. 165 Squadron being F/L Jim Porteous and F/Sgt C.M. Lawson, with three apiece.

Over the next few days no V-1s were shot down and it was felt that this was due to the squadron being given a different patrol line over the Channel. This was from

Cap Gris Nez to a point about twenty miles south-south-west. Although there were still plenty of potential targets, it was found that the vectors given by Control did not allow sufficient time to enable the Spitfires to carry out an interception before they were over the gun belt along the south coast. In many cases they had to break away just as they were about to close in to attack. The only other option was to run the gauntlet of the heavy anti-aircraft batteries and, not surprisingly, no one wanted to take the risk. Given this situation the pilots became rather despondent, especially as they felt that they stood a better chance of bringing the flying bombs down than the guns.

It was not until 22 July that No. 1 Squadron had further success and the point was underlined in the squadron diary (literally) that both were brought down over land. F/O J.O. 'Joe' Dalley DFM, a former photo-reconnaissance Spitfire pilot who had joined the squadron five days before, accounted for the first near Lamberhurst. The V-1 slowed suddenly and dived steeply into a field of cows, which led to a short stampede as far as the adjoining field where they continued their ruminations. The other was shot down by F/O Dennis Davy who completed the work of two Mustangs by blowing up a V-1 up in the air five miles south of Ashford. As he had only been 150 yards behind when it blew up, Davy had no choice but to fly through the blast and his Spitfire was damaged by fragments.

The next day F/Sgt H.J Vassie destroyed his third V-1 when he sent one cartwheeling into the sea ten miles off Folkstone during an early morning patrol, however it was F/O Dennis Davy who received all the plaudits as he shot down three during the course of two morning patrols. His first went into the sea eight miles north-east of Boulogne at 0710 hrs. Having refuelled and rearmed he was immediately in the air again and sent another down to the south-east of Ashford at 0824 hrs. He was then vectored onto another but had to wait his turn as two Mustangs, a Spitfire and a Tempest were chasing it. After the other aircraft had broken away the V-1 continued on its course with its engine still functioning and Davy moved in to fire a one-second burst from the port beam. This hit the fuel tanks and the flying bomb turned sharply to port and exploded on the Advanced Landing Ground at Kingsnorth near Ashford. This was occupied by the 36th Fighter Group, USAAF, and three of its P-47 Thunderbolts suffered blast damage, but there were no injuries to personnel.

The hazards to those under the flight path of the flying bombs were evident again the following day following a double strike by F/O Freddie Town and P/O Ken Foskett (Black section). Town was guided onto a V-1 approaching Folkstone and after several attacks it crashed in a wood north-east of Ashford. Ken Foskett saw another come through the gun belt but had to hold off as a Mustang went into the attack. This proved to be ineffectual so Foskett took over, his fire causing the V-1 to turn to port in a shallow dive. It crashed near a brick works and only about twenty yards from a railway line. As he turned back, to his consternation he saw that there was a train rapidly approaching and as the track was damaged it would, at the very least, derail when it got there. Foskett flew low alongside the train and tried to attract the attention of the driver by waggling his wings and raising and lowering his undercarriage. This unusual behaviour worked and he was relieved to see the train begin to slow and come to a standstill before it reached the crash site. Messages of appreciation from passengers were received and the press began to clamour for Foskett's photo and a full report of the episode.

On 25 July twenty-eight patrols were carried out. All were uneventful but the round-the-clock nature of the offensive was emphasised when four V-1s were shot down near Lympne during the night by the local artillery. The next day three more were destroyed by No. 1 Squadron. F/L Ian Maskill finally got his first when he sent one crashing down west of Maidstone. The others were shot down by F/O Dennis Davy and F/Sgt G. Tate (Yellow 1 and 2) who were patrolling the Channel off Folkstone in the early afternoon. Davy was soon vectored onto a Diver and sent it crashing into the sea. He was then warned of another and this was fired at by Tate who hit the V-1's port wing. Both pilots then attacked in turn and caused sufficient damage so that it crashed in the sea about five miles south of Lympne.

After a day of poor weather on 27 July in which only ten patrols were possible, an improvement the next day allowed twenty-eight anti-Diver patrols but it was not until the evening that there was any 'trade'. At 2145 hrs F/O Joe Dalley encountered a V-1 two miles north-east of Cap Gris Nez but its behaviour was extremely unusual. It was flying very slowly at around 110–130 mph and was only about 150 ft above sea level. It was also skidding with the port wing down before righting itself at regular intervals to fly straight and level. Dalley also considered that it was larger than the regular V-1 with a wingspan of 30–35 feet and had a longer fuselage and propulsion unit. As it was flying so slowly he had to lower his flaps prior to attacking but missed with his first burst. His second was on target and the V-1 nosed over to explode in the sea directly under Dalley's Spitfire. Luckily it did not cause any damage but his engine cut momentarily due to negative 'g' as his machine was lifted by the blast. As no 'outsize' V-1s were ever produced it appears that Dalley may have been deceived by its slow speed.

At the same time as Dalley was in combat, F/O Freddie Town was picking up another V-1, which had just passed through the gun belt. He fired several bursts trying to explode it in the air but it eventually exploded in a field two miles north of Staplehurst. Half an hour later he saw another V-1 being chased by two Mustangs and two Spitfires. By using full boost however he was able to overtake all of these aircraft and fired a burst which hit the tail unit. The V-1 went into an increasingly steep dive and exploded near a railway line to the west of Lenham.

Only nine patrols were carried out on 29 July due to bad weather but this did not stop the gun defences, which were much more effective than at the beginning of the offensive, and six V-1s were destroyed in the Lympne area. By now the guns were using proximity fuses and this led to a much higher success rate so that the majority of the V-1s that made it as far as the UK were now being shot down. Having had a successful campaign thus far, No. 1 Squadron had its first reverse on 30 July when F/Sgt G. Tate, who had only been with the squadron a short time, failed to return from an anti-Diver patrol over the Channel near Cap Gris Nez. He was flying as Yellow 2 to Dennis Davy but called up to say that his engine was beginning to run roughly. They were ordered by Control to return to base but shortly afterwards his engine began to cut and he informed his leader that he was losing height and would have to bale out. Owing to haze Davy lost sight of him and the next thing he saw was a large splash as Tate's Spitfire (MJ422) hit the water. Davy orbited the spot but could see no sign of parachute or dinghy. Another section and a Walrus were scrambled to continue the search but he was not located and it had to be concluded that he had been killed (his body was eventually found and he is buried at the Leopoldsburg War Cemetery).

A further period of inclement weather meant that the next combat did not occur until 3 August. It involved F/O D.R. Wallace who chased a V-1 in and out of cloud for some time before sending it down to crash in a field four miles south-west of West Malling aerodrome. The next day F/O Jack Batchelor (Black 2) intercepted a Diver five miles inland from Folkstone. As he had a 3,000 ft height advantage he caught it easily and closed to 250 yards before firing a deflection burst of three seconds from 10 degrees port to line astern. The V-1 slowed appreciably to about 250 mph and dropped its starboard wing so that Batchelor had to pull up to avoid overshooting. On pulling away after a second attack the flying bomb did some 'aerobatics' and then crashed at Eastwell Park, north of Ashford. There was further evidence of problems as a result of using 150-octane fuel and higher boost pressures when W/O J.W. McKenzie had to force-land at Thane in Kent due to engine failure. He escaped with superficial cuts and bruises but his Spitfire (NH466) was a write-off.

The last V-1 to be destroyed by No. 1 Squadron was shot down by F/L J.J. Jarman on 9 August. Flying as Red 2 to F/L Ian Maskill, he intercepted a V-1 just inland from the gun belt and attacked from astern and above from 400 yards down to 100 yards. A one-second burst was enough to send it into a dive and although a Tempest also went after it, it was not seen to fire and the flying bomb crashed just south-west of Hailsham. This brought the squadron total to forty-seven with another shared, which amounted to nearly 100,000 lbs of high explosive that had failed to reach the capital. Although the main V-1 offensive would continue to early September, No. 1 Squadron's part in it ended on 10 August when it moved back to Detling (not Hawkinge as had been rumoured) for offensive operations. This was greeted with enthusiasm, as although everyone had never lost sight of the importance of shooting down V-1s, it was after all a defensive operation and the squadron much preferred to be operating on the other side of the Channel. It was also expected that in addition to escorting bombers, the squadron would be able to carry out armed reconnaissance missions once again. Only time would tell.

CHAPTER SIXTEEN

Bomber Escorts and the Spitfire F.21

Having settled back in at Detling No. 1 Squadron flew its first bomber escort mission on 11 August when it accompanied 120 Lancasters bombing the marshalling yards at Lens. It was assisted in this task by Nos 165 and 504 Squadrons, the bombers achieving good results despite accurate heavy flak on the way in and over the target. A second operation later in the day was rather more modest and involved escorting ten Halifax bombers attacking a 'Noball' site near Cassel.

Over the next few days the squadron flew one or two operations each day and escorted a variety of medium bombers (Mitchells, Marauders and Bostons). The behaviour of the bombers often left a lot to be desired and at times caused problems for the escorting fighters. This was highlighted on 14 August when twelve Spitfires of No. 1 Squadron (together with a similar number from No. 165 Squadron and led by W/C Peter Powell) acted as close escort to thirty-six US Bostons attacking a railway junction at Frevent. The bombers were late at the rendezvous and instead of crossing over the coast at Furnes, they did so just west of Ostend. They then seemed uncertain as to the location of the target and flew to Courtrai – Lille – Arras before eventually finding the target after three wide circuits. The bombing was not particularly concentrated but on leaving the target area instead of turning for home, the Bostons headed north-east towards Brussels at which point W/C Powell lost patience and with fuel running low took his Spitfires back to Detling. Such indiscipline could have proved costly but the *Luftwaffe* was now hopelessly overstretched and their actions went unpunished.

Although the Fw 190s and Bf 109s that defended occupied Europe were now significantly outnumbered, they were still a viable force as No. 1 Squadron found to its cost on 17 August. In the afternoon W/C Powell led the Detling Wing as escort to thirty-six Mitchells bombing a fuel dump in the Forêt de Bretonne (Ramrod 1211). Heavy flak accounted for one of the Mitchells and also had the effect of splitting the formations up so that on the way back the first and last aircraft were separated by ten miles. A number of Fw 190s of III/JG 26 led by Lt Wilhelm Hofmann had been scrambled and these were able to bounce Yellow section, which was right at the back of the bomber formation and had been reduced to three aircraft (one having returned earlier with R/T trouble). Despite a shouted warning, W/O J.W. McKenzie (Yellow 2) and W/O H.G. Wallace-Wells (Yellow 4) were both hit, the former force-landing near Yvetot. Wallace-Wells glided out over the Channel at Fecamp, his aircraft streaming glycol, but had to bale out when only four miles off the French coast. Fixes were given by other squadron members and before leaving he was seen waving from his dinghy. He was picked up after an hour in the water. Hofmann undoubtedly accounted for one of the Spitfires shot down, the other being despatched by Uffz Erich Klein or Uffz Hans-Joachim Borreck who both filed claims (McKenzie evaded capture and returned to the UK the following month).

The next day the Detling Wing provided target cover for forty-five Lancasters and five Mosquitos bombing an MT depot north-east of Ghent but there followed several days of low cloud and rain and the next operation was not until 23 August. This was a sweep by Nos 1 and 165 Squadrons routeing Beauvais – Creil – Laon and although a deviation was made to Amiens as Control reported that there were 'bandits' in the area, nothing was seen. Further short periods of bad weather led to an attack by US Bostons on a fuel dump at St Just being cancelled twice and it was not until the morning of 26 August, at the third time of asking, that it finally went ahead. Later in the day two armed reconnaissance missions were flown. On the first, one aircraft had to land at Manston due to engine trouble but the others shot up two barges south of Dixmunde. During the second, Yellow section led by F/O H.L. Stuart (ML258), with F/L J.J. Jarman (NH200) as his No. 2, attacked three railway trucks, while Blue section went for a laden barge north of Ypres. F/O Tommy Wyllie (MK867 – Blue 1) raked the barge from bow to stern during a five-second burst and this was followed up by his wingman, W/O E.R. Andrews (MK926).

On 27 August the squadron paid its first visit to the Ruhr on what was a historic day as it marked the first major daylight raid by Bomber Command on Germany since 12 August 1941 when Blenheims attacked power stations near Cologne. The target on this occasion was the Rheinpreussen synthetic-oil refinery at Homberg/Meerbeck. As this involved a deep penetration (for Spitfires at least) the escorting fighters were fitted with 90-gallon overload tanks, which more than doubled internal fuel capacity. The overall flight time was 2 hours 25 minutes. In the evening Nos 1 and 165 Squadrons provided close escort to B-26 Marauders bombing rail targets north-east of Laon.

After another Marauder escort mission to fuel dumps north-east of Compiègne on 28 August, No. 1 Squadron carried out an armed reconnaissance of the Calais – Ghent – Aulnoye area on 30 August. Led by W/C Powell, the ten Spitfires crossed the coast at Blankenberge and west of Ghent attacked a stationary tug that had two barges attached. In the same area F/O H.L. Stuart (ML258 – Yellow 3) attacked several army lorries, one of which had a large gun in tow. One of these vehicles was eventually left burning furiously. The sheer numbers of Allied fighter-bombers now swarming over northern Europe was putting the German supply network under severe strain so that targets were not as plentiful as they had been. Nothing else was seen and having continued to the north-west of Lille, the coast was crossed again at Nieuport. The month of August was rounded off when the squadron acted as withdrawal cover on the 31st for Lancasters and Halifaxes bombing sites near Abbeville where it was thought V-2 rockets were being stored.

In early September only two escort missions were possible as bad weather severely affected the offensive against German transport and other targets. The operations that were possible consisted of an attack by forty-eight Mitchells on Givet marshalling yards on the 1st and one by 100 Lancasters on Deelen aerodrome in Holland on the 3rd. The break offered by the weather at least allowed the squadron to welcome back two of its members who had been shot down earlier in the year. W/O Neil Howard returned on 8 September, having evaded capture after force-landing near Tergnier on 2 March, and W/O J.W. McKenzie also turned up none the worse for his experience following his force-landing on 4 August. The day was also notable as the first V-2 rocket fell on Chiswick at 1843 hrs to mark the opening of a new terror campaign. Unlike the V-1 flying bomb, there could be no defence against the V-2 other than to find and destroy the launch sites. This was to involve No. 1 Squadron and at first light on 9 September twelve Spitfires equipped with 90-gallon overload tanks took off on an anti 'Big Ben' patrol (Big Ben was the code name give to the V-2). The Spitfires swept the Rotterdam – Amsterdam – Den Helder area but there was no sign of the elusive new weapon.

This area of Holland was visited again by the squadron the next morning and having made a landfall at Ijmuiden at 7,000 ft the Spitfires descended to look for targets of opportunity. On this occasion they did not have long to wait as a large locomotive pulling forty to fifty trucks was seen and attacked. As Pat Lardner-Burke and his section disabled the engine, the rest of the squadron went for the wagons, which were sprayed with cannon fire the full length of the train and left in flames. A radar station was also shot up at Egmond and the remainder of the morning's 'bag' were an observation post, three gun posts and electric power pylons. Light flak was experienced at various times but no aircraft were hit. In the evening a similar operation was launched, one that took in the area around Rotterdam and Amsterdam but this proved to be uneventful.

By now the bombing campaign against German oil facilities was being intensified and on 11 September No. 1 Squadron formed part of the escort to 100 Halifaxes attacking the synthetic-oil plant at Gelsenkirchen/Nordstern. Although no *Luftwaffe* fighters were seen, the flak defences were formidable as usual and scored a direct hit on one of the bombers. The following day it was the turn of the Wanne-Eickel plant in the Ruhr. For this raid No. 1 Squadron flew from Manston and provided withdrawal cover as the bombers were returning. Whenever the weather permitted the squadron's schedule now consisted of an armed reconnaissance in the morning with a bomber escort later in the day. On 12 September twelve Spitfires (45-gallon tanks) carried out a low level attack on a suspected Big Ben target north-east of The Hague. A wooded area was thoroughly strafed and a flak post was shot up on the way home. In the afternoon twelve Spitfires (90-gallon tanks) flew as escort to Halifaxes returning to the Nordstern oil plant at Gelsenkirchen. As on previous occasions the Germans laid a smoke screen over the target but this proved to be futile against the blind bombing techniques (H2S and Oboe) employed by Lancasters and Mosquitos of No. 8 (Pathfinder) Group. Vivid orange flames were seen through the smoke screen and a pall of black smoke rose above the plant.

On 16 September the squadron flew an armed reconnaissance in the area of The Hague – Utrecht – Den Helder but the locality was eerily quiet with no signs of rail or road traffic. Once again there were no German aircraft to be seen anywhere. Later in the day W/C Powell led the squadron as it provided target and withdrawal support to Invaders, Bostons and Marauders bombing a viaduct on the Dutch Islands. The next day two aircraft flew a shipping recce in the area of Dunkirk – Flushing but the only naval activity to be seen consisted of Allied craft off Ostend. The pilots did however report a vertical condensation trail at a height estimated at 20,000 ft. This was undoubtedly the squadron's first sighting of a V-2 rocket and appeared to have come from a site to the north of the Dutch Islands.

For the rest of September the squadron was mainly engaged in connection with Operation *Market Garden*, which involved the dropping of a massive airborne force into the area around Arnhem with the intention of securing a number of vital bridges. These were to be held while Montgomery's Army made a rapid thrust through Holland and Belgium to join up. If all had gone according to plan, there would have been nothing to prevent an advance to the Rhine and beyond. By such means it was hoped that the war could be ended before the year was out, but events were to conspire against the Allies and the operation quickly turned into a disaster. The extent of the operation was evident from the arrival of the operational order (Form D) in the early hours of 17 September as it was over 12 ft long. The squadron's role was to be low level escort of Dakota transports carrying paratroops, or tug and glider combinations. The sky was 10/10 Allied aircraft (as one pilot put it) and the *Luftwaffe* was again largely absent, although it was able to inflict some losses. The German flak defences once again caused the greatest hazard, especially for the transport aircraft, and gun posts were strafed as required.

On D+1 the squadron again performed an escort and anti-flak patrol and went down low over Dutch territory on the lookout for flak positions but saw none. Despite initial successes the situation of the Allied troops in the Arnhem area soon became desperate as the expected reinforcements failed to arrive. Their situation was also not helped by a significant deterioration in the weather. On 19 September (D+2) No. 1 Squadron was detailed for further escort and anti-flak work, but with a solid overcast at 1–2,000 ft, with another layer at 4–5,000 ft and poor visibility, a return had to be made when near Manston. Patrols were possible on D+3, however the next two days were again washed out. It was not until 23 September (D+6) that the squadron was able to play an active role once again by patrolling from Bourg Leopold to Eindhoven. After another day of low cloud and rain, what was left of the Allied ground forces began to withdraw on 25 September, the operation having cost the elite airborne units between 15,000 and 17,000 men killed. Those that had survived were in desperate need of supplies and on the 26th No. 1 Squadron escorted thirty-six Dakotas, which landed on a strip about six miles south-west of Nijmegen.

Despite continued unfavourable weather a fighter sweep was laid on for 27 September. This got off to an inauspicious start as long-range tanks had to be dropped just over the Dutch coast when a formation of fighters was seen, however these aircraft turned out to be Spitfires. As the Schelde Estuary was approached conditions became even worse and soon F/O Tommy Wyllie and W/O E.R. Andrews (Blue 3 and 4) were heard on Channel C calling Manston for a homing. They were given a course of 288 degrees and although Wyllie acknowledged the call, nothing further was heard from them. The remainder of the squadron returned to base despite an 'unpleasant tussle' with the weather. This was indeed a black day as Tommy Wyllie was a deputy flight commander and a first class pilot. The squadron diary also noted that Andrews 'had what it takes' to be a fighter pilot and expressed the opinion that the two would be extremely difficult to replace. Both were killed and it is not inconceivable that they collided at some point over the North Sea.

There was little improvement in the weather towards the end of the month and an adverse report from a weather recce by four aircraft on 29 September was actually listened to for once and no shows were forthcoming. On the 30th twelve Spitfires took off from Detling at 1605 hrs prior to escorting thirty-six B-26 Marauders bound for the bridge at Arnhem. Rendezvous was made at Schouwen Island, however most of the bombs were seen to burst on the northern approach to the bridge and despite the target area being covered in smoke, the bridge itself was undamaged. Some flak was experienced around Arnhem but none of No. 1 Squadron's Spitfires were hit.

The new month of October brought no respite from the weather and frequent low pressure systems coming in from the Atlantic produced wind and rain on a regular basis. As the previous month had been much wetter than average, concern began to be expressed as to the serviceability of Detling and the state of the aerodrome would soon become critical. Before then the squadron escorted twenty-four Bostons on 2 October to attack a target at Cleves. Apart from heavy flak when approaching the target area the operation passed uneventfully although F/L P.W. Stewart (NH253) had to land at Brussels-Evere due to oil trouble. He was accompanied by his No. 2, F/O J.W. Still in MK733. A further escort was laid on in the afternoon, which led to a leadership crisis as Pat Lardner-Burke was temporarily grounded with a heavy cold. With Ian Maskill on leave and F/L Stewart stranded for the time being in Brussels, it fell to F/O H.L. Stuart to lead the squadron. He had taken over from Tommy Wyllie as the deputy commander of 'B' Flight and the target on this occasion was a rail junction adjacent to the River Waal in Holland.

With the Allied armies making steady progress on the Continent there was now an increasing number of VIPs heading for Europe and on 3 October Flight Lieutenants R. Brown and F.H. James flew to Hendon in the early morning to escort a Dakota to Brussels. This flew at 5,000 ft but having crossed the French coast at Le Treport, cloud was encountered and the two Spitfire pilots lost contact with it. Although they made a thorough search, they could not locate the Dakota and eventually had to return to base. Thankfully a message was later received that the aircraft had landed safely at Brussels. In the afternoon W/C Powell led eleven Spitfires of No. 1 Squadron as escort to Bostons bombing enemy positions south of Arnhem. For a change there was no flak at any stage of the operation.

Although the squadron had always achieved high levels of serviceability, the extra strain on the Merlin engines as a result of using 150-octane fuel allied to increased sortie times meant that the ground crews were struggling to have enough aircraft on line each day. This situation was not helped by the fact that replacement aircraft had thus far failed to materialise. On 7 October the squadron was only able to put ten aircraft in the air as part of the close escort for 340 Lancasters and ten Mosquitos of 1, 3 and 8 Groups attacking Emmerich. The bombers were picked up eight miles inland from The Hague and covered all the way to the target. Accurate heavy flak was experienced and one fighter from another formation was seen to go down having been hit. The bombing attack was extremely accurate and huge columns of black smoke rose above the town from oil fires.

This was the last operation to be successfully completed for a week as bad weather either prevented any flying at all or resulted in cancellations. During this period of inactivity F/O Arthur Adams DFC joined No. 1 Squadron on 9 October. He was an extremely experienced fighter pilot having flown with No. 111 Squadron in the Middle East. He had joined this unit in February 1943 as a Sergeant pilot and was promoted to Flying Officer in the space of six months. During this time he claimed three German fighters destroyed with another five probables. Following the sad loss of Tommy Wyllie it was hoped that he would be a considerable asset to the squadron.

There was an early start on 14 October as the squadron provided escort to a large-scale attack on Duisberg. This was Operation *Hurricane*, the aim of which was to demonstrate the massive superiority of Allied air power by co-ordinated strikes by RAF Bomber Command and the US 8th Air Force. On the morning of the 14th the RAF despatched just over 1,000 Lancasters, Halifaxes and Mosquitos and this force was followed by 1,251 American heavy bombers which attacked Cologne. No. 1 Squadron's contribution got off to a bad start when Pat Lardner-Burke and his wingman, Dennis Davy (MK714), had to return with an oiled up windscreen and oxygen failure respectively. As it turned out the fact that the squadron was down on strength hardly mattered as no enemy fighters were seen. During the operation F/L J.J. Jarman also had problems and had to land at St Omer/Fort Rouge with a rough engine. He managed to get a lift in a Dakota and was back at Detling in the early evening having left his Spitfire (MK726) behind for attention.

Following two escort missions on 15 and 17 October (Mitchells to Deventer and Lancasters to Westkapelle) further heavy rain meant that Detling became unusable and the next operation did not take place until 25 October. This was an attack by 243 Halifaxes and Lancasters on the synthetic-oil plant at Homberg/Meerbeck and although the target was covered by cloud the bombing was reasonably concentrated on the markers dropped by the Pathfinders. Although twelve Spitfires took off, only eight made it to the target however due to various unserviceabilities. W/O D.M. Royds (Blue 2 – EN636) returned early with R/T trouble and Iain Hastings (Red 4 – NH246) also had to turn back with a misfiring engine. F/L P.W. Stewart (NH253) who was leading Yellow section was forced to put down at Manston, again due to engine problems, and was escorted by his No. 2 W/O John Morden (MK901). The remaining aircraft had a quiet time, which was only enlivened by another V-2 sighting in the distance when the Wing was near Diest.

Further bad weather at the end of the month led to Detling becoming unserviceable once again and after an early afternoon release on 29 October many of the squadron members headed for the ever popular Star Hotel in Maidstone and the adjoining dance hall. The weather situation did not improve so on the 31st Operation *Goody Goody* came in to force with another mass invasion of Maidstone, its cinemas proving a popular choice to while away what was a thoroughly miserable afternoon. In the evening 'Dining-In' night at Detling was a great success and having eaten an excellent meal and made numerous toasts the Station Commander, W/C Michael Crossley DSO DFC, led the assembled throng in a traditional RAF sing-song. This went down well as Crossley was an accomplished musician, being proficient on the saxophone, guitar and harmonica. As a finale the squadron challenged No. 165 Squadron to a game of Mess rugger. Having already won 3–0 at football two weeks before, No. 1 Squadron came out victorious again with a score of 2–1.

Around this time Detling received a new Wing Leader in W/C Bobby Oxspring DFC** as W/C Powell had been injured on 10 October when his car collided with an Army lorry, a crash which killed F/L T.D. Tinsey of No. 165 Squadron. Oxspring had joined the RAF in March 1938 and after completing his flying training was posted to No. 66 Squadron, the unit his father had flown with during the First World War. He had considerable combat success with No. 66 Squadron during the Battle of Britain and later led No. 72 Squadron in the Middle East. His final posting before taking over at Detling was as leader of 141 Wing.

On 2 November W/C Oxspring led the squadron on Ramrod 1357 when 184 Lancasters of 3 Group carried out a G-H attack on the oil plant at Homberg. No. 1 Squadron's involvement was as target and withdrawal support and although it appeared to them that no bombers had been hit by flak, five were in fact lost during the raid. Another V-2 contrail was seen arcing into the upper atmosphere having been launched to the east of Antwerp. On 5 November White section comprising F/O Jack Batchelor and F/O Arthur Adams escorted a twin-engined Lockheed aircraft from Hendon to Paris. This was too good an opportunity to miss and with a weather forecast predicting 100 mph winds both pilots made sure to pack their 'Sunday best' in case of an enforced stay. The rest of the squadron led by Ian Maskill supported 176 Lancasters of 3 Group, which bombed Solingen. After fulfilling their duties to the bombers the squadron then swept the local area at 25,000 ft before returning. Due to high winds at altitude, height was lost on the way back and the Channel was crossed at zero feet. This proved to be one of the longest trips so far on Spitfires as the squadron landed at 1435 hrs having been airborne for 2 hours 45 minutes. (Pat Lardner-Burke was unable to lead on this occasion due to a cracked rib. Whether this was caused by the game of Mess rugger a few days before is not recorded!)

Predictably Jack Batchelor and Arthur Adams had to stay the night in Paris and spent a very pleasant evening in Montmartre. Unfortunately the following day was a Monday and most of the shops were closed so they were unable to buy what were considered to be 'essentials'. They did manage however to bring back a bottle of champagne each and when they added up the figures on their return found that they had somehow managed to make a profit on the trip. During 6 November the squadron flew as escort to a formation of 216 Halifaxes, which was part of an overall force of 738 heavy bombers attacking the Nordstern oil plant at Gelsenkirchen. On this occasion the bombers flew in a more compact formation and in consequence were covered much more easily. Over the target pilots reported seeing two 'scarecrows' but these were undoubtedly aircraft exploding in the air after being hit by flak (although RAF bomber crews in particular believed that the Germans fired such 'scarecrows' to simulate aircraft blowing up, no evidence has ever been found that they existed).

As the squadron was now operating mostly with 90-gallon overload tanks, which allowed operations well into Germany, difficulties were being experienced as regards radio communications. To get round this problem one of the squadron's Spitfires would act as a relay aircraft by orbiting in the Brussels area where it could pass on information from Control. On 8 November thirteen aircraft took off at 0930 hrs of which twelve acted as target cover to 136 Lancasters of 3 Group which had been briefed for another raid on the Meerbeck oil plant at Homberg. The remaining Spitfire was the relay aircraft and on this occasion F/L J.J. Jarman was 'Dogbite Relay' in MK644. Despite a report from Control that enemy fighters were approaching the target area, none were seen. In the evening a dozen or so V-1 flying bombs passed over Detling at low level, which caused a certain amount of consternation as these had not been seen for some time. As most of the launch sites had now been overrun by the Allied ground forces they had most likely been air-launched, the Heinkel 111 bomber having been modified to carry a V-1 under either wing.

The airfield surface at Detling deteriorated even further over the next week and the only flying carried out was by the squadron Tiger Moth. F/L W.S. Wallace, the squadron doctor, had been taking flying instruction from F/L J.J. Jarman who was known to all as the 'Tiger King'. After 7½ hours dual he was sent solo and despite taking off in poor visibility, landed in excellent style. This momentous event was to cost him dear in the Mess bar in the evening. After three cancellations and postponements on 16 November the squadron finally managed to get airborne on Ramrod 1372. Bomber Command had been requested to attack three German towns (Duren, Julich and Heinsburg) that were immediately behind the German lines and were about to be attacked by the American First and Ninth Armies. No. 1 Squadron accompanied the raid on Duren, which was virtually destroyed and 3,127 of its inhabitants were killed. The attacking force comprised 485 Lancasters and thirteen Mosquitos of 1, 5 and 8 Groups of which three Lancasters (one each from Nos 166, 207 and 625 Squadrons) were seen to blow up in the target area. There were no survivors from any of these aircraft.

By 20 November the aerodrome at Detling resembled a quagmire so it came as something of a surprise to discover that an operation had been laid on for the following day. Despite the state of the ground the squadron's Spitfires took off at 1400 hrs without incident bound once more for Homberg. Although the oil plant there had already been attacked on several occasions the damage caused had not been decisive but this was put right by 180 Lancasters of 3 Group. Although the bombing was initially scattered, it became much more concentrated as the raid progressed and a large fire was created that produced a column of black smoke that rose to a great height. The escort fighters had a grandstand view of the destruction being wrought below and also of more V-2 launches with two rising up over The Hague, another two over Munster and a fifth from the Dorsel area.

Operations were now only possible on a sporadic basis and the next did not occur until 27 November. Top cover was provided for 169 Lancasters of 3 Group, which bombed the Kalk Nord marshalling yards at Cologne. On 29 November the squadron formed part of the escort for 294 Lancasters attacking the synthetic-oil plant at Dortmund. When in the Eindhoven area two Messerschmitt Me 262s appeared but neither made any attempt to interfere with the bombers and flew off at high speed. This was the first time that No. 1 Squadron had encountered the *Luftwaffe's* new jet fighter which, thanks to a directive from Hitler, was mostly being used in the fighter-bomber role. As was now becoming customary, two more V-2 launches were reported.

There was still no improvement in the weather and it was not until 3 December that the squadron was briefed for another Lancaster escort mission. However, Detling's role had to be cancelled at the last moment as the aerodrome was deemed unfit for operations. A keen frost on the following night at least hardened up the ground so that the Wing could take part in Ramrod 1391 in the afternoon of 4 December. Although conditions were considered to be acceptable for take-off, it was thought that the Spitfires might have to land at Manston on the way back. The attack was by 160 Lancasters of 3 Group on Oberhausen but as the target was covered by cloud no results could be seen. Having patrolled at 20,000 ft in the target area the squadron gradually lost height on the way back and crossed the

Belgian coast at 600 ft. The Spitfires were able to land at Detling after another trip lasting 2 hours 45 minutes but great care had to be taken on landing to avoid accidents with the ever present danger of nosing over on patches of soft ground.

On 5 December W/C Bobby Oxspring led the squadron as escort to fifty-six Lancasters from 3 Group, which attempted to bomb the Schwammenauel Dam on the River Roer near Hasenfeld. As the target was obscured by cloud only two aircraft bombed. The next day an example of the latest version of the Spitfire, the Mark 21, was flown into Detling for everyone to have a close look at. Although there was a pressing need for re-equipment No. 1 Squadron would have to wait for another five months to get its hands on the new aircraft as testing had shown that its directional and longitudinal handling characteristics left a lot to be desired. The lengthening of the nose to accommodate the Rolls-Royce Griffon engine, together with the use of larger propellers of increased blade area to absorb the extra power available, had destabilised the aircraft to an unacceptable degree. Various modifications to the rudder and elevators led to the Spitfire 21 eventually being accepted for service but due to the delays it was destined not to play an active part in the war.

At 0845 hrs on 8 December the squadron was briefed for an escort and target cover role to 233 Lancasters of 5 Group and five Mosquitos of 8 Group, which were to attack the Urft Dam near Heimbach. This was a large reservoir dam in the Eifel region, the destruction of which would have prevented the Germans from releasing water to flood certain areas ahead of the American advance. Fourteen Spitfires were scheduled to take part, however the relay aircraft and one other had technical problems on start up and only twelve were able to take off. W/C Bobby Oxspring flew with the squadron once again but by way of a change he flew Blue 4 in the section led by Pat Lardner-Burke. Hits were scored on the dam but no breach was made and the Germans were later able to disrupt the movement of American troops by releasing large quantities of water. The squadron suffered further technical problems as Ian Maskill had to land at Brussels-Melsbroek with a rough-sounding engine. He was accompanied by his No. 2 F/O H.L. Stuart and they were soon joined by the rest of the squadron who also had to land at Brussels due to worsening weather.

The Detling Wing took off again in the late afternoon but had to land at Manston in the gathering gloom. They also had to contend with fog but were able to take advantage of FIDO, which had recently been installed. This stood for 'Fog, Intensive Disposal Of' and consisted of burners running along each side of the runway, which burnt fuel in prodigious quantities to heat the air above and improve visibility. Once switched on the fog soon lifted, the twin lines of fire also acting as a beacon so that the Wing had little difficulty in landing, however the welcoming glow also attracted several other squadrons, which resulted in an uncomfortable night on a greatly overcrowded station. The next day the Wing attempted to return to base but as the fog persisted there were several scares. Having taken off, F/L P.W. Stewart decided to return to Manston and finally made it back to Detling in the early afternoon at the third attempt. The biggest fright had nothing to do with the weather though as the engine of Bobby Oxspring's Spitfire cut just as he was about to take off. As he was holding on a fair amount of rudder to counteract engine torque he was unable to prevent his aircraft veering in front of that flown by Pat Lardner-Burke. Only the quick reactions of the latter prevented a major accident as he pulled back on the stick to hop over the errant Spitfire.

The next two weeks were extremely disappointing as Detling's involvement in several operations was cancelled for various reasons (usually weather). This led to envy at times as on 12 December when it was discovered that Mustangs that had been escorting Lancasters to the Ruhr had encountered enemy fighters and had shot down six. The next day No. 1 Squadron discovered that it would shortly be moving to Manston and that No. 165 Squadron, with which it had been associated for so long, would be going to Bentwaters. This breaking up of the Wing was very much regretted as was the fact that the squadron was leaving Detling, which had proved to be one of the better stations. The only good news was that Bobby Oxspring was to remain as Wing Leader. The move was scheduled to take place on 16 December but due to poor visibility it did not take place for another two days.

No. 1 Squadron replaced No. 118 Squadron and its new 'Wing mates' were No. 91 Squadron led by S/L P.M. Bond and No. 124 Squadron under S/L G.W. Scott AFC. One requirement at Manston was that the squadrons had to provide two sections to carry out early morning weather reconnaissance flights. Each squadron performed this duty in turn and these so-called 'Dogsbody patrols' took in France, Holland and Belgium so that the weather could be assessed for the day's operations. Unfortunately the conditions remained poor and it was not until 23 December that the first operation from Manston took place when the squadron gave target and withdrawal cover to Lancasters bombing objectives at Trier. The next day it was Dusseldorf, an operation that was uneventful except that F/O Pete Crocker (MK726) had to return early with a misfiring engine.

On 25 December Rodeo 407 was flown, which took in the area Aachen – Bonn – Liege. One aircraft had to abort due to a jammed hood but the remainder completed the task. A Messerschmitt Me 262 was seen over Bonn but it stayed well clear and made no attempt to attack. On return the pilots were dismayed to discover that the bar was closed and that there was hardly any food available apart from a few leftover sausage rolls. A few headed for local hostelries but on the whole Christmas Day was rather an anti-climax. Boxing Day proved to be rather better as the cancellation of an escort operation allowed everyone to head back to their old station at Detling, which provided an excellent spread with plenty to drink to remind the squadron just what it was missing.

After an escort mission to Cologne/Gremberg on 28 December the squadron escorted a Bomber Command attack on the railway yards at Koblenz. This was intended to create as much disruption as possible behind the Ardennes battlefront and came after an American raid the previous day. On the way home W/O D.M. Royds (Blue 4 – ML258) called up to say that his engine was cutting out intermittently. He was at 20,000 ft at the time but the situation soon became much more serious and he was last seen diving steeply at 15,000 ft with an engine that was obviously dead. Iain Hastings (Blue 3) turned back to search for him but saw nothing and there was no further R/T contact. It later transpired that Royds had been able to bale out and he spent the last few months of the war as a prisoner.

For some weeks there had been rumours that Pat Lardner-Burke would soon be on his way and this was finally confirmed on 30 December when he returned from two days away at 11 and 12 Groups. He was able to inform everyone that he had been promoted to Wing Commander and was set to take over the Coltishall Wing. His replacement was F/L David Cox DFC* CdG who had been flying with No. 1 Squadron for several weeks as a supernumerary. Cox was twenty-four years of age and had been educated at Bournemouth Collegiate School. His RAF career had had a faltering start as he initially failed his medical but to improve his fitness he got a job at Billingsgate fish market. His second attempt to join up in April 1939 was successful and after flight training he was posted as a Sergeant pilot to No. 19 Squadron at Duxford in May 1940. During the Battle of Britain he incurred the wrath of S/L Douglas Bader on one occasion even though he had just shot down a Bf 109E. His own Spitfire was riddled with holes and Bader made the point that a one-for-one ratio was 'not so f——g good'. He later served with No. 72 Squadron in the Middle East when this unit was led by Bobby Oxspring and during a third tour he commanded No. 222 Squadron. His final posting prior to joining No. 1 Squadron was as a test pilot with No. 84 Ground Support Unit (GSU). During his time as leader David Cox often flew ML119, which had previously been the preferred choice of Pat Lardner-Burke.

The last operation of the year took place on 31 December with No. 1 Squadron providing target and withdrawal support to 155 Lancasters of 3 Group, which carried out a G-H raid on marshalling yards at Vohwinkel near Solingen. Strong winds over the target badly affected this attack and much of the bombing missed the rail yards and struck the town of Solingen. All but two of No. 1 Squadron's Spitfires returned to Manston. Due to fuel shortage F/L R.D. Scrase and P/O Iain Hastings landed at Ursel (B-67) in Belgium, an airfield that the squadron would become well acquainted with in the coming weeks.

The New Year began in disappointing fashion as Manston's involvement in an attack on the Dortmund-Ems canal on 1 January had to be cancelled when the weather suddenly 'clamped' from the sea. 'Dogsbody' patrols were flown at first light on 3 January during which two more V-2 contrails were seen near The Hague. Two Ramrod operations were scheduled for later in the day but both had to be postponed due to worsening weather. In the afternoon there was another departure when the ever-popular Jack Batchelor left to become a flight commander with No. 229 Squadron at Coltishall.

On 5 January the squadron took off at 1040 hrs and led by S/L David Cox flew to Ursel to refuel prior to escorting 160 Lancasters of 3 Group to the marshalling yards at Ludwigshafen. The use of forward airfields in Belgium allowed the unit's

Spitfires to fly deeper into Germany so that escort operations could be undertaken to the majority of targets in the north-west of the country. Having taken off from Ursel four aircraft had to return to Manston with various maladies. F/O J.W. Still returned having damaged the rudder of his Spitfire (MK733) when taxiing, and Ian Maskill (NH200) had to abort due to an oxygen leak. Once in the air F/L P.W. Stewart discovered that his overload tank was not transferring fuel as it should and he was accompanied back to Manston by his No. 2, F/O Arthur Adams (ML423). The remainder patrolled the target area at 20,000 ft before returning to Ursel where they stayed the night.

With half the squadron at Manston and the rest at Ursel it was, perhaps, inevitable that the weather would intervene. The eight aircraft that had night stopped tried to get back to Manston on 6 January but only five made it at the first attempt as S/L David Cox and F/O Pete Crocker had to land at Friston with mist and low cloud closing in fast. F/L K.C. Pedersen did not even make it back over the Channel and had to spend another night at Ursel. 'Dogsbody' patrols on the 7th reported conditions that were wholly unsuitable for large-scale operations and the squadron was released for training, however another VIP trip to Brussels was flown around midday by Yellow section comprising F/L Joe Dalley (MH774) and F/L R. Brown (MK988). Having successfully shepherded the anonymous personage to the Continent they then had to fly back through a snowstorm in very poor visibility. This was the onset of severe winter weather with significant snow falls, which put a stop to operations for a while but led to some highly competitive snowball fights between pilots and ground crews. During this period there was cause for celebration when W/O J.W. McKenzie received his commission. Joe Dalley was also well toasted as he was about to get married.

The next successful operation did not take place until 17 January when the squadron flew a sweep (Rodeo 409) in the Rheine – Lingen area. They landed at Ursel and night stopped and should have flown a strafing mission from there the following day but this was cancelled due to the weather. The squadron then became weather bound in Belgium and did not return to Manston until 20 January by which time most pilots were wearing several days growth of beard and were thoroughly cold and fed up. Again they did not all make it back as F/O F.D. Thiele became lost and returned to Ursel and P/O J.W. McKenzie had to stay behind as his Spitfire (ML117) needed a new propeller. Further heavy falls of snow meant that they did not get back to Manston until 22 January by which time the squadron had moved to different dispersals which were closer to those of No. 91 Squadron. Although the accommodation was restricted, the squadron's Spitfires were at least closer to the runway and were able to repose on excellent hard standings so there was no chance of bogging down.

On 24 January the squadron welcomed P/O W.E. Recile from Trinidad and Tobago who joined from No. 64 Squadron at Bentwaters. The day was also notable for a rapid thaw that led to mist and fog, however temperatures then plummeted overnight to –12 degrees Centigrade and all the snow that had melted during the day froze solid, and the roads became treacherous with ice. The weather was so bad that even the 'Dogsbody' sections could not get off the ground and there was more snow overnight on 27 January. This did not stop two Ramrod operations being laid on over the next two days but both were cancelled with the pilots already in their cockpits and ready to go. Towards the end of the month there was another rise in temperature but on this occasion it was maintained, which gave hope that February might be rather more productive in terms of operational flying.

The first operation for two weeks took place on 1 February when the squadron took off shortly after 1500 hrs to carry out a sweep to assist a raid by 160 Lancasters of 3 Group on Munchen-Gladbach. Although the target was covered by a layer of cloud at 4–5,000 ft the bombers were able to attack using the G-H blind bombing system. As far as No. 1 Squadron was concerned the operation was straightforward, although the return to Manston in conditions of low cloud and poor visibility, together with the approaching dusk was anything but. Another new pilot arrived on this day in the shape of P/O R.C. Bahadurji from India who had previously flown with No. 63 Squadron. His name was more than anyone could cope with so he was promptly nicknamed Barry.

On 3 February the squadron, led by Bobby Oxspring, took off in the early afternoon to carry out a sweep in the Rheine area, however two aircraft failed to make it as F/L R. Brown (MK997) had to return with a jammed hood and F/L Joe Dalley (MH744) had to abort before take-off. Some heavy flak was experienced from the front line but otherwise the operation was uneventful and the squadron landed at Ursel where they were joined later by Brown and Dalley who had had their snags rectified. It had been hoped to carry out an operation from the Belgian airfield the following day but this had to be cancelled due to adverse weather and a return was made to Manston on 5 February. The next day the squadron could only muster seven aircraft for a sweep in connection with an attack by Lancasters of Nos 9 and 617 Squadrons on railway viaducts at Bielefeld and Altenbeken. This was the first of several attempts to destroy these targets using 12,000 lb Tallboy bombs but on this occasion cloud cover led to the bombers being recalled. The Spitfires returned to Manston after refuelling at Ursel.

The oil plant at Wanne-Eickel was the scheduled target on 7 February although wintry weather disrupted the bombing attack and also affected the escort fighters. The force of 100 Lancasters became widely scattered and only seventy-five were able to carry out their bombing runs. Due to thick layers of cloud the rendezvous with the fighters was missed and No. 1 Squadron had to return after a fruitless search for the bombers. After an early release due to bad weather on 8 February the squadron did a sweep of the area around Osnabruck the following day before landing at Ursel to stay the night. Once again there was little to get excited about, the squadron diary lamenting that there was 'no flak, no Huns, no nothing'. From Ursel a sweep was made from Munster to the Zuider Zee on 10 February in which intense light flak that was extremely accurate was experienced near Leiden. Luckily all of the nine Spitfires (one having returned with engine trouble) came through unscathed. The squadron also had the clearest view yet of a V-2 launch as one was seen leaving the ground near The Hague. Back at Manston the rest of the squadron had provided the obligatory 'Dogsbody' patrols with two sections flying to Rotterdam, Borkum, Schouwen, Brussels and St Quentin.

The next escort operation did not take place until 14 February and involved another attempt by Nos 9 and 617 Squadrons to knock down the Bielefeld and Altenbeken viaducts. This attack fared no better than the previous one and again had to be abandoned due to cloud. No. 1 Squadron had little to report on return to Ursel except that F/L Neville Brown (Yellow 1) indicated that he had seen two jet fighters twenty miles south of Zwolle at 15,000 ft. These had approached to within four miles of the formation before dashing away eastwards. After a day weatherbound at Ursel, the squadron escorted 100 Lancasters of 3 Group in an attack on Wesel. As there was little in the way of cloud the bombing was excellent and no aircraft were lost. The squadron flew back to Ursel having been in the air for 2 hours 10 minutes and spent the night before returning to Manston the next day.

On 19 February the squadron was cheered when it received information that it was to provide the escort for Winston Churchill who was due to fly to the Continent in his special C-54 Skymaster. It was therefore extremely disappointing to discover that there had been a last-minute change and the job had been given to Bentwaters instead. As way of consolation the squadron could at least console itself with a party to celebrate the promotion of F/O H.L. Stuart (otherwise known as Bert) to Flight Lieutenant. Although no one on the squadron could compare with the likes of Des Perrin and Moose Mossip of the previous generation, Stuart was one of the longest-serving members of the current unit having joined at Predannack. Although a show was intended for the 21 February it was subsequently cancelled and this allowed David Cox the opportunity to give the squadron some formation practice. As No. 1 was Brighton's own squadron he led the Spitfires over the town, an event that was welcomed by everyone on the ground lucky enough to see it. For those who had missed it the local press published photographs the following day of the squadron flying in immaculate formation.

Having had a few days off it was back to the grind of escort operations on 22 February when eighty-five Lancasters bombed a power station at Gelsenkirchen. The attack was well concentrated, however the squadron had the misfortune to witness one Lancaster blow up after being hit by flak. This was an aircraft of No. 218 Squadron flown by F/O J.E.G. Muschamp who was killed along with two of the crew. Although four others baled out successfully all four were mistreated by a member of the Gestapo before being taken to a prisoner of war camp (Sgt J. Halsall was so badly beaten that he never fully recovered from the injuries that were inflicted on him and he died in 1950). After another night at Ursel the squadron was back over Gelsenkirchen the following day although on this occasion it was rather understrength as three aircraft had to make early returns with various snags, these being escorted by a fourth. The target was the Alma Pluto benzol plant, however on this occasion the bomber force, which consisted of 133 Lancasters of 3 Group, was badly straggled at 18,000 ft and in an effort to provide adequate cover the squadron climbed to 22,000 ft and orbited west of Krefeld but the cloud tops were higher still. Heavy flak came up from the target area to burst in the clouds but no aircraft were hit.

On 24 February ten Spitfires took off from Ursel to provide part of the escort to 340 bombers of 4, 6 and 8 Groups attacking a synthetic-oil plant north of Kamen. Problems were experienced as the bombers were late at the rendezvous and failed to make up any time prior to reaching the target which was bombed through cloud on Oboe and H2S markers. One Halifax (NP936 of No. 415 Squadron) was hit by flak and was seen to break up in mid air. There were no survivors. All but one of No. 1 Squadron's Spitfires returned to Manston after the raid, the exception having to put down at Ursel short of fuel. On 26 February twelve Spitfires took off at 1500 hrs for Maldegem (B-65), which was the other Belgian airfield that had been allocated for use by 11 Group squadrons. After night stopping, the squadron gave penetration and withdrawal cover to 149 Lancasters returning to the Alma Pluto benzol plant at Gelsenkirchen. The operation went according to plan and a return was made to Maldegem. They were back at Gelsenkirchen the next day as escort to Lancasters bombing the Nordstern synthetic-oil plant before returning to Manston.

Having escorted 151 Lancasters of 3 Group to an oil plant at Kamen on 1 March, the squadron flew to its former base at Northolt at 1725 hrs to prepare for a VIP escort the following day. Although they had missed out on taking Winston Churchill to the Continent ten days before, No. 1 Squadron had the honour of escorting him on 2 March as he flew to Brussels. On their return however the pilots were confronted with a strong crosswind and a particularly violent gust caught MK644, which was being flown by S/L David Cox. The Spitfire turned over trapping its unfortunate pilot, but help was quickly at hand and he was pulled clear with only minor injuries.

This was the last operation to be carried out for several days, which allowed plenty of time for the organisation of a large squadron party that was to take place in Ramsgate on 5 March. As David Cox was still at Northolt, F/O W.R. Harrison took off in the squadron's newly acquired Auster (LB369) with the intention of picking him up. Low cloud and poor visibility made low level navigation extremely difficult and Harrison mistook Heston for Northolt and landed there. By the time he had discovered his error and taken off again it was nearly dark when he finally made it to Northolt. Despite his late arrival David Cox was determined to make it to the party and having ignoring warnings concerning the weather and the dangers of night flying in a machine as basic as an Auster, the intrepid pair set off. Later an Observer Corps post reported that they had heard a light aircraft flying in the Herne Bay area and by the aid of searchlights the Auster was able to land at Manston. The party was a huge success and was attended by several former members of the squadron including Pat Lardner-Burke and Jack Batchelor.

On 6 March two Spitfires escorted another VIP (this time to Le Bourget) and this proved to be the only operational sorties of the day. Two days later it was announced that F/L Ian Maskill was leaving the squadron having been given the command of No. 91 Squadron. Maskill had been with No. 1 Squadron for nearly a year and his leadership skills would be sorely missed, although as No. 91 Squadron was still based at Manston he would still be around from a social point of view. On 10 March after a VIP escort to Brussels carried out by F/L Joe Dalley and F/O W.R. Harrison the squadron was released for training but at very short notice it was then instructed to move to Maldegem to spend the night there prior to a 'show' the next day. This was a raid on Essen by 1,079 Lancasters, Halifaxes and Mosquitos, which marked the largest number of aircraft sent by the RAF to a single target so far. With the eclipse of the German fighter force there was little to stop the destructive power of Bomber Command and 4,461 tons of bombs were dropped with great accuracy on sky-markers dropped by the Pathfinder force using Oboe. Widespread devastation was caused which added to that from previous raids and as a result the city was virtually paralysed. After carrying out its escort role No. 1 Squadron's Spitfires returned to Maldegem as a similar operation had been planned for the following day.

The record achieved by Bomber Command against Essen was broken on 12 March when 1,108 heavy bombers attacked Dortmund in which 4,851 tons of bombs were dropped. On this occasion No. 1 Squadron was led by Bobby Oxspring, however two of its number had to return early. The Spitfire of F/O J.W. Still (MK733) developed fuel feed trouble over the Ruhr and he had to use his hand pump throughout the return journey. He made a good landing but was just about on the point of collapse due to the physical effort involved and could hardly get out of the cockpit. He was accompanied back by F/L R.D. Scrase in NH255. The rest of the squadron escorted the bombers as planned and were back at Maldegem at 1755 hrs having been airborne for 2 hours 30 minutes.

The next day Ramrod 1493 took No. 1 Squadron's Spitfires to Wuppertal/Barmen as 354 heavy bombers of 4, 6 and 8 Groups attacked the town. During the last three daylight attacks Bomber Command had despatched 2,541 sorties and only five aircraft had been shot down. Once again No. 1 Squadron had few concerns, although F/L Neville Brown (Yellow 1 – MJ411) reported that his engine was down on power as he could only get –6 lbs boost pressure. He was instructed by Bobby Oxspring to put down at Brussels and as the rest of the squadron flew back to Manston he landed there with his No. 2 P/O W.E. Recile (NH246).

The pace was maintained on the 14 March as the squadron took off from Manston to escort 169 Lancasters of 3 Group attacking benzol plants at Datteln and Hattingen near Bochum. After night stopping at Maldegem the target on the 15th was another benzol plant, this time at Castrop-Rauxel. The bombing appeared good and black smoke could be seen from the Dutch Islands on the way back to Manston. There were no operations the following day and the only excitement involved two scrambles, one to shepherd a damaged Mosquito into Manston and the other to investigate an unidentified aircraft which turned out to be a Gloster Meteor. In the evening an impromptu party celebrated Bob Bridgman being able to put up his second ring, his promotion to Flight Lieutenant following soon after that of his fellow Australian, and great friend, F/L Pete Crocker.

On 17 March Ramrod 1500 took place in the afternoon when twelve Spitfires equipped with 90-gallon overload tanks flew over to Maldegem and then escorted seventy-five Lancasters attacking a benzol plant at Dortmund-Derne. This operation provided very little in the way of drama for both fighters and bombers, although P/O Bahadurji (Barry) had to return early with de-icer trouble. It proved to be one of the longer trips and the Spitfires finally touched down at Manston after 3 hours 20 minutes in the air. Having been released for training on 18 March another escort operation was provided the next day when Lancasters raided the benzol plant at Gelsenkirchen. This was flown from and to Ursel and was notable for the amount of flak that was put up not only from the target, but from the front line as well. On 20 March it was the marshalling yards at Recklinghausen with No. 1 Squadron escorting the rear of a force of Halifaxes drawn from 4 and 6 Groups. This was not one of the more successful attacks as a strong wind badly affected the marking carried out by the Pathfinders and the bombing was very scattered. After fulfilling their duty, No. 1 Squadron's Spitfires returned to Manston.

There was an early start on 21 March as the squadron took off just after first light to fly to Ursel to await the call for further escort duties. This came around midday when 160 Lancasters of 3 Group made for Munster. At the same time a similar number were heading for Rheine and the intention was to cause the maximum disruption in the area to the north-east of the Allied advance into Germany. Although the bombers were late at the rendezvous and over the target, the operation went well and several large fires were started including one huge conflagration to the south of the town. One bomber was seen to crash in the target area, but unseen by No. 1 Squadron pilots another two also went down (all three were from 75 Squadron, which was based at Mepal).

The next day it was more of the same and having flown to Ursel in the morning the squadron attempted to escort a force of Halifaxes. These however failed to make the rendezvous so the squadron took 100 Lancasters of 3 Group to Bocholt instead. Two Spitfires flown by P/O Bahadurji and Iain Hastings did not make it due to engine problems and a malfunctioning overload tank respectively. Having returned to Manston the pilots were given just enough time to eat and change their clothes before flying to Northolt (fourteen aircraft including two spares). They arrived a little after 1800 hrs in conditions of haze and poor visibility and P/O W.E. Recile was unfortunate enough to end up off the end of the runway in NH246. He was not hurt although his aircraft was damaged Cat B. Being so close to London, the pilots grasped the opportunity that had been given to them and wasted no time in organising excursions to their favourite haunts during the evening.

The reason for the squadron being at Northolt became clear the following day as it had been chosen once again to escort Winston Churchill, this time to Venlo aerodrome in Holland. His transport on this occasion consisted of a Dakota and having orbited overhead as it landed and taxied to its dispersal, the squadron flew to Ursel to spend the night. This was in preparation for Operation *Varsity*, which took place on 24 March and involved two airborne divisions being dropped behind German lines to facilitate the crossing of the Rhine by Field Marshal Montgomery's 21st Army Group. No. 1 Squadron's role was to patrol the route taken by the airborne forces and although there was a fair amount of flak, no enemy fighters were seen. Afterwards the Spitfires returned to Ursel before flying back to Manston.

On 25 March twelve aircraft, led by Bobby Oxspring, took off at 0640 hrs and landed at Ursel half an hour later. They were airborne again at 0925 hrs to escort 151 Halifaxes of 4 and 6 Groups to Munster. Heavy accurate flak was put up over the target area and this accounted for three of the bombers. No. 1 Squadron pilots saw two go down in flames, one of which was NP804 of No. 408 Squadron from which only the tail gunner survived. The other was MZ907 of 415 Squadron but here, again, there is evidence of atrocities carried out against surviving crew members. Although five parachutes were seen to open, only two airmen were to become prisoners of war as three of the crew of MZ907 were shot by an SS officer. At one point during the raid a warning was received of enemy aircraft approaching and although a formation of unidentified aircraft was seen flying at an altitude estimated at 35,000 ft, these made no attempt to interfere. A return was made to Manston and the Spitfires landed just before midday.

With the advance of the Allied armies deeper into Germany, in the majority of cases even the use of Ursel and Maldegem was now not enough for No. 1 Squadron to be able to accompany bombers all the way to the target. On 31 March the objective was the Blohm & Voss shipyards in Hamburg but having taken off from Maldegem the squadron's Spitfires were only able to assist by carrying out a sweep of the area Lingen – Osnabruck – Munster – Wesel, which was well to the south of the bomber stream. For once the *Luftwaffe* was able to take advantage of the lack of fighter cover over the target and eleven bombers were shot down from a force of 469, mostly by Me 262 jet fighters. After refuelling at Maldegem, No. 1 Squadron returned to Manston later in the day.

The first two days of April were characterised by gale force winds which put a stop to operational flying although it did not halt the progress of No. 1 Squadron's all-conquering football team, which beat No. 91 Squadron by 3–0. On 2 April three new pilots arrived from Hunsdon in W/O L.J. Vickery, W/O D.G. Murphy and F/Sgt E.T. Snowball. All three had previously flown with No. 154 (Mustang) Squadron, which had just been disbanded. On the 3rd the squadron flew to Maldegem with the intention of providing withdrawal cover to 247 Lancasters of 1 Group attacking Nordhausen. This operation was not an unqualified success as despite being slightly early at the rendezvous point the bombers failed to turn up at the appointed time and the squadron eventually landed at Maldegem and spent the night. Nordhausen was hit again the following day but on this occasion the Lancasters were located and were brought back safely.

On 4 April No. 1 Squadron bade farewell to another CO as S/L David Cox was about to head off for the Far East having been promoted to Wing Commander. He was replaced by S/L Ray Nash DFC who came from 61 OTU but before that had spent over two years with No. 91 Squadron. During the anti-Diver operations of the previous year he had had much success flying the Spitfire XII and ended the campaign with a score of seventeen, plus another three shared. His arrival coincided with that of W/O A.G. Cameron who arrived straight from training with 57 OTU at Eshott in Northumberland and at the same time F/O Duncan McIntosh, who had been with the squadron since 1 December 1943, was promoted to Flight Lieutenant.

After two days in which there was no operational flying, word was received that another move was imminent, this time to Coltishall in Norfolk. This was carried out on 8 April and having settled in most pilots flew sector recces the following day. These were followed by two patrols by sections of two aircraft to the Amsterdam area on the lookout for any movement by road, rail, sea or canal. The first was flown in the afternoon by F/L Pete Crocker (ML175) with W/O D.G. Murphy (ML414) as his No. 2, and the other took place in the evening and involved F/L H.L. Stuart (NH255) and F/O Arthur Adams (ML423). Nothing of any interest was seen and all four aircraft returned without having fired their guns.

Following a day of low cloud and mist, the squadron's Spitfires, led by W/C Bill Douglas DFC, the Coltishall Wing Leader, took off at 0800 hrs on 11 April for the new forward airfield at Petit Brogel (B-90) in north-east Belgium. In the early afternoon they were airborne again as escort to 129 Halifaxes of 4 Group on their way to bomb rail targets at Nuremberg. The bombers were again late at the rendezvous but the trip was uneventful and the squadron landed at Petit Brogel to spend the night before returning to Coltishall the next day. On 13 April what should have been called Operation *Wild Goose Chase* took place when F/L P.W. Stewart led fourteen Spitfires to Turnhouse aerodrome to the west of Edinburgh, as four Dakotas loaded up with ground crews and equipment followed. It had been expected that the squadron would remain at the Scottish base for several days but just before lunch an order was received for everyone to return to Coltishall. The Dakotas had to turn back before actually arriving and eventually touched down at Coltishall having been in the air for just over four hours. Although it had all been a complete waste of time the ground crews had at least enjoyed the views. In the evening F/L R. Brown and F/Sgt T. Jeffrey did another recce over Holland, taking in The Hague – Utrecht – Amsterdam – Egmond. Once again there was no surface movement at all and the area was described as being 'utterly desolate'.

With daylight attacks now taking place as far afield as Swinemunde in the Baltic the chances of taking part in any of these were becoming increasingly remote. It was not until 16 April that the squadron was called upon again, but having flown to Petit Brogel in expectation of a bomber escort mission the following day, nothing was forthcoming. On the 18th however 969 heavy bombers attacked the German naval base at Heligoland and No. 1 Squadron's Spitfires acted as part of the target cover. On the way back W/O L.J. Vickery's aircraft (NH356) developed engine trouble and eventually the motor stopped altogether. He carried out a force-landing near Arnhem and although he was uninjured, his Spitfire was a write-off. The next day the squadron took off mid morning for Helmond (B-86) in Holland prior to escorting Lancasters of Nos 9 and 617 Squadrons attacking Heligoland. Each Lancaster carried a Tallboy bomb and the objective was the coastal gun batteries, which were badly damaged. After the raid No. 1 Squadron returned to Helmond but as the chance of further operations began to recede the Spitfires returned to Coltishall on 21 April.

The squadron's last operational sorties of the war took place on 25 April, a rather unfortunate choice of date as the unit's football team had been due to take on No. 603 Squadron in the evening and several of its key players found themselves heading for Petit Brogel instead. From here they set out to escort 482 heavy bombers bound for Wangerooge, one of the Frisian Islands, as they attempted to knock out gun batteries that protected the approaches to Bremen and Wilhelmshaven. Although the bombing was extremely accurate and the target area resembled a lunar landscape after the attack, the heavily fortified gun positions were hardly damaged. No. 1 Squadron's pilots saw a Halifax hit by flak over the target area, which was NP921 of 347 Squadron. However, four more Halifaxes and two Lancasters were lost, all as a result of mid-air collisions despite ideal weather conditions. From the crews of these seven aircraft there was only one survivor. No. 1 Squadron returned to Petit Brogel but as Wangerooge was to be the last daylight attack by Bomber Command there was nothing for it to do and a return was made to Coltishall.

As the Allied and Soviet armies carved up what was left of Germany No. 1 Squadron remained at Coltishall and flew practice formations with S/L Ray Nash in the lead. Some of the more experienced pilots also got their hands on the new Spitfire F.21, the first examples of which had arrived to replace the Mark IXs. The new Spitfire had finally been approved for service having had its longitudinal and directional handling problems sorted and these provided a welcome increase in performance, especially in top speed and climb rate. For No. 1 Squadron the end of the war on 8 May 1945 came as something of an anti-climax as there was no large-scale celebration at Coltishall, the station commander preferring a period of sober reflection, which was in marked contrast to everyone else's desire to hold the party of all parties. F/L Joe Dalley was however able to negociate that the bar in the Sergeants' Mess could remain open until midnight, but that in the Officers' Mess was to close at the regular time. Although these rules were strictly adhered to, the enterprising NCOs made sure that the contents of their bar had been poured into buckets well before midnight so that the celebrations could continue into the small hours.

For the officers there was no alternative but to celebrate in local pubs before returning to the Mess after midnight. Here they were joined by Pat Lardner-Burke who managed to smuggle some beer in so that the celebrations could continue a little longer. The station commander would probably never have known had it not been for someone deciding to draw Hitler's face on the clock in the ante-room before inviting those present to shoot at it. It is safe to assume that a considerable amount of drink had been consumed by this time as the clock was only hit at the fifth attempt. The following day Joe Dalley was ordered to see the station commander who promptly fined him three times the cost of the clock when he admitted to having been the one to finally hit it (he was not left out of pocket as the others had a whip-round to raise the money).

And so No. 1 Squadron's war ended in censure rather than congratulation. Unlike many other units it had been active from start to finish and was joined only by Nos 56 and 164 Squadrons in flying three of the RAF's principal fighters in the Hawker Hurricane, Hawker Typhoon and Supermarine Spitfire. During the course of the war it had shot down 234 enemy aircraft and had also caused much damage to transportation and other targets in occupied Europe. In addition it had destroyed forty-seven V-1 flying bombs, which saved many innocent lives in London. However, this impressive record has to be set against the loss of fifty-one pilots from all over the free world who died during active service with No. 1 Squadron.

At the start of the war the unit epitomised the pre-war RAF in that its members were an elite group of individuals, highly trained in their respective tasks. The high standards that had been set during those times of austerity were however maintained and the quality of those who, but for the war, would never have served with No. 1 Squadron, were a credit not only to themselves, but to the excellence of the training organisation that produced them. For those few that remain there is the satisfaction that not only did they serve their country during time of war, they did so with the RAF's top fighter squadron, No. 1.

CHAPTER SEVENTEEN

The Post-war Years

No. 1 Squadron's first task after the end of the war was to fly to Warmwell from where it provided cover as German forces in the Channel Islands surrendered. Although other units were also involved, it was fitting that the squadron that had been the first to go to war should be on hand at the final act of the European war. The rest of the year was spent converting to the Spitfire F.21, including four examples that featured contra-rotating propellers. These were much easier to fly as torque reaction was eliminated. Although in some ways VE Day had been rather a disappointment, VJ Day on 15 August 1945 more than made up for it. By this time No. 1 Squadron was based at Hutton Cranswick near Driffield in Yorkshire and the occasion was celebrated in style. The other big event of the year was the Battle of Britain Flypast over London on 15 September in which No. 1 Squadron flew with around 300 fighters over the capital.

On 9 January 1946 S/L Ray Nash handed command of the squadron over to S/L H.R. 'Dizzy' Allen DFC, a former Battle of Britain veteran who had flown with No. 66 Squadron. Allen had plenty of contacts at the Air Ministry and he set about finding a way for No. 1 Squadron to be returned to Tangmere. As many former pilots had now reached high rank in the RAF his proposal was looked upon favourably and on 30 April No. 1 Squadron found itself heading south once more. Later in the year it was announced that the squadron would be converting to jets and in October the first Meteor III was received. Unfortunately for Dizzy Allen he was posted to India shortly after the Meteors began to arrive and was replaced by S/L Colin MacFie DFC.

Having taken part in a major exercise in Germany, the unthinkable happened in August 1947 when No. 1 Squadron ceased to be a fighter squadron. For once it appeared as though it had been deserted by its friends in high places as it was reduced to an instrument training outfit flying Harvards and Oxfords. This sorry state of affairs lasted until 1 June 1948 when it was restored to its rightful place and began to receive the more powerful Meteor IV. In October 1948 Major Robin Olds joined the squadron, initially as a flight commander, however he was to take over as CO early the following year thereby becoming the first USAF exchange officer to command an RAF fighter squadron. Olds was a highly experienced pilot whose rise had been dramatic to say the least as he had attained the rank of Major at the age of only twenty-two. During the Second World War he shot down thirteen enemy aircraft and was awarded the US Silver Star, Legion of Merit and DFC, as well as a British DFC and French *Croix de Guerre*. His standing was further enhanced as he was married to the US film actress Ella Raines. Although he was only a member of the squadron for ten months, his influence was profound and during this time there was a marked improvement in No. 1 Squadron's gunnery scores.

In 1950 the squadron resurrected its four-aircraft aerobatic team but tragedy struck on 19 April when its leader, F/L P.W. Speller, was killed when his aircraft collided with that flown by PIII D.C. Harpham. The following month P/O R.W.M. Dixon was killed on the 25th when he lost control and crashed during an asymmetric approach. Later in the year the squadron received its first F.8, an improved version of the Meteor, which it was to fly for the next four years. Although the Meteor F.8 had uprated Rolls-Royce Derwent 8 engines, which delivered ample power, it was limited to Mach 0.82 by its airframe and was rapidly becoming obsolescent. It could not compete with the swept-wing F-86 Sabre flown by the USAF or even the high-flying Canberra bomber that was entering service with the RAF.

One of the highlights of the early 1950s was the presentation of the Squadron Standard at Tangmere on 24 April 1953. The Standard was handed over by Air Vice-Marshal Sir Charles Longcroft KCB CMG DSO AFC who had been the squadron's second commanding officer back in 1914. Many former members of the squadron were invited to the ceremony, including Johnny Walker (by now a Group Captain) and Prosser Hanks and Billy Drake who were both Wing Commanders. This was not the only ceremonial occasion that No. 1 Squadron took part in as it flew in the Coronation Review over London on 2 June and also participated in the Queen's Review of the RAF, which took place at Odiham on 15 July.

No. 1 Squadron soldiered on with its Meteors until February 1955 when the first Sapphire-engined Hawker Hunter F.2 was delivered. By the end of July conversion onto the Hunter was complete but by this time the squadron was flyng the F.5, which had a slightly uprated version of the Sapphire. In many ways the squadron was fortunate to receive this mark of Hunter as the F.1, which was powered by the Rolls-Royce Avon, was suffering from engine surge when the Aden cannons were fired. The Hunter was not supersonic in level flight, but it could exceed Mach 1.0 in a shallow dive and it was not long before the villages around Tangmere were experiencing sonic bangs for the first time as the pilots aimed sonic dives directly at the aerodrome.

The Hunter was received just in time as the following year No. 1 Squadron moved to Akrotiri in Cyprus as relations deteriorated with Egypt over the Suez Canal. This culminated in the nationalisation of the Canal by Colonel Gamal Nasser on 26 July 1956, which ultimately led to an invasion by Britain and France on 31 October. No. 1 Squadron flew sweeps over Egypt, however these were soon abandoned due to limited fuel reserves and the Hunters then provided defensive cover over Cyprus. Due to American pressure the Suez crisis was quickly brought to an end and Britain and France were forced to pull its military forces out of the area.

The next crisis for No. 1 Squadron turned out to be home-grown as the infamous 1957 Defence White Paper issued by Duncan Sandys outlined massive defence cuts that would see advanced fighter projects cancelled and fighter squadrons disbanded, all to be replaced by missile systems. This misguided policy resulted in the closure of Tangmere as a fighter base although No. 1 Squadron survived, albeit at the expense of No. 263 Squadron. This unit was based at Stradishall in Suffolk and flew the Hunter F.6, which had the more powerful Rolls-Royce Avon 203 offering 10,000 lbs thrust. No. 263 Squadron disbanded on 1 July 1958 and was re-numbered as No. 1 Squadron with two pilots transferring from the old No. 1 to provide some element of continuity.

The Hunter continued to be flown for the next eleven years, however the traditional fighter role gradually became a thing of the past as No. 1 Squadron began to specialise in ground-attack. The FGA.9 variant was used from early 1960, which allowed the carriage of drop tanks of up to 230 gallons and various combinations of bombs and rockets. In December 1961 No. 1 Squadron moved to Waterbeach near Cambridge and together with No. 54 Squadron formed the ground-attack Wing of No. 38 Group. As high levels of mobility were required, No. 1 Squadron flew regularly to the Middle East, and even ventured as far as Pakistan. In August 1963 the squadron moved again to West Raynham in Norfolk, which was to be its home for the next six years.

At a special occasion in July 1965 Whitbreads presented No. 1 Squadron with a sign that had previously hung outside The True Briton pub near Lympne. This establishment had been a particular favourite of wartime pilots so it was fitting that the ceremony should be attended by Roy Wilkinson who had commanded the squadron when it moved to Lympne in March 1943. At the same time the squadron museum, which contained trophies collected over the years, was officially opened. These included the gun that Arno Frankenberger had used to shoot down the Hurricane of Pussy Palmer in November 1939.

In March 1967 No. 1 Squadron took part in strikes against the oil tanker *Torrey Canyon*, which had struck Pollard's Rock in the Seven Stones reef between the Scilly Isles and Land's End. These attacks were intended to set fire to the oil that was pouring from the stricken vessel but despite bombing by Royal Navy Buccaneers and napalm and rocket attacks by No. 1 Squadron Hunters, the fires that were created soon went out. No. 1 Squadron hit the headlines again the following year when one of its Hunters was flown through Tower Bridge. The fiftieth anniversary of the RAF occurred on 1 April 1968 but there was to be no celebratory flypast over London, a fact that was particularly resented by F/L Alan Pollock who at the time was No. 1 Squadron's 'B' Flight commander. On a flight from Tangmere to West Raynham, Pollock managed to slip away from the three Hunters he was flying with and descended to low level. Having flown over

Dunsfold aerodrome he picked up the Thames and flew towards the centre of the city where he circled the Houses of Parliament three times. He then flew along the river again towards the east and saw Tower Bridge ahead. Although he could easily have flown over the bridge, he made an instant decision to fly through it as had four other pilots before him, albeit not in jet fighters. Pollock continued along the Thames before turning north, beating up Wattisham, Lakenheath and Marham prior to landing at West Raynham. Public reaction to his protest varied tremendously but Pollock's days in the RAF were numbered and he was eventually forced out of the service.

In June 1969 No. 1 Squadron moved to its former Second World War base at Wittering where it became the first unit to fly the revolutionary Hawker Harrier GR.1. This aircraft was powered by a Rolls-Royce Pegasus 101 of 19,000 lbs thrust allowing vertical take-off via four swivelling nozzles that could be rotated from the vertical to the horizontal position for conventional flight. The capability of the Harrier allowed the book on tactical operations to be re-written and in 1982 it gave outstanding service during the Falklands campaign. As Royal Navy Sea Harriers provided cover, No. 1 Squadron Harriers flew ground attack operations on the aerodrome at Port Stanley and Argentinian positions. These missions were particularly hazardous and four aircraft were lost to ground fire and surface-to-air missiles.

No. 1 Squadron was next in action over northern Iraq during operations to protect the Kurds in the north of the country after the first Iraq war. To carry out this task (Operation *Warden*) the squadron's Harriers flew from Incirlik in Turkey. No. 1 Squadron was also involved in operations over Bosnia from November 1995 and deployed to Gioia Del Colle in Italy. In 1999 the squadron took part in the NATO air campaign over Kosovo and was ultimately to fly over 800 combat missions. Targets included aerodromes, air defence systems and other military installations in Serbia, together with Serb forces operating in Kosovo. Flying the advanced Harrier GR.7, No. 1 Squadron was able to operate by day or night using laser-guided munitions. At the end of the campaign in June 1999, No. 1 Squadron's CO, W/C Andy Golledge, was awarded the Distinguished Service Order, the first DSO awarded to the squadron since that given to James MacLachlan back in May 1942.

With the re-organisation of the Harrier force in 1999/2000, No. 1 Squadron moved to Cottesmore in July 2000 and at the time of writing is still based at the Leicestershire aerodrome. In recent years it has flown in Operation *Telic*, the invasion of Iraq in 2003, and in December 2004 it made its first deployment to Afghanistan as part of Operation *Herrick*. It continues to operate from Kandahar for about four months each year and now flies the upgraded Harrier GR.9.

As No. 1 Squadron nears its centenery it remains, as it always has done, at the forefront of British military aviation. Its rich history is a measure of the achievements of those who served in the past and their exemplary record provides inspiration to a new generation to continue the story. Those who served in No. 1

Squadron during the Second World War were fortunate to be part of the RAF's premier fighter squadron, however they amply repayed the honour that had been bestowed on them. By their actions they lived up to the squadron motto and were indeed In All Things First.

Envoi

Peter Boot
Left No. 1 Squadron on 18 October 1940 and spent much of the rest of the war as an instructor. He retired from the RAF in 1946 and died in 1984.

Richard Brooker
In January 1942 he was posted to the Far East and commanded No. 232 Squadron in Singapore. Subsequently he led No. 77 (RAAF) Squadron but later returned to the UK to become leader of 123 Wing on Typhoons. He was shot down by flak when attacking a radar site near Dieppe on 23 May 1944 but was rescued from the Channel by an ASR Walrus. Having flown during the Allied invasion of Europe he became tour expired but took over 122 Wing in January 1945. He was killed on 16 April 1945 when his Tempest (NV641) was shot down by Fw 190s near Wittenberge. After his death Brooker was awarded a posthumous bar to his DSO (having already been awarded the DFC and bar).

Hilly Brown
After leaving No. 1 Squadron on 17 May 1941, Brown was an instructor at 58 OTU, Grangemouth, before transferring to 57 OTU, Hawarden. On 5 November 1942 he took over as the Wing Leader at Takali in Malta but seven days later he was killed during a low level attack on Gela airfield in Sicily when his aircraft was hit by fire from the ground. At the time of his death Brown was one of the top-scoring Canadian pilots having shot down fifteen German aircraft with another four shared.

Johnny Checketts
Having been Wing Leader at Horne on Spitfire Vs (during which time he shot down two V-1s) he returned to New Zealand and served in the RNZAF until 1954. He was then involved in aerial crop-spraying and later worked as a salesman for a firm producing agricultural chemicals. He then joined a company making leather-stamping tools before retiring in 1982, however he remained active and became a member of the RNZAF Museum in Christchurch, helping to restore aircraft for flight and static display. He died on 21 April 2006 at the age of ninety-four.

Charles Chetham
Left No. 1 Squadron on 11 December 1940 and was posted overseas shortly

afterwards. He served with No. 33 Squadron in Greece but was killed on 15 April 1941 when he was shot down near Larissa airfield by a Bf 109E of II/JG 77 flown by Lt Jacob Arnoldy. This combat also led to the death of Arnoldy who was shot down by F/O John Mackie who was in turn shot down and killed by Arnoldy's wingman, Fw Otto Kohler. Chetham is buried at the Phaleron War Cemetery near Athens.

Darky Clowes
On being rested in April 1941 he became an instructor at 56 OTU, Heston, but within a month moved to 53 OTU. He later led No. 79 Squadron before commanding No. 601 Squadron in North Africa. He subsequently took command of No. 94 Squadron but during a Mess party in late 1943 a prank went disastrously wrong and he was blinded in one eye, thus ending his operational career. He remained in the RAF after the war but died of cancer on 7 December 1949.

Basil 'Buck' Collyns
Having achieved his first combat success with No. 1 Squadron, he was posted to No. 243 Squadron in June 1942 after a period as an instructor. Following a spell with AFDU at Duxford he joined No. 65 Squadron on Mustang IIIs. He later went on to fly with No. 19 Squadron and, in all, claimed another four enemy aircraft destroyed with two shared. On 22 June 1944 he baled out after his aircraft was hit by flak but on 20 August he was killed when his Mustang (FB194) was shot down near Rouvres by Fw 190s. He was posthumously awarded a DFC, which was gazetted on 16 October 1944.

Harry Connolly
Later flew with No. 32 Squadron as a Flight Lieutenant but was killed on 19 August 1942 during the Dieppe Raid when he collided with his No. 2 (Sgt H. Stanage), his Hurricane (HL860) crashing in flames.

David Cox
Took over as Wing Leader of 909 (Spitfire) Wing in the Far East in April 1945. With the end of hostilities against Japan he served for a time at HQ RAF Siam. On leaving the RAF in March 1946 he joined MAC Fisheries, a part of Unilever, as a trainee manager and by the time he retired in 1980 he was Chief Buyer. He died in 2004 at the age of eighty-three.

Dennis Davy
Stayed with No. 1 Squadron until August 1945 when he went to India. After a period instructing with 22 APC he flew Tempest IIs with 20 Squadron. On returning to the UK in 1947 he served with the Day Fighter Leaders' School before being posted to the Flying College at Manby in March 1950. On 18 February 1951 he was killed when flying in a Vickers Valetta, which crashed on landing at Bromma in Sweden.

Jean-François Demozay
After moving to No. 242 Squadron he flew with No. 91 Squadron. His second tour

commenced in June 1942 and this saw him return to No. 91 Squadron as its CO. His last combat victories occurred on 31 October 1942 when he shot down two Fw 190s, thus bringing his score to eighteen. He later served at HQ 11 Group (as a Wing Commander) and subsequently worked with the French Air Ministry. Shortly after the end of the war he was appointed Deputy Commander of the French Air Force's flying training schools. He was killed in an air accident on 19 December 1945. In addition to a DSO and DFC, he was awarded the *Croix de Guerre* by France and Belgium, and also received a US DFC and Czech War Cross.

Con Devey

On completing his rest period as an instructor he commenced his second tour with No. 263 Squadron in January 1945. He continued to fly with this unit until 17 April 1945 when he crashed at B-105 Drope in Germany. The port tyre of his Typhoon (RB398) burst on take-off and his aircraft veered to the left before rolling onto its back. Devey was pulled clear with lacerations to his scalp and arms, which prevented him from flying again before the war ended. (The following day Walter Ramsey (see below) was injured in a road accident as he was travelling to see his friend in hospital. As a result he also played no further part in the war.)

Billy Drake

After recovering from his wounds, Drake flew with 421 Flight on reconnaissance missions over the Channel seeing further combat success. After a period instructing, he commanded No. 128 Squadron in Africa before leading No. 112 Squadron in the desert. By the end of 1942 he was a Wing Commander and in June 1943 was posted to Malta. He then returned to the UK and led 20 Wing on Typhoons. After a time in the USA, he served in SHAEF HQ for the remainder of the war. He stayed in the RAF and was CFI at the Day Fighter Leaders' School before becoming Wing Commander Flying at Linton-on-Ouse. His final posting was as station commander at Chivenor and he retired from the RAF in 1963.

Tim Elkington

Had a short spell as an instructor at 55 OTU, Usworth, before joining No. 601 Squadron in May 1941. In late July he was posted to No. 134 Squadron, which was transferred shortly afterwards to Russia where it operated from Vaenga, near Murmansk, until November 1941. He joined the Merchant Ship Fighter Unit at Speke in April 1942 before rejoining No. 1 Squadron in August. After a month he transferred to No. 539 Squadron, which operated Hurricanes and Turbinlite Havocs, but when this unit disbanded in January 1943 he was posted to No. 197 Squadron on Typhoons. At the end of 1943 he went to India and flew with No. 67 Squadron, subsequently commanding the AFDU and TWDU at Amarda Road and Ranchi. In 1948 he married Patricia Adamson who was a witness to the last major daylight raid on London on 20 January 1943 (see page 165). He remained in the RAF until 1975 when he left the service with the rank of Wing Commander. At the time of writing he lives in retirement in the Cotswolds.

John 'Jack' Finnis

Later flew with Nos 229 and 302 Squadrons. By mid-1942 he was a flight commander with No. 127 Squadron in Egypt and went on to command No. 33 Squadron from 20 July to 31 October 1942. Having been awarded a DFC, he began conversion to heavy bombers at No. 5 Lancaster Finishing School, Syerston, in 1944 but did not complete the course and returned to Rhodesia (now Zimbabwe) before the end of the war. He later became an Air Traffic Controller and it has been recorded that he committed suicide in 1954.

Ernie Glover

On his return from PoW camp at the end of the war he returned to Canada and after leaving the RCAF for a time, rejoined in 1948. After flying P-51D Mustangs with 416 Squadron, he went to the 334th. Fighter Interceptor Squadron, USAF, on an exchange posting and flew the F-86 Sabre during the Korean War. During this conflict he shot down three MiG-15 fighters to become the top-scoring Canadian pilot. He went on to fly the Sabre with the RCAF and eventually retired from the service in April 1970. He died on 9 September 1991.

George Goodman

Having been awarded a DFC for his exploits during the Battle of Britain, he was posted to No. 73 Squadron in November 1940 and flew to Egypt via the Takoradi route after being taken to West Africa by HMS *Furious*. He made a number of further claims over the desert but was shot down by ground fire on 9 April 1941, returning to his unit. He was shot down again on 14 June 1941 along with two other Hurricanes that were attacking the airfield at Gazala, but on this occasion he was killed. His victory tally at the time stood at ten, plus six shared for which he was awarded the DFC.

Colin Gray

Flew with No. 616 Squadron before being rested in February 1942. Six months later he became CO of No. 64 Squadron on Spitfire IXs but moved to No. 81 Squadron in early 1943, this unit operating in North Africa. In June he took over 322 Wing completing his second tour in September 1943. He was later CO of the Fighter Leaders' School at Milfield and Wing Leader at Detling. At the end of the war he was the top-scoring New Zealand pilot with twenty-seven destroyed plus two shared and was awarded the DFC** and DSO. He stayed in the RAF post war and commanded Church Fenton from 1954–56. He left the service in 1961 and returned to New Zealand where he worked for Unilever, retiring as Personnel Director in 1979. He died in August 1995.

Bull Halahan

After returning from France he was posted to 5 OTU as an instructor, taking over command shortly afterwards. In April 1941 he travelled to Malta for fighter control duties but had to leave two months later following an incident in which pilots of No. 249 Squadron were thrown in jail after becoming drunk. He then served at HQ,

Middle East before commanding 250 Wing. However, a disagreement with ACM Sir Trafford Leigh-Mallory led to him retiring from the service in November 1943. After spending time in Tanganyika after the war he returned to the UK and was involved in civil defence. He died on 12 November 1982.

Pat Hancock
In April 1941 he flew to Malta where he served with Nos 261 and 185 Squadrons before instructing with 71 OTU in the Sudan. He returned to operations with No. 250 Squadron on Kittyhawks and continued to serve with this unit until March 1943, receiving a DFC. After being attached to the Turkish Air Force as a liaison officer, he was seconded to the Royal Egyptian Air Force before joining HQ, 216 Group, Transport Command, at Heliopolis in February 1945. He remained in the RAF after the war serving for a time in the Far East before returning to the UK, his last posting before retirement in August 1958 being at HQ, Bomber Command. He was awarded an OBE in 1991 and died in April 2003.

Prosser Hanks
Another ex No. 1 Squadron pilot to serve with 5 OTU at Aston Down, he subsequently flew with No. 257 Squadron before commanding No. 56 Squadron in 1941. He was then Wing Leader at Duxford and Coltishall before taking over similar duties at Luqa in Malta. He made several more claims over Malta in October 1942 to bring his victory tally to thirteen. At the end of the war he was commander at his former station of Aston Down and in 1948 he was Wing Commander Flying at Wunstorf in Germany. He was later to command the Day Fighter Leaders' School at West Raynham. He retired to South Africa and died on 31 January 1986.

John Holderness
Also flew with Nos 229 and 248 Squadrons during the Battle of Britain. He survived the war and returned to his native southern Rhodesia (now Zimbabwe). He died in a road traffic accident in South Africa on 16 April 2008 at the age of ninety-six.

Bob Hornall
After leaving No. 1 Squadron he flew Typhoons with No. 245 Squadron before moving to No. 184 Squadron as a flight commander. He received a DFC, which was gazetted on 13 February 1945.

Vaclav Jicha
Left No. 1 Squadron on 17 November 1940 on posting to No. 17 Squadron with whom he was commissioned. He later flew with No. 313 (Czech) Squadron and was awarded a DFC in September 1942. In early 1943 he was posted to Castle Bromwich as a production test pilot and stayed there for two years during which time he was awarded an AFC. Here he flew with legendary test pilot Alex Henshaw who rated him as the best Spitfire pilot that he had at Castle Bromwich. On 1

February 1945 Jicha was flying as a passenger in an Anson bound for Kinloss when it crashed on a hillside in a snowstorm. Although he survived, he froze to death before a rescue party was able to help.

Killy Kilmartin

After a period instructing he returned to No. 43 Squadron as a flight commander and was awarded the DFC. In April 1941 he was CO of No. 602 Squadron before moving to No. 313 (Czech) Squadron. By May 1943 he was Wing Leader at Hornchurch and at the time of D-Day he was commander of 136 Wing (Typhoons). He later served as Wing Commander Ops (Fighter) at HQ, 2 TAF. He retired from the service in July 1958 having commanded No. 249 Squadron on Tempests at Habbaniyah in Iraq. He died on 1 October 1998.

Bedrich Kratkoruky

On completion of his tour he was posted to 61 OTU at Heston as an instructor. His second fighter tour commenced with No. 313 (Czech) Squadron at the end of 1942 by which time he was a Flying Officer. During the escort of a Circus operation on 16 January 1943 he collided over the Channel with another of the squadron's Spitfire VBs flown by F/Sgt J. Blaha and both pilots were killed.

Karel Kuttlewascher

Was posted to No. 23 Squadron where he flew the Mosquito but moved to Maintenance Command in September 1942 on liaison duties. In mid-1943 he flew to the USA for a lecture tour, returning at the end of the year and for the remainder of the war he served as a test pilot at St Athan. He went back to Czechoslovakia in August 1945 but returned to the UK the following year. Towards the end of 1946 he joined British European Airways with whom he flew the Viking, Ambassador and Viscount airliners. He died on 17 August 1959 after suffering a heart attack.

Pat Lardner-Burke

On leaving No. 1 Squadron in December 1944 he took over as Wing Leader at Coltishall. Having received a bar to his DFC, he was then made base commander at Horsham St Faith, before taking over as Wing Leader at Church Fenton. After a spell in Aden he moved to Acklington in Northumberland where he was in charge of flying in the early 1950s. On retirement from the service he moved to the Isle of Man and ran a public house for a number of years. He died on 4 February 1970. (Lardner-Burke is noted for having flown Spitfire IX MH434 of the Old Flying Machine Company at Duxford. On 5 September 1943 when flying with 222 Squadron he shot down an Fw 190 with this aircraft.)

Romas Marcinkus

After being shot down and captured on 12 February 1942 he was sent to *Stalag Luft* III at Sagan where he was involved in the mass breakout on 24 March 1944 known as the 'Great Escape'. Travelling with three other officers he got as far as Danzig where they were captured and handed over to the *Gestapo*. All four men were shot on 29 March 1944.

Peter Matthews

In April 1941 he began a rest period as an instructor at 52 OTU, Debden, having received a DFC at the end of his tour. He took over as CO of No. 74 Squadron in November 1941, this unit then transferring to the Middle East, but not long after arriving he was transferred to No. 145 Squadron (Spitfire V) where he had considerable combat success. Having survived being shot down on 3 November 1942 he served with 71 OTU in the Sudan before leading No. 111 Squadron in August 1943. Later in the year he was badly injured in a road crash and spent much of the rest of the war at Fighter Command HQ. He continued in the RAF post war and retired from the service on 8 May 1966. As a civilian he spent fifteen years as Director of Olympia and Earls Court exhibition centres. He died on 2 October 1991.

Henry Merchant

Left No. 1 Squadron on 26 November 1940 for the Central Flying School at Upavon and went on to serve as an instructor for the rest of the war. He left the service in 1945 by which time his rank was Flight Lieutenant.

Moose Mossip

After leaving No. 1 Squadron he flew with No. 245 Squadron but was killed on 7 March 1945 when his Typhoon (JP936) crashed after hitting high tension cables south-west of Soest.

Boy Mould

On his return to the UK from France, Mould became an instructor at 6 OTU but soon moved to 5 OTU at Aston Down. He was posted to Malta in March 1941 where he commanded No. 185 Squadron but was killed on 1 October 1941 during combat with Italian Macchi C.202 fighters. At the time of his death his combat score stood at eight destroyed with another shared.

Jarda Novak

By 1943 he was a Flying Officer serving with No. 312 (Czech) Squadron. He was killed on 14 May of that year when his Spitfire VC (EP539) was shot down by flak during an attack on shipping in St Peter Port, Guernsey.

Pussy Palmer

After serving in France he returned to the UK to become an instructor serving with 6 OTU. He returned to operations as a supernumerary with No. 234 Squadron on 6 October 1942 by which time he was a Squadron Leader. On 27 October of that year he was shot down and killed in Spitfire VB BM527 by Fw 190s during a Rodeo in the Isle de Batz area.

Otto Pavlu

Later flew with No. 310 (Czech) Squadron and was killed on 28 April 1943 when his Spitfire VC (EE635) was hit by flak during a Roadstead operation in the English Channel.

Des Perrin

After serving with No. 1 Squadron he flew with No. 198 Squadron as a flight commander but was killed on 10 September 1944 when his Typhoon (MP116) burst a tyre on take off from B-35 Merville and crashed.

George Plinston

Subsequently flew with Nos 607 and 85 Squadrons in France before being posted to No. 242 Squadron. In 1941 he volunteered to join a Merchant Ship Fighter Unit and the following year went to the Middle East where he flew with Nos 250 and 3 (RAAF) Squadrons before commanding No. 601 Squadron. For the last two years of the war he delivered transport aircraft to operational theatres. In 1968 after the unauthorised flight of a No. 1 Squadron Hunter through Tower Bridge he wrote a letter to *Flight International* magazine commenting on the adverse reaction to this event as recorded in the press. Part of his letter was as follows – 'What on earth is the matter with the youth of today? In my day we used to fly whole squadrons of aeroplanes through bridges. At Rouen all of No. 1 Squadron's Hurricanes flew under the transporter bridge one behind the other!'

Josef Prihoda

In early 1942 he was posted to No. 111 Squadron but having added to his score by shooting down a Bf 109 during the Channel Dash by the *Scharnhorst* and *Gneisenau* on 12 February 1942 he was on the move again to No. 313 (Czech) Squadron. He remained with this unit until 6 March 1943 when he was shot down and killed near Brest by Fw 190s of JG 2 during the escort of B-24 Liberators.

Walter Ramsey

After taking an instructors course at 7 FIS Upavon, he was promoted to Flying Officer and posted to 21 (P) AFU at Tatenhill near Burton-on-Trent on 7 April 1944 to fly Oxfords. On 21 November he was transferred to 1534 BAT Flight at Shawbury (again on Oxfords) before commencing a second fighter tour with No. 263 Squadron at Fairwood Common on 11 January 1945. This unit was equipped with Typhoons and left the UK for B-89 (Mill) in early February, however shortly after arriving he was posted to No. 257 Squadron, which was also based at B-89. He continued to fly with No. 257 Squadron until it was disbanded on 5 March and then returned to No. 263 Squadron. His last operatonal sortie took place on 18 April 1945 and involved a shipping strike west of Borkum in which he scored a direct hit on one of the ships. After the war he re-trained as a teacher and was deputy head at East Road School, Northallerton in Yorkshire, before taking over as head teacher at Topcliffe Primary. He died of cancer on 9 January 1977.

Paul Richey

On returning from France he became a fighter controller at Middle Wallop before being posted to 55 OTU at Aston Down as an instructor. He returned to operations in April 1941 as a flight commander with No. 609 Squadron on Spitfires and then joined No. 74 Squadron as CO. He returned to No. 609 Squadron as its commander in June 1942 by which time it had converted to Typhoons. He then served in the Far East but suffered a period of ill health and was invalided home. On recovery he was posted to SHAEF with whom he served until March 1945. He left the RAF the following year but returned to flying with No. 601 Squadron of the RAuxAF. Here he flew Spitfire LF.16es and de Havilland Vampires and was CO from 1950–52. He died on 23 February 1989.

Harold 'Sammy' Salmon

On leaving No. 1 Squadron he flew with No. 229 Squadron during the Battle of Britain but later became a pilot with Ferry Command. On 6 December 1943 he and a three-man crew were flying a Mitchell II (FW159) that went missing on a flight from Goose Bay in Newfoundland to Reykjavik in Iceland. His daughter was to become well known as the actress Joanna Pettet who featured in the film *Casino Royale* (1967) and a number of other films and TV series including Knots Landing.

Les Scott

After being posted to No. 198 Squadron in August 1943 he was shot down by flak on one of his first sorties on the 28th of that month. His Typhoon (JP516) came down near Knocke during a Ramrod operation and he spent the rest of the war as a prisoner.

Bill Sizer

Left No. 1 Squadron in June 1941 and had short spells with No. 91 Squadron and 1 PRU before joining No. 152 Squadron as a flight commander, moving with this unit to North Africa in November 1942. Two months later he was given command of No. 93 Squadron and took part in the invasion of Sicily in July 1943. He often flew with Raymond Baxter (later to achieve fame as a TV presenter) who claimed that Sizer saved his life on at least two occasions and described him as 'an outstanding character and fighter leader'. He left the RAF in 1946 having been awarded a bar to his DFC but rejoined two years later and went on to command No. 54 Squadron. He left the service in August 1963 and worked for Marconi Radar in the Middle East, retiring in 1985. He died on 22 December 2006.

Frank Soper

Was commissioned on his return from France and became an instructor at 6 OTU before returning to operations as a flight commander with No. 257 Squadron in June 1941. Three months later he took over as CO and around this time was awarded a DFC. His last combat victory was a half share in the destruction of a Ju 88 off the Suffolk coast on 5 October 1941, however it would appear that his Hurricane was hit by return fire as he failed to return. It was later confirmed that he had been killed.

Charles Stavert

After being posted from No. 1 Squadron in September 1940 he flew with No. 504 Squadron during the Battle of Britain. He ended the war as a Flight Lieutenant and stayed in the service, being awarded an AFC in June 1953. He retired from the RAF in August 1964 and died at the age of eighty-six in 2008.

Bill Stratton
Did not return to operations until February 1943 when he was posted to No. 134 Squadron as a supernumerary Squadron Leader. He took over full control of this unit four months later when it moved to the Far East to operate in Burma. In 1944 he transferred to the RNZAF and had a long post war career that saw him rise to the rank of Air Vice-Marshal as Chief of the Air Staff. In addition to his wartime decorations of DFC and bar, he was made CB, CBE. He died in January 2006.

Alex Vale
After being shot down on 22 May 1944 he was taken in by a local farmer but was arrested after the *Gestapo* received a tip off as to his whereabouts. He was taken to *Stalag Luft* III but was later force-marched to Luchenwald near Berlin before being released by the Russians. After the war he enrolled in the Metropolitan Police before joining the CID. He later specialised in fingerprints and also spent time on this type of work in Uganda. He worked for a time training detectives in Botswana before returning to the UK in 1971 to work with the Construction Industry Training Board. He died on 22 September 2007.

Johnny Walker
Yet another of No. 1 Squadron's pre-war pilots to join 5 OTU as an instructor on returning from France. He went on to lead No. 253 Squadron and in mid-1942 was Wing Leader at Tangmere, receiving a DSO for his role in the Dieppe Raid of 19 August 1942. For the first nine months of 1943 he held a staff appointment at HQ, 11 Group, before taking over command of the Central Gunnery School at Sutton Bridge (later Catfoss). After the war he was base commander at Fassberg in Germany and retired from the RAF on 6 March 1964 as a Group Captain. He died in the early 1980s.

Ken 'Tony' Weller
Left the RAF in 1946 and after spending time as a pupil at East Farm, Bincombe, near Weymouth, he joined a local business and was responsible for sales of the new Massey Ferguson tractor. In 1962 he joined Massey Ferguson as a Regional Manager and in 1967 joined the Board of Directors of an M-F Distributor in the south-west, initially as Machinery Director. He retired in 1986 having become the firm's Managing Director in 1975. He is married with one son and has three grandchildren. He lives in Cornwall.

Roy Wilkinson
After leaving No. 1 Squadron in May 1943 he took over as CO of Gravesend for ten months before commanding 149 Mobile Airfield up to and beyond D-Day. In August 1944 he travelled to Australia to command the Spitfire Wing at Darwin and returned to a staff posting at the Air Ministry after the war had ended. He left the

service in 1946 (by which time he had been awarded an OBE) but he retained an interest in aviation in the post war years and was involved in the transition from military to civil flying at Stansted. Later he operated the Elstree Flying Club for a time before running a garage business on the Isle of Sheppey. He died in 1992.

Antonin Zavoral
Was posted to No. 312 Squadron on 9 April 1941. Just over six months later he moved to No. 607 Squadron but was shot down and killed by anti-aircraft fire during a Ramrod operation on 31 October 1941.

Glossary

AA – Anti-aircraft

AASF – Advanced Air Striking Force

ACM – Air Chief Marshal

AI – Airborne Interception (radar)

AOC – Air Officer Commanding

AVM – Air Vice-Marshal

AFC – Air Force Cross

AFDU – Air Fighting Development Unit

APC – Armament Practice Camp

ASR – Air-Sea Rescue

ATS – Auxiliary Territorial Service

BAFF – British Air Forces in France

BAT – Beam Approach Training

BEF – British Expeditionary Force

BFTS – British Flying Training School

Bomphoon – Bomb-carrying Typhoon

CdG – *Croix de Guerre*

Cdr – Commander

CFI – Chief Flying Instructor

C-in-C – Commander-in-chief

Circus – RAF operation comprising a few bombers escorted by large numbers of fighters

CO – Commanding Officer

DFC – Distinguished Flying Cross

DFM – Distinguished Flying Medal

Diver – British code name given to V-1 flying bomb

DSO – Distinguished Service Order

E-Boat – German fast torpedo boat

EFTS – Elementary Flying Training School

ETA – Estimated Time of Arrival

FIS – Flying Instructors' School

F/L – Flight Lieutenant

F/O – Flying Officer

Form D – RAF operational order

F/Sgt – Flight Sergeant

FTS – Flying Training School

Fw – *Feldwebel* (German equivalent of RAF Sgt)

GCI – Ground Controlled Interception

Gefr – *Gefreiter* (German equivalent of RAF Aircraftman First Class)

G-H – A British radio navigation system

H2S – A type of blind-bombing aid

HMT – His Majesty's Troopship

Hptm – *Hauptmann* (German equivalent of RAF F/L)

IAS – Indicated Airspeed

IFF – Identification Friend or Foe

Instep – RAF patrol over the sea looking for long-range *Luftwaffe* fighters

Jabos – Derived from *Jagerbombers* or fighter-bombers

JG – *Jagdgeschwader* (*Luftwaffe* fighter Wing)

KG – *Kampfgeschwader* (*Luftwaffe* bomber Wing)

LAC – Leading Aircraftman

LG – *Lehrgeschwader* (*Luftwaffe* operational training Wing)

LR – Long-Range

Lt – *Leutnant* (German equivalent of RAF P/O)

MT – Motor Transport

NCO – Non-commissioned Officer

NJG – *Nachtjagdgeschwader* (*Luftwaffe* night-fighter Wing)

Noball – British code name given to V-1 construction sites

Oberstlt – *Oberstleutnant* (German equivalent of RAF W/C)

Obfw – *Oberfeldwebel* (German equivalent of RAF Flight Sergeant)

Obgfr – *Obergefreiter* (German equivalent of RAF Leading Aircraftman)

Oblt – *Oberleutnant* (German equivalent of RAF F/O)

Oboe – A type of blind-bombing aid

OTU – Operational Training Unit

(P) AFU – (Pilot) Advanced Flying Unit

Pancake – Code word for aircraft to return to base and land

P/O – Pilot Officer

PoW – Prisoner of War

PRU – Photographic Reconnaissance Unit

Prune – Character in the RAF training manual *Tee Emm*

RAAF – Royal Australian Air Force

RAE – Royal Aircraft Establishment

Ramrod – RAF attack by bombers (or fighter-bombers) with fighter escort

Ranger – RAF deep penetration by fighters to attack targets in a designated area

R-Boat – Small German minesweeper

RFC – Royal Flying Corps

Rhubarb – RAF operation by small numbers of fighters looking for targets of opportunity

RNZAF – Royal New Zealand Air Force

Roadstead – RAF operation to attack enemy shipping

Rodeo – RAF fighter sweep

RP – Rocket Projectile

R/T – Radio Telephony

Sgt – Sergeant

SHAEF – Supreme Headquarters Allied Expeditionary Force

SKG – *Schnellkampfgeschwader* (*Luftwaffe* Fast-bomber Wing)

S/L – Squadron Leader

Stab – Or staff, used to designate a *Luftwaffe* headquarters unit

TAF – Tactical Air Force

TEU – Tactical Exercise Unit

Turbinlite – A form of airborne searchlight used in Douglas Havoc aircraft

TWDU – Tactical Weapons Development Unit

Uffz – *Unteroffizier* (German equivalent of RAF Corporal)

USAAF – US Army Air Force

VHF – Very High Frequency

Visual Lorenz – Aerodrome approach path lighting

W/C – Wing Commander

Whirlibomber – Bomb-carrying Whirlwind

W/O – Warrant Officer

ZG – *Zerstorergeschwader* (*Luftwaffe* destroyer Wing – Bf 110)

ZZ Landings – Form of instrument approach

Select Bibliography

Aces High, Christopher Shores and Clive Williams, Grub Street, 1994

Aces High, Volume 2, Christopher Shores, Grub Street, 1999

Battle of France Then and Now, The, Peter D. Cornwell, After the Battle, 2007

Billy Drake, Fighter Leader, with Christopher Shores, Grub Street, 2002

Broken Eagles, Bill Norman, Pen and Sword, 2001

Fighter Pilot, Paul Richey, Pan Books, 1969

Fighter Pilot's Summer, Norman Franks and Paul Richey, Grub Street, 1993

Flying Sailor, The, Andre Jubelin, Hurst and Blackett, 1953

Night Hawk, Roger Darlington, William Kimber, 1985

Number One in War and Peace, Norman Franks and Mike O'Connor, Grub Street, 2000

One-Armed Mac, Brian Cull and Roland Symons, Grub Street, 2003

Rolls-Royce on the Front Line, Tony Henniker, Rolls-Royce Heritage Trust, 2000

Those Other Eagles, Christopher Shores, Grub Street, 2004

Tony's War, Britta von Zweigbergk, Vanguard Press, 2007

Twice Vertical, Michael Shaw, Macdonald, 1971

Appendix One – Aircraft Losses

Hawker Hurricane

Date	Pilot	A/c	Remarks
23/11/39	F/O C.D. Palmer	L1590	Damaged by return fire from a Do 17 and force landed near Moiremont, pilot safe
2/3/40	P/O J.S. Mitchell	L1971	Crashed during attempted force landing after combat with Do 17 in the vicinity of Metz, pilot killed
2/3/40	F/L H.M. Brown	L1843	Damaged during combat with Do 17 and force landed near Fenetrange, pilot safe
2/4/40	F/O C.D. Palmer	N2326	Shot down near St Avold by a Bf 109E of III/JG 53 flown by Lt Werner Mölders, pilot baled out safely
20/4/40	F/O J.I. Kilmartin	L1843	Shot up during combat with Ju 88 and crash landed near Paris, pilot safe
10/5/40	F/O L. Lorimer	L1689	Damaged by return fire from an He 111 of KG 53, pilot baled out safely
10/5/40	F/L P.R. Walker	N2382	Damaged during combat with a Do 17 of III/KG 2 and force landed near Verdun, pilot safe
11/5/40	F/O P.H.M. Richey	L1679	Force landed at Mezieres after combat with Do 17, pilot safe
11/5/40	F/O P.H.M. Richey	L1685	Shot down by a Bf 110, pilot baled out safely
12/5/40	F/O R. Lewis	L1688	Badly damaged during combat with Bf 109Es of JG 27, pilot baled out safely near Maastricht
12/5/40	S/L P.J.H. Halahan	L1671	Shot up during combat over Belgium and crash-landed, pilot safe
12/5/40	Sgt F.J. Soper	L1686	Damaged in combat with Bf 109Es, force landed, pilot safe (a/c later abandoned)
13/5/40	F/O B. Drake	'P'	A/c damaged during combat with Bf 110s, pilot baled out injured
13/5/40	F/O L. Lorimer	L1681	Hit by return fire from He 111s, crash-landed near St Loupe, pilot safe
13/5/40	F/O L.R. Clisby	L1694?	Landed next to He 111 that the pilot had just shot down, a/c damaged and abandoned
14/5/40	F/L P.P. Hanks	N2380	Shot down by Bf 110s of ZG 26 near Sedan. Pilot baled out safely
14/5/40	F/O L. Lorimer	L1676	Shot down by Bf 110s of ZG 26 near Sedan, pilot killed

14/5/40	F/O L.R. Clisby	P2546	Shot down by Bf 110s of ZG 26 near Sedan, pilot killed
15/5/40	F/O P.H.M. Richey	L1943	Shot down by Bf 110s of ZG 26 near St Hilaire-le-Grand, pilot baled out safely
15/5/40	F/L P.R. Walker	?	Damaged by return fire from Bf 110 of III/ZG 26 and force landed, pilot safe
17/5/40	Sgt F.J. Soper	L1905	Shot down by Bf 110s, pilot safe
17/5/40	F/O C.D. Palmer	P2820	Badly damaged during combat with Bf 110s near Reims, pilot baled out safely
18/5/40	Sgt R.A. Albonico	L1856	Hit by ground fire near St Quentin, pilot PoW
18/5/40	P/O C.M. Stavert	?	Crash landed out of fuel at Vraux after combat, pilot safe
19/5/40	F/O P.H.M. Richey	P2694	A/c damaged during combat with He 111s near Chateau-Thierry, pilot baled out wounded
19/5/40	Sgt F.J. Soper	L1925	Set on fire by return fire from He 111 of 8/KG 27, crash landed, pilot injured
23/5/40	F/L F.E. Warcup	?	Damaged during combat with Bf 109Es of 2/JG 3, pilot safe
25/5/40	P/O D. Thom	P2880	Shot down, possibly by AA fire, pilot PoW
26/5/40	P/O R.H. Dibnah	?	Hit by AA fire during patrol, crash-landed near Nancy, pilot wounded
5/6/40	P/O H.B.L. Hillcoat	?	Damaged during combat with Bf 110s and crash landed on fire, pilot safe
5/6/40	P/O N.P.W. Hancock	P3590	Damaged during combat and struck Blenheim on landing at Rouen-Boos, pilot safe
5/6/40	P/O J.A. Shepherd	?	Shot down during combat with Bf 109Es, pilot killed
14/6/40	F/L F.E. Warcup	?	Shot down over St Nazaire, pilot PoW
14/6/40	F/L M.H. Brown	?	Shot down over St Nazaire, force landed near Caen, pilot safe
19/7/40	P/O D.O.M. Browne	P3471	Hit by return fire from He 111, a/c crash-landed on fire near Brighton, pilot safe
11/8/40	P/O J.A.J. Davey	P3172	Damaged during combat with Bf 110s, crashed on Sandown golf course during attempted force-landing, pilot killed
15/8/40	Sgt M.M. Shanahan	P3047	Shot down by Bf 109E off Harwich during patrol, pilot killed
15/8/40	P/O D.O.M. Browne	?	Shot down by Bf 109E off Harwich during patrol, pilot killed

15/8/40	F/L H.M. Brown	R4075	Shot down by Bf 109E off Harwich during patrol, pilot baled out and rescued
16/8/40	P/O J.F.D. Elkington	P3173	Shot down during combat with Bf109Es over Thorney Island, pilot injured
19/8/40	P/O C.N. Birch	P3684	Became lost during night patrol over London, hit balloon cable, pilot baled out safely
24/8/40	Sgt H.J. Merchant	P2980	Ran out of fuel during night patrol and hit trees in force-landing at Withyham in Kent, pilot safe
27/8/40	P/O C.A.C. Chetham	P3897	Lost control during night patrol when lit up by searchlights, pilot baled out safely
31/8/40	Sgt H.J. Merchant	V7375	Shot down during combat with Bf 110s over Halstead, pilot baled out wounded (burns)
1/9/40	F/Sgt F.G. Berry	P3276	Shot down by a Bf 109E over Tonbridge, pilot killed
3/9/40	F/L H.B.L. Hillcoat	P3044	Shot down when in combat near Maidstone, pilot killed
3/9/40	P/O R.H. Shaw	P3782	Shot down when in combat near Maidstone, pilot killed
6/9/40	P/O G.E. Goodman	P2686?	Shot up during combat with Bf 110 near Penshurst in Kent, pilot baled out safely
9/10/40	Sgt S. Warren	V7376	Failed to return from training flight in the Wash area, pilot killed
29/10/40	Sgt W.T. Page	P3318	Damaged during combat with Do 17 near Peterborough and force-landed, pilot safe
29/10/40	Sgt J.D. Dygryn	V7302	Crashed on landing at Wittering, pilot safe (aircraft salvaged and converted to Mark.II BV164)
2/11/40	S/L D.A. Pemberton	P2751	Crashed near Wittering in bad visibility, pilot killed
5/2/41	F/O R.G. Lewis	P3920?	Shot down by Bf 109Es over the Channel, pilot killed
19/3/41	Sgt J. Stefan	Z2810	Shot up during combat with a Bf 109E of I/LG 2 and crash-landed, pilot safe
19/3/41	P/O A. Kershaw	Z2759	Shot up during combat with a Bf 109E of I/LG 2, pilot baled out but parachute failed to open
9/5/41	F/L H.B.L. Hillcoat	Z2919	Crashed during force landing 1m east of Redhill
10/5/41	P/O J. Behal	Z2921	Shot down during night patrol near Sanderstead in Surrey, pilot killed

21/5/41	F/L J.C.E. Robinson	Z2764	Shot down by Bf 109E of JG 51 during Circus operation over the Pas de Calais, pilot killed
16/6/41	Sgt A. Nasswetter	Z3460	Shot down over the Channel, pilot badly injured and died later
21/6/41	P/O V.A. Kopecky	Z2909	Shot down over the Channel during a Circus operation, ditched near Folkstone, pilot rescued
21/6/41	P/O N. Moranz	Z3461	Shot down during Circus operation, pilot PoW
29/6/41	P/O B. Horak	Z3240	Spun into ground on approach to Gatwick, pilot killed
16/7/41	F/L A. Velebnovsky	Z3902	Flew into hill near Petworth, Sussex at night, pilot killed
27/8/41	Sgt E. Bloor	Z3843	Crashed near Horsham whilst on searchlight co-operation, pilot killed
29/8/41	Sgt G.S. Metcalf	Z3842	Crashed on landing at night, pilot safe and aircraft repaired
11/9/41	Sgt A.C. Smith	BD950	Failed to return from night flying practice, presumed down in Channel, pilot killed
2/10/41	F/Sgt S. Merryweather	Z3844	Crashed on landing at Langley, pilot safe
21/10/41	Sgt R.H. Oakley	?	Crashed near Martlesham, pilot killed
18/11/41	Sgt E. Ruppel	BE576	Flew into hill when practicing night landings, pilot killed
22/11/41	Sgt L.J. Travis	BD940	Collided with Z3899 over the Isle of Wight following a scramble at dusk, pilot killed
22/11/41	Sgt D.P. Perrin	Z3899	Collided with BD940 over the Isle of Wight following a scramble at dusk, pilot baled out
11/2/42	Sgt E.G. Parsons	BD945	Crashed when landing at night, pilot killed
12/2/42	Sgt E.F.G. Blair	Z3774	Shot down by flak during the Channel breakout by the *Scharnhorst* and *Gneisenau*, pilot killed
12/2/42	P/O R. Marcinkus	BD949	Shot down by flak during the Channel breakout by the *Scharnhorst* and *Gneisenau*, pilot PoW
3/4/42	P/O H. Connolly	BD947	Crashed into the sea off Selsey during a night patrol, pilot rescued
5/4/42	Sgt Z. Bachurek	BE647	Crashed during night patrol, pilot injured
10/4/42	Sgt J. Vlk	Z3970	Crashed whilst carrying out night approaches, pilot killed
24/4/42	Sgt V. Machacek	BE573	Crashed during a night intruder operation to Bretigny, pilot killed

3/6/42	F/Sgt G.C. English	Z3897	Spun into the ground near Bersted, Sussex during practice attack, pilot killed
4/6/42	W/O Dygryn-Ligoticky	Z3183	Failed to return from night intruder operation to St Andre, pilot killed
26/6/42	W/O G. Scott	HL589	Failed to return from night intruder operation to Gilze Rijen, pilot killed

Miles Magister

| 22/4/41 | Sgt C.M. Stocken | T9680 | Flew into hill in bad visibility near Kingsdown in Kent, pilot killed |
| 16/2/42 | P/O E.S.G. Sweeting | V1013 | Spun into ground on approach to Tangmere, pilot and passenger (George Martin) killed |

Hawker Typhoon

5/9/42	Sgt A.E. Pearce	R8690	Force landed near RAF Longtown due to engine failure; aircraft burnt out, pilot safe
21/10/42	P/O P.N. Dobie	R7861	Collided with R7867 over North Sea 4m off Amble, pilot killed
21/10/42	Mr P.E.G. Sayer	R7867	Collided with R7861 over North Sea 4m off Amble, pilot killed
9/11/42	P/O T.G. Bridges	R7868	Damaged beyond repair in ground collision with R8630, pilot safe
21/11/42	P/O C.H. Watson	R7862	Caught fire in air and force landed near Charterhall; aircraft burnt out, pilot safe
9/2/43	Sgt E. Crowley	DN241	Overshot landing at Southend due to hydraulics failure, pilot safe
13/2/43	Sgt R.W. Hornall	R7864	Crash-landed near Danehill, Sussex due to engine failure, pilot safe
6/3/43	P/O G.C. Whitmore	DN615	Collided with R8942 in cloud during defensive patrol near Tenterden, pilot killed
6/3/43	Sgt H.R. Fraser	R8942	Collided with DN615 in cloud during defensive patrol near Tenterden, pilot killed
19/3/43	P/O C.H. Watson	DN335	Overshot on landing at Lympne and overturned, pilot safe
29/3/43	F/O C.L. Bolster	R7876	Shot down by Fw 190s of JG 2 to the south of Beachy Head, pilot killed
28/4/43	Sgt H. Bletcher	R8634	Force landed on Pevensey marshes due to engine failure, pilot safe
19/5/43	P/O E.A. Glover	R7863	Shot down by flak during Rhubarb operation in the Lille area, pilot PoW
2/6/43	F/Sgt W.H. Ramsey	R8752	Damaged during Rhubarb operation, force landed on return, pilot safe

16/6/43	F/L L.S.B. Scott	R7919	Shot up by Fw 190s of JG 26 during Rhubarb operation, pilot wounded
16/6/43	P/O S.P. Dennis	DN585	Shot down by Fw 190s of JG 26 near Douai, pilot PoW
6/7/43	P/O C.H. Watson	EJ982	Crashed on take off from Lympne, pilot safe
15/7/43	P/O J.M. Chalifour	EK228	Lost tail in dive when returning from patrol, crashed near Paddlesworth, Kent, pilot killed
16/8/43	F/O L.J. Wood	EK176	Crash landed near Lydd due to engine failure, pilot killed
23/8/43	P/O H. Gray	R7856	Spun into ground shortly after take off from Tangmere, pilot killed
25/11/43	F/O J.W. Wiley	JP592	Shot down by flak near Martinvast during Ramrod operation, pilot killed
7/12/43	W/O J.D. Fairbairn	EK113	Flew into hill in bad weather after overshoot from Hawkinge, pilot killed
12/12/43	Not known	JP795	Damaged in flying accident, not repaired
21/12/43	F/Sgt S.D. Cunningham	JR144	Crashed into the Channel off Dover following engine failure during an ASR sortie, pilot killed
22/12/43	W/O F.J. Wyatt	JP961	Failed to return from Ramrod operation to the St Pol area, pilot PoW
22/12/43	P/O J.W. Sutherland	JR237	Failed to return from Ramrod operation to the St Pol area, pilot PoW
26/1/44	F/Sgt H. Bletcher	EK139	Engine failed on take off from Lympne, aircraft crashed into a wood, pilot safe
29/1/44	F/Sgt L.E. Watson	JP498	Shot down during Ramrod operation to Amiens, pilot killed
30/1/44	W/O J.W. McKenzie	JP841	Undershot due to engine failure when landing at Lympne, pilot safe
2/3/44	W/O N.D. Howard	JP483	Force landed near Tergnier following engine failure during Ramrod operation, pilot evaded
23/3/44	F/O H.T. Jackson	EK245	Crashed into the sea near Orfordness after engine failure during ASR operation, pilot killed

Supermarine Spitfire

20/4/44	F/O R.G. Ward	MK725	Lost tail in collision with Spitfire flown by F/O F.H. Cattermoul and crashed, pilot killed
22/5/44	Sgt E.F. Jacobsen	MK890	Hit by flak during Rhubarb operation, pilot killed

22/5/44	F/L A.A. Vale	MK796	Hit by flak during Rhubarb operation, pilot PoW
22/5/44	F/O J.R. Campbell	MK919	A/c damaged by flak during Rhubarb operation, pilot safe
22/5/44	F/Sgt K.C. Weller	MK644	A/c damaged by flak during Rhubarb operation, pilot safe
1/6/44	F/O F.H. Cattermoul	MK798	Hit by flak during Rhubarb operation, pilot PoW but died later
30/7/44	F/Sgt G. Tate	MJ422	Engine trouble during an anti-Diver patrol over the Channel, pilot baled out but was not picked up
4/8/44	W/O J.W. McKenzie	NH466	Engine failure during anti-Diver patrol and force landed, pilot injured
17/8/44	W/O Wallace-Wells	NH201	Shot down by Fw 190s of JG 26 during Ramrod operation, pilot safe
17/8/44	W/O J.W. McKenzie	MK744	Shot down by Fw 190s of JG 26 during Ramrod operation, pilot evaded
27/9/44	W/O E.R. Andrews	MJ481	Failed to return from a sweep near Arnhem, pilot killed
27/9/44	F/O T. Wyllie	MK867	Failed to return from a sweep near Arnhem, pilot killed
29/12/44	W/O D.M. Royds	ML258	Engine trouble during Ramrod operation, pilot baled out near Koblenz and PoW
2/3/45	S/L D.G.S.R. Cox	MK644	Crashed on landing at Northolt when caught by a strong gust of wind, pilot slightly injured
22/3/45	P/O W.E. Recile	NH246	Ran off end of runway at Northolt, damaged Cat B, pilot safe (a/c repaired and sold to Turkey)
18/4/45	W/O L.J. Vickery	NH356	Engine lost power during Ramrod operation and crash landed near Genappe, pilot safe

Appendix Two – Details of Selected Operations/Squadron Moves

Squadron patrol over Saarbrucken – 15 October 1939 (1100-1230)

S/L P.J.H. Halahan	L1905	F/L P.R. Walker	L1971	F/L G.H.F. Plinston	L1960
F/O C.G.H. Crusoe	L1676	F/L P.P. Hanks	L1969	F/O C.D. Palmer	L1925
F/O L.R. Clisby	L1693	F/O B. Drake	L1590	F/O M.H. Brown	L1974
P/O P.W.O. Mould	L1842	P/O S.W. Baldie	L1843	Sgt A.V. Clowes	L1688
Sgt F.J. Soper	L1681	Sgt F.G. Berry	L1673	Sgt R.A. Albonico	L1927

Squadron move to Berry-au-Bac – 11 April 1940 (1710-1740)

S/L P.J.H. Halahan	L1905	P/O R.G. Lewis	L1689	F/L P.P Hanks	N2380
F/O B. Drake	L1590	P/O P.W.O. Mould	L1856	Sgt R.A. Albonico	L1927
Sgt F.G. Berry	P2451	F/O C.D. Palmer	P2546	Sgt A.V. Clowes	L1969
F/O C.G.H. Crusoe	L1685	F/L P.R. Walker	N2382	F/O W.H. Stratton	P2678
F/O J.I. Kilmartin	L1843	F/O G.P.H. Matthews	L1679	Sgt F.J. Soper	L1681

P/O R.H. Shaw in Magister P2434

Squadron Patrol – 11 August 1940 (Take off 0940)

F/L M.H. Brown	P3047	P/O C.A.C. Chetham	P2548	P/O D.O.M. Browne	R4075
P/O J.A.J. Davey	P3172	F/O G.P.H. Matthews	P2980	P/O H.J. Mann	P3043
P/O R.H. Shaw	P3405	P/O G.E. Goodman	P2686	P/O C.N. Birch	P3684

Squadron Patrol – 1 September 1940 (1045-1145)

F/L H.B.L. Hillcoat	P3044	F/Sgt F.G. Berry	P3276	P/O R.H. Shaw	P3782
F/O G.P.H. Matthews	P3395	P/O P.V. Boot	P3169	P/O C.A.C. Chetham	P2548
P/O N.P.W. Hancock	P3396	F/O H.N.E. Salmon	V7256	P/O C.N. Birch	V7376

Night Operations over London and Redhill – 11 May 1941

S/L R.E.P Brooker	Z2625	F/L W.H. Sizer	Z3072	Lt J-F Demozay	Z3240
Sgt J. Plasil	Z2764	F/L K.C. Jackman	Z2834	P/O W. Raymond	Z2482
Sgt B. Kratkoruky	Z2490	Sgt J. Dygryn	Z2687	Sgt J. Novak	Z2746
Sgt J. Prihoda	Z3165	Sgt O. Pavlu	Z2764	P/O F. Behal	Z2921

Intruder Operations – 1 May 1942

Sgt G.S.M. Pearson	BE150	0115-0330	Sgt J.R. Campbell	BD983	0320-0525
P/O D.P. Perrin	BN205	0040-0240	P/O G.H. Corbet	BD262	0325-0505
F/Sgt C.F. Bland	BN205	0320-0530	F/L L.S.B. Scott	Z3455	0330-0520

Mitchell Escort to Rouen Power Station – 16 September 1943 (1745-1900)

S/L A. Zweigbergk	JP498	Sgt W.A. Booker	JP679	F/L F.W. Murray	R7877
F/Sgt W.H. Ramsey	JP592	F/L D.P. Perrin	JP685	F/Sgt R.W. Hornall	EJ983
F/Sgt C.J. Devey	DN502	Sgt A.H. Browne	EK113		

Ramrod Operation to Martinvast – 10 November 1943 (1145-1245)

F/L F.W. Murray	JP841	F/Sgt S.D. Cunningham	JP592	F/O J.H. McCullough	JP679
P/O J.W. Sutherland	JR237	F/O H.T. Mossip	JP677	F/O J.R. Campbell	JR144
F/O G.J. King	R8882	P/O W.H. Ramsey	EK210	F/Sgt E. Crowley	DN490
F/L D.P. Perrin	JP685	P/O C.J. Devey	DN502	F/O H.J. Wilkinson	JP483
F/O J.W. Wiley	JP961	P/O W.H. Dunwoodie	JP795	P/O G. Hardie	JP738
F/Sgt N. Howard	DN432	W/O D. Fairbairn	JR147		

Ramrod 603 over Holland – 29 February 1944

F/L D.P. Perrin	JR522	P/O R.W. Hornall	JP738	W/O N.D. Howard	JP483
F/O F.H. Cattermoul	JR328	F/O H.T. Jackson	JP677	F/O W.F. Anderson	JR126
F/O D.V. McIntosh	JR380	F/O N.E. Brown	MN124		

Ramrod 609 – B-26 Marauder Escort – 2 March 1944 (1050-1230)

F/L D.P. Perrin	R8882	W/O M.J. Gullan	JR380	F/Sgt H.H. Price	JR126
F/O H.T. Jackson	JP677	F/O R.W. Bridgman	MN124	F/O A.A. Vale	JP679
P/O R.W. Hornall	JP738	F/O R.A. Miller	JP483	F/O E.N.W. Marsh	JP685
P/O H. Bletcher	JR328				

Rodeo 141 to Kerlin Bastard and Vannes – 14 May 1944 (1400-1550)

S/L H.P. Lardner-Burke	ML119	F/O N.E. Brown	MK583	F/L I.P. Maskill	MK846
F/O D.V. McIntosh	MK901	F/O F.H. Cattermoul	MK798	F/O K.M. Langmuir	MK926
P/O H. Bletcher	MK867	F/O E.G. Hutchin	MK986		

Ramrod 1211 – Mitchell Escort – 17 August 1944

Red Section		Blue Section		Yellow Section	
S/L H.P. Lardner-Burke	ML119	F/L T.D. Williams	MK583	F/L I.P. Maskill	NH200
F/O D.H. Davy	MK659	W/O E.R. Andrews	ML423	W/O J.W. McKenzie	MK744
F/O J.O. Dalley	MK919	F/O K.R. Foskett	MK846	F/O H.L. Stuart	NH246
F/O D.R. Wallace	MK926	F/L R. Brown	MK988	W/O Wallace-Wells	NH201

Rodeo 411 to Rheine Area – 3 February 1945

Red Section		Blue Section		Yellow Section	
W/C R.W. Oxspring	MK644	F/L I.P. Maskill	NH200	S/L D.G.S.R. Cox	ML119
S/L H.W. Harrison	MK988	P/O W.E. Recile	MK726	F/L R.D. Scrase	NH255
F/L K.C. Pedersen	NH246	F/O D.V. McIntosh	EN636	F/O A.J. Adams	ML423
F/L J.O. Dalley *	?	F/O D.H. Davy	ML117	F/L R. Brown +	MK997

* Failed to take off   + Abortive

Ramrod 1555 to Wangerooge – 25 April 1945

Red Section		Yellow Section		Blue Section	
F/L P.W Stewart	ML119	F/L N.E. Brown	NH200	F/O A.J. Adams	ML423
F/L D.V. McIntosh	MJ244	F/L R.W. Bridgman	NH401	W/O L.J. Vickery	MK515
F/L P.E. Crocker	NH209	F/L D.H. Davy	MJ627	F/L R. Brown	MH774
		F/L K.C. Pedersen	MJ873	F/O W.R. Harrison	ML242

Appendix Three – Operational Career of Sgt (later P/O) Walter Ramsey (1st Tour – No.1 Squadron)

The following information has been compiled from Walter Ramsey's Logbook and the Squadron ORB

Date	A/c serial	Code	Up	Down	Remarks
10/9/42	R7865	JX-F	1540	1635	Scramble 15,000 ft (F/Sgt Glover) – nothing seen
19/10/42	R7861	JX-D	1250	1325	Scramble (P/O Campbell) no contact
23/10/42	R7877	JX-K	1250	1320	Scramble (P/O Pearson) nothing seen
22/12/42	R8752	JX-L	1040	1050	Scramble White section – recalled (a/c friendly)
22/1/43	DN241	JX-H	1625	1645	Patrol Farne Islands (F/Sgt Mossip)
27/1/43	DN241	JX-H	0945	1005	Scramble (Sgt Sutherland) no contact
24/2/43	DN490	JX-G	0740	0915	Patrol Dungeness – flak from shore batteries
24/2/43	R7877	JX K	1405	1540	Patrol Beachy Head (F/O Bolster)
26/2/43	R8752	JX-L	1025	1140	Patrol Beachy Head (S/L Wilkinson) divert Ford
27/2/43	R7877	JX-K	1130	1315	Patrol Beachy Head (S/L Wilkinson) divert Tangmere
8/3/43	DN244	JX-I	0815	0940	Patrol Beachy Head (Sgt Crowley)
8/3/43	DN335	JX-B	1310	1440	Patrol Beachy Head (Sgt Crowley)
9/3/43	DN385	JX-D	1435	1610	Patrol Beachy Head (P/O McCullough)
9/3/43	DN385	JX-D	1800	1840	Patrol Beachy Head (Sgt Shawyer)
10/3/43	DN335	JX-B	1025	1150	Patrol Beachy Head (F/O Bolster)
11/3/43	DN385	JX-D	0725	0855	Patrol Beachy Head (P/O McCullough)
13/3/43	DN451	JX-E	1435	1550	Patrol Beachy Head (Sgt Shawyer)
13/3/43	DN451	JX-E	1750	1915	Patrol Beachy Head (Sgt Shawyer)
17/3/43	DN335	JX-B	1120	1150	Convoy Patrol – Dungeness (P/O Glover)
17/3/43	DN335	JX-B	1410	1510	Patrol Beachy Head (F/O Bolster) – fired on by AA
19/3/43	DN385	JX-D	1200	1310	Patrol Beachy Head (F/O Bolster)
19/3/43	EJ982	JX-H	1805	1900	Patrol (F/O Bolster) * Detached 'B' Flight 23/3/43
24/3/43	R8630	JX-U	1350	1525	Patrol Beachy Head (W/O Dunwoodie)

25/3/43	R7923	JX-X	1000	1130	Patrol Beachy Head (W/O Dunwoodie) vector no joy
25/3/43	R8708	JX-Q	1310	1435	Patrol Beachy Head (P/O Dennis)
25/3/43	R8634	JX-P	1730	1850	Patrol Dungeness (P/O Dennis) – two duff vectors
28/3/43	DN432	JX-O	1005	1145	Patrol (F/O Perrin) – trouble with u/c
28/3/43	DN432	JX-O	1600	1735	Patrol (F/O Perrin) – interception friendly (6 a/c)
29/3/43	DN432	JX-O	0700	0830	Patrol Beachy Head (F/O Perrin)
29/3/43	R8630	JX-U	1245	1350	Patrol Beachy Head (F/O Perrin) – returned R/T u/s
30/3/43	DN432	JX-O	0825	0915	Patrol Beachy Head (Sgt Hornall) – vector, no joy
30/3/43	R8708	JX-Q	1420	1530	Patrol Beachy Head (Sgt Hornall)
31/3/43	R7923	JX-X	1115	1200	Patrol Beachy Head (Sgt Hornall)
1/4/43	R7921	JX-Z	0645	0740	Patrol North Foreland (Sgt Hornall) intercepted four friendly patrols
1/4/43	R7921	JX-Z	1210	1325	Patrol Beachy Head (Sgt Hornall)
2/4/43	R8708	JX-Q	1355	1525	Scramble Patrol (F/Sgt Devey) no joy, weather bad
3/4/43	R7923	JX-X	0930	1050	Patrol Dungeness (F/Sgt Devey)
3/4/43	R7921	JX-Z	1230	1340	Patrol Dungeness/Beachy Head (F/Sgt Devey) vectors, no joy. 12 e/a bombed Eastbourne
3/4/43	R8708	JX-Q	1635	1805	Patrol Beachy Head (P/O Higham) chase to 10,000 ft over French coast, no joy
4/4/43	R7923	JX-X	0850	0950	Patrol North Foreland, Dover, Cap Gris Nez (F/Sgt Devey) returned with u/s generator
5/4/43	R8708	JX-Q	0800	0905	Patrol Dungeness (F/O Perrin)
5/4/43	R7923	JX-X	1400	1520	Patrol Dungeness (Sgt Hornall)
5/4/43	R8634	JX-P	1940	2105	Patrol Dungeness (Sgt Hornall) dusk landing
6/4/43	R8630	JX-U	1055	1220	Patrol Dungeness (Sgt Hornall)
6/4/43	R8630	JX-U	1630	1740	Patrol Dungeness (W/O Dunwoodie)
7/4/43	R7923	JX-X	1155	1325	Patrol Beachy Head (W/O Dunwoodie) very bumpy
9/4/43	R8634	JX-P	1655	1815	Patrol Beachy Head (F/Sgt Fraser) 4 190's bombed Folkstone, chase, no joy, ops 'finger in'

9/4/43	R8634	JX-P	1940	2020	Scramble – join sweep to Gris Nez, Bob Hornall got 1 Fw 190. 611 Spits got 2 and 4 damaged. Shaky Do!!
10/4/43	R7922	JX-N	1155	1315	Patrol Beachy Head (F/Sgt Fraser)
10/4/43	R8630	JX-U	1635	1800	Scramble Hastings (F/Sgt Fraser) chased Huns south of Rye to Le Touquet. No joy
11/4/43	R7922	JX-N	0850	1025	Patrol Dungeness (F/Sgt Fraser)
11/4/43	R7922	JX-N	1455	1615	Patrol Dungeness (F/Sgt Fraser)
11/4/43	R8630	JX-U	2013	2018	Scramble base 4,000 ft (F/Sgt Fraser) patrol Beachy Head/Dungeness – 6+ bandits stooging Deal-Margate
13/4/43	R8630	JX-U	0745	0855	Patrol Beachy Head (F/Sgt Fraser)
13/4/43	R7923	JX-X	1300	1410	Patrol Dungeness (F/Sgt Fraser)
13/4/43	R7923	JX-X	1855	2020	Patrol Dungeness (F/Sgt Fraser)
14/4/43	R7922	JX-N	0710	0820	Patrol Dungeness (F/Sgt Brown)
14/4/43	R8708	JX-Q	1255	1355	Patrol Beachy Head (F/Sgt Brown)
14/4/43	R7919	JX-R	1850	2020	Patrol Dungeness/Beachy Head (F/Sgt Brown) vectors, no joy
15/4/43	R7922	JX-N	1105	1225	Patrol Dungeness to Beachy Head (F/Sgt Brown)
16/4/43	R8708	JX-Q	1355	1505	Patrol Dungeness (P/O Chalifour)
17/4/43	R8630	JX-U	1455	1620	Patrol Dungeness (F/O Perrin)
17/4/43	R8630	JX-U	1850	1900	Scramble – 4 a/c (F/L Murray, F/O Perrin, F/O Higham) after 6 Huns on ASR. Recalled due to presence of Spits
17/4/43	R8630	JX-U	2025	2130	Patrol Dungeness (F/O Perrin) vector, no joy. Dusk landing
18/4/43	R8630	JX-U	0955	1120	Patrol Dungeness (Sgt Hornall) vector, no joy
18/4/43	R7923	JX-X	1555	1715	Patrol Dungeness (Sgt Hornall)
19/4/43	R8708	JX-Q	0715	0815	Patrol Dungeness (Sgt Hornall)
19/4/43	R7921	JX-Z	1330	1430	Patrol Dungeness (Sgt Hornall) vector, no joy
20/4/43	R7921	JX-Z	0800	0910	Patrol Dungeness (Sgt Hornall)
20/4/43	R7921	JX-Z	1400	1505	Patrol Dungeness (Sgt Hornall) Huns about – no joy
20/4/43	R7921	JX-Z	1925	2045	Patrol Dungeness (Sgt Hornall) * return to 'A' Flight
29/4/43	R8752	JX-L	0800	0935	Patrol Beachy Head (Sgt Shawyer)
1/5/43	R8752	JX-L	1400	1510	Patrol Dungeness (Sgt Sutherland)

4/5/43	DN385	JX-D	2055	2130	Patrol Dungeness – Folkstone (Sgt Shawyer)
5/5/43	R8752	JX-L	1250	1400	Patrol Beachy Head (Sgt Shawyer) vectored to Boulogne
5/5/43	R7877	JX-K	1850	2010	Patrol Dungeness – Folkstone (Sgt Shawyer)
7/5/43	DN385	JX-D	1350	1520	Patrol Dungeness – Dover (Sgt Shawyer)
7/5/43	R7877	JX-K	?	?	Patrol Dungeness (Sgt Shawyer) bags of Huns – vectors, no contacts
9/5/43	R8752	JX-L	1655	1750	Shipping recce Dieppe – Boulogne – Calais (F/L Murray)
13/5/43	R8752	JX-L	0855	1020	Patrol Dungeness – North Foreland (P/O Glover)
13/5/43	R8752	JX-L	2115	2140	Scramble 4 a/c patrol Dungeness – Gris Nez (F/L Scott, F/O Perrin. P/O Glover)
14/5/43	R8752	JX-L	1540	1645	Scramble (P/O Glover) tried to intercept Huns returning from East Anglia
15/5/43	R8752	JX-L	1750	1810	Scramble 'A' Flt 6+ Huns coming up from Gris Nez
16/5/43	DN490	JX-G	1620	1710	Scramble (Sgt Sutherland) bandit S of Beachy Head
20/5/43	DN451	JX-E	0615	0635	Scramble (F/Sgt Brown) bandits over Folkstone, Huns ran for home from 7,000 ft
20/5/43	R7877	JX-K	1145	1220	Rodeo to Abbeville – bad weather, aborted
23/5/43	R8752	JX-L	1300	1325	Scramble (F/O Watson) – Fw 190 Destroyed
25/5/43	R7877	JX-T	1735	1835	Patrol Beachy Head – Hastings
26/5/43	R8752	JX-L	1540	1635	Scramble (F/O Perrin, F/O Watson, P/O Miller) to Dunkirk – bags of duff vectors
28/5/43	R8631	JX-C	1255	1310	Scramble Dungeness (Sgt Sutherland)
29/5/43	R8752	JX-L	1540	1650	Scramble 4 a/c patrol Dungeness (F/O Watson, F/S Hornall, Sgt Gray) Huns turned back
1/6/43	R8752	JX-L	2115	2220	Scramble 4 a/c cover patrol Dover – Dungeness (F/O Baker, P/O Miller, Sgt Booker)
2/6/43	R8752	JX-L	0940	1030	Rhubarb (P/O Mossip) a/c damaged Cat E
4/6/43	DN490	JX-G	1615	1730	Patrol North Foreland (P/O McCullough)
5/6/43	R7856	JX-M	1925	2010	Scramble patrol Dover - Dungeness
7/6/43	EK210	JX-F	1305	1425	Scramble patrol Dungeness (P/O McCullough)

7/6/43	EJ982	JX-H	1935	2045	Patrol Dover – Dungeness (P/O McCullough)
10/6/43	DN451	JX-E	2030	2115	Scramble patrol Beachy Head (Sgt Cunningham) 12+ Huns turned back
11/6/43	DN451	JX-E	0630	0750	Patrol Dungeness (Sgt Booker)
12/6/43	DN451	JX-E	0605	0715	Patrol Dungeness (Sgt Sutherland) * two weeks leave
26/6/43	R8631	JX-C	2000	2125	Scramble patrol Hastings 4 a/c
29/6/43	R8631	JX-C	0630	0640	Scramble (Sgt Crowley) 'bogeys' were friendly a/c
1/7/43	R7877	JX-T	1440	1525	Escort to Bomphoons of 3 Sqn - abortive
1/7/43	EK210	JX-F	2200	2225	Scramble (Sgt Crowley) abortive
2/7/43	R7877	JX-T	2040	2105	Scramble base (Sgt Crowley) two lots of Huns heading north, turned back
6/7/43	R7877	JX-T	1220	1305	Scramble by 'A' Flt 20m S of Dungeness – bags of Huns after ASR but turned back
8/7/43	EK210	JX-F	2125	2150	Scramble (Sgt Crowley) two bandits S of Dungeness, chased them in at Hardelot – 4m behind
25/7/43	DN490	JX-G	1820	1925	Scramble Dungeness (P/O Jackson)
31/7/43	EK210	JX-F	1130	1150	Scramble by 'A' Flt, Huns approaching – too many Spits about!
4/8/43	DN490	JX-G	1000	1050	Scramble Dungeness (F/Sgt Crowley) a/c friendly
4/8/43	EK210	JX-F	1505	1605	Scramble by 'A' Flt, ASR patrol Ostend – Zeebrugge over two launches
4/8/43	EK210	JX-F	2040	2110	Patrol by 'A' Flt to Boulogne 9,000 ft, vectors, no joy, S/L Zweigbergk leading
5/8/43	R7877	JX-T	1640	1735	Calibration (F/O Wood) mid Channel sweep 15,000 ft
11/8/43	DN490	JX-G	2045	2110	Scramble
14/8/43	R7877	JX-T	1135	1245	Patrol – Dungeness (F/Sgt Crowley)
29/8/43	R7877	JX-T	1045	1125	Scramble S of Dover (F/O King)
1/9/43	JP498	JX-K	1535	1555	Scramble (F/Sgt Crowley) bandit N of Calais
2/9/43	JP677	JX-C	0725	0840	Shipping Patrol – Operation Pontoon (Starkey)
3/9/43	JP679	JX-E	0730	0800	Shipping Patrol – Operation Pontoon (Starkey)
5/9/43	JP592	JX-L	1335	1500	Shipping Patrol – Operation Pontoon (Starkey)

6/9/43	JP592	JX-L	0915	1045	Shipping Patrol – Operation Pontoon (Starkey)
9/9/43	JP592	JX-L	1900	1905	Scramble – abortive
16/9/43	JP592	JX-L	1745	1900	Close Escort to Mitchells – Rouen power station
26/9/43	JP592	JX-L	1215	1330	ASR (F/Sgt Crowley) Walrus taxiing off Le Touquet and launches
8/10/43	JP592	JX-L	1520	1625	Close Escort to Mitchells – St Omer/Longuenesse – 10/10 cloud, bombers turned back
9/10/43	JP592	JX-L	1310	1350	Withdrawal Cover to Mosquitos – weather bad
22/10/43	JP592	JX-L	1515	1625	Withdrawal Cover to Bostons – Courcelles, bags of flak – picked up bombers at Knocke
10/11/43	EK210	JX-F	1155	1240	Ramrod to Gris Nez – escort to Bomphoons – 11 bombers 7 fighters – flak!!
10/11/43	EK210	JX-F	1455	1515	Channel sweep – a/c u/s – early return
11/11/43	EK210	JX-F	1355	1520	Operation George patrol Sevenoaks – Brooklands 10,000 ft – cover to HM King and Queen
23/11/43	JP679	JX-E	1420	1445	Ramrod – V-1 target Augingham, bombed and strafed gun positions, escorted by 609 Sqn
25/11/43	JR144	JX-D	1035	1115	Ramrod 331 – Audingham, bombed and strafed gun positions and buildings on coast, escort by 609 Sqn – landed Tangmere
25/11/43	JR144	JX-D	1445	1605	Ramrod 332 – V-1 target Martinvast, heavy flak. Bombed and attacked Bofors guns and huts, strafed blockhouse.
14/12/43	EK210	JX-F	1450	1515	Ramrod 366 – V-1 target Losterberne – heavy flak
17/12/43	JP679	JX-E	1505	1545	Ramrod 371 – V-1 target Fruges – attacked flak positions S of Hardelot – a/c hit by flak
30/12/43	JP498	JX-K	1445	1525	Ramrod 400 – V-1 target Linghem – attacked train
1/1/44	JP679	JX-E	1235	1320	Ramrod 407 – V-1 target nr Hesdin – escorted 184 Sqn RP Hurricanes to target then bombed – engine trouble
4/1/44	JP679	JX-E	1015	1105	Ramrod 417 – V-1 target Ligescourt – escorted 184 Sqn then bombed, engine cut again, stbd main tank not draining as usual
4/1/44	EJ983	JX-R	1415	1455	Ramrod 420 – escort to sqn by section of 2 a/c

5/1/44	JP498	JX-K	1420	1455	Ramrod 426 – V-1 target Bois Rempre – bombed through broken cloud over target – no excitement
11/1/44	JP679	JX-E	0945	1025	Ramrod 447 – V-1 target Losterberne – heavy intense flak, bombed (wizard prang) – a/c damaged

Appendix Four _ Operational Career of F/Sgt (later P/O) Ken Weller (2nd Tour – No.1 Squadron)

The following information has been compiled from Ken Weller's Logbook and the Squadron ORB

Date	A/c serial	Code	Up	Down	Remarks
1/5/44	MK988	JX-O	1910	2030	Scramble – 30m S of Land's End – nothing seen
3/5/44	MK659	JX-A	2005	2050	Scramble – nothing seen
5/5/44	MK988	JX-O	2020	2200	Patrol – Start Point to Lizard, uneventful
6/5/44	MK988	JX-O	0620	0630	Patrol – early return, R/T trouble
6/5/44	MK988	JX-O	1245	1355	Convoy Patrol – S of Land's End
8/5/44	MK744	JX-K	2035	2225	Standing Patrol – Lizard to Start Point
9/5/44	MK846	JX-G	1600	1705	Patrol - uneventful
11/5/44	MK659	JX-A	1930	2010	Scramble to 5-10m from French coast
11/5/44	MK659	JX-A	2100	2140	Convoy Patrol
12/5/44	MK659	JX-A	0615	0710	Patrol – uneventful
12/5/44	MK659	JX-A	1955	2220	Instep Patrol – 150m WNW Lizard 'zero' feet
14/5/44	MK659	JX-A	1035	1130	Patrol – uneventful
14/5/44	MK846	JX-G	1900	2105	Patrol – uneventful
17/5/44	MK744	JX-K	1400	1505	Patrol – uneventful
17/5/44	MK744	JX-K	1615	1705	Patrol – uneventful
18/5/44	MK659	JX-A	0930	1035	Shipping recce to Ushant
18/5/44	MK659	JX-A	1220	1305	Patrol - uneventful
19/5/44	MK659	JX-A	1825	1940	Shipping recce – Ushant to Brest
20/5/44	MK659	JX-A	0655	0750	Patrol – uneventful
20/5/44	MK659	JX-A	2045	2205	Roadstead – close escort to Beaufighters
22/5/44	MK644	JX-M	1500	1710	Rhubarb Vannes – Quimper – Chateaulin – Morlaix
23/5/44	MK901	JX-E	1410	1505	Patrol – uneventful
23/5/44	ML119	JX-B	1750	1830	Patrol – uneventful
24/5/44	MK659	JX-A	0925	1235	Patrol of destroyers on 'anti U-Boat' search
28/5/44	MK659	JX-A	2130	2235	Ranger in search of R-Boats off Ushant
29/5/44	MK659	JX-A	1950	2055	Patrol – uneventful

29/5/44	MK659	JX-A	2225	2300	Patrol – uneventful
8/6/44	MK644	JX-M	1200	1340	Ranger – attacked trains
10/6/44	MK926	JX-L	1150	1155	Ranger – early return due to oiled up windscreen
12/6/44	MK926	JX-L	0525	0710	Rodeo 168 to Kerlin Bastard
12/6/44	MK659	JX-A	1855	2125	Rodeo 171 Nantes – Vannes
16/6/44	MK846	JX-G	2145	2250	Shipping recce – Ile de Batz
17/6/44	MK733	JX-T	1655	1805	Bombed radar station
18/6/44	MK867	JX-W	1745	1850	Patrol – uneventful
20/6/44	NH246	JX-H	1645	1820	Escort to bombers – dive bombed radar station
20/6/44	MK901	JX-E	2150	2305	Armed patrol to Cherbourg – jettisoned bombs in sea
21/6/44	ML117	JX-D	0810	0940	Convoy patrol – S of Plymouth
24/6/44	MK744	JX-K	1455	1625	Convoy patrol
24/6/44	MK867	JX-W	2200	2230	Anti-Diver patrol
25/6/44	MK901	JX-E	0510	0625	Anti-Diver patrol (F/Sgt Hastings)
27/6/44	ML258	JX-L	?	?	Anti-Diver patrol (F/O Bridgman and F/Sgt Hastings) V-1 destroyed
27/6/44	MK987	JX-U	1250	1410	Bomber escort
28/6/44	ML258	JX-L	2100	2205	Anti-Diver patrol (F/L Jarman)
29/6/44	ML258	JX-L	0605	0720	Anti-Diver patrol (F/L Jarman)
29/6/44	ML258	JX-L	0825	0935	Anti-Diver patrol (F/L Jarman)
29/6/44	ML258	JX-L	1240	1330	Anti-Diver patrol (F/O Langmuir)
30/6/44	ML258	JX-L	1435	1500	Anti-Diver patrol (F/L Jarman)
30/6/44	ML258	JX-L	1630	1725	Anti-Diver patrol (F/L Jarman)
4/7/44	ML258	JX-L	1915	2010	Anti-Diver patrol (F/O McIntosh) V-1 destroyed
4/7/44	ML258	JX-L	2155	2300	Anti-Diver patrol (F/O McIntosh)
5/7/44	ML258	JX-L	1510	1610	Anti-Diver patrol (W/O McKenzie)
6/7/44	ML258	JX-L	2005	2030	Anti-Diver patrol
7/7/44	MK644	JX-M	1355	1500	Anti-Diver patrol (W/O McKenzie)
8/7/44	ML258	JX-L	0800	0900	Anti-Diver patrol (W/O McKenzie)
8/7/44	ML258	JX-L	0950	1100	Anti-Diver patrol (W/O McKenzie)
8/7/44	ML258	JX-L	2005	2110	Anti-Diver patrol (P/O Turner)
9/7/44	MK644	JX-M	1415	1435	Anti-Diver patrol (W/O McKenzie)
10/7/44	MK744	JX-K	0725	0825	Anti-Diver patrol (F/L Jarman)

10/7/44	MK744	JX-K	0905	1005	Anti-Diver patrol (F/L Jarman)
12/7/44	ML258	JX-L	2005	2110	Anti-Diver patrol (W/O McKenzie)
13/7/44	ML258	JX-L	1635	1710	Anti-Diver patrol (W/O McKenzie)
14/7/44	ML258	JX-L	1530	1640	Anti-Diver patrol (W/O McKenzie)
15/7/44	ML258	JX-L	?	?	Anti-Diver patrol
16/7/44	ML258	JX-L	1300	1410	Anti-Diver patrol (W/O McKenzie)
17/7/44	ML258	JX-L	1705	1825	Anti-Diver patrol (W/O McKenzie)
17/7/44	ML258	JX-L	2000	2120	Anti-Diver patrol (W/O McKenzie)
18/7/44	ML258	JX-L	1400	1520	Anti-Diver patrol (F/Sgt Tate)
18/7/44	ML258	JX-L	1635	1715	Anti-Diver patrol
19/7/44	ML258	JX-L	?	?	Anti-Diver patrol
19/7/44	ML117	JX-D	1105	1205	Anti-Diver patrol (F/Sgt Tate)
20/7/44	ML258	JX-L	0610	0720	Anti-Diver patrol (F/Sgt Tate)
20/7/44	ML258	JX-L	0815	0940	Anti-Diver patrol (F/O Crocker)
20/7/44	ML258	JX-L	?	?	Anti-Diver patrol
22/7/44	ML258	JX-L	1530	1630	Anti-Diver patrol (W/O McKenzie)
23/7/44	ML258	JX-L	0955	1115	Anti-Diver patrol (W/O McKenzie)
23/7/44	ML258	JX-L	1200	1320	Anti-Diver patrol (W/O McKenzie)
25/7/44	MK846	JX-G	1705	1815	Anti-Diver patrol (F/Sgt Tate)
25/7/44	MK846	JX-G	1900	1945	Anti-Diver patrol (F/Sgt Tate)
25/7/44	ML258	JX-L	2050	2205	Anti-Diver patrol (F/Sgt Tate)
28/7/44	ML258	JX-L	1310	1410	Anti-Diver patrol (F/Sgt Hastings)
3/8/44	ML258	JX-L	1355	1500	Anti-Diver patrol (W/O Bush)
3/8/44	ML258	JX-L	1600	1710	Anti-Diver patrol (W/O Bush)
3/8/44	ML258	JX-L	1905	2020	Anti-Diver patrol (W/O McKenzie)
4/8/44	ML258	JX-L	0950	1105	Anti-Diver patrol (W/O McKenzie)
6/8/44	ML258	JX-L	1800	1915	Anti-Diver patrol (F/Sgt Hastings)
6/8/44	ML258	JX-L	2010	2115	Anti-Diver patrol (F/Sgt Hastings)
7/8/44	ML258	JX-L	1350	1505	Anti-Diver patrol (W/O Bush)
7/8/44	ML258	JX-L	1700	1810	Anti-Diver patrol (W/O Bush)
8/8/44	ML258	JX-L	1200	1310	Anti-Diver patrol (F/O McIntosh)
9/8/44	ML258	JX-L	1500	1620	Anti-Diver patrol (W/O Bush)
11/8/44	ML258	JX-L	1545	1715	Ramrod 1186 – escort Lancasters to Lens
11/8/44	ML258	JX-L	1900	2020	Ramrod 1188 – escort Halifaxes to target nr Cassel

12/8/44	ML258	JX-L	1205	1340	Ramrod 1191 – ammunition dump NW of Beauvais
13/8/44	ML258	JX-L	1835	2035	Ramrod 1196 – escort to Marauders
10/9/44	ML258	JX-L	0825	1020	Armed recce Amsterdam – Den Helder
10/9/44	ML258	JX-L	1835	2020	Armed recce Rotterdam – Amsterdam
12/9/44	ML258	JX-L	1300	1520	Ramrod 1274 – withdrawal cover to Halifaxes
13/9/44	ML258	JX-L	1725	1945	Ramrod 1280 – escort Halifaxes to Gelsenkirchen
16/9/44	ML258	JX-L	1300	1450	Armed recce The Hague – Utrecht – Den Helder
17/9/44	MK988	JX-O	1225	1435	Escort patrol – Operation Market Garden
19/9/44	ML258	JX-L	1455	1510	Escort – bad weather return
20/9/44	ML258	JX-L	1635	1900	Escort to glider tugs
27/9/44	ML258	JX-L	1620	1750	Sweep over Holland
30/9/44	ML258	JX-L	1605	1840	Ramrod 1303 – escort Marauders to Arnhem
2/10/44	ML258	JX-L	1555	1820	Ramrod 1307 – escort Bostons to Nijmegan
3/10/44	ML258	JX-L	1545	1800	Ramrod 1309 – escort Bostons to Arnhem
16/11/44	ML258	JX-L	1410	1650	Ramrod 1372 – escort Lancasters to Duren
21/11/44	ML258	JX-L	1400	1635	Ramrod 1375 – escort Lancasters to Homberg
27/11/44	MH414	JX-E	1345	1625	Ramrod 1379 – withdrawal cover to Lancasters
5/12/44	?	R-O	1000	1250	Ramrod 1394 – withdrawal cover to Lancasters
23/12/44	ML258	JX-L	1315	1535	Ramrod 1414 – withdrawal cover to Lancasters
25/12/44	ML258	JX-L	1320	1530	Rodeo 407 Aachen – Bonn – Liege
5/1/45	EN636	JX-F	1350	1635	Ramrod 1427 – withdrawal cover to Lancasters
11/1/45	EN636	JX-F	1345	1455	Ramrod 1430 – escort, bad weather return
15/1/45	EN636	JX-F	1325	1345	Ramrod 1434 – escort, bad weather abort
17/1/45	MK659	JX-A	1035	1235	Rodeo 409 Rheine – Lingen
6/2/45	EN636	JX-F	0915	1140	Ramrod 1453 – sweep route of Lancasters - Paderborn
9/2/45	NH246	JX-H	1400	1620	Rodeo 413 – sweep of Osnabruck area

10/2/45	NH246	JX-H	1420	1615	Rodeo 414 – sweep of Munster – Zuider Zee area
14/2/45	NH246	JX-H	0930	1150	Rodeo 415 – sweep of Osnabruck area
16/2/45	NH246	JX-H	1500	1710	Ramrod 1463 – cover to Lancasters – Wesel
27/2/45	MK726	JX-K	1350	1540	Ramrod 1474 – withdrawal cover to Lancasters
28/2/45	MK726	JX-K	1120	1320	Ramrod 1475 – withdrawal cover to Lancasters
1/3/45	ML175	JX-J	1340	1650	Ramrod 1476 – withdrawal cover to Lancasters
2/3/45	NH246	JX-H	1100	1330	VIP escort to Brussels – Winston Churchill
17/3/45	MJ627	JX-D	1350	1640	Ramrod 1500 – escort Lancasters to Dortmund
19/3/45	MJ411	JX-M	1515	1715	Ramrod 1504 – escort Lancasters to Gelsenkirchen
20/3/45	MJ411	JX-M	1215	1455	Ramrod 1506 – escort Halifaxes to Recklinghausen
21/3/45	MJ873	JX-A	1200	1455	Ramrod 1507 – escort Lancasters to Munster area
23/3/45	ML414	JX-E	1440	1730	VIP escort to Venlo – Winston Churchill
24/3/45	MJ873	JX-A	1030	1305	Patrol – Operation Varsity
25/3/45	MJ873	JX-A	0925	1150	Ramrod 1515 – escort Halifaxes to Munster
31/3/45	MJ873	JX-A	0705	0930	Ramrod 1523 – sweep in Osnabruck area
3/4/45	MJ873	JX-A	1540	1810	Ramrod 1527 – withdrawal cover to Lancasters
4/4/45	MJ873	JX-A	0840	1100	Ramrod 1528 – withdrawal cover to Lancasters
11/4/45	MJ873	JX-A	1340	1640	Ramrod 1537 – escort cover Lancasters to Nurnberg
19/4/45	NH209	JX-F	1530	1815	Ramrod 1546 – escort cover Lancasters to Heligoland

Index

Luftwaffe

General